CW01011084

365 Tasty Mayonnaise Recipes

(365 Tasty Mayonnaise Recipes - Volume 1)

Ebony Garcia

Content

365 Awesome Mayonnaise Recipes

***

1. Big Apple Stuffed Burger

Serving: Makes 4 | Prep: | Cook: |Ready in:

Ingredients

- 12 Nathan hotdog or any brand you like
- 2 eggs
- 1-1/2 pounds grd beef sirloin,
- 2 teaspoons salt
- 1-1/2 cups mayonnaise
- 1- 8 ounces pkg Pastrami
- 1- 8 ounces chive and onion cream cheese spread
- 2 cups sliced iceburg lettuce
- 1/2 cup cilantro, chopped
- 1/2 cup thinly sliced red onion
- 4 toasted buns on both sides
- 4 teaspoons fennel seeds, toast for 3 minutes in small skillet
- 1/2 cup finely chopped onion
- 4 teaspoons Grill Mates Mesquite seasoning

Direction

- Grill hotdogs for 10 minutes, turn around after 5 minutes, to get rid of excess fat, in oven or stove top grill.
- Divide 6 hotdogs into 2, crosswise, if doing the stuffed burger, 3 halves per burger. Chopped the rest of hotdog to combine with ground meat.
- Beat eggs in same bowl where ground beef will be mix. Combine ground beef and chopped hotdogs into the beaten eggs. Mix well to evenly distribute the hotdogs. Add salt, fennel seeds and mesquite seasoning and mix.
- Place 2/3 cup of ground beef mixture into the bottom of press. Press the burger using the top, to make a dent/well for the stuffing. Add the 3 pcs of hotdog in the center of burger, then add 1/3 cup of mixture on top and press to seal.
- Grill for 3 minutes on both sides for the stuffed burger on medium-low; for single burger, grill for 2 minutes on a stove top grill or cast iron skillet.
- While burgers are cooking, toast the bread, then mixed lettuce, cilantro, red onion and salt, to make the flavor of cilantro blend with the lettuce.
- Before assembly, place 1-1/2 Tbsp cream cheese spread on top end of pastrami and roll. Make 3 pastrami rolls per bun. Set aside.
- To assemble, spread mayonnaise on both sides of the bun. Place burger on the bottom bun, top with the pastrami rolls and then the salad. Serves 4 for stuffed ones, about 8 for single burgers.

2. Hearty Salad From Your Fridge And Pantry

Serving: Serves 4-6 | Prep: | Cook: |Ready in:

Ingredients

- • 2 cups rice fresh cooked or leftover
- • 1 tablespoon canola oil
- • 1 lemon or lime juiced
- • Zest of 1 lemon
- • 1 teaspoon salt
- • ½ teaspoons freshly ground black pepper
- • 4-5 chopped scallions
- • ½ cup mayonnaise
- • 1 can (15 ounces) pink salmon, drained, flaked and chilled

- • 1 thinly sliced celery rib with the lives
- • 1 tablespoon chopped dill or parsley
- • ½ cup petted olives halved

Direction

- Toss the rice with oil to coat and separate them. If fresh cooked, cool for about 1 hour.
- In a salad bowl mix lemon juice, salt, black pepper, scallions (leave about a tablespoon of the green part for garnish), celery, mayonnaise and olives.
- Gently mix-in the rice, half of the salmon, dill and lemon zest.
- Spoon to a platter or a nice shallow salad bowl.
- In the center arrange the remaining salmon.
- Garnish with lemon wedges or rounds, and sprinkle with the reserved green part of the scallions.

3. Orzo Pasta Chicken And Dates Salad

Serving: Serves 2-3 | Prep: | Cook: | Ready in:

Ingredients

- 2 cups Store bought grilled diced chicken breast
- 1/4 Small-medium sweet onion, peeled
- 14-16 Dried pitted dates
- 1/4 cup Slivered almonds
- 1/4 cup Orzo pasta
- 4 tablespoons Balsamic vinegar
- 4 tablespoons Mayonnaise
- 3 tablespoons Olive oil
- Salt and black pepper to taste

Direction

- Cook orzo pasta followed by the directions of the package. Then drain in a colander and set aside.

- Slice onion thinly and put into a microwave-safe plate or bowl. Microwave on high for 60-90 seconds or until soft. Set aside.
- Cut each date into half-forth lengthwise (depends on the size of each date).
- Make dressing. In a large bowl, mix together balsamic vinegar, mayonnaise and olive oil.
- Put the orzo pasta into the dressing bowl. Then add chicken, onion, dates and slivered almonds to the bowl. Mix to combine. Add salt and black pepper to taste and mix to combine.

4. Potato Salad (Salad E Oliveh)

Serving: Serves 6 to 8 | Prep: | Cook: | Ready in:

Ingredients

- 6 to 8 potatoes (I like Yukon Gold. If the potatoes are large, use 6. If they're medium-small, use 8.)
- 1 cup cornichons, chopped
- 1 small chicken (baked or boiled and shredded; you could use leftover chicken too)
- 4 hard-boiled eggs, chopped
- 1/4 cup freshly-squeezed lemon juice (about 1 lemon)
- 1/4 cup olive oil, plus more for serving
- 1 to 2 cups mayonnaise (homemade or store-bought)
- Salt and pepper, to taste
- 1 cup canned, fresh, or frozen baby peas
- Bread of your choice, for serving. I like with either warmed flat bread or baguette drizzled with olive oil and toasted.
- Lemon wedges
- Chopped chives, for serving

Direction

- Peel potatoes and boil them whole, until they are fork tender but not falling apart. Drain and rinse with cold water to stop the cooking process. Mash with a hand-held masher.

- Chop the cornichons. In a large bowl, mix the cornichons, shredded chicken, hard-boiled egg, and potatoes. Add the lemon juice, olive oil, and 1 cup of mayonnaise. Add more mayonnaise according to your taste. Salt and pepper to taste. Then, add the peas, gently incorporating so you don't mash them.
- Refrigerate overnight. When you serve, heat your bread. Squeeze lemon and drizzle olive oil over the salad and garnish with chives. Scoop with the warm bread.

5. Traditional Vegan Caesar Salad

Serving: Serves 4 (but can easily be doubled) | Prep: | Cook: | Ready in:

Ingredients

- For the salad and dressing:
- 1 head romaine lettuce, washed, dried, and torn or chopped into bite-sized pieces
- 1 garlic, finely minced or grated on a microplane
- 2 tablespoons olive oil
- 1/4 cup vegan mayonnaise
- 1/2 teaspoon sea salt
- 1 tablespoon lemon juice
- 1 tablespoon red wine vinegar
- 1 teaspoon vegan Worcestershire sauce
- 1 tablespoon drained capers
- 2 tablespoons nutritional yeast
- 1 teaspoon Dijon mustard (optional; it's less traditional, but I think it makes for the best flavor)
- Freshly ground black pepper
- For the croutons:
- 1/2 baguette, cut into 1-inch cubes (about 3-4 cups)
- 1-2 tablespoons tablespoons olive oil (as needed)
- 2 teaspoons finely minced garlic
- Coarse salt and freshly grated black pepper

Direction

- To make the croutons, preheat your oven to 350°F and line a baking sheet with parchment. Place the bread cubes in a mixing bowl and add the garlic and olive oil. Toss the cubes well to coat. Transfer them to the baking sheet and sprinkle generously with salt and pepper. Bake for 12-15 minutes, or until the cubes are crisp, stirring the cubes on the sheet halfway through cooking to help them brown evenly.
- While the croutons are roasting, whisk together the garlic, oil, vegan mayonnaise, salt, lemon, vinegar, Worcestershire sauce, capers, nutritional yeast, and mustard, if using. Taste the dressing and add freshly ground black pepper and additional salt as needed. (You can also add a bit of lemon if you're like me, and prefer very tart dressings.)
- Add the dressing to the romaine and toss well to combine. Fold in the croutons. Serve.

6. "Little Green Devils" Deviled Eggs

Serving: Makes 16 green deviled eggs | Prep: | Cook: | Ready in:

Ingredients

- 8 hard boiled eggs - use your own best method - sliced lengthwise and the yolks removed
- 4 strips very crispy bacon, finely crumbled
- 1 ripe avocado, chopped in medium chunks
- 2 teaspoons Dijon mustard
- 4 teaspoons mayonnaise
- 4 teaspoons fresh lime juice
- 4 dashes cayenne pepper, plus more for decorating the deviled eggs
- sea salt and ground pepper to taste
- 8 cherry tomatoes; halved crosswise
- 16 small pieces of crumbled feta or blue cheese to fill the tomato halves

Direction

- Place the hard-boiled egg yolks, the chopped avocado, Dijon mustard, mayonnaise, lime juice, and cayenne pepper into a large glass bowl. With a potato masher combine all the ingredients to make an almost smooth filling. Then use a fork to further pulverize the bits of yolk and avocado. Add salt and pepper to taste. The filling does not have to be completely smooth! Use a small spatula to scoop the filling into a pastry bag to pipe into the egg whites, or use a large Ziploc bag with a corner tip cut off after you fill the bag.
- Place the equivalent of 1/4 strip of bacon into the well of each egg white.
- Pipe the filling into each egg white. Try to hide the bacon bits.
- Gently squeeze the juice and seeds out of each tomato half. Then, press a cheese crumble into each tomato half. Carefully place the cheese-filled tomatoes atop each deviled egg.
- Sprinkle the little green devils with more cayenne pepper if you would like. I like lots of cayenne, but you be the judge.

7. AUTHENTIC BUFFALO CHICKEN WINGS

Serving: Serves 4 | Prep: | Cook: | Ready in:

Ingredients

- 1 cup flour
- 1 teaspoon salt
- 1 teaspoon paprika
- 1 teaspoon garlic powder
- 1 teaspoon cayenne powder
- 1/2 teaspoon black pepper
- 20 chicken wings
- 3/4 cup salted butter
- 1/4 cup hot sauce (I use Tabasco)
- 2/3 cup mayonnaise
- 1/3 cup sour cream (14%)

- 1 cup blue cheese, crumbled
- 1 teaspoon white vinegar
- salt and pepper

Direction

- Combine all dry ingredients in a bowl. Toss wings to coat. Refrigerate for 1 hour. Remove from fridge and coat again. In a large pot, or deep fryer, put enough vegetable or peanut oil to completely cover the wings and heat oil to 375 degrees. Deep fry the wings 8 to 10 at one time for 13 minutes or until nicely crisp. Meanwhile melt the butter and the hot sauce together in a large fry pan. Once wings are nice and crispy, quickly remove from fat, shake off any oil, and place in fry pan with melted butter and hot sauce. Let stay in pan for 3 minutes, then remove with a slotted spoon and put in warm oven (about 250F). Once all the wings have cooked, place all the wings back into the hot sauce for another minute before serving. Ratio for hot factor: Mild 3/4 cup butter - 1/4 cup hot sauce. Hot: 1/4 cup butter - 3/4 hot sauce. Mix together the sour cream, mayonnaise, blue cheese and vinegar to make the traditional dip to go along with the wings.

8. Always Requested Roasted Potato Salad

Serving: Serves 8 | Prep: | Cook: | Ready in:

Ingredients

- 2 pounds potatoes, yukon gold or other thin-skinned
- 2 tablespoons olive oil
- 1 teaspoon salt
- 1/2 cup low fat sour cream or yogurt
- 1/2 cup mayonnaise
- 1 teaspoon dijon mustard
- 1 teaspoon celery seeds
- 2 teaspoons celery salt

- 1 teaspoon white pepper
- 2 teaspoons seasoning salt
- 1/2 teaspoon sugar
- 1/2 cup sweet onions, finely chopped (soak onions in cold water to reduce bite if desired)
- 1 cup celery, finely chopped
- 4 tablespoons dill, chopped
- 1/4 cup cooked and chopped bacon, optional

Direction

- Preheat oven to 350 degrees. Wash potatoes and place in a baking dish. Put the oil over the potatoes, coating thoroughly. Bake for 45 minutes-1 hour until potatoes are tender but not mushy. Refrigerate until cool.
- Make the dressing: Add the sour cream, mayonnaise, mustard, all the seasonings, and the chopped vegetables. Stir thoroughly to blend and adjust seasoning to taste as necessary. Add the bacon if using. Refrigerate.
- When the potatoes are cool, remove the skins if desired by easily pulling them away from the potato. The skins can be left on; I usually leave on the skins of a few potatoes. Cut potato in half, then into batons, then into 1 inch chunks.
- Test seasoning on the dressing and adjust if necessary. Add the potato chunks and stir to mix thoroughly.
- Add the dill, mix, and serve!

9. Apple Salad

Serving: Serves 4-6 | Prep: 0hours30mins | Cook: 1hours0mins | Ready in:

Ingredients

- 3 cups Gala apples (about 3-4 medium apples)
- 3 cups Honeycrisp apples (2 large or 3 medium apples)
- 1/2 cup Celery
- 1/4 cup Fresh lemon juice
- 1 cup Red seedless grapes

- 3/4 cup Toasted pecans
- 1/4 teaspoon Celery seed
- 1/4 teaspoon Sea salt
- 1/8 teaspoon Fresh cracked black pepper
- 1 cup Olive oil mayonnaise

Direction

- Wash, dry, core, apples. Dice into one in pieces (skin on).Toss with lemon juice.
- Wash and slice celery, including leaves, into 1/2 inch pieces.
- Toast pecans 350 degrees about 5 minutes. Cool and roughly chop.
- Wash and cut grapes in half lengthwise.
- Toss apples, celery, pecans, grapes, celery seed, salt and pepper.
- Add mayonnaise and gently fold into apple salad mixture.
- Cover with plastic wrap. Refrigerate at least an hour before serving.

10. Avocado BLT Salsa

Serving: Serves 4 | Prep: | Cook: | Ready in:

Ingredients

- 1 large ripe tomato, chopped
- 2 cups finely chopped bacon, cooked until crisp (12-14 slices)
- 1/2 cup scallions, chopped
- 1 cup diced avocado
- 1/2 cup paleo mayonnaise
- 1 tablespoon freshly squeezed lemon juice
- 1/2 teaspoon sea salt
- 1/2 teaspoon freshly ground black pepper
- 2 romaine leaves, finely chopped

Direction

- To make the salsa, mix the tomatoes, bacon, scallions, avocado, mayonnaise, lemon juice, salt, and pepper in a large bowl. Cover and refrigerate.

- When ready to serve, add in chopped romaine lettuce

11. Avocados Stuffed With Hot Smoked Salmon, Cilantro And Lemon Chipotle Mayonnaise

Serving: Serves six as an appetizer | Prep: | Cook: |Ready in:

Ingredients

- 1 teaspoon minced chipotle in adobo sauce (more adobo sauce can be added to taste)
- 2 tablespoons light mayonnaise
- 2 tablespoons light sour cream
- 1/2 teaspoon cumin seeds, toasted and ground to a fine powder
- 1 teaspoon real maple syrup
- 2 lemons, one juiced and one cut into six sections to be used for garnish
- 8 ounces hot smoked salmon*, skin removed and flesh broken into bite-sized pieces
- 1/2 cup frech bell pepper, diced in 1/4-inch pieces
- 1/4 cup chives, chopped
- 1/4 cup cilantro, chopped, plus more cilantro sprigs for garnish
- 3 ripe Haas avacados, halved with pits removed

Direction

- In a small bowl, whisk together mayonnaise, sour cream, cumin, maple syrup and one teaspoon of lemon juice. Put the pieces of hot smoked salmon in a medium bowl and add the diced bell pepper and chopped chives and coriander. Set both bowls aside momentarily.
- Take one avocado half and using a sharp knife take a thin slice of skin and flesh (no more than 1/8 inch) off the roundest part of the underside of the fruit. Turn the avocado over and rest it on its newly flattened backside.

- Using the small end of a melon baller, remove four balls of flesh from around the hole left by the pit. Place the avocado balls into the bowl with the salmon. You are simply trying to make the naturally round hole a bit more oval in shape. Take care not to remove too much flesh as you want to see a nice expanse of green once you place the salad into the hole.
- Using a pastry brush, lightly paint lemon juice across all exposed avocado flesh to prevent it turning that unappetizing shade of grey. Set the prepared avocado on a single salad plate that you will end up serving it on. Repeat this process with all remaining avocado halves.
- Gently fold the mayonnaise mixture into the salmon salad. It may take a bit of time to get all the components of the salad well coated with the limited amount of mayonnaise you've made. But don't be tempted to whip up more and add it to the mix as it will overpower the other ingredients in this dish quite quickly.
- Fill each avocado hole with about 1/3 cup of salmon salad. Garnish with cilantro springs and lemon slices. These prepared avocado halves can stay chilled in the refrigerator for a short time, but serve them within 30 minutes so that the mayonnaise doesn't separate.
- *NOTE: The "hot" in this ingredient does not describe its spiciness, but rather, the method by which the fish was smoked. Hot smoked fish is prepared differently from traditional cold smoked salmon (the kind you'd put on a bagel with cream cheese, for example) in that it is smoked over hot coals to a temperature of 145 degrees Fahrenheit so that it is fully cooked. Cold smoked salmon is smoked to a temperature of 80 degrees, so while it is cured, it is still technically raw.

12. BEST CHICKEN SALAD SANDWICH RECIPE

Serving: Serves 4 | Prep: 15hours0mins | Cook: 10hours0mins |Ready in:

Ingredients

- 20 ounces Chicken breasts
- ½ cups grape
- 2/3 cup cherry tomato
- 1 cup mayonnaise
- 3 tablespoons olive oil
- 2 tablespoons salt
- 2 tablespoons scallion
- 2   small cucumbers
- 1 tablespoon chopped onion

Direction

- Step 1: Preparation. Chop up the cherry tomatoes in quarters, and cucumbers in small dices. Cut the grapes in halves and get rid of their seeds. Roughly chop the celery, dill, scallion and cilantro.
- Step 2: Season the chicken. Rub the mixture of peppers, 1 tbsp. olive oil, 1 tbsp. salt and dill over the chicken breasts.
- Step 3: Toast the sandwiches. Get 4 sandwich slices toasted in 1 tbsp. olive oil until they turn golden brown. Let them chill, finely dice into cubes of ½ inch square.
- Step 4: Make the salad dressing. In a small mixing bowl, add in mayonnaise, 1 tbsp. olive oil, ½ vinegar, 1tbsp scallion, mustard, cilantro, dill and chopped onion. Stir everything together for a luscious salad dressing.
- Step 5: Fry the chicken breasts. Heat your pan to 350°F with enough oil to lightly coat the chicken. Put the chicken breasts in to fry in approximately 10 minutes. Remember to turn over evenly for both sides. Once done, drain them on paper towels and let chill. Use your hands to tear them in small threads.
- Step 6: Complete the salad. Combine the sandwich dices, cucumbers, cherry tomatoes, green peas, grapes and celery together with the fried splits of chicken breasts in a large bowl. Toss them together with the mayonnaise dressing that has been done at Step 4. Stir them all up until everything is evenly coated.

- Step 7: Serve. Occasionally, you can have this chicken salad spread on some toasted slices of sandwiches or seasoning crackers. You can even serve it over a bed of lettuce or just traditionally wrap it up and sink your teeth into. Don't forget to sprinkle some of your own leafy greens or nuts for a mega-flavorful side dish. Or just, you know, give it in. Go grab a monster scoop off the spoon. It worths the bursts!

13. BLT Fritters With Jalapeño Aioli

Serving: Makes 24 fritters | Prep: | Cook: |Ready in:

Ingredients

- BLT Fritters
- 2 cups All purpose flour
- 1/2 cup Crumbled cooked bacon [approximately 6 slices]
- 1-1/2 teaspoons Baking powder
- 1/2 teaspoon Salt
- 2 tablespoons Shortening
- 2   Eggs, slightly beaten
- 1/3 cup Milk
- 1/2 cup Oil-packed sun dried tomatoes, drained and finely chopped
- 2-3   Fresh Romaine lettuce leaves, center rib removed
- Cooking oil
- Jalapeño Aioli
- 1-1/2 cups Mayonnaise
- 2 tablespoons Extra virgin olive oil
- 1   Garlic clove, finely minced
- 1 tablespoon Finely minced fresh jalapeño (or to taste)
- 1 tablespoon Jalapeño-flavored pepper sauce (or to taste)
- 1 tablespoon Fresh lime juice
- 1 teaspoon Honey or agave

Direction

- BLT Fritters

- In a medium bowl stir together flour, crumbled bacon, baking powder, and salt. Using a pastry blender cut in shortening until flour mixture resembles fine crumbs. Make a well in center of flour mixture.
- In a small bowl combine eggs and milk. Add to flour mixture all at once. Stir just until dough clings together.
- On a lightly floured surface gently knead dough about 1 minute or until smooth. Divide dough in 24 portions; shape each portion in a ball. Cover dough; let rest for 20 minutes.
- Finely chop tomatoes and lettuce; combine thoroughly. On a lightly floured surface roll each ball in a 4-inch circle. Place a 1/2-teaspoon dollop of tomato-lettuce filling off-center of dough circle and fold dough over to form a half-circle; crimp edges with a fork to ensure they are thoroughly sealed.
- In a heavy 10-inch skillet pour cooking oil to a depth of 3/4 inch; heat to 375 degrees F. (Submerge end of thermometer in hot oil.) Fry fritters, 2 or 3 at a time, in hot oil for 2 to 3 minutes or until golden, turning once. Drain on paper towels. (Keep warm on a baking sheet in a 300 degrees F oven while frying remaining fritters.) Serve with Jalapeño Aioli.
- Jalapeño Aioli
- In a small bowl, whisk together mayonnaise, olive oil, garlic, minced jalapeño, pepper sauce, lime juice and honey. Transfer to a serving bowl and refrigerate until use.

---

14. BLT Panzanella

Serving: Serves 4 | Prep: | Cook: | Ready in:

Ingredients

- For the Salad
- 1/2 large loaf ciabatta bread, cubed
- 3   small to medium sized tomatoes, largely diced
- 3 ounces slab bacon, cut into cubes
- 3 handfuls arugula, roughly chopped

- Creamy Lemon Dressing
- 1/2 lemon, juiced
- zest of 1/4 lemon
- 1 teaspoon Dijon mustard
- 1 teaspoon leftover bacon drippings
- 3 tablespoons extra virgin olive oil
- 2 teaspoons mayonnaise
- Salt and fresh cracked pepper, to taste

Direction

- Preheat oven to 350.
- In a single layer on a cookie sheet, place cubed bread. Toast in oven until golden and dried through completely.
- In a medium sized sauté pan, cook bacon until slightly crispy and nicely browned. Remove to paper towels, reserve 1 tsp drippings.
- Combine the Dijon, lemon juice, zest, salt and pepper to taste.
- Whisk together bacon drippings and olive oil, then add in a slow stream to Dijon mixture.
- Once dressing is emulsified, whisk in mayonnaise until fully incorporated and slightly creamy.
- Toss tomatoes, bacon, bread, salt and fresh cracked black pepper with dressing.
- Just before serving, toss in arugula. Check for seasoning, serve.

---

15. BLT Pasta Salad

Serving: Makes 1 big bowl | Prep: | Cook: | Ready in:

Ingredients

- 1 pound Pasta (Shells, Farfalle, Orecchiette)
- 1 pound Thick cut bacon
- 2 cups Grape tomatoes, cut in half
- 3 cups Fresh baby spinach
- 1/2 - 3/4 cups Mayonnaise
- 1/2 Lemon - Juice and zest
- Salt and Pepper to taste

Direction

- Cut bacon into ¼ inch pieces and render over medium low heat until fairly crispy. Drain bacon on paper towels and set aside.
- While the bacon is cooking, prepare the pasta as directed on the package. You can use any type of pasta, but you want something that will catch some of the bacon in "pockets". For this reason, my favorites to use are orecchiette or farfalle pasta, although in this case, I used penne, which also worked just fine.
- After you drain the pasta, toss it with 1 tbsp. of olive oil to keep the pasta from sticking together and let the pasta cool for at least 20 minutes.
- Toss the pasta, bacon, tomatoes, mayonnaise, lemon juice, and lemon zest together and fold in the fresh spinach. Season with salt and pepper. Chill and serve.

16. BLT Potato Wedge Salad

Serving: Serves 6 | Prep: | Cook: | Ready in:

Ingredients

- 6 (medium-size) Idaho red potatoes
- 1/2 cup mayonnaise
- 2 tablespoons heavy cream
- 2 teaspoons tarragon vinegar
- 3 ounces crumbly blue cheese like Roquefort or Danish blue
- 1/2 teaspoon kosher salt
- 1/4 teaspoon freshly ground black pepper
- 1 large vine ripened tomato, seeded and diced
- 4 scallions, thinly sliced
- 3 tablespoons chopped flat leaf parsley
- 6 slices bacon, cooked crisp and crumbled
- 1/2 head iceberg lettuce, thinly sliced

Direction

- Cook potatoes in boiling salted water just until tender; drain and cool. Slice each potato into 6 wedges; place in a large bowl.

- In food processor combine mayonnaise, heavy cream, vinegar, 2/3 of the blue cheese, ¼ teaspoon salt and ¼ teaspoon black pepper; process just until combined.
- Add dressing, tomatoes, scallions, 2 tablespoons parsley and ¾ of the bacon to the potatoes; toss well. Taste and season with remaining salt, if needed.
- Line serving platter with lettuce. Spoon potato salad on top of lettuce. Sprinkle with remaining blue cheese, bacon and parsley.

17. BLT A La Italiana

Serving: Serves 2 to 3 servings or more | Prep: | Cook: | Ready in:

Ingredients

- 1 pound pecan wood smoked organic thick-sliced bacon
- 1 large loaf fresh ciabatta bread
- fresh baby arugula
- baby tri-color sweet peppers (yellow, red and orange)
- sun dried tomatoes preserved in olive oil
- good quality store variety mayonnaise
- fresh vine-ripe beefsteak tomatoes, sliced

Direction

- De-seed and clean the baby sweet peppers, leave them whole and layer onto a large baking sheet. Drizzle with olive oil, season with salt. Roast in a 450 degree oven until they begin to soften and the edges blacken a bit, the aroma will tell you when they are close to done.
- Remove from the oven, place in a bowl to cool. In the same 450 degree oven, place the slices of bacon on a large baking sheet spaced evenly and bake until sizzling and golden brown and crispy (I love mine extra crispy with some darker edges.)

- Remove from the oven and drain the slices carefully on paper towel on a large flat platter to remove excess oil, etc.
- Toast large sections of the ciabatta bread sliced in half until crispy and golden brown. Depending on the size of your loaf of bread you can make up to three sandwiches with this recipe.
- Take the roasted peppers (approx. 1/4 cup or more to taste) along with a good measure of the sun dried tomatoes (drained a bit, approx. 1/4 cup or more to taste.)
- Add about 3/4 to 1 cup of mayonnaise to the food processor bowl, and if desired add a cut up garlic clove to taste.
- Pulse this mixture until all the ingredients are well-blended. Taste for seasoning (add salt, pepper, etc.) and add more roasted peppers and/or sun dried tomatoes to your personal taste.
- Arrange your sandwiches by slathering a good amount of the flavored mayonnaise on the top slice of the toasted ciabatta, arrange several slices of the bacon strips on the bottom slice of toasted ciabatta, two to three tomato slices, and a good handful of fresh arugula.
- You can add more mayonnaise if desired and gently press down on the entire sandwich to meld the flavors together. Serve immediately.

18. BSP

Serving: Makes one sandwich | Prep: | Cook: | Ready in:

Ingredients

- 2 slices of whole grain bread
- 1 strip of bacon fried until crisp
- 1/2 tablespoon mayonnaise
- 1 peach sliced into 8 wedges
- 1 handful washed and dry spinach leaves

Direction

- Toast the bread and set aside.

- Cook the bacon in a skillet until crisp. Drain excess fat from the strips.
- Spread mayonnaise on one side of both pieces of toast.
- Pile a handful of washed and dry spinach on one piece of toast.
- Slice a whole peach into quarters and then slice the quarters in half. Place the eight peach slices on top of the spinach in an even layer.
- Break bacon into smaller pieces and layer on top of the peaches.
- Place the second piece of toast with mayonnaise layer on top.

19. BYOwnBob's BBT

Serving: Serves 1 | Prep: | Cook: | Ready in:

Ingredients

- The sandwich
- 4 pieces thick-sliced bacon (Neuskie's is nice)
- 1/2 teaspoon cracked black peppercorns
- 10-12 large fresh basil leaves
- 1 medium ripe tomato, peeled and thick-sliced
- salt and fresh ground black pepper to taste
- 2 slices Italian style bread
- The mayonnaise
- 2-3 tablespoons mayonnaise
- 6 large fresh basil leaves, chiffonade

Direction

- Fry bacon over medium low heat until evenly done, not too crisp. Season bacon slices with cracked black pepper as they crisp.
- Stack and roll 6 basil leaves into a cylinder and thinly slice (chiffonade) the basil. Add to mayonnaise in a small bowl and combine. Season lightly with salt and pepper.
- Divide and spread the basil mayo on both slices of bread. Divide and arrange 10-12 whole basil leaves on the 2 slices of bread. Arrange the sliced tomato on one slice and

season tomatoes with salt and freshly ground black pepper to taste.

- Drain bacon slices on paper towels and place on top of the tomato. Top the bacon with the second bread slice with basil to make a sandwich.
- Slice in half and enjoy with a tall glass of iced lemon-limeade.
- Double the ingredients to make the number of sandwiches you need.

20. Babe's Cole Slaw

Serving: Serves 4 | Prep: | Cook: | Ready in:

Ingredients

- 1 Small Cabbage
- 1/4 Onion
- 1 Small Carrot
- 4 tablespoons Salt
- 1 tablespoon Lemon juice
- 1 splash Milk
- 2 tablespoons Mayonnaise
- Pepper

Direction

- Finely chop cabbage, onion and carrot in food processor or use small grate on box grater
- Place Ingredients in colander over bowl
- Sprinkle the mix generously with salt
- Stir salt into mixture and wait 20 to 30 minutes until water drains from mix
- By hand, squeeze as much water as you can from the mix
- Taste the mix to see if the salt needs to be rinsed off. Most of the salt leaves the mix with the water, if not, rinse and squeeze excess water once again
- In a large bowl, add lemon juice and milk. Add mixture to bowl, stir together. Add mayonnaise a little at a time until it is the consistency you like. Season with less salt more pepper.

21. Bacon "Lettuce" And Peach Sandwich With Basil Mayo

Serving: Serves 2 | Prep: | Cook: | Ready in:

Ingredients

- Basil Mayonnaise
- 1/2 cup mayonnaise
- 2 tablespoons fresh chopped basil
- BL"P" sandwich
- 4 3/4 inch slices hearty white bread
- 2 ripe peaches, peeled and cut into slices
- 1 cup fresh arugula
- 8 slices cooked bacon

Direction

- In a small bowl, combine the mayonnaise and basil. Set aside.
- Place the bread under the broiler and toast until golden brown, Flip the bread slices over and continue to toast until golden.
- Transfer the bread to a platter or plate and spread the basil mayonnaise liberally on one side of each slice being sure to cover the entire surface. Layer two slices of bread with peaches and top each with 1/2 cup arugula. Top the arugula with the bacon and the remaining slice of bread. But the sandwich on an angle, corner to corner and serve immediately.

22. Bacon And Cheddar Stuffed Burgers

Serving: Serves 4 | Prep: | Cook: | Ready in:

Ingredients

- 4 slices bacon, diced
- 1 large red onion, halved and sliced thin

- 1/2 cup red wine
- 1 tablespoon fresh thyme leaves
- 1   large ripe tomato
- 1 1/2 pounds ground beef (with at least 16% fat)
- 1/2 cup (about 2 ounces) grated cheddar cheese
- 4   hamburger buns or small ciabatta rolls
- 2 tablespoons butter
- 1/4 cup mayonnaise
- 1/4 cup barbecue sauce
- Kosher salt and freshly ground pepper
- 4   romaine lettuce leaves

Direction

- Put the bacon in a skillet and cook over medium-low heat until the bacon is browned and crispy, 5 to 7 minutes. Transfer to a paper towel-lined plate with a slotted spoon. Discard the drippings.
- Return the pan to medium-low heat. Add the onion and cook until the onion is evenly browned and tender, about 20 minutes. Add the wine, increase the heat to high and bring to a boil. Cook until dry, 2 to 3 minutes. Stir in the thyme and remove from the heat
- While the onions are cooking, divide the ground beef into 8 equal portions and shape into 1/4-inch-thick patties. Use the bottom of a small bowl or plate to mark a spot for the stuffing.
- Cut the tomato into four thick slices and arrange in a single layer on a paper towel. Sprinkle with salt. Let sit. (This helps to eliminate the liquid and concentrate the flavors.)
- Preheat a gas grill to medium-high heat.
- Combine the bacon and cheese in a small bowl. Divide into 4 portions and shape each into a patty small enough to fit in the center of a patty. Top each with the remaining patties and press the edges together to seal.
- Spread the butter evenly over the tops and bottoms of the buns. Put on the grill, crust-side up. Cook until toasted, about 1. Transfer to a cutting board and spread equal amounts of

mayonnaise and barbecue sauce over the bottom half of each roll.
- Season the patties with salt and pepper and put on the grill. Cook, covered, until browned on both sides, about 4 minutes per side for medium rare. Divide among the rolls, top each with one-quarter of the onions, a tomato slice, lettuce leaf and the top of the bun. Serve immediately.

23. Bacon And Egg Salad

Serving: Makes egg salad for 2 sandwiches | Prep: | Cook: | Ready in:

Ingredients

- 2   hard boiled eggs
- 2   rashers of crispy bacon, coarsely crumbled
- 2   small stalks of celery, sliced in half lengthwise, and then finely chopped
- 6   bread and butter sweet pickle slices, preferably small batch, chopped
- 2   grindings Himilayan salt, or other favorite salt
- 2 dashes celery seed
- 1 heaping tablespoons good mayonnaise
- 1/2 teaspoon Dijon mustard

Direction

- With a fork, crumble the hard boiled eggs in a medium sized bowl. Add the crumbled bacon, the chopped celery, the chopped pickles, the salt, and the celery seed. Mix well with a fork.
- Add the mayonnaise and mustard and stir until all ingredients are well bound. Taste for seasoning.
- Serve as a sandwich, or place on good, crisp crackers (my preference).

24. Bacon And Egg Salad Sandwich With Dukkah And Peppery Greens

Serving: Makes 1 sandwich, but can be doubled, tripled, etc. | Prep: | Cook: | Ready in:

Ingredients

- The Sandwich – Makes one sandwich, but can be doubled, tripled, etc.
- 2 hard cooked eggs, peeled and cooled
- 1 tablespoon aioli or good mayonnaise + more for spreading on the bread, if desired
- 1 teaspoon Dijon or stoneground mustard (if not using an aioli with a strong mustard flavor)
- A healthy pinch or two of dukkah, or more, or less, to taste
- 2 slices good sandwich bread, toasted (See note, below.)
- 1 or 2 slices of natural bacon, cooked until crisp (optional)
- Small handful of watercress or arugula
- Dukkah – Makes a bit more than ¼ cup
- 2 tablespoons raw pepitas or pumpkin seeds
- 2 teaspoons whole cumin seeds
- 2 teaspoons whole coriander seeds
- 2 tablespoons raw sesame seeds
- 1 ½ teaspoons good black peppercorns or grains of paradise (I like Malabar black pepper for this, but a Tellicherry will also do just fine.)
- ½ teaspoon flaky sea salt, or more to taste

Direction

- The Sandwich – Makes one sandwich, but can be doubled, tripled, etc.
- Halve the eggs, remove the yolks and put them in a small bowl.
- Add the aioli and mustard (if using) and mash together well, using the back of a fork. Coarsely chop the whites of the eggs and stir them into the mashed yolks, with the dukkah. Taste, and add more salt, or more dukkah, or both, if necessary. (If adding both, add the dukkah first, taste again, and then add salt if necessary. Remember, the dukkah has salt in it.)
- If you want a bit of extra aioli or mayonnaise on the toasted bread, spread some on one or both slices.
- You can either chop the bacon up and stir it into the egg salad, or put the strips on the sandwich itself. Either way, heap the egg salad and greens on the toasted bread. Other.
- Put the sides together, then cut in half.
- Enjoy!! ;o)
- Dukkah – Makes a bit more than ¼ cup
- Toast the pepitas or pumpkin seeds in a small heavy skillet until they just start to darken and release their fragrance. Remove immediately from the pan and allow them to cool a bit.
- Toast the cumin and coriander seeds, each in turn, in the same skillet, removing from the pan as soon as they start to darken. Do not tarry, as they can burn easily in the hot pan, even when removed from the stove.
- Toast the sesame seeds in the same skillet, shaking periodically to make sure they brown evenly. Remove when they start to darken just a bit.
- Grind the pepitas in a spice mill to a coarse powder. Don't worry if there are a few larger pieces. Remove from the mill and put into a medium bowl.
- Grind the spices together until fine, and then add to the bowl with the ground pepitas.
- Grind the peppercorns coarsely and add to the bowl.
- Add the sesame seeds and salt and stir well until the blend is thoroughly combined.
- Store, tightly covered, in the refrigerator. It should hold for several weeks at least, depending on the freshness of the pepitas and sesame seeds.
- Enjoy!! ;o)

25. Bacon, Lettuce & Strawberry Sandwich

Serving: Makes 1 sandwich | Prep: 0hours10mins | Cook: 0hours10mins | Ready in:

Ingredients

- 4 to 6   ripe strawberries, tops removed and halved or quartered vertically
- Kosher salt and freshly ground black pepper
- 2   thick slices bacon, halved
- 2   slices bread
- 4   leaves iceberg lettuce
- Mayonnaise, to taste

Direction

- Add the strawberries to a bowl and sprinkle with a pinch each of salt and pepper. Toss, then let hang out while you work on the rest of the sandwich.
- Add the bacon to a cast-iron skillet and set over medium heat. Cook, shuffling around and flipping until crisp, 6 to 8 minutes.
- Use tongs to transfer the bacon to a plate, then immediately add the bread to the pan. Cook for 1 to 2 minutes per side, lowering the heat if needed, until the bread is toasty and golden-brown. Transfer the bread to a plate and let cool for a couple minutes.
- Spread each slice of bread with mayo, then build the sandwich in this order: strawberries, bacon, lettuce. Slice in half and eat immediately.

26. Bacon, Lettuce And Tomato/Mayo

Serving: Serves one sandwich per person | Prep: | Cook: | Ready in:

Ingredients

- 1   tomato per person
- mayonnaise to desired taste and consistency
- 2 to 3   strips crisp bacon
- 1 or 2 leaves   lettuce – whatever you like
- 2   sliced bread – toasted
- salt and pepper to taste

Direction

- Core and dice the tomato. Place in a strainer and allow the juice to drain out. 15 minutes should be enough. You can do it longer if you think it needs it.
- Mix the drained tomato dice with mayonnaise to a consistency that you like. Add salt and pepper to taste.
- Toast the bread if that is how you like it.
- Assemble your sandwich as usual – bread, lettuce, bacon and tomato/mayo mix. Cut in half as usual. Eat as usual.

27. Bacon Stuffed Burgers With Pimento Cheese And Avocado

Serving: Makes 4 burgers | Prep: | Cook: | Ready in:

Ingredients

- 2   slices bacon, diced
- 1   large white onion, halved and sliced paper-thin
- 1/4 cup   rice wine vinegar
- 1 teaspoon   granulated sugar
- 1 teaspoon   kosher salt
- 3 ounces   cream cheese, room temperature
- 4 ounces   extra-sharp cheddar cheese, grated
- 1   large jalapeño, minced
- 1 tablespoon   finely chopped pickled jalapeño
- 1 tablespoon   chopped pimentos
- 1 pinch   cayenne
- 1 1/4 pounds   ground beef (15% fat)
- 4   Dutch Crunch or other sturdy rolls, split in half
- 2 tablespoons   mayonnaise
- 1   large avocado, diced

- Lettuce mix

Direction

- Put the bacon in a skillet and cook over medium-low heat until the bacon is browned and crispy, 5 to 7 minutes. Transfer to a paper towel-lined plate with a slotted spoon and discard the drippings.
- Slice the onion and put it into a deep, narrow bowl. Add the vinegar, sugar, and salt, and stir to combine. Refrigerate at least 20 minutes.
- Put the cream cheese in the bowl of a food processor. Add the cheddar cheese.
- Add the fresh and pickled jalapeño to the cream cheese and cheddar cheese mixture. Add the pimentos and a pinch of cayenne. Pulse until thoroughly combined.
- Divide the ground beef into 8 equal portions and shape into 1/4 inch-thick patties. Use the bottom of a small bowl or plate to mark a spot for the stuffing. Divide the bacon among four of the patties. Top each with one of the remaining patties and press the edges together to seal. Set aside.
- Preheat a gas grill to medium-high heat.
- Put the buns on the grill, cut side-down. Cook until toasted, about 1 minute, moving as needed to prevent burning.
- Transfer the buns to a cutting board and spread 4 of them with mayonnaise. Mash one-quarter of the avocado on top of the mayonnaise on each roll. Top with a small handful of the lettuce mix and a scoop of the onions.
- Spread the other four rolls with equal amounts of the pimento cheese. (You may want to use less than the entire recipe. Any leftover can be refrigerated for up to one week.)
- Season the patties with salt and pepper and put on the grill. Cook, covered, until browned on both sides, about 4 minutes per side for medium-rare. Divide the patties among the rolls. Arrange the top half of the buns over each burger. Serve immediately.

28. Bagels To Go.

Serving: Makes 12 | Prep: | Cook: | Ready in:

Ingredients

- Red salmon filling:
- 12 plane, stale mini bagels
- 2 cups milk
- 2 cups caned red salmon, drained
- 1 medium white onion (fine diced)
- 2 hard-boiled eggs (fine diced)
- 3/4 cup prepared mayonnaise mixed with juice and zest of 1 large lemon and 2 teaspoons fresh dill (chopped)
- 1 cup shredded cheese (optional)
- Sausage and Sun-Dried Tomatoes filling:
- • 4 Bratwurst or Italian sausages, casings removed
- • 1 medium onion, chopped
- • 1/4 cup chopped sun-dried tomatoes (if very dry, soaked in hot water and drained first)
- • Coarse salt and freshly ground pepper
- • 1 large egg beaten
- • 1 cup shredded mozzarella cheese
- • 2 tablespoons freshly chopped parsley

Direction

- In a large glass baking dish lay out the bagels in one layer. Pour the milk over the bagels and soak them until puffed. Turn bagels a few times or press down. Meanwhile make the filling. In a mixing bowl steer eggs, onion, mayonnaise until well combined.
- To make the sausage filling: In a large skillet over medium-high heat, cook sausage, stirring occasionally, and breaking up meat with a spoon, until browned, 8 to 10 minutes.
- Add onion; cook stirring, until soft, 8 to 10 minutes. Stir in sun-dried tomatoes and parsley. Transfer to a plate; let cool to room temperature. Mix in the beaten egg to bind the filling.
- To assemble with red salmon filling: Preheat oven to 375 degrees F. Cover a large baking

sheet with parchment paper, spray with cooking spray, and lay out the bagels. In the center mount 1 heaping tablespoon salmon mixture and sprinkle with cheese. If not using cheese, cover the filling with about 1 teaspoon mayonnaise or bread crumbs sautéed in butter. Bake for about 10- 15 minutes or until golden brown.

- To assemble with Sausage filling: In the center mount 1 heaping tablespoon Sausage mixture and sprinkle with cheese. Bake for about 10- 15 minutes or until golden brown.

29. Baja Fish Tacos

Serving: Serves 4 | Prep: | Cook: | Ready in:

Ingredients

- Beer Batter Fish
- 1 cup all purpose flour
- 1 teaspoon salt
- 1/2 teaspoon dried oregano
- 1 cup beer
- 1 1/2 pounds skinless haddock, or other mild light fish, cut into 1-inch wide x 4-inch long strips
- 1- 2 tablespoons Malaysian Palm Oil, for frying
- 12   (6-inch) soft corn tortillas, warmed
- Tomato Salsa and and Crema
- 2 tablespoons Malaysian Palm Oil
- 1   small red onion, coarsely chopped
- 4   large ripe tomatoes, chopped
- 1   serrano chili
- 1   jalapeno, sliced
- 1 tablespoon chipotle hot sauce
- 1 tablespoon Mexican oregano
- 1/4 cup chopped fresh cilantro leaves
- 3 tablespoons mayonnaise
- 3 tablespoons sour cream
- 1 teaspoon grated lime rind
- 1 1/2 teaspoons fresh lime juice

Direction

- Beer Batter Fish
- Mix the flour, salt and oregano together in a medium bowl. Gradually add the beer, whisking until the batter is smooth with no lumps. Set aside.
- In a medium skillet, over medium heat, add enough palm oil to reach a depth of 1/2-inch. Heat the oil until a deep-fry thermometer registers 350 degrees F, or when the end of a wooden spoon sizzles when dipped into the oil.
- Working in batches so as not to crowd the pan, dip the fish strips in the beer batter and coat on both sides. Let the excess batter drip off, then fry the fish in the hot palm oil until golden brown and cooked through, about 2 minutes per side or an internal temperature of 140 degrees Fahrenheit is reached. Transfer to a plate lined with paper towels to drain.
- Tomato Salsa and Crema
- For Crema: Combine mayonnaise, sour cream, grated lime rind, fresh lime juice and let flavors blend.
- For tomato salsa combine remaining ingredients and let sit to marry the flavors.
- Place a strip of fish in each tortilla, serve with lime wedges, salsa, crema,

30. Baked "Coronation" Style Chicken

Serving: Serves 4-6 | Prep: | Cook: | Ready in:

Ingredients

- 8   bone-in chicken legs and thighs
- 1 1/2 cups yogurt, plain
- 1/2 cup mayonnaise
- 2/3 cup mango chutney
- 1   chopped apple
- 1   lemon, zested and juiced.
- 1   onion, chopped
- 1   garlic clove, crushed

- 1 tablespoon curry powder
- 1 teaspoon cumin
- salt and pepper to taste

Direction

- Mix the yogurt, mayonnaise, chutney, apple, lemon zest and juice, onion, garlic and spices together thoroughly.
- Make 1-2 deep slashes in each piece of chicken so the marinade can penetrate to the bone.
- Marinate chicken thighs in a ziptop plastic bag or a bowl for at least 4 hours or overnight.
- Preheat oven to 350 degrees. Bake chicken skin-side down, turning skin side up after 30 minutes. Chicken is finished when internal temperature reaches 165 degrees, approximately 1 hour.

31. Balsamic Chicken Sandwich With Peach Jam And Brandied Onions

Serving: Serves 4 | Prep: | Cook: |Ready in:

Ingredients

- For the chicken and brandied onions:
- 1 pound boneless free-range chicken breast, cut into strips
- 1 cup balsamic vinaigrette
- Sea salt, to taste
- Freshly cracked pepper, to taste
- Olive oil
- 1 red onion, thinly sliced
- 1 tablespoon brandy
- 1 loaf of bread from the bakery (I used French bread), sliced
- Peach jam (see below)
- Your favorite mayonnaise (or a vegan substitute)
- 1 head of lettuce (Boston, green, or red leaf would work)
- For the peach jam:

- 1 peach, peeled and chopped
- 2 tablespoons organic sugar
- 1 teaspoon brandy
- 1 pinch sea salt

Direction

- For the chicken and brandied onions:
- Marinate the chicken for at least one hour and up to 12. When you're ready to cook, preheat a grill or a grill pan over medium-high heat. Drizzle the grill with a little olive oil and cook chicken strips for 4 minutes per side. Remove and set aside.
- Meanwhile, in a small pan, heat a glug of olive oil over medium heat and add the onion slices. Season with salt and pepper and cook for 6 to 7 minutes, stirring often.
- Add the brandy and continue to cook until the alcohol is absorbed, about 2 to 3 minutes. Remove from the heat and set aside.
- Lay out the slices of bread. Spread the jam on one side and the mayonnaise on the other. On top of the jam, add the chicken, onion, then the lettuce. Voilà!
- For the peach jam:
- Add the ingredients to a pan set over high heat. Bring to a boil, then reduce heat to medium and continue to cook for about 7 minutes. Using a potato masher, smash the peaches until the big lumps are gone.
- Turn off heat and transfer to a jar to cool. The jam will keep for up to 3 weeks in the refrigerator (if you don't eat it all first!).

32. Banh Mi Soft Tacos

Serving: Serves 6 | Prep: | Cook: |Ready in:

Ingredients

- 1 daikon radish, cut into matchsticks
- 3 carrots, cut into matchsticks
- 1/4 cup cup white vinegar
- 1/4 cup unseasoned rice vinegar

- 1 cup water
- 1/4 cup sugar
- 1 tablespoon salt
- 1 cup mayonnaise
- 2 tablespoons sriracha
- 2 teaspoons Maggi seasoning
- 2 pounds chicken thighs, boneless
- 1 cup Thai barbecue sauce or teriyaki sauce
- 1 package taco-size soft corn tortillas
- 1 English cucumber, chopped
- 2 jalapeño peppers, chopped
- 1 bunch cilantro, chopped
- 1 queso fresco cheese round, broken into small pieces (optional)

Direction

- Make the pickled vegetables: Put the white vinegar, rice vinegar, water, sugar, and salt into a canning jar or container with a lid and stir until the sugar is dissolved. Add the daikon and carrot matchsticks. Make sure all the vegetables are covered. Refrigerate up to a month.
- Make the "sauce": Mix the mayonnaise, sriracha, and Maggi seasoning together until combined. Refrigerate.
- Marinate the chicken in the Thai or teriyaki sauce for at least an hour or overnight. Barbecue, broil, or bake the chicken until brown and the internal temperature reaches 165 degrees. Cool and shred the chicken into small pieces.
- To assemble tacos: Warm corn tortillas directly over a gas burner, under the broiler, or on the grill. (You can also wrap them in a wet paper towel two or three at a time and microwave for 30 seconds.)
- Spread about 1/2 teaspoon of the sriracha sauce on each warm tortilla, then put shredded chicken on top. Add the pickled vegetables and chopped cucumbers and jalapeños. Sprinkle with chopped cilantro. Add more sriracha sauce on top.
- If desired, sprinkle tacos with the soft queso fresco cheese.

- This recipe is great with marinated beef or pork strips, too!

33. Beef On A String

Serving: Serves 4 to 6 | Prep: | Cook: | Ready in:

Ingredients

- 8 cups home made vegetable stock
- 1/4 teaspoon fennel seed
- 1/4 teaspoon Sechuan peppercorns
- 1/2 teaspoon black peppercorns
- 8 whole cloves of garlic, peeled and trimmed
- 8 carrots, washed, peeled and cut into 2 inch long pieces
- 8 fingerling or small potatoes, peeled
- 2 celery roots, peeled and cut into 2 inch batons
- 1 or 2 onions depending on size, trimmed, root end left on then cut into wedges
- 2 to 2 1/4 pounds center cut piece of beef tenderloin, trimmed and cleaned of sinew, buyer can do this for you, trussed
- 2 tablespoons Pommery whole grain mustard
- 3 tablespoons Mayonnaise
- 1 tablespoon flat leaf parsley, very finely minced
- 1/2 to 1 teaspoons fresh lemon juice
- kosher salt and fresh ground black pepper

Direction

- Remove the trimmed and trussed tenderloin from the fridge and let it come to room temperature. This will take about an hour.
- Place a 4 quart heavy bottomed pot onto the stove. Place the tenderloin into the pot and add enough stock to cover it by an inch. You may or may not use all the stock. Remove the beef tenderloin from the stock and place it onto a plate. Pate the tenderloin dry and season it with salt.
- Add the garlic, fennel, Sechuan and black peppercorns to the vegetable stock. Season the

stock with a teaspoon kosher salt and a few grinds fresh ground black pepper. Bring the stock to a boil then turn off the heat. Now trim all your vegetables and prep everything else while you let the stock steep with the spices.

- Combine the mustard, mayo, parsley and lemon juice. Mix it well. Add some salt and pepper. Set aside.
- Add the trussed tenderloin to the pot.
- If you have big chunks of vegetables and some smaller ones you will want to add the veggies in stages. If the carrots are the largest add them first and so on. If they are all about the same size just add them all.
- Turn the heat to medium high and bring the pot to a boil then immediately reduce the heat to a simmer. Set a timer for 10 minutes. At the end of 10 minutes turn the tenderloin if it is floating and check for doneness. Set the timer again for 10 minutes.
- The tenderloin will start to look split at the edges and if you look into the cracks and see bright red you need to cook it longer. The usual way of checking the beef by squeezing works ok but the tenderloin is much squishier since it is being poached and therefore harder to gauge.
- I found 30 minutes was a perfect medium rare for the tenderloin I cooked but that time may vary a little depending on size. So be careful with your cooking time and don't be afraid to remove the beef to a plate, cover it and let it rest while everything else is finishing up.
- Remove the beef from the pot, let it rest covered then slice it into 1/2 inch medallions. Do not ladle hot stock over the top of the beef but instead ladle it on to the plate first. If you ladle it over the top it will cook the beef and it won't look as appealing. Place the medallions onto a platter surrounded by vegetables and stock. Serve with Maldon salt and the mayonnaise on the side.

Serving: Serves 3 | Prep: | Cook: | Ready in:

Ingredients

- 3   onions
- 10 ounces beer (300 mililiters)
- 2 teaspoons brown sugar
- 1 teaspoon balsamic vinegar
- 3   burger patties
- 3   buns
- 1   tomato
- 1/2 cup shredded lettuce
- 3 teaspoons barbecue sauce
- 2 teaspoons mayonnaise
- 1 teaspoon mustard
- 2-3 tablespoons flour
- salt, pepper
- oil for frying

Direction

- Peel and thinly slice 2 onions. Heat a tea spoon of oil in a pan to medium, then add onion slices and lightly fry until the onions are translucent. Add about 1/3 of beer and let it simmer until the beer has cooked down. Add brown sugar and balsamic vinegar, stir together, then add another 1/3 of beer and cook for 5-10 minutes, until the onions are soft, lightly brown and in a creamy sauce. Season with salt and pepper to taste. Remove from stove and set aside.
- While the onions are cooking, prepare Beer Batter Crispy Onion Rings: mix together about 2-3 tbsp. of flour and about 1/3 of beer. Season the batter with salt and pepper. Peel an onion and cut into slices. I made thin slices, but you can make them wider. Add onion slices to the beer batter and stir in gently, making sure the onion slices are covered in batter. Heat up oil for frying, then add onion slices one by one. Make sure the onions have enough room to float around in oil. Fry for about a minute on each side, or until the onion rings and golden-

brown and crispy, then remove from pan and set on a plate, covered with a paper towel.

- Heat up the grill pan and rub with a bit of oil. Place burger patties on grill and cook about 4 minutes until golden brown, then turn around and grill another couple of minutes on the other side. Remove from pan and set aside. Cut buns in half and place them on the grill pan to grill for a couple of minutes. Remove from pan.
- In a small bowl, mix together mayonnaise and mustard. Wash and dry tomato, then cut into slices.
- Start assembling your burgers. Take the bottom bun slices and spread with the mayonnaise mix. Add burger patty on top and a tomato slice, then top with beer braised onions. Add about 1 tsp. of barbecue sauce (I used store-bought), then top with a few crispy onion rings and some lettuce. Finish the burger with the top bun slice and stick through with a bamboo stick or knife. Serve.

35. Black Bean Burgers

Serving: Serves 4 | Prep: | Cook: |Ready in:

Ingredients

- For the Burgers
- 1 cup canned black beans, pureed
- 1 pound lean ground beef
- 1/2 cup chopped spinach
- 1/2 cup quoina, cooked
- 1 egg
- 1 tablespoon crushed garlic
- 1 teaspoon smoked paprika
- 4 Burrito-size tortillas
- For the Spread
- 1/4 cup mayonnaise
- 1/4 cup sour cream
- 1 tablespoon cumin
- 1/4 cup chopped cilantro
- 1 avacado

- 1 teaspoon ancho chili powder

Direction

- Combine black bean puree and next 6 ingredients in a large bowl. Shape into 4 patties.
- Heat a large sauté pan with 2 Tbsp. olive oil over med. high heat. Add 4 patties. Cook about 7 minutes per side, or until just slightly pink in center.
- Meanwhile, combine mayonnaise and next 5 ingredients in a food processor. Puree and chill.
- Heat tortillas in microwave about 15 seconds each. Spread each with 2 Tbsp. sauce and top with a burger patty.
- If desired, serve with chopped green cabbage, chopped plum tomatoes, and grated sharp cheddar cheese.
- Enjoy!

36. Black Bean Pumpkin Burgers With Cilantro Yogurt Sauce

Serving: Makes 10 burgers | Prep: | Cook: |Ready in:

Ingredients

- For the burgers:
- 2 cups cooked black beans
- 1.5 cups pumpkin puree
- 1.25 cups whole wheat bread crumbs
- 2 tablespoons chipotle sauce (I use La Morena brand)
- 1 medium garlic clove, roughly chopped
- 1 egg, beaten
- A generous handful of cilantro leaves
- A few dashes of hot sauce
- 0.5 teaspoons ground cumin
- 0.25 teaspoons sea salt
- 0.25 teaspoons freshly ground black pepper
- 3 tablespoons organic canola oil
- For the sauce and assembly:
- 5 ounces full fat plain Greek yogurt

- 1 tablespoon mayonnaise
- 1 teaspoon lime juice
- 1/3 cup packed cilantro leaves
- Pinch of salt
- Romaine leaves
- Sandwich rolls, halved

Direction

- For the burgers:
- In a food processor, combine all ingredients except canola oil. Pulse to combine. Do not puree - mixture should remain a bit chunky.
- Heat a large nonstick skillet over medium heat and add enough canola oil to coat the bottom. Using your hands, divide mixture into burger-sized patties. Working in batches, cook patties until browned and crisp on the bottom, about 5 minutes, flip, and cook for another 5 minutes.
- For the sauce and assembly:
- In a blender, combine yogurt, mayonnaise, lime juice, cilantro and salt. Puree until smooth. Taste and season with more salt or lime juice, if needed.
- To assemble, place romaine leaves on bottom sandwich roll halves and top with pumpkin burgers. Spread yogurt sauce on top sandwich roll halves, assemble into burgers and serve immediately.

37. Blackened Barramundi Sliders With Lemon Tartar Sauce

Serving: Makes 12 | Prep: | Cook: | Ready in:

Ingredients

- 2/3 cup mayonnaise
- 1 small shallot, minced
- 1/4 cup minced dill pickles
- 1 lemon, zested and juiced
- 2 tablespoons capers, drained, rinsed and minced
- 2 tablespoons finely minced parsley
- freshly cracked pepper, to taste
- 12 small slider rolls, sliced in half lengthwise
- 2 tablespoons salted butter
- 12 small pieces of little gem, bibb, or other delicate lettuce
- 2 plum tomatoes, cut into 12 even slices
- 1 pound skinless barramundi fillets, cut into 12 2-inch squares
- 2 tablespoons blackening seasoning
- 1 tablespoon vegetable oil
- 12 toothpicks, for serving

Direction

- In a small bowl, whisk together the mayonnaise, shallot, pickles, lemon zest, lemon juice, capers, parsley and pepper, then cover and refrigerate until ready to serve.
- Melt butter in a large skillet over medium heat, then place the slider rolls in the pan cut side down. Cook until lightly browned and toasted, about 2 minutes. Remove to a serving platter and top each bottom roll with a small piece of lettuce and a slice of tomato.
- Coat the barramundi pieces all over with blackening seasoning. Heat vegetable oil in a large skillet (cast iron works best) over high heat. Cook the barramundi pieces until blackened on one side, about 2 minutes, then flip and cook on the other side until opaque throughout, about 1-2 minutes more.
- Place a piece of fish on each bun on top of the tomato, then spoon a generous amount of lemon tartar sauce on top. Place the top bun over the sauce and secure with a toothpick. Serve immediately.

38. Bolognese Burger

Serving: Serves 6 | Prep: | Cook: | Ready in:

Ingredients

- 1 small carrot, roughly chopped
- 1 small celery stalk, roughly chopped

- 1/4 yellow onion, roughly chopped
- 2 teaspoons olive oil
- 1/2 cup dry red wine (preferably one you wouldn't hesitate to drink)
- 2 cups strained tomatoes (such as Pomi)
- 1 teaspoon salt, plus more to taste for the burger patties
- 1 tablespoon dark brown sugar, packed
- 1/2 cup mayonnaise
- 1/4 cup grated parmesan, packed
- 2 small garlic cloves, peeled and smashed
- 1 1/4 pounds ground beef, at least 15% fat content
- 12 ounces ground pork
- 4 ounces pancetta, finely diced
- 6 ounces young fontina cheese, grated
- 6 lightly toasted burger buns, either regular white or brioche
- 1 1/2 cups fresh arugula, packed
- 1/2 red onion, sliced into thin rings

Direction

- To make the aioli: place mayonnaise, parmesan, and garlic in a food processor. Blend until mostly smooth and only small flecks of parmesan remain. Transfer to a small bowl, cover, and refrigerate until use.
- To make the tomato sauce: place the chopped carrot, celery, and onion in a food processor, pulse until the mixture is minced. In a medium saucepan, heat up olive oil on medium high. Add vegetable mixture and cook until most of the liquid has been absorbed, 6 to 8 minutes. Add red wine and cook for 1 minute. Add strained tomatoes, salt, and sugar. Turn down the heat to medium low and simmer for 35 minutes, stirring every few minutes to prevent scorching, until the sauce has reduced by 1/3 to 1/2. Transfer about 1/3 cup of sauce to a small bowl and reserve for burger assembly, set the rest aside by your stove for brushing burger patties with while they are cooking.
- To make the burgers: combine ground beef, ground pork, and pancetta in a large bowl and mix well with either your hands or a spoon. Form the mixture into six 6 oz. patties. Place

an indent in the middle of each patty so it doesn't puff up in the middle while cooking.
- Heat up a cast iron griddle or skillet on medium high (or have your outdoor grill ready). Have the tomato sauce and a brush close at hand. Liberally salt one side of each patty and place, salt side down, on the griddle. Salt the other exposed side, cook for 2 minutes then gently flip. Generously brush the top of each patty with tomato sauce, cook for another 2 minutes and flip again. Generously brush the other side with tomato sauce, cook for 2 minutes then flip one final time so the tomato sauce on both sides gets a chance to come into contact with the pan and caramelize. Add 1 oz. of grated fontina on top of each patty and cook for 1 to 2 more minutes (covered, if you want the cheese to get really melty), for a total cooking time of 7 to 8 minutes for medium burgers. Adjust cooking times as necessary for your desired doneness.
- To assemble: place a spoonful of the reserved tomato sauce on the bottom bun. Place burger patty on top. Add a heaping handful of arugula and a few rings of sliced red onion. Smear some aioli on the top bun and finish off the burger by placing it on top.

39. Boston Greens With Tarragon Buttermilk Dressing, Red Pears, And Toasted Hazelnuts

Serving: Serves 4 | Prep: | Cook: | Ready in:

Ingredients

- Fresh Tarragon Buttermilk Dressing
- 3 tablespoons buttermilk
- 2 tablespoons mayonnaise
- 1.5 teaspoons olive oil
- 1 teaspoon minced shallot
- 1.5 teaspoons finely chopped fresh tarragon
- freshly ground black pepper (4-5 turns on the mill - finest setting)

- salt (3-4 turns on the mill - finest setting)
- Hazelnut Preparation and Salad Assembly
- 1/3 cup hazelnuts
- 3 red pears
- 2 heads of Boston lettuce, washed and torn into medium-large sized pieces
- coarse pink or red sea salt (such as Alaea Hawaiian)
- freshly ground black pepper

Direction

- Fresh Tarragon Buttermilk Dressing
- Whisk together buttermilk and mayonnaise until smooth; whisk in olive oil until well incorporated; add shallot, tarragon, salt and pepper.
- Hazelnut Preparation and Salad Assembly
- Roast hazelnuts in a single layer in a 350 oven for about 10 minutes, or until they start to lightly brown; remove from oven, and roll hazelnuts in dish towel to remove the papery skins; allow hazelnuts to cool, then coarsely chop and set aside
- Thinly slice the pears, being sure to keep a good sliver of the red peel on each slice; arrange the pears in a single layer on 4 salad plates, with the peel edges facing outward
- Toss the lettuce in about half the dressing, adding more, as necessary, to nicely coat all pieces; pile the lettuce in a tall mound on top of the pears (be sure to keep the red pear peals visible)
- Top each salad with freshly ground pepper, a small handful of the toasted hazelnuts, and a little pinch of the crunchy sea salt.

40. Bourbon Onion Mayonnaise

Serving: Makes 2 cups | Prep: | Cook: | Ready in:

Ingredients

- 2 tablespoons Canola Oil
- 1 tablespoon Butter
- 1 Large Yellow Onion (Sliced)
- 1/2 teaspoon Sea Salt
- 1/8 teaspoon Black Pepper
- 1/4 cup Beef Au Jus
- 1/2 cup Bourbon
- 1 cup Mayonnaise

Direction

- Heat oil over medium heat.
- Add butter and brown slightly.
- Add sliced onions and cook while stirring for about 10 minutes or until onions just begin to caramelize.
- Add Brown Sugar, Salt and Pepper. Stir well, reduce heat to medium low and continue cooking for 20-30 minutes.
- When onions are caramelized, add the Beef Au Jus and Jim Beam Black Bourbon.
- Cook until onions have a nice brown color.
- Remove from heat and cool slightly.
- Place onions in food processor and pulse until smooth.
- Combine in mixing bowl with mayonnaise and mix until smooth.

41. Breakfast Egg Salad

Serving: Serves 4 | Prep: | Cook: | Ready in:

Ingredients

- 6 large eggs
- 2 tablespoons full-fat mayonnaise
- 2 tablespoons plain 2% Greek yogurt
- 2 teaspoons Dijon mustard
- 4 slices cooked bacon, crumbled
- 3 tablespoons finely chopped red onion
- 1 tablespoon finely chopped fresh chives
- 1/4 teaspoon salt
- 1/4 teaspoon freshly ground black pepper
- 4 pieces 100% whole-grain bread, toasted

Direction

- Put the eggs in a medium saucepan, cover with 1 inch of water, and bring to a boil over high heat. Remove the pan from the heat, cover, and let stand for 12 minutes. Immediately transfer the eggs to an ice bath for 5 minutes. Peel and chop the eggs.
- In a medium bowl, combine the eggs, mayonnaise, yogurt, mustard, bacon, red onion, chives, salt, and pepper. Serve on toast. The egg salad will keep in an airtight container in the refrigerator for 1 day.

42. Briny Mediterranean Deviled Eggs

Serving: Makes 2 dozen pieces | Prep: | Cook: |Ready in:

Ingredients

- 12 hard boiled eggs
- 3/4 cup mayonnaise
- 1 tablespoon white wine vinegar
- 1.5 tablespoons anchovy paste
- 1 tablespoon aleppo pepper, or smoked paprika, plus additional for garnish
- 1/3 cup pitted kalamata olives, finely chopped
- 1 tablespoon lemon zest
- 1 teaspoon salt
- 1 teaspoon freshly ground black pepper
- 12 anchovies (one 2 oz. tin) packed in olive oil, halved for garnish
- Parsley leaves, for garnish

Direction

- Carefully slice the hard boiled eggs in half, and place the yolks in a mixing bowl for the filling. Set the whites aside.
- Mash up the egg yolks with a fork until finely crumbled.
- In the same bowl, add the mayonnaise, white wine vinegar, anchovy paste, aleppo pepper, kalamata olives, and lemon zest. Combine all ingredients with a fork until well combined.

- Add salt and pepper, taste for seasoning, and add more aleppo if you like more spice. Use the fork to vigorously combine the mixture until smooth.
- Using a piping bag or simply a teaspoon, fill the egg white halves with the yolk mixture. Garnish each egg with a parsley leaf and half an anchovy. Sprinkle on a little more aleppo pepper and serve.

43. Broccoli Cheese Casserole Recipe

Serving: Serves 2 | Prep: | Cook: |Ready in:

Ingredients

- 1/4 ounce Can of condensed cream of mushroom soup
- 1/4 cup Mayonnaise
- 1/4 Egg (beaten)
- 1 tablespoon Finely chopped onions
- 3/4 ounce Frozen chopped broccoli
- 1/2 pinch Paprika

Direction

- Preheat oven to 350 degrees F (175 degrees C).
- Butter a 9x13 inch baking dish.
- In a medium bowl, whisk together condensed cream of mushroom soup, mayonnaise, egg and onion.
- Place frozen broccoli into a very large mixing bowl. (I like to use my large stainless steel bowl to mix this recipe thoroughly.)
- Break up the frozen broccoli.
- Using a rubber spatula, scrape soup-mayonnaise mixture on top of broccoli, and mix well.
- Sprinkle on cheese and mix well.
- Spread mixture into prepared baking dish, and smooth top of casserole.
- Season to taste with salt, pepper and paprika
- Bake for 45 minutes to 1 hour in the preheated oven.

44. Broccoli Salad & Egg Persillade Dressing

Serving: Serves 3 generously – can easily be doubled | Prep: | Cook: | Ready in:

Ingredients

- Persillade Dressing
- 3 tablespoons fresh Italian parsley
- 4 cloves pressed garlic
- 1/8 teaspoon kosher salt
- Zest from one lemon
- Fresh ground pepper
- Yolks from 3 jumbo hard boiled eggs
- 4 tablespoons of a good mayonnaise (I use Best Foods)
- 1 teaspoon yellow prepared mustard
- 1 tablespoon olive oil
- 1-1/2 teaspoon fresh lemon juice
- Salad Ingredients
- 2-1/2 cups bite size broccoli and stems
- Whites from 3 jumbo hard boiled eggs, sliced bite size
- 4 large cherry tomatoes, sliced in thirds (or 8 small sliced in half)
- 6 Kalamata olives, sliced in thirds
- 1 cup celery, sliced on slight diagonal
- 1/4 cup sweet bell pepper, any color - optional
- 2 tablespoons chopped Italian parsley for garnish - if desired

Direction

- Persillade Dressing
- Prepare the Persillade mixture: Combine the parsley and its stems, pressed garlic, salt, lemon zest and ground pepper on a flat surface, chop and grind the ingredients together. Set aside.
- Hard boil the eggs in your usual manner, run under cold water a few minutes, then shell and cut in half. Remove the yolks from the whites. Reserve the whites for the salad.
- Combine the yolks and Persillade mixture in a bowl and crush with a fork creating a coarse paste.
- Add in the mayonnaise, mustard, olive oil and lemon juice, whisk to incorporate, creating a creamy dressing. Set aside until needed.
- Salad Ingredients
- Prepare the broccoli: wash, shake off excess water, pat dry with paper towel; using a vegetable peeler shave away the outside skin of the thick stalk. Lay it on a cutting board; begin to thinly slice the stalk at a slight diagonal, as you cut the florets will begin to fall off, cut them into bite size pieces.
- Add the broccoli and rest of the salad ingredients to a bowl.
- Pour the dressing over the top, toss with a spoon, coating all ingredients evenly.
- Cover and refrigerate at least 2 hours.
- Before serving, toss gently and add a few grinds of fresh ground pepper. Garnish with chopped Italian parsley, if desired.

45. Broccoli Salad With A Mustard Vinaigrette & Roasted Pumpkin Seeds

Serving: Serves 3 | Prep: | Cook: | Ready in:

Ingredients

- 1 large head of broccoli chopped into small pieces
- 35ml red wine vinegar
- 45ml mayonnaise
- 1.5 tsp honey
- 1 tsp mustard (I use Colemans Savora)
- salt & pepper to taste
- 3 chopped spring onions as garnish
- roasted pumpkin seeds as garnish

Direction

- Chop your broccoli into small bite size pieces.

- Prepare the vinaigrette dressing. Mix together vinegar, honey, mayonnaise, salt, pepper and mustard in a small bowl. I prefer my vinaigrette more on the vinegar-y side, so add more honey if you'd like it sweeter, more mayonnaise to cut the sharpness of the vinegar, and more mustard to add spice.
- Pour over top the chopped broccoli in a plastic container that you can close. Shake the broccoli to coat it in the dressing. Place in fridge overnight.
- The next day, serve the broccoli and garnish with spring onions and roasted pumpkin seeds.

46. Broccoli Bean Salad

Serving: Serves 8 to 12 | Prep: | Cook: |Ready in:

Ingredients

- 3 to 3 1/2 cups finely chopped raw broccoli
- 1 15-ounce can black beans, rinsed and drained
- 1 10-ounce bag frozen shelled edamame, cooked and cooled
- 1/4 cup finely chopped red onion, rinsed and drained
- 1/3 cup roasted and salted sunflower seeds
- 1/3 cup dried cranberries, finely chopped
- 1/2 cup mayonnaise
- 3 tablespoons red wine vinegar
- 1 tablespoon sugar
- 1/4 teaspoon salt
- 1/4 teaspoon coarsely ground black pepper

Direction

- In 2-quart glass bowl, combine broccoli, beans, onion, seeds and cranberries.
- In small bowl, whisk together mayonnaise, vinegar, sugar, salt and pepper.
- Stir dressing into salad. Cover and chill at least 4 hours or overnight.

47. Brown Rice Sushi Balls

Serving: Makes 12 to 15 rice balls | Prep: | Cook: |Ready in:

Ingredients

- For the rice balls:
- 1 cup short grain brown rice, prepared according to package directions and cool enough to handle comfortably
- 1 tablespoon black sesame seeds
- 1 tablespoon white sesame seeds
- 2 tablespoons minced, toasted seaweed (I used Annie Chun's sesame seaweed snacks)
- 1 ounce toasted almonds, finely chopped
- 3 tablespoons minced chives, divided
- For the spicy mayonnaise:
- 1 tablespoon mayonnaise
- 1 teaspoon sriracha hot chili sauce
- 1 dash soy sauce
- 1 dash lemon juice

Direction

- Some filling ingredient options: small cubes of avocado tossed with a little lemon juice (to keep them from turning brown), tiny cubes of sashimi grade ahi tuna or salmon, pickled ginger, spicy mayonnaise.
- Line a container or platter with parchment paper and set aside.
- Combine all rice ball ingredients - reserving 1 tablespoon of the chives for garnish - in a large bowl. Season to taste with fine sea salt.
- Line a small, deep cup with plastic wrap. Scoop in enough of the rice mixture to fill about 2/3 full. Make an indentation in the center of the rice and fill with your choice of ingredients (see suggested combinations above). Gather the plastic wrap straight up from the sides and use your fingers to gently cover the filling with rice. Lift the ball from the bowl and gently twist it, letting any air escape. Use your fingertips and opposite palm to shape a round ball. Gently remove the ball

from the plastic wrap and place in container or on platter. Repeat with remaining rice mixture (you'll get the hang of it after a few balls). Sprinkle with reserved chives for garnish.

- Filling them is the fun part: sashimi grade ahi tuna + avocado + spicy mayonnaise - avocado + spicy mayonnaise + pickled ginger - sashimi grade ahi tuna + avocado + pickled ginger - or - How about sashimi grade salmon, crab, or even solid rice balls topped with a thin slice of ahi or salmon (similar to nigiri); you see where I'm going with this. So many options!
- For dipping (optional): 2 parts soy sauce to 1 part sesame oil +soy sauce + wasabi paste to taste

---

48. Brussel Sprout Salad With Creamy Garlic Dressing

Serving: Serves 4 | Prep: | Cook: |Ready in:

Ingredients

- For the dressing
- 3 heads of garlic
- olive oil
- Kosher salt
- freshly ground black pepper
- 1/2 cup mayonnaise
- 3 tablespoons Parmesan cheese
- 2 1/2 tablespoons heavy cream
- 2 tablespoons lemon juice
- For the salad:
- stale bread, cut into squares, resulting in about 1 1/2 cups of croutons
- olive oil
- Kosher salt
- freshly ground black pepper
- 3 slices thick cut bacon, chopped into 1/2 inch pieces
- 3/4 pound brussel sprouts, trimmed and halved
- 9 ounces romaine lettuce
- 1/2 cup blue cheese

Direction

- Preheat oven to 325. Slice off a ½ inch of the top of the garlic head and peel off a little of the skin, making sure that the cloves stay together. Place on baking sheet, cut side up, and sprinkle with olive oil, salt, and pepper. Flip garlic so it's cut side down and bake for an hour. Let cool completely.
- Squeeze out garlic cloves and mash into a paste using a fork or mortar and pestle.
- In a small bowl, whisk together mayonnaise, garlic mash, Parmesan, cream, and lemon juice. Taste and adjust seasoning. If dressing is too thick, thin out with a little additional lemon juice. Set aside. Note that this makes about 3 times the amount of dressing you need for the salad, but it's great for dipping vegetables or using for a different salad.
- Increase oven temperature to 400. Lay bread pieces single layer on a baking sheet. Drizzle with olive oil, salt, and pepper. Bake for 10-15 minutes until bread has browned. Let cool completely.
- Cook bacon in a large skillet until crispy. Transfer bacon bits to a paper-towel lined plate.
- Add brussel sprouts, cut side down, to skillet with bacon fat. Cook until they are bright green and slightly crispy. Remove from heat.
- Toss lettuce leaves with about ⅓ of dressing. Top with brussel sprouts, bacon bits, blue cheese, and croutons.

---

49. Buffalo Chicken Potato Skins

Serving: Makes approximately 40 bite-size potato skins | Prep: | Cook: |Ready in:

Ingredients

- 1 pound fingerling potatoes (larger is better)
- Olive oil
- Salt

- 1 pound boneless, skinless chicken thighs, cut into small 1/4-inch cubes
- 1/4 cup cornstarch
- Grapeseed oil
- 1/2 cup Frank's RedHot hot sauce (or your favorite hot sauce)
- 2 tablespoons butter
- 1/4 cup crumbled blue cheese (I used Stilton)
- 1/4 cup sour cream
- 1 tablespoon mayonnaise
- 1 teaspoon white wine vinegar
- A handful of thinly sliced chives

Direction

- Preheat the oven to 425° F. Place the potatoes on a foil-lined rimmed baking sheet, drizzle them with olive oil so they are barely coated, and season with salt. Cook for approximately 20 minutes, until they are tender when pierced with a fork. When the potatoes are cool enough to handle, slice them in half, and using a small spoon, remove about 2/3 of the flesh from the inside of each potato. You can discard this potato flesh or save it for another purpose.
- Arrange the potato skins on a foil-lined rimmed baking sheet, drizzle each one with a tiny bit of olive oil, and roast in the oven for an additional 8 to 10 minutes at 425° F, until the edges of the potatoes appear crispy and brown. Remove the potatoes from the oven and set aside.
- In a large mixing bowl, season the chicken with salt, and then toss it with the cornstarch so that the pieces of chicken are lightly dusted. Set a large skillet over high heat, and add grape seed oil until the bottom of the skillet is covered with 1/8 inch of oil. When the oil begins to lightly smoke, add the chicken. Be aware that the hot oil may splatter. Stir the chicken regularly, and cook until the chicken begins to brown and become crispy. If you cannot cook all of the chicken in a single even layer, cook it in batches—otherwise your chicken will not get crispy. When the chicken is crispy, remove it to a rimmed baking sheet

lined with paper towels to drain any excess fat.
- Set a large skillet over medium heat. Add the hot sauce and the butter, and when the butter melts, stir to combine. Add the chicken, and toss to fully coat. Set aside.
- In a mixing bowl, beat together the blue cheese, sour cream, mayonnaise, and white wine vinegar. Fill each potato skin with a small about of the blue cheese mixture. Top each potato skin with a few small pieces of chicken. Place the filled potato skins into the oven at 425° F, and cook until the cheese mixture begins to bubble, approximately 5 minutes. Transfer the potato skins to a serving platter, garnish with chives, and enjoy.

50. Buffalo Chicken Sandwich With Blue Cheese & Hot Sauce

Serving: Makes about 4 sandwiches | Prep: | Cook: | Ready in:

Ingredients

- 4 ounces blue cheese, plus more for serving, if you'd like
- 2/3 cup mayonnaise
- 1/4 cup sour cream or thick yogurt
- 1/4 cup well-shaken buttermilk
- 1 tablespoon white wine vinegar
- 1 teaspoon runny honey
- 1 tablespoon minced fresh chives, scallions, or garlic scapes
- Freshly ground black pepper
- 2 pounds boneless, skinless chicken thighs, cut into 1-inch cubes
- 1/2 cup cornstarch
- Grapeseed oil, for frying
- 1 cup Frank's RedHot hot sauce, or your favorite hot sauce, plus more for serving
- 4 tablespoons butter

Direction

- If you like a smooth dressing, grab a medium bowl and mash the blue cheese into the mayonnaise with the back of a fork. If a chunky dressing is preferred, keep the blue cheese aside and proceed. Mix the mayonnaise with the sour cream, most of the buttermilk, and all of the vinegar and honey. Add the chives to the bowl, along with the blue cheese if making the chunkier style. Fold to combine, and season with pepper. Taste for seasoning, adding more buttermilk, vinegar, honey, and pepper, as necessary. You can use the dressing right away but it's even nicer after a day in the fridge, which gives the flavors a chance to round out. The dressing will thicken as it sits, but can be thinned with a few drops of water.
- In a large mixing bowl, season the chicken with salt, and then toss it with the cornstarch so that the pieces of chicken are lightly dusted. Set a large skillet over high heat, and add 1/8 inch of grape seed oil. When the oil begins to lightly smoke, add the chicken. Be aware that the hot oil may splatter. Stir the chicken regularly, and cook until the chicken begins to brown and become crispy. If you cannot cook all of the chicken in a single even layer, cook it in batches—otherwise your chicken will not get crispy. When the chicken is crispy, remove it to a rimmed baking sheet lined with paper towels to drain any excess fat.
- Set a large skillet over medium heat. Add the hot sauce and the butter, and when the butter melts, stir to combine. (If your chicken will not all fit in the skillet, you'll want to work in batches here, too.) Add the chicken and toss to fully coat. Set aside.
- To assemble the sandwiches, top buns or subs with chicken, then drizzle on blue cheese dressing and as much hot sauce as you'd like. Crumble over any remaining blue cheese.

Serving: Serves 1 | Prep: 0hours10mins | Cook: 0hours10mins | Ready in:

Ingredients

- Buffalo-glazed salmon
- 1 center-cut salmon fillet (about 6 to 8 ounces)
- 1 tablespoon your favorite hot sauce, especially a vinegary one like Tabasco or Frank's RedHot
- 1 tablespoon mayonnaise
- 1 teaspoon granulated sugar
- Freshly ground black pepper, lots of it
- Blue cheese kale salad
- 1 ounce blue cheese, at room temperature
- 1 tablespoon mayonnaise
- 2 teaspoons malt vinegar
- 3 tablespoons olive oil
- 1 pinch celery seed, optional
- Kosher salt and freshly ground black pepper, to taste
- 1 small bunch Tuscan kale (also known as lacinato or dinosaur), cut into bite-size pieces

Direction

- For the salmon, whisk together the hot sauce, mayonnaise, sugar, and black pepper and marinate the fillet in this for 10 minutes or so.
- Heat a nonstick pan and fry the salmon (no oil required, as the mayo will melt into its oily base) for 4 minutes on its first side, then another 2 to 3 minutes on its second side. (Though, it's important to cook your fillet based on its thickness rather than on its weight, which is to say: the thicker the fillet, the longer the cooking time.) Raising the heat to high, add any leftover marinade and let it bubble up into a sticky glaze.
- Meanwhile, for the salad, whisk together the blue cheese, mayo, vinegar, olive oil, celery seed, salt, and pepper until amalgamated into a dressing. Massage this dressing into the kale.

Crack some more black pepper overtop for good measure and enjoy with the salmon.

---

52. Bulgogi

Serving: Serves 4-6 | Prep: 4hours30mins | Cook: 0hours25mins | Ready in:

Ingredients

- Marinade
- 1 pound Sliced Beef (Top Sirloin, Hanger Steak, Skirt Steak, Flat Iron, Short rib), or Boneless Pork Loin, or Skinless Boneless Chicken Breasts or Thighs
- 3 tablespoons Soy Sauce
- 2 tablespoons Brown Sugar
- 1 tablespoon Honey
- 2 tablespoons Sake, Red Wine, Korean Wine
- 1 tablespoon Sesame Oil
- 2 tablespoons Garlic, minced
- 1 tablespoon Ginger, minced
- 1 tablespoon Gochujang
- 1 teaspoon Black Pepper
- 2 teaspoons Sesame Seeds
- 1 tablespoon Green Onion, chopped
- 1/2-1 Asian Pear or Bosc Pear, pureed
- Ssam, Sssamjang Sauce, and Toppings
- 1 bunch Bib Lettuce, Living Lettuce, Boston Lettuce, Red Cabbage for Ssam
- 2 tablespoons Soybean Paste such as Doenjang or Miso
- 1 tablespoon Gochujang
- 1 teaspoon Garlic, minced or grated
- 1 teaspoon Ginger, minced or grated
- 1 teaspoon Green Onion, finely chopped
- 1 tablespoon Sesame Seeds
- 2 tablespoons Mayonnaise
- 1 teaspoon Sesame Oil
- Suggested Toppings: Broccoli Slaw featuring Shredded Carrots, Broccoli and Red Cabbage. Red Bell Pepper. Asian or Bosc Pear. White Rice. Green Onion.

Direction

- Marinade: Slice your choice of meat very thin. Place in a Ziploc gallon size bag. Mix marinade ingredients together. Pour over meat in the bag. Marinate 4 hours up to overnight
- For the sauce; mix all ingredients together. Add more mayonnaise if sauce is too spicy. Cut the toppings small in order to be able to stuff it into a cabbage wrap.
- To cook the meat: Heat pan over medium heat. Add half the meat and cook until it's just starting to brown and is quite tender. Remove first batch from pan and cook second batch. Serve with toppings and Ssamjang sauce.

---

53. Buttermilk Mayonnaise, Ranch Style

Serving: Serves 4 | Prep: | Cook: | Ready in:

Ingredients

- buttermilk mayonnaise
- 1/3 cup buttermilk
- 2 cloves garlic, pressed (or 4 cloves roasted)
- 2/3 cup oil, neutral (may substitute up to 1/4 cup with olive oil)
- salt and pepper to taste
- Ranch dip
- 1 bunch batch buttermilk mayonnaise from above
- 2 tablespoons yogurt
- 2 teaspoons fresh dill
- 1 tablespoon chives or scallions
- 1 tablespoon other fresh herbs
- 1/2 teaspoon black pepper

Direction

- Buttermilk mayonnaise
- Add pressed garlic to buttermilk and blend with immersion blender.
- Add oil slowly in a thin stream. Once mixture begins to emulsify it is safe to add oil more

rapidly. I haven't broken this emulsion once (though I've messed up traditional mayonnaise several times).

- If mixture hasn't formed a "thick dressing" consistency after adding all the oil add a bit of lemon juice or other acid (no more than 1/2 tsp.) and blend fully. I've had different results with different buttermilks.
- Salt and pepper to taste.
- Ranch dip
- Chop herbs to smallish pieces which won't wind around the immersion blender.
- Blend all ingredients until smooth. If mixture isn't thick enough add additional yogurt and oil and reblend.

54. Bánh Mì Style Turkey Sandwich

Serving: Serves 2 with leftover vegetables | Prep: | Cook: | Ready in:

Ingredients

- 1 teaspoon peeled, finely minced ginger
- 1/4 cup brown sugar
- 1/4 cup white or rice wine vinegar
- 1/4 teaspoon kosher salt
- 1 medium carrot, peeled and coarsely shredded
- 1/2 seedless cucumber, cut crosswise in pieces about the same lngth as the rolls you are using, and sliced thinly lengthwise (this is most easily done with a mandolin)
- 2 tablespoons mayonnaise
- 1/8 teaspoon Sriracha or similar hot sauce
- 4-5 drops sesame oil
- 4 pieces cooked and drained bacon
- 2-4 ounces thinly sliced turkey per sandwich
- 2 tablespoons roughly chopped flat leaf parsley and celery leaves
- 2 French rolls

Direction

- In a medium bowl, whisk together the minced ginger, brown sugar, vinegar, and salt. Add the shredded carrots and sliced cucumbers and allow to marinate for 20-30 minutes.
- In the meantime, blend the mayonnaise, hot sauce, and sesame oil together in a small bowl.
- After the vegetables have finished marinating, drain them in a sieve set over a small bowl. Split the rolls almost all the way through and open them out. Slather the spicy mayonnaise over each side of the rolls. Layer 2 slices of bacon, then the turkey and the drained vegetables on the bottom half of the roll. Sprinkle the chopped parsley and celery leaves over top and close the roll. Slice in half diagonally and serve with a cold beer or a cup of herbal tea. (Leftover pickled vegetables can be stored in the refrigerator for a day or two).

55. CHA! Battered Fish With Spicy Lemon Mayonnaise

Serving: Makes 4 each 6 ounce fillet | Prep: | Cook: | Ready in:

Ingredients

- Batter
- 1 cup All Purpose Flour
- 1/2 cup MIlk
- 1/2 cup Water
- 1/4 cup Baking Powder
- 1 teaspoon Salt
- 3 tablespoons CHA! by Texas Pete
- Flavored Mayonnaise
- 1/3 cup Mayonnaise
- 2 teaspoons Dijon Mustard
- 1 bunch 2 lemons- minced-lemon zest (squeezed)
- 2 tablespoons CHA! by Texas Pete
- 1 quart Vegetable Oil- for deep frying

Direction

- Trim the fish if necessary and keep refrigerated until ready to use. Preheat the deep fryer to 350 degrees.
- Prepare the batter: In a small mixing bowl combine the flour, milk, water, baking powder and the salt. Mix well. Refrigerate the batter for 1 hour before using. Do not add the CHA! By Texas Pete® until just before you are ready to batter the fish after refrigerating.
- Prepare the flavored mayonnaise. Combine the mayonnaise, Dijon mustard, lemon zest, lemon juice and the CHA! by Texas Pete®. Mix well. Season with a pinch of salt and pepper and keep refrigerated until ready to use.
- When you are ready to fry the fish add the CHA! by Texas Pete® into the batter and mix well.
- Pat the fish fillets dry with paper towels before dipping them into the batter. Dip the fish fillets into the batter and lightly shake off excess batter. Carefully place the battered fillets into the deep fryer.
- Do not move the battered fish fillets until the batter has set and the fish begins to float up from the bottom of the fryer. Touching the fish too soon will cause the batter to fall off the fish.
- Fry the fish for approximately 4 minutes or until golden brown, crispy and fully cooked with an internal temperature of 150 degrees. When the fish is cooked it will float to the top of the oil. Carefully remove the fillets from the fryer and place them on paper towels to absorb excess grease and season them with salt and pepper.
- Portion the spicy mayonnaise into four ramekins and serve with the CHA! Flavored Battered Fish.

56. CHA! Giardiniera Mayo Stard

Serving: Makes 6 | Prep: | Cook: |Ready in:

Ingredients

- 3/4 cup Mayonnaise
- 1/2 cup Italian style Giardiniera, drained well, minced
- 1 tablespoon Dijon mustard
- 1 tablespoon CHA! By Texas Pete
- 1 splash salt and pepper (to taste)

Direction

- Place the mayonnaise into a small mixing bowl.
- Add the drained and minced Italian style Giardiniera, Dijon mustard, CHA! by Texas Pete® and a pinch of salt and pepper to the bowl and mix well.
- Place in an airtight storage container and keep refrigerated until ready to use.

57. CHICKEN SALAD WITH GRAPES & PECANS

Serving: Serves 4 servings | Prep: | Cook: |Ready in:

Ingredients

- 1/2 cup Light or Regular Mayonnaise
- 1/2 cup Light or Regular Sour Cream
- 1 tablespoon Fresh Lemon Juice
- 1 teaspoon Sea Salt
- 1/2 teaspoon freshly Ground Pepper
- 2 pounds Skinned & boned Chicken Breasts, cooked & chopped
- 1-2 Ribs Celery, chopped
- 2-3 cups Red & White Seedless Grapes, halved
- 1 cup Chopped Pecans, toasted or Walnuts
- Lettuce Leaves (optional)

Direction

- Stir together 1/2 cup mayonnaise and next 4 ingredients in a large bowl. Add chopped chicken and grapes, tossing gently to coat. Cover and chill at least 1 hour. Stir in nuts just before serving. Serve in stemware lined with lettuce leaves, if desired.

- Serve this fruity, nutty chicken salad with assorted crackers and grapes for a filling lunch or a delicious brunch.

- Cover with plastic wrap and refrigerate. Serve with a baguette or crackers. Use a small spoon to serve.

58. CONFETTI CAULIFLOWER

Serving: Serves a small gathering | Prep: | Cook: | Ready in:

Ingredients

- 1 white cauliflower
- 1/2 cup mayonnaise (preferably homemade, but Best Foods/Hellmans if not)
- 1 tbs curry powder
- 1/2 cup shelled and roasted pistachio nuts
- 1/2 cup dried cranberries
- s & p

Direction

- Freeze the cranberries...it will make them easier to process into small pieces in a food processer. Otherwise they will be gummy. When firm enough, process them until they are tiny bits.
- Process the pistachios into little bits.
- Trim the bottom of the cauliflower so that it sits flat. You can carefully remove the head from the leaves so that they remain a "bowl" of leaves.
- In a large pot, steam the cauliflower head until very tender...about 10 to 15 minutes. Cool.
- Mix 1/2 cup of mayonnaise with 1 tbs of curry powder.
- "Frost" the cauliflower head completely with the mayonnaise.
- Sprinkle the cauliflower head with the pistachio nuts and then with the cranberry bits pressing to firmly stick them into the mayonnaise.
- Sprinkle with a little salt and pepper.
- Place the head back into the bowl of cauliflower leaves.

59. Cabbage And Fennel Or Leeks Pie

Serving: Serves 12 | Prep: | Cook: | Ready in:

Ingredients

- Ingredients for the batter:
- • 1 cup all purpose flour
- • 1 cup sour cream
- • 1 cup mayonnaise
- • 1 teaspoon baking powder
- • ½ teaspoon baking soda
- Zest of 1 lemon
- • 5 extra large eggs room temperature
- For the filling:
- • • 1 medium cabbage head shredded
- • 1 medium onion sliced
- •1 medium fennel bulb or 4 small leeks thinly sliced
- • 1 teaspoon salt
- • ¾ teaspoons freshly ground black pepper
- • ½ cup fresh parsley chopped
- • ¼ cup fresh dill chopped
- • 1 cup goat cheese
- Juice of 1 lemon

Direction

- Directions: Preheat the oven to 350 degrees. Butter and sprinkle with some breadcrumbs the bottom of a 12by 71/2 casserole or glass baking dish. In a large bowl mix cabbage, onion, fennel or leeks, lemon juice, parsley, dill, salt and pepper set aside.
- To another bowl sift the flour, baking powder, baking soda. In a large mixing bowl, whisk sour cream, mayonnaise and lightly beaten eggs, fold in to the flour mixture. Pour 2/3 of the batter in the baking dish, then squeeze with your hands the excess moisture from the

cabbage and fennel or leeks filling and spread it on top of the batter. Crumble goat cheese evenly over the top, and cover with the remaining 1/3 of the batter.

- Bake for 1 hour, or until the pie is golden brown and the sides are slightly pulled from the dish. Serve at room temperature.
- Cut cooled pie in 12 portions, wrap each slice in wax paper, pack in a food container and enjoy with your family or friends.

60. Caesar Parmesan Chicken

Serving: Serves 6 | Prep: | Cook: |Ready in:

Ingredients

- 6 chicken breasts; boneless and skinless
- 1/2 cup caesar salad dressing
- 1/2 cup mayonnaise (Hellman's!)
- 1 cup parmesan cheese, finely grated
- 1 packet garlic or caesar croutons, crushed into crumbs

Direction

- Preheat oven to 350 degrees. In a medium bowl, mix together salad dressing, mayonnaise, and 3/4 cup of cheese.
- In a baking dish, lay out chicken breasts. Spread salad dressing mixture over chicken.
- Crush croutons into crumbs by bashing them with a rolling pin while still in the sealed bag (very therapeutic). Place crushed croutons in a bowl, and mix in remaining 1/4 cup of cheese.
- Sprinkle crouton mixture over chicken breasts. Bake for 30 minutes or until sauce is bubbly and crouton topping is browned.
- Of course, serve with Caesar salad, or grilled romaine brushed with Caesar dressing.

61. Calamari Mimosa Salad

Serving: Serves 8-10 | Prep: | Cook: |Ready in:

Ingredients

- For the salad.
- • 1 pound Calamari (Squid) cleaned, washed, and pat dry
- • 2 medium shallots or 1 red onion sliced in very thin rounds
- • 5 hard boiled eggs
- • 1 tablespoon oil
- • 2 carrots cut in thin strips and blanched
- • Salt & freshly ground pepper to taste
- Lemon Tarragon Dressing:
- • 3 lemons, juiced
- • 3 tablespoons prepared mayonnaise
- • 1 teaspoon Dijon mustard
- • ½ cup olive oil
- • Salt& freshly ground pepper
- • 1 tablespoon capers in vinegar (drained)
- • 1 tablespoon chopped fresh tarragon leaves

Direction

- To make the dressing: Whisk together lemon juice, mayonnaise, mustard, salt and pepper in a medium bowl. Slowly whisk in olive oil until emulsified, mix- in capers and tarragon.
- Organize the cooking with the final assembly in mind. 1. Boil the eggs, cool and peel; and then cut in half lengthwise. 2. Separate yolks from the whites. Slice the egg whites in thin half-moon slices. Blanch the carrot strips in salted water for 10 minutes. 4. Slice only calamari body's in1/8-inch rounds, leave the tentacles whole. 5. Heat a frying pan over medium-high heat, add the tablespoon oil. 6. When oil is hot add the calamari slices and stir-fry just for (about 11/2 to 2 minutes). 7. Transfer to a plate lined with paper towels to drain, sprinkle with salt and pepper. 8. Repeat the same with the tentacles. Drain on another plate, you will need them later for decoration.
- To assemble the salad: 1. On a nice platter layer all ingredients in this order: egg whites,

carrots, shallots, and squid. 2. In between each layer spread lemon dressing. 3. Repeat as many times as you need to use-up all the ingredients, and dressing. 4. The top layer should be crumbled egg yolks. 5. Decorate with the reserved fried tentacles.

62. Capitol Hill Burgers

Serving: Serves 6 burgers | Prep: | Cook: | Ready in:

Ingredients

- 3/4 cup Stilton cheese, crumbled
- 1/4 cup mayonnaise
- 2 tablespoons Dijon mustard
- 1 tablespoon sherry vinegar
- 18 pieces thick cut pepper bacon
- 2/3 cup packed light brown sugar
- 2 pounds ground chuck
- 1   small sweet onion, grated
- 2 tablespoons chopped fresh rosemary
- 1 tablespoon grated garlic
- 1 tablespoon Worcestershire sauce
- 2 teaspoons kosher salt
- 1 teaspoon black pepper
- 1/2 teaspoon allspice
- 2   firm pears, thinly sliced
- 3 cups washed arugula, gently torn
- 2 tablespoons vegetable oil
- 6   Brioche buns, split horizontally

Direction

- Make a medium/hot fire in a charcoal grill with a cover, or preheat a gas grill to medium high.
- To make the Creamy Stilton Spread, mix the Stilton, mayonnaise, mustard, and vinegar in a small bowl until well combined. Refrigerate until serving.
- To make the brown sugar bacon, place the bacon in a large skillet on top of the middle of the grill. Turn the bacon once the bottom is crisp, about 4 minutes. Cook on this side for

about three minutes, until almost completely crisp. Sprinkle the bacon with the brown sugar, turning to coat evenly. Cook until the sugar has melted and bacon is glazed on both sides, about two minutes. Remove bacon to a plate. Cover and set aside.

- To make the patties, add the beef, onion, rosemary, garlic, Worcestershire sauce, salt, pepper, and allspice to a medium bowl. Combine, mixing gently so that the meat does not get compacted. Divide into 6 equal portions and gently shape into patties that equal the size of the Kaiser rolls. Refrigerate until grilling.
- To grill the patties, brush the grill rack with oil. Place patties on the rack, cover and grill approximately 4 minutes, until golden brown on the bottom. Turn the patties gently, and grill an additional 3-4 minutes, or until meat reaches an internal temperature of 165 degrees on an instant-read thermometer. Remove from the grill and let rest tented with foil, about three minutes.
- While the patties rest, place the brioche buns, cut side down on the grill and toast lightly, about 2 minutes.
- To assemble the burgers, thinly spread all bun tops and bottoms with Creamy Stilton Spread, evenly divide pear slices and arugula and place on top of roll bottoms, and top with patties. Top each patty with three slices of Brown Sugar Bacon. Add the bun tops and serve.

63. Caprese Pesto Pasta Salad

Serving: Serves 8 | Prep: | Cook: | Ready in:

Ingredients

- 1 cup fresh basil, gently packed, stems removed
- 1   small garlic clove
- 1/2 cup ground almonds
- 1 teaspoon kosher salt

- 1/4 teaspoon freshly ground black pepper
- 1/2 cup olive oil
- 1 cup freshly grated Parmesan cheese
- 1/4 cup mayonnaise
- 1/4 cup white balsamic vinegar
- 1 pound rigatoni pasta
- 1 cup cherry tomatoes, halved
- 1/2 cup mini bocconcini cheese
- kosher salt and freshly ground black pepper, to taste
- fresh basil, to garnish

Direction

- For the pesto, place the basil, garlic, almonds, salt and pepper in a food processor. Process 10 seconds to chop. Scrape down the sides of the bowl. With the machine running, slowly pour in the olive oil in a steady stream until mixture is smooth, about 20 seconds. Add the Parmesan cheese, mayonnaise and white balsamic vinegar, processing just until incorporated.
- For the pasta, bring a large pot of lightly salted water to a boil. Cook pasta until tender, drain well and transfer to a large serving bowl. Let cool slightly.
- Toss pesto with cooked pasta, tomatoes and bocconcini. Add salt and pepper to taste and garnish serving bowl with fresh basil.

---

64. Caramelized Pork Bánh Mì

Serving: Serves 4-6 | Prep: 1hours15mins | Cook: 0hours15mins | Ready in:

Ingredients

- Caramelized Pork and Bánh mì Assembly
- 1 pound pork tenderloin (up to 1 1/2 pounds)
- 3 tablespoons Fish sauce
- 2 tablespoons Maple Syrup
- 1 tablespoon brown sugar
- 2 tablespoons soy sauce
- 1/2 teaspoon sesame oil

- 2 garlic cloves, minced
- 1 slice ginger, minced
- 1 green onion, sliced thinly
- 1/2 teaspoon black pepper
- 2 tablespoons vegetable oil
- 1 loaf sweet French baguette (thin) or french bread sandwich rolls. Try to get the kind of French bread with a crisp crust and tender light center.
- 3 pieces red leaf lettuce
- 1 handful pickled carrot and radishes (see below)
- 2 pieces sliced jalapeno chili peppers
- 5 sprigs cilantro
- 1 tablespoon Pâté (optional, but recommended)
- 1 tablespoon mayonnaise
- Pickled Carrots and Radishes
- 1/4 pound carrots, peeled
- 1 bunch red radishes, preferably breakfast radishes (daikon are more traditional. I just think red radishes are beautiful.)
- 1/2 cup water
- 1 cup apple cider vinegar
- 1 tablespoon salt
- 2 tablespoons sugar

Direction

- Caramelized Pork and Bánh mì Assembly
- Cut tenderloin across the grain of the meat into ½ inch pieces. Flatten each piece to an even ¼ inch between two pieces of saran wrap using a meat pounder, rolling pin, or large bottle.
- Mix ingredients from fish sauce to black pepper. Taste and adjust seasoning – it should be sweet and savory so add more soy, salt, or sesame oil as you like. Add marinade to the meat and use your hands or large spoon to make sure all pieces of meat are coated in marinade. Marinate for 10-30 minutes.
- You can cook the pork on the grill outdoors (best) or indoors using a grill pan or cast iron pan, something that you can get very hot. Heat grill or grill pan to high and turn on that vent fan! Add vegetable oil to meat and stir to coat.

Sear first side of meat until very dark brown on one side, then flip and sear on the second side. Be careful not to overcook it. The meat is thin so it cooks quickly, one or two minutes on each side.

- To assemble sandwiches, slice baguette and spread mayonnaise on one side, pâté on the other. Add lettuce, meat, pickled vegetables, cilantro and peppers. Dig in!
- Pickled Carrots and Radishes
- Slice carrots and radishes into quarters (or sixths for thicker guys) lengthwise. Mix all ingredients together. Taste for seasoning. Let stand as little as an hour or up to overnight. They keep for several days.

65. Carpaccio Of Blood Oranges With A Green Salad

Serving: Serves 4 | Prep: | Cook: |Ready in:

Ingredients

- 2 cups blood orange juice (reserve 3-4 tablespoons for the dressing)
- 2 teaspoons unflavoured gelatine powder
- 1/2 cup caster sugar
- 1 1/2 cups water
- 2 cups mixed green salad leaves
- 1/2 teaspoon (wholegrain) mustard
- 1 tablespoon Mayonnaise
- 3-4 tablespoons olive oil
- 2 tablespoons chopped fresh mint
- 50 - 100g crumbled feta cheese
- Pinch of cayenne pepper (Optional)

Direction

- Grease an 11 & 7 inch pan lightly with oil. In a bowl, whisk half of the orange juice with the gelatin till smooth and well combined. Set aside for five minutes to soften.
- Then heat the sugar and water till dissolved and bring to the boil. Reduce heat and simmer for a couple of minutes.

- Take off the heat and stir in the juice-gelatin mixture. Whisk/stir again well. Add the remaining half cup of juice and a pinch of cayenne, (if using). Whisk well to combine. Pour the mixture into the greased pan and refrigerate till set.
- Make the salad dressing by combining the mustard, mayonnaise, olive oil and blood orange juice. Taste and season with some cayenne pepper, if you like.
- Plating this per person is easier than serving in a large bowl. If you want to serve in a large bowl though, slice the gelee into small pieces and sprinkle them on the leaves. Then follow Step 7 and 8
- Otherwise, using a round cookie cutter (3 inch diameter/smaller), cut out blood orange capriccios and place one or two on each plate.
- Place some salad on top of the 'Carpaccio'. Sprinkle some chopped mint and crumbled feta on top. Drizzle some dressing over the salad but also spoon some unto the plate.
- Garnish with wedges of blood orange and some whole mint leaves

66. Causa Rellena

Serving: Serves 8-10 | Prep: | Cook: |Ready in:

Ingredients

- Causa Rellena
- 3 pounds (about 6) russet potatoes, peeled and sliced into 1/2-inch rounds
- 1/4 yellow onion, peeled
- 2 large garlic cloves, peeled and lightly crushed
- 1 pound poached chicken breast, chopped
- 1 cup mayonnaise
- 1/3 cup diced carrots, cooked until tender
- 1/3 cup green peas, cooked until tender
- 1/4 teaspoon garlic powder
- Salt and pepper, to taste
- Juice of 4 limes

- 2 tablespoons vegetable oil plus extra for greasing the pan
- 2 tablespoons ají amarillo paste
- Sliced avocado, hardboiled eggs, and pitted botija or kalamata olives to garnish
- Salsa Golf
- 1/2 cup mayonnaise
- 2 tablespoons tomato ketchup
- 1/4 teaspoon Worcestershire sauce
- 1 tablespoon pisco, brandy, or vodka

Direction

- Causa Rellena
- Place potatoes in a large, heavy bottomed pot. Fill pot with enough cold water to cover potatoes and add yellow onion and garlic cloves.
- Bring the pot to a boil over high heat. When boiling, reduce the heat to medium low and simmer until potatoes are cooked through, about 15 minutes. To test for doneness, use a knife to pierce a slice of potato. If it goes through easily, the potatoes are cooked.
- When the potatoes are cooked through, turn off the burner, and drain the water from the pot. Place the pot back onto the burner and cover with lid. Let the potatoes sit for about 15 minutes to finish cooking the potatoes. You want the potatoes to be mostly dry.
- After the 15 minutes, uncover the pot. Pass potatoes along with the onion and garlic through a ricer or food mill into a large bowl and set aside to cool to room temperature.
- Meanwhile, prepare the chicken salad. Place the poached chicken, peas, carrots, mayonnaise, and garlic powder into a bowl and mix thoroughly. Season to taste with salt and freshly ground black pepper.
- When riced potatoes have cooled to room temperature, add 2 tablespoons vegetable oil, lime juice, and ají amarillo paste and continue to mix until potatoes are a uniform yellow color. Add salt to taste. Adjust lime juice and/or ají amarillo paste, if necessary. The flavor of the potatoes should be tart and somewhat spicy.
- Lightly grease the inside of a 9-inch springform pan with oil, being sure to coat the sides. Use your hands or a spatula to evenly spread 1/3 of the potato mixture inside the pan.
- Now add the chicken salad and spread evenly over the potatoes. Cover with the remaining potato mixture, spreading out evenly and smoothly. Cover pan with plastic wrap and place in the refrigerator for at least 1 hour or up to 8 hours to chill and set.
- When ready to serve, remove causa from the refrigerator. Remove plastic wrap and place on a serving platter. Unfasten the latch of the springform pan. Remove the side of the pan from the causa. Smooth the top and sides of the causa, if necessary. Garnish with sliced avocado, hardboiled eggs, and olives. Drizzle entire causa with salsa golf, if using, and slice it like a cake to serve.
- Salsa Golf
- Thoroughly combine all of the ingredients in a small bowl. You can either drizzle this sauce onto the causa with a spoon or transfer to a squeeze bottle for more control.

67. Celery Remoulade With Golden Beets & Beet Greens

Serving: Serves 8 | Prep: | Cook: | Ready in:

Ingredients

- 2 small golden beets, peeled, leaves & stems reserved
- 1/4 cup parsley leaves
- 1 large celery root, about 1.5 lbs, trimmed & peeled
- 1 cup mayonnaise
- 2 tablespoons creme fraiche
- 2 tablespoons Dijon mustard
- 2 tablespoons lemon juice
- 1 teaspoon salt
- Black pepper, to taste

Direction

- Wash and dry the beet greens and stems. Slice stems into 1/2" pieces. Thinly slice beet greens and parsley leaves. Using a box grater or the shredder disc of a food processor, grate the beet and celery root.
- Combine the mayonnaise, crème fraiche, mustard, lemon juice, and salt in a large bowl. Add black pepper to taste, whisk together and set aside.
- Transfer the celery root and beets to the mayonnaise mixture. Add the parsley, beet greens and stems and toss to coat. Season to taste with salt and pepper and serve.

68. Cevapcici With Lime Mayo Dip

Serving: Serves 6 | Prep: | Cook: | Ready in:

Ingredients

- 1 pound lean ground beef
- 1 pound ground lamb
- 2 large cloves garlic, minced
- 1/4 cup onion, minced
- 2 tablespoons finely chopped fresh parsley
- 2 tablespoons finely chopped fresh basil leaves
- 2 teaspoons sweet paprika
- 1 teaspoon salt
- 1/2 teaspoon freshly ground black pepper
- 2 eggs, lightly beaten
- 1/2 cup mayonnaise
- 1/4 cup sour cream
- zest of 1 lime
- 3 tablespoons freshly squeezed lime juice
- 1 teaspoon sweet paprika
- Pinch black pepper
- 3 tablespoons olive oil

Direction

- In a large bowl mix together the first 10 ingredients with your hands until well combined
- With your hands shape meat mixture into long 1 inch thick rolls and cut into 3-inch long strips, making the cigar shaped cevapcici meatballs, set aside for a few minutes
- In a small bowl blend together mayonnaise, sour cream, lime zest and juice, paprika and pepper, then refrigerate until ready to serve as a dipping sauce for the cevapcici
- In a large frying pan heat olive oil on medium heat and cook meatballs, in batches, for about 10 minutes, turning often to brown evenly on all sides
- Serve with dipping sauce or with your favourite salad

69. Char, Fast And Slow

Serving: Serves 2 | Prep: | Cook: | Ready in:

Ingredients

- 3 tablespoons mayonnaise
- 1 tablespoon chopped fresh herbs (e.g. parsley, tarragon, dill)
- zest of 1 small lemon
- 1 teaspoon freshly squeezed lemon juice
- salt and freshly ground black pepper
- 1 pound arctic char (or salmon) fillet, skin on, cut into 2 equal portions

Direction

- Position a rack in the top third of the oven and set it to 250°F. In a small bowl, stir together the mayonnaise, herbs, lemon zest and juice, and pepper to taste.
- Season the flesh side of the fish generously with salt and pepper and slather with about two thirds of the lemon herb mayonnaise, making sure to cover all of the fish. Gently turn over the fillets and place them, skin side up, in a shallow baking dish just big enough to

hold them. Put in the oven for 15 to 20 minutes, until the fish is just beginning to turn opaque around the edges (cooking time will vary according to the thickness of the fillets). Remove from the oven.

- About five minutes before you are ready to eat, turn on the broiler. Gently turn over the fish (you can probably do this with your hands, as the fish will not be very hot) so that the flesh side is facing up and slather on the rest of the mayonnaise mixture. Broil for a minute or so, until the top of the fish just starts to brown and it sizzles a bit. (You do not want to broil it for much longer than this, as the fish will overcook.) Serve immediately.

70. Cheese Ball With Pecans And Dried Cranberries

Serving: Makes 4 large cheese balls | Prep: | Cook: | Ready in:

Ingredients

- 2 teaspoons extra-virgin olive oil
- 3 to 5 large shallots, finely chopped (about 1/2 cup)
- 4 cloves garlic, peeled and grated or finely chopped
- 1 teaspoon creamy Dijon mustard
- 2 tablespoons apricot jam (any large chunks removed or chopped up)
- 2 teaspoons Worcestershire sauce
- 1 teaspoon lemon zest
- 1 tablespoon lemon juice
- 1 teaspoon Champagne vinegar
- 1 tablespoon Sriracha (or Tabasco), more to taste
- 1 teaspoon kosher salt
- 4 tablespoons unsalted butter, room temperature
- 8 ounces cream cheese, room temperature
- 2 tablespoons mayonnaise

- 5 cups grated cheddar cheddar (I recommend a combination of mellow and sharp)
- 1/2 cup creamy blue cheese (I use Mountain Gorgonzola)
- 1/2 cup pecans, chopped
- 1/3 cup dried sweetened cranberries, chopped
- 2 tablespoons fig jam

Direction

- Turn heat to medium under a medium-sized frying pan. Add olive oil. When the oil is hot and shimmery, add the shallots. Cook until they soften and just start to get crispy (about 10 minutes). Turn to low heat and add the garlic. Cook for one minute. Turn off the heat and stir in mustard, apricot jam, Worcestershire sauce, lemon zest, lemon juice, Champagne vinegar, hot sauce, and salt. Set aside.
- Place butter and cream cheese in a standing mixer bowl. With the paddle attachment, whip until smooth and light (about 2 minutes). Scrape down the sides. Add mayonnaise, cheddar, and blue cheese. Whip again on medium for about 30 seconds. Scrape down the side. Add shallot/garlic mixture. Mix for another 30 seconds. Taste. Adjust. It might need more salt. Add more Sriracha if it doesn't have enough kick. And often, I need to add some acid (more lemon juice or vinegar). Mix well after adjusting the balance.
- At this point, you should chill the mixture so it's easier to handle. Or go for it and just brave the sticky mess. The thing to remember is you will be rolling it in nuts and dried fruit so it doesn't have to be perfect looking. After an hour or so in the fridge, use saran wrap to shape the mixture into any size balls and/or logs. Chill in the fridge for a few hours or overnight. Or freeze for a few months.
- Take the cheese balls out of the fridge about 30 minutes before serving it (a few hours before if frozen). Place chopped nuts and cranberries on a large plate. Use your hands (fun!) to cover the ball with a thin and even coating of fig

jam. Place cheese ball on nut/cranberry plate. Wash your hands. Then go to town rolling the ball in the pecans and cranberries. You might need to use your hands a bit to make sure the goodies stick. Serve immediately with classic round butter crackers.

71. Cheesy Crab & Hammy Sammy

Serving: Serves 2 | Prep: | Cook: | Ready in:

Ingredients

- 4 ounces fresh cooked crab leg chunks
- 2 slices deli ham, diced
- 1 tablespoon sliced green onion
- 1/3 cup chopped artichoke hearts
- 1/3 cup cole slaw mix
- 2 ounces light cream cheese, softened
- 1/4 cup light mayonnaise
- 1 teaspoon dijon mustard
- 2 slices smoked cheddar cheese
- 4 slices Italian bread
- 1 tablespoon butter, olive oil or coconut oil

Direction

- In a medium bowl, combine crab, ham, onion, artichokes, slaw mix, cream cheese, mayonnaise and mustard. Onto each of 2 pieces of bread, place 1 slice of cheese, followed by ½ of the crab/ham mixture. Top with the remaining slices of bread. In a medium hot skillet or griddle, melt ½ tablespoon butter or oil over medium heat. Add one sandwich and cook until golden brown on both sides, about 2-4 minutes per side. Repeat with remaining sandwich.

72. Chicken Cakes

Serving: Serves 3 | Prep: | Cook: | Ready in:

Ingredients

- 2 cups diced, uncooked chicken
- 1/3 cup Italian bread crumbs
- 1/2 cup diced celery
- 1/2 cup diced sweet onion
- 1-2 cloves of garlic, smushed and chopped finely
- 1-2 tablespoons butter, for sauteing
- 1-2 pinches salt and pepper
- 1 egg
- 1/4 cup heavy cream
- 1/4 cup chopped, fresh parsley
- 1/4 cup mayonnaise

Direction

- Sauté onions, garlic and celery in a mixture of half olive oil and half butter until golden, dark-ish brown. Set aside and let cool.
- Put chicken in large mixing bowl. Add cream, mayonnaise Italian bread crumbs, the egg, a generous pinch of salt and pepper and the parsley. Then I add the slightly cooled sautéed onions, garlic and celery and mix this all up. The consistency should be meatloafish. The only way I can figure to adequately combine all these ingredients is to mix with my hands. My very clean hands. Once that's all mushed up I let it rest for a few minutes.
- In the same pan that you sautéed your veg in, on medium-high heat. Add a little bit more of the olive oil.
- Grab about a 1/2 cup of your chicken mixture and pat into little cakes. I keep them between 1/2 and 3/4 of an inch thick.
- When the oil is hot, throw in as many cakes as you can fit in the pan. Cook about 4 minutes or so on each side- careful not to over brown them.
- I serve these hot, with some store bought horse radish cream- they are also good with a little sour cream on top, and some people have been known to eat them with ranch dressing- go figure. I like to top them with some fresh, chopped parsley. I'm serving them with risotto- soooooo good!

73. Chicken Mustard Croquettes

Serving: Serves 4 | Prep: | Cook: | Ready in:

Ingredients

- Chicken Croquettes
- 1 pound chicken meat, raw, boneless and without skin
- 2 tablespoons chopped parsley
- 1 teaspoon grated fresh ginger
- 3   small shallots chopped finely
- 1   garlic clove
- 3 tablespoons Extra Virgin Olive Oil
- 2 teaspoons granulated Mustard
- 1 cup bread without the crust
- 1/4 cup whole milk
- salt
- pepper
- 1/2 cup bread crumbs
- 1   egg whole
- Vegetable oil for frying
- Honey Mustard Mayonnaise
- 3/4 cup mayonnaise
- 2 tablespoons wholegrain mustard
- 2 tablespoons honey, clear and runny
- 1/4 cup fresh cream
- salt
- pepper
- 1 pinch paprika

Direction

- For the Honey Mustard Mayonnaise: Whip the mustard with the honey and the mayonnaise. Add the cream and season with the paprika, salt and freshly grated pepper. Cover and chill.
- For the Chicken croquettes: Chop the shallots very finely. Peel the garlic, cut in half, remove the green inside, and chop very finely.
- In a sauté pan, add the olive oil and the onions and fry until translucid. Add the garlic, fry an

extra 1 minute and remove from the heat. Let cool completely.
- Cut the inside of the bread (without the crust) in small pieces and measure 1 cup. Put in a bowl and add the milk. Mix with your hands until the milk is totally absorbed.
- Cut the chicken meat in small pieces making sure there are no bones. In a food processor pulse the chicken meat until is ground. Add the mustard, bread with milk, chopped parsley, cooled sautéed shallots and garlic, and grated fresh ginger. Add some salt and freshly ground pepper. Pulse until combined. Check the seasoning. Chill for 30 minutes.
- Beat 1 whole egg in a bowl. Put the breadcrumbs in a plate. Make the croquettes taking some chicken mince and giving them a shape of a cylinder 1 1/2 inches long by 3/4 inches thick.
- Roll the croquettes in the egg and then in the bread crumbs. At this point you can chill them and wait until serving time, or freeze them in a tray and when frozen put them in a plastic bag.
- Heat the oil to medium temperature (the oil should be deep enough to come to half the height of the croquettes). Fry the croquettes slowly as you need to make sure the inside is well cooked. When golden on one side turn them over and continue frying until golden on the other side.
- Remove from the oil and put on kitchen paper towel to absorb excess oil.
- Serve with a green salad, mashed potatoes and the Honey Mustard Mayonnaise on the side.
- The croquettes can also be serve at room temperature for a picnic or made smaller (half the size) and served as finger food.

74. Chicken Nanban

Serving: Serves 2 | Prep: | Cook: | Ready in:

Ingredients

- FOR THE CHICKEN KARAAGE
- 300 grams (10 oz) skin-on boneless chicken thighs, excess fat trimmed, flesh poked many times with a fork, then cut into nugget-sized pieces
- 1 fat garlic clove, minced
- 2.5 cm (1 inch) ginger, finely chopped/ minced
- 2 tablespoons light soy sauce
- 1 tablespoon rice wine
- 4 tablespoons corn starch
- canola oil, for frying
- FOR THE VEGETABLES
- 1 small carrot, julienned
- 1/2 red capsicum, julienned
- 1 medium onion, cut in half then thinly sliced
- 1 tablespoon canola oil
- FOR THE NANBAN BROTH
- 3 tablespoons water
- 4 tablespoons rice vinegar
- 1 tablespoon mirin
- 1 tablespoon light soy sauce
- 1 1/2 tablespoons brown sugar
- 1/4 teaspoon granulated dashi
- 1 red bird's eye chilli, deseeded (or not) then thinly sliced
- 1 pinch salt
- FOR THE TARTAR SAUCE
- 1/2 tablespoon capers, drained and roughly chopped
- 1 gherkin, finely chopped (a small food processor/ immersion blender would do the job perfectly), drained of excess liquid
- 4 tablespoons good quality mayonnaise (I used Kewpie)
- 2 tablespoons plain yoghurt

Direction

- First, MARINADE THE CHICKEN. In a ziploc bag, mix ginger, garlic, soy sauce, rice wine and chicken pieces together. Give it a shake and leave to marinade in the fridge for an hour or so.
- In the meantime, heat 2 tablespoons oil in a medium pan and stir-fry THE VEGETABLES over medium heat for about 5 minutes, just enough to wilt the vegetables a bit and cook the onions. You still want a bit of crunch to them. Lift from the pan and set aside.
- Now MAKE THE TARTAR SAUCE. In a small bowl, mix mayonnaise and yoghurt together. Slowly fold in the capers and gherkin. Taste for salt. Refrigerate.
- ON TO THE NANBAN BROTH: heat water, light soy sauce, rice vinegar and mirin in a small saucepan over low heat. Add in the brown sugar and granulated dashi and stir to dissolve. Bring to a boil then add the chilli slices. Taste for salt. Transfer broth to a serving bowl and TOSS IN THE RESERVED VEGETABLES. Set aside.
- When you're ready TO FRY THE CHICKEN, grab another ziplock bag and place the corn starch inside. Put marinated chicken pieces in the new corn starch filled ziplock (discarding any excess liquid from the marinade) and shake vigorously. In a medium pan (that has been used for stir-frying the veggies earlier) heat canola oil over medium heat until it reaches 180 degrees C (350F). If you don't have a thermometer, stick a wooden chopstick into the hot oil and if bubbles instantly appear, you're good to go. When the oil is hot enough, deep-fry the chicken pieces until golden. Whatever you do, don't crowd the pan. You may need to do this in batches. When all chicken pieces are golden and crispy, toss them into the nanban broth, coating well.
- Serve with hot jasmine rice and tartar sauce. Itadakimasu!

Serving: Serves 6-8 | Prep: | Cook: |Ready in:

Ingredients

- Fried Chicken Nuggets (Regular & Spicy)
- 1 tablespoon dijon mustard

- 1/4 cup pickle juice (or substitute: 1/4 c. vinegar, 1 tbsp. honey, 1 tbsp. Kosher salt, and 2 tsp. black pepper)
- 2 tablespoons extra virgin olive oil
- 2 pounds boneless chicken breasts, cut into 1 1/2-inch pieces
- 5 ounces Napa cabbage kimchi (for Spicy Nuggets)
- 1 cup rice flour (+ 1/2 cup for first coating)
- 1 tablespoon Kosher salt
- 1 tablespoon black pepper
- 1 cup rolled oats
- 1/4 cup onion powder
- 3 tablespoons garlic powder
- 1/2 tablespoon smoked paprika
- 1 tablespoon brown sugar
- 1 teaspoon gochugaru, Korean red pepper flakes (for Spicy Nuggets)
- 1/4 teaspoon ground cayenne pepper (for Spicy Nuggets)
- 3 eggs
- 1 cup vegetable oil
- Kimchi Bacon Ranch Dip
- 5 ounces napa cabbage kimchi (reserved from the Spicy Nuggets recipe, if they were priorly made)
- 4 strips of bacon, cooked & broken-up
- 1/2 cup sour cream
- 1/2 cup mayonnaise
- 2 tablespoons fresh chives, minced
- 1 teaspoon white vinegar
- 1 teaspoon runny honey or agave nectar
- 1/2 teaspoon onion powder
- 1/4 teaspoon mustard powder
- Kosher salt
- black pepper
- 1 pinch fresh dill or parsley, chopped (optional)

Direction

- Fried Chicken Nuggets (Regular & Spicy)
- In a small bowl, mix together the mustard, pickle juice, and extra virgin olive oil. Take your cut chicken pieces and place them in a resealable plastic storage bag. Pour the marinade on top, seal the bag, and massage the meat to fully coat the chicken pieces. Store in the refrigerator overnight, or for at least 6-hours. FOR SPICY NUGGETS: Drop the Napa cabbage kimchi into the resealable plastic storage bag with the chicken pieces, seal the bag, massage the meat together with the kimchi. Store in the refrigerator overnight, or for at least 6 hours.
- Once the nuggets have marinated, take out a medium-sized bowl and drop in 1/2 cup of rice flour. Season it well with salt & pepper, and whisk it together. Transfer the nuggets to the bowl and coat them lightly. (For spicy nuggets, separate the kimchi from the chicken.)
- In a food processor, combine the rice flour mix, rolled oats, onion powder, garlic powder, smoked paprika, brown sugar, Kosher salt, and pepper. For spicy nuggets, add in the gochugaru and cayenne pepper as well!) Pulse until the mixture is very fine and combined. Transfer the oat-rice flour mixture into a bowl (or rimmed plate), and set aside.
- In another medium-size bowl, whisk together the eggs with a splash of water to create your egg wash, and set aside.
- Set up your dredging stations, and dredge in this order: rice flour-coated chicken > egg wash > seasoned oat-rice flour > clean plate. Remove a few pieces of chicken at a time from the flour, dip each into the egg wash, then the oat-rice flour, gently pressing the crumbs into the chicken, and set on a clean plate. Repeat steps with the remaining chicken pieces.
- In a large frying pan, heat the vegetable oil over medium-high heat for approximately 8-minutes. To test and see if the oil is hot enough, you can take a speck of leftover egged-breading and put it in the oil. If it sizzles / bubbles, it should be ready for frying.
- Carefully add the chicken nuggets to the pan in batches. Don't crowd them! Cook the nuggets on each side for about 3-4 minutes each or flipping as the edges look crisped up, using a spatula or chopsticks to flip them. Once the nuggets are cooked, transfer the chicken nuggets to a paper-towel-lined plate,

- or you can do as I do sometimes, and drop them to cool on a cooling rack with paper towels underneath.
- Season with a little salt on top while the nuggets are still hot, let them cool for a few minutes. Serve with Kimchi Bacon Ranch Dip!
- Kimchi Bacon Ranch Dip
- Lightly coat a small frying pan with olive oil, and set it over medium heat. Sauté the Napa cabbage kimchi for about 5-minutes, or until the kimchi is softened and the liquid reduced by at least half. Lower the heat, and mix in about a teaspoon of the sour cream to the sautéed kimchi, letting it continue to cook for about another minute. Turn the heat off, transfer the sautéed kimchi to a plate and let it cool for about 10-minutes.
- In a food processor, combine the kimchi, cooked bacon pieces, sour cream, mayonnaise, chives, onion powder, honey or agave nectar, vinegar (and chopped parsley and /or dill, if you decided to use them!) and season with salt and pepper. Blitz the mixture until it reaches a smooth texture, remembering to stop and taste frequently and adjusting seasonings however if you'd like them to be.
- Serve with your fresh-made chicken nuggets, or however you'd like it! Enjoy!

---

76. Chicken Wraps With Corn, Red Bell Pepper And Basil Arugula Parsley Aioli

Serving: Serves 4 people | Prep: | Cook: |Ready in:

Ingredients

- 2   bone-in breast halves, about 1 pound
- 1   small onion, halved
- 1   bay leaf
- 1 cup corn, cut off the cob or frozen, thawed
- 1   red bell pepper, finely diced
- 4 cups arugula, about half of a 5-oz pkg
- 1 cup Italian flat-leaf parsley
- 1 cup fresh basil leaves
- 1 1/2 teaspoons anchovy paste
- 3   small scallions, white and green parts, lightly chopped
- 1   clove garlic, peeled
- 1/2 cup mayonnaise
- 1/2 cup plain yogurt, preferably Greek
- 1 teaspoon cider vinegar
- zest and juice of 1 lemon
- 1/2 teaspoon kosher salt
- 1/2 teaspoon freshly ground black pepper
- 4   12-inch spinach or whole wheat tortillas
- 1 cup romaine lettuce, chopped into chiffonade
- 1 cup arugula
- 1/4 cup fresh basil leaves, chopped into chiffonade

Direction

- Place chicken breast halves in a large saucepan, along with the onion and bay leaf. Just barely cover the chicken with water and bring to a boil over high heat. Reduce heat and gently simmer partially covered for 20 minutes. Remove from heat, cover completely and let chicken cool in the broth. Remove chicken, discard skin and pull meat from the bones. Shred meat and place in a bowl with the corn and red pepper.
- While chicken cooks, combine arugula, parsley, basil, anchovy, scallions and garlic in a food processor. Pulse to chop well. Add mayonnaise, yogurt, vinegar, lemon zest and juice, salt and pepper and process mixture until smooth.
- Combine the aioli with chicken, corn and red pepper. Toss well. Check and adjust seasonings.
- To assemble wraps, spread a quarter of the chicken mixture on each tortilla, leaving a ½-inch border. Sprinkle ¼ c romaine lettuce chiffonade, 1/4 c arugula and a pinch of the basil chiffonade over each tortilla. Roll up the tortillas, secure with a pick and cut each sandwich in half, diagonally. Serve and enjoy!

77. Chicken For A Crowd Of All Ages

Serving: Serves 12 at least | Prep: | Cook: |Ready in:

Ingredients

- 4 onions, two white turnips, two parsnips, 8 carrots, one bag of celery, one large leek, fresh dill and parsley to taste.
- 4 onions
- 2 white turnips
- 2 parsnips
- 8 carrots
- 8 pieces celery
- 1 leek
- 3 sprigs fresh parsley
- 3 sprigs fresh dill
- Chicken breasts bone in place with skin on, skinless chicken breasts
- 6 whole chicken breasts, bone in skin on
- 8 skinless, boneless, cubed chicken breasts
- Tablespoon salt to taste
- 6 tablespoons Extra Virgin Olive oil
- one whole head of escarole
- one pound egg noodles
- one store bought pie crust
- one bunch green grapes
- one cup low fat mayonnaise or plain greek yogurt
- one whole wheat loaf of bread, toasted

Direction

- Wash, peel, and chop all of the vegetables and put into a very large stock pot with olive oil on the bottom of the pan. Saute them until the vegetables begin to soften. Cube the skinless, boneless, chicken breasts and cook with vegetables. Add the whole chicken breasts and brown the skin. Add enough fresh water to cover all of the ingredients. Bring to a rapid boil for 5 minutes, turn the heat down and cook at moderate temperature for one hour. Salt the broth to taste. Test meat with

thermometer to make sure it reaches 180 degrees. Remove the cubed chicken and set aside. Remove the whole chicken breasts, shred the chicken and set aside. Remove half of the cooked vegetables and set aside. Put one half of the shredded chicken breasts back into the pot and one head of cleaned, sauteed with olive oil escarole. (Make sure to remove the skin which may be in pot from whole breasts.) Add one pound of pre-cooked egg noodles. You now have Chicken noodle soup. Next take the cubed chicken and place them in a bowl with one cup broth and some of the vegetables from the soup. Add one table spoon of cornstarch to one half cup cold water and mix together. Add this to the chicken and vegetables. Mix it until it thickens together. Put into eight individual ramekins and top with piece of pie crust to cover the top. Place the ramekins on a cookie sheet and you have 8 individual chicken pot pies. Cook for 20 minutes until pie crust is slightly browned. Take the shredded chicken and add prewashed, sliced green grapes, chopped raw celery, fresh chopped dill. Add mayonnaise or plain low-fat Greek yogurt to taste and desired consistency. Toast the whole wheat bread put the chicken salad on the bread and cut into four sections.

- This recipe uses very few utensils, it is very easy to follow and because of the chicken dishes it produces it appeals to many different ages. It is very cost effective and your shopping list is very short. We often make this when there is a challenging weather system. It has been referred to as snow storm soup, hurricane soup, or rain storm soup. The kids can help participate as you tell them the tale of "catching the eye of the storm" throwing it into the big pot and covering it with a lid.

78. Chicken Amba (Mango Condiment) Sandwiches With Lime Mayonnaise

Serving: Makes 4 sandwiches | Prep: | Cook: | Ready in:

Ingredients

- For the Amba:
- 2 mangoes, peeled and diced
- 1 teaspoon kosher salt
- 2 tablespoons safflower oil
- 1 1/2 teaspoons black mustard seeds
- 1 fresh red (Fresno) chili pepper, seeded and minced
- 3/4 teaspoon ground fenugreek
- 1 teaspoon ground cumin
- 1 teaspoon sumac
- 1/2 teaspoon cayenne pepper or to taste
- Juice of 1/2 lime
- Water as needed (have ready 1 cup)
- 2 tablespoons (packed) brown sugar
- For the Sandwiches
- 1 pound leftover roast chicken (weighed before boning), boned and torn into strips
- 8 slices sourdough or other crusty bread
- 4 tablespoons mayonnaise
- Soft-leaf lettuce or arugula for garnish
- 1 teaspoon ground cumin
- 1 teaspoon lime juice
- 1/2 Vidalia onion, sliced thinly
- Sliced tomato for garnish

Direction

- To make the amba condiment, stir together the salt and mangoes in a nonreactive bowl. Cover and chill overnight.
- The next day, heat a 3-quart heavy saucepan over low-medium heat and add the oil. Stir in the mustard seeds and heat until they sizzle and start to pop, then stir in the hot red pepper. Stir once or twice then add the mango and spices. Stir in the brown sugar, lime juice, and about 1/4 cup of water, bring to a simmer, and simmer, stirring occasionally to prevent sticking and adding water as needed, until

tender and cooked through. Remove from heat and set aside.

- Stir mayonnaise with lime juice and cumin and spread on each slice of sourdough bread. Layer each half with tomato slices, chicken, a dollop or two of amba, onion slices, and lettuce, and top each sandwich with remaining slice of bread, then serve.

79. Chickpea Chicken Salad

Serving: Serves 8 | Prep: | Cook: | Ready in:

Ingredients

- Tofu "Mayonnaise"
- 14 ounces extra firm tofu
- 2 teaspoons whole grain or Dijon mustard
- 2 teaspoons brown rice vinegar
- 2 teaspoons lemon juice
- 4 teaspoons umeboshi plum vinegar
- Chickpea Salad
- 30 ounces canned chickpeas, drained and rinsed
- 12-16 dill pickles, finely minced
- 8 scallions, finely minced
- 1 cup parsley, finely minced
- 8 stalks celery, finely minced
- 1 1/4 cups tofu "mayonnaise"
- 2 teaspoons stone ground mustard
- 1/2 teaspoon garlic powder
- 2 teaspoons tamari

Direction

- First, prepare the tofu mayonnaise by combining all the ingredients in a blender and slowly blending until pureed. Adjust seasonings to taste.
- Next, add the chickpeas to a medium size bowl and mash them with a fork. Add the rest of the ingredients and mix well.

80. Chipotle And Duck Confit Deviled Eggs With Microgreens

Serving: Serves 8 (2 halves each) | Prep: | Cook: | Ready in:

Ingredients

- 8 eggs (boiled, cut in half, and yolks removed)
- 1/3 cup mayonnaise
- 2 tablespoons Hickory Farms chipotle ranch sauce
- Spice Lab's smoked chipotle sea salt (to taste)
- 1/2 teaspoon GOOD paprika
- 1 5oz D'Artagnan duck leg confit, shredded
- microgreens

Direction

- In a bowl, break the yolks up as fine as possible. Then mix in the chipotle ranch, mayonnaise, paprika, and sea salt to taste. Mix well until very smooth. Scoop out into a sandwich or piping bag for filling.
- Shred the meat from the duck leg and don't trim off any of the fat. It tastes great and helps the meat crisp. On medium high heat, warm the shreds through until just crispy and place on a plate to drain/cool.
- Lay out your egg halves and fill the cavities with the yolk filling followed by a few pieces of duck meat. Sprinkle some extra paprika or smoked chipotle sea salt over top if desired. I chose paprika.
- When you're serving them, add a few pieces of micro greens to each plate.

81. Chocolate Mayonnaise Cake

Serving: Serves 8-12 | Prep: | Cook: | Ready in:

Ingredients

- Chocolate Mayonnaise Cake

- 2 ounces dark chocolate, chopped
- 2/3 cup cocoa powder
- 1 3/4 cups boiling water
- 2 3/4 cups flour
- 1 1/4 teaspoons baking soda
- 1/4 teaspoon baking powder
- 1 cup sugar
- 1 cup brown sugar, packed
- 1 1/3 cups mayonnaise
- 2 eggs
- 1 teaspoon vanilla
- Chocolate Frosting
- 10 ounces dark chocolate, chopped
- 1 1/2 cups unsalted butter
- 3 cups powdered sugar
- 1 tablespoon vanilla

Direction

- Chocolate Mayonnaise Cake
- Preheat the oven to 350. Butter and flour your cake pans and set them aside. Combine the chopped chocolate and cocoa powder in a glass bowl then pour over the boiling water. Whisk together until the mixture is smooth.
- Whisk together the flour, baking soda, and baking powder. Using an electric mixer or your beaters, beat both the sugar and mayonnaise until well blended, about 2-3 minutes. Add eggs 1 at a time then beat in vanilla.
- Scrape down the bowl then add in flour and chocolate, alternating about 3-4 times starting with the flour. Beat well after each addition and scrape down the sides in the middle and at the end to make sure everything is incorporated. Divide batter among prepared cake pans and bake until a toothpick comes out clean. Start with 20 minutes for 3 9" pans or 25-30 for 8" pans.
- When the cakes are done cool them in the pan for 20 minutes then run a knife along the side and invert them onto a cooling racks to cool.
- Chocolate Frosting
- Place chopped chocolate in a medium metal or glass bowl. Place the bowl over a saucepan of simmering water and stir until the chocolate is

melted. Remove from the heat and allow the chocolate to cool so it won't melt the butter. Stirring it often helps as you want it to be lukewarm- a good step to do when you place the cakes in the oven or while they are cooling!

- Beat the butter in a bowl until smooth and creamy. Add powdered sugar and beat until blended well, about 2 minutes. Beat in vanilla and then add your chocolate and combine until nice and smooth. Scrape down the sides to make sure everything is combined.
- Place one cake on a platter (maybe with some wax paper under the edges which you can remove when you're done frosting) and spread about 3/4 cup of the frosting onto the cake, add another cake and another 3/4 cup frosting. Add the final layer and your remaining frosting all around the sides.

82. Chopped Potato Salad

Serving: Serves 8 as a side | Prep: | Cook: | Ready in:

Ingredients

- 6 yellow (or white) potatoes
- 6 carrots
- 1/2 a sweet onion
- 3 dill pickles (not the huge deli kind, the medium size jarred kind)
- 1 can of sweet peas
- 3 tablespoons mayonnaise (adjust this to your mayo preferences, you may want a bit more or a bit less)

Direction

- Start carrots and potatoes in cold water. Bring to a boil and cook until they can be pierced with a fork (don't overcook!). They may have slightly different cooking times. Remove them from the water and let the carrots and potatoes come to room temperature (or pop them in the fridge).

- Add all of the chopped ingredients to a mixing bowl along with the can of peas and the mayonnaise and give it all a good stir. Salt to taste (but usually the pickles take care of that for you). Enjoy!

83. Citrus & Spice Pork Sandwich

Serving: Serves 8 | Prep: | Cook: | Ready in:

Ingredients

- 2 3/4 to 3 pounds Fresh, boneless country-style ribs, 8 ribs total
- 1 teaspoon Kosher salt
- 1 teaspoon Citrus pepper
- 1 teaspoon Olive oil
- 1 teaspoon Butter
- 2.5 quart Electric slow cooker
- 2 Small white onions, thinly sliced
- 1 teaspoon Olive oil
- Glaze:
- 1 tablespoon Olive oil
- 1 teaspoon Apple cider vinegar
- 1/4 teaspoon Freshly ground nutmeg
- 1/4 teaspoon Cinnamon
- 1/4 teaspoon Garlic powder
- 1/2 teaspoon Citrus pepper
- 1/2 teaspoon Orange zest
- 2 tablespoons Brown sugar
- 1/2 teaspoon Soy
- Citrus Salsa:
- 1 Large orange, peeled, seeded, and chopped
- 1 Tangerine, peeled, seeded, and chopped
- 2 Roma tomatoes, seeded, and chopped
- 1/2 to 1 Jalapeno pepper, seeded, and finely diced (adjust to your taste)
- 1 tablespoon Red onion, grated
- 1 teaspoon Honey
- 1/2 teaspoon Apple cider vinegar
- 1/4 teaspoon Kosher salt
- 1 tablespoon Fresh Italian parsley, chopped
- Sandwich rolls:
- 8 Ciabatta rolls, split

- 1 1/2 tablespoons Softened butter
- 1 1/2 tablespoons Wasabi-flavored mayonnaise
- 1/2 cup Citrus salsa

Direction

- Season ribs on both sides with 1/2-teaspoon salt and pepper. Set aside.
- Slice 2 small white onions into thin slices. Set aside.
- Combine all ingredients for glaze in a small bowl.
- Combine all ingredients for Citrus Salsa in a small bowl, except parsley. Refrigerate while pork is cooking.
- Heat electric slow cooker casserole on high for 4 minutes. Add 1 teaspoon Olive oil to coat bottom of casserole. Spread one-half of onion slices in casserole.
- Heat large skillet on medium-high heat. Add 1-teaspoon each: Olive oil and butter. Quickly sear ribs on each side, remove from heat and place 4 ribs on top of onion slices in slow cooker. Spoon one-half of glaze over the ribs in the slow cooker. Top with remaining 4 ribs, onion, and glaze. Cover. Cook 1 hour on high heat, reduce heat to "low" and cook for 4 hours. Remove pork from slow cooker and place on cutting board. Cover with foil and let rest for ten minutes.
- Preheat oven to 350 degrees F.
- Butter Ciabatta buns and toast butter-side up in oven for 4-5 minutes until light brown.
- Using two forks, shred pork, discarding any visible fat.
- Add parsley to salsa and stir before topping on buns.
- Remove buns from oven. Spread each bun top with a thin layer of mayonnaise. Divide pork among eight buns. Top pork with a heaping tablespoon of Citrus Salsa. Place bun-top on each sandwich. Slice sandwich in half.
- Serve with dill pickles and sweet potato salad as sides.

84. Classic Coleslaw

Serving: Serves 6 | Prep: | Cook: |Ready in:

Ingredients

- 1 medium-sized head of cabbage
- 2 medium carrots, trimmed and peeled
- 1/2 cup mayonnaise (or Vegenaise or Miracle Whip)
- 3 tablespoons apple cider vinegar
- 3 tablespoons sugar
- 2 teaspoons kosher salt
- Black pepper to taste (I like lots)
- 1/2 teaspoon celery seed
- 1 tablespoon chives, minced

Direction

- Carefully cut the cabbage in half. Remove the core with a knife, then cut the cabbage into pieces small enough to fit into the tube of your food processor. If you are doing this by hand, it is still a good idea to cut the cabbage into manageable pieces.
- Grate the cabbage as finely as you can with a food processor, grater, or by hand, then do the same with the carrots.
- Combine the carrots and cabbage in a strainer or colander and season them with the salt. Toss to combine. Place the strainer in a bowl or leave it in the sink to drain for an hour.
- After about an hour, squeeze the cabbage by hand or by twisting it in a clean dish towel to remove as much moisture as you can.
- In a large bowl, combine the sugar and apple cider vinegar. Whisk them together until the sugar has dissolved. Add the mayonnaise (or Vegenaise or Miracle Whip) along with the celery seed, chives, and black pepper. Whisk the dressing again. Taste and adjust the seasoning to your preference.
- Squeeze the cabbage mixture one more time. Add it to the dressing and mix until the dressing is evenly distributed throughout the cabbage. Serve.

85. Classic Ranch Dressing

Serving: Makes 1 pint | Prep: 0hours10mins | Cook: 1hours0mins | Ready in:

Ingredients

- 4 teaspoons dried parsley
- 2 teaspoons minced toasted onion
- 1-1/2 teaspoons dill weed
- 1 teaspoon granulated garlic
- 1 teaspoon kosher salt
- 1 teaspoon dried minced chives
- 1/2 teaspoon granulated onion
- 1 teaspoon red bell pepper flakes
- 3/4 cup mayonnaise
- 3/4 cup labneh (or yogurt)
- 1/4 cup milk

Direction

- Mix together all the dry ingredients. I put them in a jar and shake them up.
- Combine the labneh (or yogurt) with the mayonnaise. Add 2 tablespoons of the herb mix to the white stuff, and mix. Thin with milk to your desired consistency, which may change based on the kind of yogurt or labneh you use. Add more herb mix to taste. Refrigerate for an hour to allow herbs to hydrate and flavors to blend. Great on everything!
- I like to triple this recipe and keep the jar of herb mix handy to use in meat and vegetable recipes.

86. Classic Waldorf Salad

Serving: Serves 4 as an appetizer | Prep: | Cook: | Ready in:

Ingredients

- 1 cup diced apples
- 1/2 cup diced celery
- 1/2 cup chopped walnuts
- 1/2 cup mayonnaise
- 5 leaves escarole or chicory, chopped and stems removed
- Smoked paprika, for garnish

Direction

- In a medium bowl, mix apples, celery, walnuts, and mayonnaise. Arrange chopped lettuce on four plates and top with apple mixture. Sprinkle paprika on salad to finish.

87. Cool Cucumber Summer Sauce

Serving: Serves 2-4 | Prep: | Cook: | Ready in:

Ingredients

- 1/4 cup English Cucumber, finely diced
- 1 tablespoon Red onion, minced
- 1 teaspoon Rice Vinegar, sodium and sugar-free
- 1/3 cup Mayonnaise, homemade or Hellmann's
- 1/3 cup Sour cream, whole milk
- 1 tablespoon Wasabi style mayonnaise
- 1/4 teaspoon Natural stone ground mustard
- 1/4 teaspoon White ground pepper
- 1/2 teaspoon Kosher salt
- 1 teaspoon Lemon zest
- Pinch Garlic powder
- 1 and 1/2 teaspoons Capers, drained
- 1/2 to 1 teaspoons Sugar, to taste
- 1 teaspoon Fresh dill, finely chopped
- 3 to 5 Thinly sliced pieces of cucumber as garnish

Direction

- Dice cucumbers and place in medium bowl.

- Mince red onion and place in a small bowl, add Rice Vinegar and marinate while adding other ingredients to cucumbers.
- Add mayonnaise, sour cream, Wasabi style mayonnaise, mustard, white pepper, salt, lemon zest, garlic powder, capers, and sugar. Gently combine, and then add red onion with vinegar. Cover, place in refrigerator, and chill for two hours before serving. Fold in dill before placing sauce in serving dish. Garnish with thinly sliced cucumbers.
- Note: The sauce may be pureed in a blender and used as a dip.

88. Cool Ranch Summer Vegetable Pizza

Serving: Serves 4 people as main dish | Prep: | Cook: | Ready in:

Ingredients

- Crust
- 1 tablespoon active dry yeast
- 1 cup warm water
- 1 tablespoon oliver oil
- 1 teaspoon garlic powder
- 1 teaspoon salt
- 2.5 cups flour
- Sauce & Toppings
- 16 ounces cream cheese, softened
- 1/2 cup mayonnaise
- 1 packet dry ranch salad dressing mix
- 1/2 cup black olives, chopped
- 1/2 cup red, yellow, and green bell peppers, diced
- 1/4 cup green onions
- 1 cup broccoli, chopped
- 1 cup carrots, shredded
- 1 cup cauliflower, chopped
- 1 cup cheddar cheese, shredded

Direction

- Dissolve yeast in warm water and let sit while mixing the olive oil, garlic powder, salt and flour in a large mixing bowl. Gradually stir yeast mixture into the other ingredients and mix well. Place on floured surface and knead for five minutes or until smooth and no longer sticky. Roll out the dough and place it on a pizza stone. Bake at 400 degrees for 12-15 minutes or until fully cooked.
- While the crust is baking, make the sauce by stirring together the cream cheese, mayonnaise and salad dressing mix. You can prepare the filling up to a day in advance in order to let the flavors blend together and save time in preparing the pizza.
- Wash and dry the vegetables. Cut them into small, bite-sized pieces.
- Once pizza crust is fully cooled, spread sauce over the entire crust. Top with vegetables and cheese. Keep refrigerated until serving time. Cut into slices or squares.

89. Corn On The Cob Mexican Style

Serving: Serves 2people | Prep: | Cook: | Ready in:

Ingredients

- 2 Corn, Husked
- 2 tablespoons Mayonnaise
- 2 tablespoons Yogurt
- 1/2 teaspoon Cumin powder
- 1/2 teaspoon Cayenne pepper powder
- 1/2 of 1/4 teaspoons Salt
- 1tbs tablespoons Cilantro
- 1 teaspoon Lemon juice

Direction

- In a bowl mix mayonnaise, yogurt, cumin powder, cayenne powder, cilantro & salt. Adjust taste if needed
- Grill corn & keep aside. Allow it to cool a little. Spread each corn with the sauce & squeeze a little lemon juice. Serve & enjoy.

90. Coronation Chicken Salad

Serving: Serves 6-8 | Prep: | Cook: |Ready in:

Ingredients

- Chicken
- 4 chicken breasts
- 2 celery stalks
- 1 medium onion
- 1 carrot
- 2 bay leaves
- 3 sprigs fresh thyme
- 8 black peppercorns
- 3 cloves
- salt
- Sauce and Salad
- 1 1/2 cups mayonnaise
- 3/4 cup Greek yoghurt
- 4 tablespoons mango chutney
- 3 tablespoons curry paste
- 2 tablespoons fresh coriander leaves
- 1 lemon - juice
- 1 celery stalk
- 2 tablespoons sultanas
- 2 tablespoons flaked almonds roasted
- 2 sprigs coriander for garnish

Direction

- Chicken
- In a large pot put the chicken and all the vegetables, bay leaf, thyme, peppercorns, cloves and salt and cover the chicken with water. Bring to a boil and check for salt. Lower heat to a simmer and cook chicken for 20 minutes. Turn the heat off and allow the chicken to cool in the broth.
- Remove chicken from broth and cut in regular cubes.
- Strain the broth and keep it for other recipes - it will be very tasty.
- Sauce and Salad

- For the sauce put in a food processor the mayonnaise, the Greek yoghurt, the mango chutney, the curry paste and the coriander leaves and process until smooth. Check for seasoning and add lemon juice to your liking.
- Cut the celery stalk in regular cubes.
- Mix the poached chicken with the celery and enough sauce to coat the pieces. Add 2 tbsp. sultanas and mix. Cover and chill until ready to serve.
- Serve cold garnished with the remaining sultanas, roasted almond flakes and coriander leaves.

91. Crab Cake Eggs Benedict With Avgolemono Sauce

Serving: Serves 4 | Prep: | Cook: |Ready in:

Ingredients

- Crab Cake Eggs Benedict
- 4 - 8 large eggs
- 1 teaspoon white vinegar
- 4 English muffins
- 4 citrus crab cakes (see recipe below)
- Avgolemono Sauce (see recipe below)
- Citrus Crab Cakes and Avgolemono Sauce
- 2 tablespoons butter
- 1 shallot, finely chopped
- 1 garlic clove, finely chopped
- 1/4 teaspoon dried thyme
- 1 cup Japanese Panko breadcrumbs
- 1/3 cup low-far mayonnaise
- 3/4 teaspoon each lemon zest, finely grated and lemon juice
- 1/2 teaspoon hot chili sauce
- 1 cup lump crab meat, moisture removed
- 3 tablespoons green onions or chives, finely chopped
- 1 egg, lightly beaten
- 1 teaspoon Dijon mustard
- salt and pepper to taste
- 2-3 eggs separated

- 1 tablespoon of water
- 2-3 lemons, juiced
- 1-2 cups hot beef or chicken broth or stock)

Direction

- Crab Cake Eggs Benedict
- In a large saucepan of simmering water, add 1 teaspoon (5 ml) of white vinegar. Add eggs and poach to desired doneness. Toast and butter English muffins. Place crab cake onto toasted muffin half. Remove and drain poached eggs on a towel and place onto crab cake. Top with warm avgolemono sauce and serve immediately.
- Citrus Crab Cakes and Avgolemono Sauce
- Preheat oven to 425 F (220 C). In a large skillet, melt butter over medium heat and sauté shallot, garlic and thyme until fragrant. Add bread crumbs and stir often until light golden. Transfer to shallow dish. In a bowl, mix together mayonnaise, citrus zest and juice and chili sauce. Add crabmeat, green onions, egg and mustard to mayonnaise mixture and stir. Season to taste. Using about 4 tbsp. (60 ml) of the mixture, make 1/2 in (1 cm) thick patties. Press lightly into bread crumb mixture, coating all sides. Place cakes on parchment-lined baking sheet and bake for 15 minutes, turning once, or until crisp and golden. Avgolemono Sauce: Beat the egg whites until foamy. Beat in egg yolks, water, lemon juice, and 2-3 ladlesful of heated broth, a little at a time, beating (or whisking) continuously. The sauce will thicken and when it coats the spoon it is ready. Cover with a towel for a few minutes and serve.

92. Crab Cakes With Chipotle Lemon Mayo

Serving: Makes 16 crab cakes | Prep: | Cook: |Ready in:

Ingredients

- Chipotle Lemon Mayo
- 2 cups mayonnaise
- 1/2 tablespoon chipotle powder
- 1 tablespoon lemon juice
- 1/2 teaspoon lemon zest
- Crab Cakes
- 2 tablespoons olive oil
- 4 ounces diced red onion
- 5 ounces diced red pepper
- 4 ounces diced eggplant
- 1/2 teaspoon salt
- 1/4 teaspoon black pepper
- 2 teaspoons Worcestershire sauce
- 1/2 teaspoon Tabasco sauce
- 1 teaspoon Old bay seasoning
- 3 tablespoons chopped fresh parsley
- 1 tablespoon lemon juice
- 1/2 teaspoon lemon zest
- 2 pounds lump crabmeat
- 1 cup mayonnaise
- 1.5 cups plain breadcrumbs
- 4 eggs, lightly beaten
- 1 tablespoon Dijon mustard
- 1/2 tablespoon chopped fresh basil
- 1/4 cup canola oil for frying

Direction

- Combine the mayonnaise, chipotle powder, lemon juice, and lemon zest. Whisk until incorporated. Refrigerate mixture until ready to serve.
- Preheat the oven to 250°F. Heat the olive oil in a large sauté pan over medium heat. Add the red onion, red pepper, eggplant, salt, and pepper. Cook until the vegetables have softened, about 10-12 minutes. Stir in the Worcestershire, Tabasco, Old Bay, parsley, lemon juice, and lemon zest. Cook for another 5 minutes before removing the pan from the heat to cool. Meanwhile, combine the crabmeat, mayonnaise, breadcrumbs, eggs, mustard, and basil in a large bowl. Add the cooked mixture and mix well until incorporated. Refrigerate for 30 minutes. Form 3.5-ounce crab cakes, shaping them into round patties. Pour the extra breadcrumbs into a

bowl. Place each crab cake in the bowl, coating each side with breadcrumbs. In a 12-inch frying pan, heat the ¼ cup of oil over medium heat. Fry the crab cakes until golden brown, about 4-5 minutes on each side. Keep warm in the oven until all of the cakes are cooked.

- Spoon the mayo over each crab cake, and sprinkle each with parsley and lemon zest. Alternatively, serve the crab cakes on a platter with the mayo on the side.

93. Crab Pasta With Old Bay & Saltines

Serving: Serves 2 to 4 | Prep: 0hours25mins | Cook: 0hours30mins | Ready in:

Ingredients

- 4 tablespoons unsalted butter, divided
- 2 stalks celery, thinly sliced
- 1 leek, halved lengthwise and thinly sliced
- 3 scallions, thinly sliced (both the white and green parts)
- 1 pinch kosher salt, plus more to taste
- 1/2 pound jumbo lump crab meat, drained as much as possible
- 2 tablespoons freshly squeezed lemon juice, divided
- 1/2 pound short-shaped pasta (such as shells, rigatoni, farfalle, or penne)
- 1/3 cup mayonnaise
- 1 teaspoon Old Bay
- 1 teaspoon Dijon mustard
- 1 teaspoon Worcestershire
- 10 Saltine crackers
- 1/4 cup finely chopped chives

Direction

- Set a large pot of water, covered with a lid, on the stove to come to a boil.
- Add 2 tablespoons butter to a very large skillet over medium heat. When the butter has melted and the skillet is hot, add the prepped celery, leek, and scallion. Sprinkle with a big pinch of salt and stir to coat all the vegetables in the butter. Cook for about 10 minutes, stirring occasionally, until the vegetables are soft and beginning to brown.

- Once the vegetables are tender, push them toward the perimeter of the pan, so there's a big empty circle in the center. Add another 1 tablespoon butter to melt. Now add the crab meat and sprinkle with salt. Cook the crab meat for about 4 minutes, until it's just starting to brown in places, flipping halfway through. Pour 1 tablespoon lemon juice on top of the vegetables and crab, then gently stir to incorporate. Turn off the heat.

- Is the water boiling? Great. Season it generously with salt (I estimate 1 tablespoon kosher salt per 1 quart of water). Add the pasta and cook for 8 to 10 minutes, or until al dente.

- While the pasta cooks, melt the remaining 1 tablespoon butter in a nonstick skillet over medium heat. Crush the Saltines with your hands, then add to the butter. Toss to coat. Toast the Saltine crumbs for about 3 minutes, or until golden-brown. Sprinkle with salt.

- Now, combine the mayo, Old Bay, Dijon, Worcestershire, and remaining 1 tablespoon of lemon juice in a big bowl. Taste and adjust the seasoning accordingly.

- When the pasta is done, reserve ½ cup or so of pasta water, then drain the pasta. Add the pasta to the bowl with the Old Bay sauce, give a quick toss, then add the crab-vegetable mixture, about half the chopped chives, and a tablespoon of reserved pasta water. Gingerly toss again, taking care not to break up the crab lumps. (Does it need more pasta water to loosen up? Add a small splash if so.)

- Serve immediately, with the fried Saltines and remaining chives sprinkled on top.

94. Crab And Corn Rice Salad

Serving: Serves 6 | Prep: | Cook: | Ready in:

Ingredients

- 6   crab sticks
- 1   can corn
- 2 cups white rice, cooked
- 1 cup mayonnaise
- salt and pepper, to taste

Direction

- Combine crab, corn, and mayonnaise. Add room-temperature, cooked rice gradually until thoroughly incorporated. Add salt and pepper, to taste. Don't stir the mixture too much as rice may become mushy. We went really light on the mayo, just adding enough to make it 'stick'.

95. Crab And Shrimp Avocado Salad

Serving: Serves 4 | Prep: | Cook: | Ready in:

Ingredients

- 2   Avocado's
- 1/2 cup Cooked Crab
- 1/2 cup Cooked Shrimp
- 1 tablespoon White Vinegar
- 1 tablespoon Fresh Lime Juice
- 2 tablespoons Mayonnaise
- 1 pinch Salt
- 1 pinch White Pepper

Direction

- Squeeze Lime Juice and Mix with Vinegar. Set Aside
- Remove Avocado Pit and scoop out the meat. Cut into bite size pieces
- Take the vinegar mix and pour into empty avocado shell and swirl around coating the inside.

- Then pour the vinegar mix on to the cubed Avocado and mix gently.
- In a clean bowl, mix the cooked crab and cooked shrimp.
- Add the Mayonnaise and mix well trying not to break up the crab.
- Mix the crab mixture with the Avocado mixture carefully.
- Place the mixture into the empty Avocado shells and cover with saran wrap.

96. Crab And Corn Sandwich

Serving: Serves for one person | Prep: | Cook: | Ready in:

Ingredients

- 4 ounces canned crab
- 3 tablespoons boiled corn
- 3 tablespoons mayonnaise
- 1 pinch salt
- 1 piece bread
- 2 tablespoons mayonnaise
- 1/2   cucumber
- 7 ounces broccoli sprout

Direction

- Heat corn in microwave oven for about 10minutes. Cut corn. Slice cucumber.
- Mix crab, corn, pepper, salt and 3 tbsp. mayonnaise.
- Spread 2 tbsp. mayonnaise both sides. Put filling between slices of bread.

97. Crabby Snacks W/ Avocado & Bacon

Serving: Makes 30 pieces | Prep: | Cook: | Ready in:

Ingredients

- 1 baguette, cut into 1/4-inch slices (need 30 pieces)
- Nonstick cooking spray or olive oil
- 1/4 pound smoked bacon, cut crosswise into 1/4-inch pieces
- 1/4 cup thinly sliced green onions
- 1 pound canned crab meat, drained if necessary
- 6 tablespoons mayonnaise or cream cheese
- 2 tablespoons chopped fresh parsley
- 1 tablespoon fresh lemon juice
- 1 tablespoon Worcestershire sauce
- 1 teaspoon grated lemon zest
- 1/4 teaspoon ground white pepper
- 1/8 teaspoon kosher salt
- 1 avocado, pitted, peeled and thinly sliced
- Red pepper flakes for garnish

Direction

- Preheat oven to 350°. Spray baguette slices with cooking spray or brush with olive oil. Bake 8 to 10 minutes or until crisp, turning once. Meanwhile, in a small skillet, cook bacon over medium heat 6 to 8 minutes or until crisp; drain on paper towel.
- In a medium bowl, toss together crab, mayonnaise, parsley, lemon juice, Worcestershire, lemon zest, white pepper, salt and bacon. Makes about 2 cups crab mixture.
- Top each baguette slice with a heaping tablespoon of crab mixture. Top with avocado slice and sprinkle with red pepper flakes.

98. Crabe Beninoise, Avocado And Mango Salad

Serving: Serves 2-4 | Prep: | Cook: | Ready in:

Ingredients

- 1 champagne mango
- 1 hass avocado
- 1 scallion, chopped
- zest and fresh juice of 1 Lime

- salt and pepper to taste
- 1/2 cup mayonnaise
- 1 garlic clove, minced
- 1/2 teaspoon scotch bonnet, minced
- 6 ounces jumbo lump crabmeat
- 1 tablespoon chopped fresh cilantro
- 1 plum tomato, diced

Direction

- Dice champagne mango or regular mango and set aside in a medium-sized bowl. (Champagne mangos are less fibrous and have a thin pit.)
- Split the avocado in half and remove the pit. Dice the flesh and drop into a medium-sized bowl. Add the zest and juice of lime and salt and pepper. Lightly toss.
- Combine crabmeat, chopped scallions, chopped cilantro, diced tomatoes, minced scotch bonnet, mayonnaise and salt and pepper to taste. Lightly toss.
- Use the crabmeat mixture to fill the bottom layer of a clear container. Repeat with the avocado mixture and then the diced mango. You can eat immediately, but it's best refrigerated for at least an hour.

99. Crazy Street Corn

Serving: Serves 6 | Prep: | Cook: | Ready in:

Ingredients

- 6 fresh ears of corn, husked and rinsed
- 1 tablespoon vegetable oil, if grilling
- Unsalted butter, to taste
- Mayonnaise, to taste
- 1 cup crumbled queso fresco, Cotija, farmer's cheese, or mild feta
- Kosher or coarse sea salt, to taste
- Dried ground chile, such as the piquín, ancho, chipotle, or a Mexican mix
- 3 limes, halved, for squeezing on top

Direction

- Lightly brush the ears of corn with the oil. Place over an already hot outdoor grill or indoor grill pan set over medium heat until hot. Let the corn cook and char slightly, turning every 3 minutes, until tender and cooked through, 9 to 12 minutes. Alternatively, you can cook the corn in a big pot of boiling water until tender, 4 to 8 minutes depending on the freshness of the corn.
- Remove the corn from the heat and pile on a large plate or platter, along with corn holders or thick wooden skewers. Serve with the garnishes so everyone can fix their crazy corn the way they want. The traditional way is to spread on a layer of butter, then a layer of mayonnaise. Next, thoroughly cover the corn with the crumbled cheese, either by rolling the corn on a plate of the cheese or sprinkle it on. Finish with a shower of salt and ground chile, then a squeeze or two of fresh lime juice.

---

100.   Creamy Bacon Dip

Serving: Serves 8 | Prep: 0hours5mins | Cook: 0hours20mins | Ready in:

Ingredients

- 6   pieces turkey bacon, cooked
- 8 ounces organic cream cheese
- 1 cup organic sour cream
- 1/2 cup mayonnaise
- 1/2 teaspoon salt
- 1/2 cup shredded cheddar cheese
- 6   green onions, sliced thin
- 1   tomato, finely chopped

Direction

- Combine cream cheese, sour cream, and mayonnaise in a large mixing bowl and mix until creamy and smooth.

- Finely chop the bacon in a food processor, and add half of it to the creamed mixture; mix well.
- Add the salt, mix, and transfer to a baking dish.
- Sprinkle with cheese, and bake at 375* for 20 minutes.
- Sprinkle the baked dip with the remaining bacon, green onions, and tomatoes.
- Serve with tortilla chips.

---

101.   Creamy Horseradish Duck Fat Roasted Potato Salad With Smoked Sable And Deviled Egg Topping

Serving: Makes 4 | Prep: | Cook: | Ready in:

Ingredients

- 2 tablespoons Duck fat, melted
- 3   Russet Potatoes, large dice
- 2 tablespoons Prepare Horseradish
- 1   shallot, minced
- .5 cups Creme Fraiche
- 4-8   slices smoked sable
- 4   eggs, hard boiled
- 1-2 tablespoons mayonnaise
- 1 teaspoon Horseradish Mustard
- 4   slices white bread, toasted
- 1 teaspoon smoked paprika
- 10   Chives
- Salt
- Pepper

Direction

- Preheat oven to 400 degrees. Toss diced potatoes with the duck fat and 1 teaspoon salt and.5 teaspoon pepper and smoked paprika. Roast until golden brown and crispy flipping once after 10-15 minutes. Total time about 45 minutes.

- Add half of minced chives and minced shallot along with crème fraiche to bowl. Add salt, pepper and prepared horseradish.5 teaspoons at a time to taste. I ended up using all 2 tablespoons.
- Allow potatoes to cool slightly, then mix with crème fraiche dressing and set aside.
- Cut eggs in half. Dice egg whites. Combine egg yolks with mayonnaise, mustard and season to taste with salt and pepper. Mix until quite smooth, adding additional mayonnaise if too dry. Place in a small zipper bag.
- Layer slice of toasted bread with potatoes, then sprinkle with diced egg white. Next top with a couple slices of smoked sable, and using the zipper bag pipe the yolk mixture on the top. Garnish with remaining minced chives and dusting of smoked paprika.

102. Creamy Tarragon Shrimp Salad Sandwiches

Serving: Makes 2 sandwiches | Prep: | Cook: |Ready in:

Ingredients

- 1 tablespoon olive oil
- 1/ pounds uncooked shrimp (medium size, peeled and cleaned)
- 1/4 cup mayonnaise
- 1/4 cup Greek yogurt
- 1 tablespoon lemon juice
- 1.5 tablespoons tarragon, chopped
- 1 tablespoon shallot, chopped
- 1/3 cup celery, chopped
- 4   slices pumpernickel (or rye) bread
- 1/2 cup arugula leaves

Direction

- Heat olive oil in a skillet; add shrimp, and cook 4 minutes. Turn the shrimp and cook another 2 minutes. Allow to cool 5-10 minutes.
- In a medium bowl, combine the mayonnaise, Greek yogurt, lemon juice, tarragon, shallot,

and celery. Add the cooked shrimp and stir to combine. Season with salt and pepper, then chill for at least 1 hour. Serve on a bed of arugula sandwiched between slices of pumpernickel or rye bread.

103. Crispy Parmesan Swordfish With Creamy Aioli Dipping Sauce

Serving: Serves 6 | Prep: | Cook: |Ready in:

Ingredients

- Crispy Parmesan Swordfish
- 1 1/2 pounds swordfish steak, side skin removed and cut into 1 1/2" cubes
- 1/2 cup whole wheat flour
- sea salt and freshly ground black pepper to taste
- 3 egg whites
- 1 cup grated Parmesan cheese
- 1 cup whole wheat bread crumbs
- 2 teaspoons red pepper flakes
- 1 teaspoon grated lemon zest
- extra virgin olive oil, for drizzling
- Creamy Aioli Dipping Sauce
- 1/3 cup canola mayonnaise
- 1/3 cup low fat plain yogurt
- 1 tablespoon Dijon mustard
- 1 tablespoon chopped fresh parsley

Direction

- Preheat the oven to 450 degrees F.
- Pat swordfish dry with paper towels. In a medium bowl combine whole wheat flour, salt and pepper. Place the egg whites in another bowl and beat until frothy, about 30 seconds with a fork. Combine the Parmesan, bread crumbs, red pepper flakes, and lemon zest in a third bowl.
- Coat the swordfish pieces in the seasoned flour and pat to remove any excess flour. Dip

the floured swordfish in the egg whites and then into the Parmesan mixture, gently pressing the mixture into the fish. Place the breaded swordfish pieces on an oiled baking sheet. Drizzle lightly with the olive oil. Bake for 15 minutes or until just cooked through and golden brown.

- For the Aioli Dipping Sauce: mix the mayonnaise, yogurt, Dijon mustard, and parsley in a small dipping bowl.
- Serve the crispy parmesan swordfish with the aioli dipping sauce.

---

104. Crispy Salmon Patties

Serving: Serves 4 | Prep: | Cook: |Ready in:

Ingredients

- 1 tablespoon extra-virgin olive oil
- 1 cup finely diced celery
- 1   large leek, white and light green parts only, finely diced (about ½ cup)
- Kosher salt and freshly ground black pepper
- 1-1/2 pounds skinless salmon fillet, cut into 1-inch cubes
- 1   large egg
- 1-1/2 tablespoons fresh lemon juice
- 1/4 teaspoon cayenne pepper (or a small sprinkle of crushed red pepper flakes)
- 1/3 cup mayonnaise
- 3 tablespoons capers – drained, rinsed, and coarsely chopped
- 2 tablespoons chopped fresh dill
- 1-1/2 cups panko (Japanese bread crumbs)

Direction

- Start by dicing 3 stalks of celery (about 1 cup) and 1 leek. Make sure to rinse the leek well, to get rid of sand!
- Sauté this over medium-low heat in a skillet, stirring occasionally until soft and opaque. Let it cool, while you get the salmon mixture ready.

- In a food processor, combine ~1.5 pounds of raw salmon fillet (skin removed), the juice of 1 lemon, 1 teaspoon cayenne pepper, 1 teaspoon of kosher salt, and ¼ teaspoon black pepper. Pulse this until combined to a paste, and transfer the salmon paste to a large bowl.
- Add ⅓ cup of mayonnaise, 3 tablespoons of diced capers, 2 tablespoons of chopped fresh dill, and ⅓ cup of panko bread crumbs to the bowl and stir with a spatula to combine.
- Add in the sautéed leeks and celery, and form the mixture into 8 patties, coat them with another ¾ of the panko bread crumbs, and lay them in an oiled baking pan.
- Bake the patties at 425* on convection for 20 minutes, 10 on each side. If you're baking in a regular oven, increase the temperature by 25* to 450*.

---

105. Crocchetta Di Patate Di Thanksgiving (Stuffed Potato Croquettes)

Serving: Serves as much as your leftovers allow | Prep: | Cook: |Ready in:

Ingredients

- Leftover turkey meat, finely chopped
- Mayonnaise (1 ½ tsp for each cup of chopped turkey)
- 1 bunch fresh tarragon (optional)
- Salt
- Ground black pepper
- 3   eggs
- 1/4 cup half and half
- Leftover mashed potatoes
- Leftover stuffing/dressing
- Leftover cranberry sauce
- 3 cups bread crumbs, preferably panko plus more for dusting
- 1/4 cup grated parmagiano reggiano cheese
- chopped parsley plus more for garnish
- Leftover gravy

Direction

- Incorporate mayonnaise into turkey (1 1/2 tsp mayonnaise for each cup of chopped turkey). Season to taste with salt and pepper. Optional: Season to taste with freshly chopped tarragon or other herb of choice.
- In a bowl, beat eggs and whisk in ¼ cup half and half.
- The seasoning in this step is optional. Skip the seasoning and simply use plain or seasoned breadcrumbs. Otherwise, in a bowl, combine grated parmagiano reggiano cheese and 1/4 cup chopped parsley with 3 cups of bread crumbs. Season to taste with salt and pepper.
- Oil palms of your hands, then shape ¼ cup of potato mixture into a ball. Make an indentation in the center of the ball, then flatten it into a 4" concave disk about ½" thick. Fill center with chopped turkey to within one inch of all edges. Top turkey with a thin disk of dressing. Top dressing with cranberry sauce. Take a second disk of mashed potato, formed just as the first and place over your creation. Pinch together to seal, reshaping to form a cylinder.
- Sprinkle some breadcrumbs onto the croquette and lightly press crumbs into the potato. Carefully turn the croquette over and repeat bread crumb step. Press some crumbs into the sides of the disk as well. Dip croquette into beaten egg, then into bread crumbs and place onto a baking sheet. Repeat process with remaining potato, turkey, dressing, and cranberry sauce. Refrigerate croquettes for at least 30 minutes.
- Pour oil into a deep skillet to a depth of 2 - 3" (enough for the croquette to be completely submerged) and heat until about 350° on a candy thermometer. Fry the croquettes in batches until golden brown on all sides, 3-5 minutes. Drain on paper towels.
- Serve with gravy and garnish with chopped parsley or tarragon

106.   Crumbled Bacon And Hard Boiled Egg Sandwiches

Serving: Serves 4 | Prep: | Cook: |Ready in:

Ingredients

- 6   large eggs
- 1-2 tablespoons mayonnaise
- 1   squeeze lemon juice
- 1 pinch salt and pepper
- 1/2 bunch chopped chives
- 8   slices of whole grain bread, toasted
- 8   slices bacon, cooked and crumbled into largish pieces
- 8   lettuce leaves

Direction

- Hard boil the eggs. (Which is supposed to be idiot-proof, but I am still learning. I place the eggs in the bottom of a saucepan and cover them with water. I turn the heat to medium, and wait for the water to boil. Then I turn the heat off, cover the eggs with the top [or a plate, because I can never find the right top quickly enough] and wait 15 minutes. Then I pour off the warm water add some ice cubes, and run cold water over the eggs.
- Crack and peel each egg, and put in the nice blue bowl. The colors are pure and lovely, just like Monet's dining room. Add the mayonnaise, salt and pepper, and slice through the warm eggs. Don't mix the eggs too much – this is not egg salad. Sprinkle in the chopped chives.
- You want to see all the chunks and appreciate the colors! No mush, please. Put a piece of lettuce on each piece of bread, gently spoon the egg mixture onto the lettuce, then crumble the bacon lovingly onto the egg. The lettuce will keep the bread from getting soggy, but this is a meal that is best eaten while the egg and bacon are still warm. Maybe your box lunch goes no further than the back porch, where you can watch over the bird feeder and plan the fall bulb scheme. Or it will transport

nicely to the tent that has sprung up in the living room where someone has a scratchy throat, and needs sustenance to get through the long afternoon home from school.

- And, as is the case with most sandwiches, this is greatly enhanced with a judicious handful of potato chips.

107. Crunchy Adult Rusk Spicy Sesame Flavor

Serving: Makes 40 pieces | Prep: | Cook: | Ready in:

Ingredients

- 1 loaf French bread or Baguette, 2 days old
- 4 Tablespoons mayonnaise
- 4 teaspoons Tohbanjan (chili bean paste, see Notes)
- 4 teaspoons sesame oil
- Sesame seeds, for sprinkling

Direction

- Thinly slice bread, about 1/4 inch.
- Mix mayo and tobanjan until well mixed, then add sesame oil and mix again.
- Spread the dressing on the bread slices, not too thick.
- Sprinkle with sesame seeds.
- I grilled in my microwave oven on the 'toast' cycle which was fine (about 4 minutes). I would bake rather than broil in a larger oven.
- Mayo Notes*-I used Kewpie Mayonnaise. It is soft and very smooth, and tasty. You could thin other mayos with water, but a touch of vinegar is nice too.
- Notes**- If the sesame oil is a little hard from being cold in the fridge, set it out for about 10 minutes to warm it up for mixing.
- Notes***- Make as above, then add a buttery cheese like Havarti, toast again.
- The flower is a Chocolate Orchid- it really smells like chocolate.

108. Crunchy Burdock Salad

Serving: Serves 4 | Prep: | Cook: | Ready in:

Ingredients

- Burdock Salad Vegetables
- 1 Burdock root, large, about 300 grams. See Note 1
- 1 teaspoon vinegar
- 1 carrot
- 1/2 ear sweet corn, cut from the cob, cooked
- 1/2 cup cabbage, thinly sliced, cut in 1/2-inch pieces
- 1 tablespoon white sesame seeds, half white/half black OK
- Miso Mayonnaise Dressing
- 5 tablespoons mayonnaise, see Note 3 (I recommend Kewpie 50%)
- 1 teaspoon honey or agave
- 2 teaspoons blend or medium miso, (white is OK)
- 1 teaspoon soy sauce, Lite Kikkoman recommended (opt. +1 teaspoon)
- 1 tablespoon white sesame seeds or half black/half white
- salt & pepper

Direction

- Scrub the burdock root with a vegetable brush, scratching a little of the surface peeling off. Prepare a bowl of 4 cups of water and add the vinegar. Cut the ends off and throw away (compost). Cut a section about 1 1/2 inch long, then slice in half the long way, cut into matchsticks. After cutting put in the water with vinegar. After cutting half the burdock, I change the water, adding vinegar again. Let soak about 10 minutes after cutting.
- Scrub the carrot and cut into matchsticks also. It doesn't have to go into the water with vinegar.
- Microwave or Blanche the carrots in a spoon of water. Drain. But I like raw carrots.

- Cover the burdock in water and boil for about a minute, taste, if you feel the taste is too strong, boil a little longer, another minute. You don't want to boil the 'earthiness' away. Drain.
- Mix the Mayonnaise Dressing. I like to keep the sodium down so if you need more, you could add the soy sauce, but if your mayonnaise is too runny, then just use more salt.
- Put burdock, carrots, corn and cabbage (if using) in a large bowl. Add most of the dressing. Vegetables should be lightly dressed, add rest of dressing as needed. Cool in the refrigerator for an hour or two.
- Note* BURBOCK will probably be sold in the root section of the store or your farmer's market. It is usually fresher if you can find it covered with dirt like a potato. Or in the prepared veggie section, it might be washed, possibly cut in half (to shorten to fit into a sack) but with the peeling still attached. Or in some Asian markets you may find matchstick-cut goboh which is all ready to cook (it will be in a transparent sack with liquid in it).
- Note BURDOCK 2* I always used to peel the gobo but my chef friend showed me it wasn't necessary. If you are new to goboh or squirmish about the peeling, you can use a potato peeler. If you want really white goboh, trim the peeling down to the inner black circle (like a tree-ring). Also change the water once it turns dark, don't forget more vinegar.
- Note 3* MAYONNAISE--If making your favorite recipe, make it a little thinner than usual. If using a bottled mayonnaise, I like to add lemon juice or water to thin. American-style mayonnaise is very thick. Japanese Kewpie Mayonnaise (no thinning necessary) comes in different proportions of oil in the mayonnaise--50 is 50% oil is cut; 75% is cut even more. It is very delicious, try it and you may not go back...Great on BLT and Koreans like to eat on French fries!

Serving: Serves 12 | Prep: | Cook: | Ready in:

Ingredients

- 4 cups cornflakes
- 3/4 cup slivered almonds
- 3/4 cake sesame seeds
- 3/4 cup sugar
- 1 1/2 tablespoons crushed red pepper
- 2 tablespoons Kosher Salt
- 2 cups mayonnaise
- 1 cup chopped cilantro (1 bunch w/o stems)
- 2 tablespoons fresh lime juice
- 4 garlic cloves, minced
- 3 Jalapeño peppers, seeded, finely chopped
- 1/2 teaspoon black pepper
- 16 cups pkg. fresh coleslaw mix
- 3 pounds boneless, skinless chicken breasts
- 8 eggs, beaten
- 1 cup milk
- 2 cups all purpose flour
- 6 cups oil, for frying
- 12 10-inch Flour Tortillas or 24 (6-inch) Tortillas

Direction

- In Food Processor, combine cornflakes, almonds, sesame seeds, sugar, red pepper and kosher salt. PULSE on and off only till coarsely chopped; do not over process. Leave crunchy. Transfer mixture to a pie plate, as needed. (If making day before, store in tightly covered container)
- Combine mayonnaise, cilantro, lime juice, garlic, jalapeño and pepper; mix well. Stir in coleslaw mix and chill. Can be made day before and refrigerated covered overnight.
- Cut Chicken lengthwise into 1-inch wide strips. Combine your eggs and milk in one pie plate (as needed). Place flour in another pie plate. Set out your 3rd pie plate with cereal crumb mixture. Set a rack over a rimmed baking sheet to place your dredged chicken

strips on. Dredge chicken first in flour, then egg mixture and finally cereal mixture; place on rack. Continue till you finish dredging process. (You can chill these lightly covered with waxed paper overnight to set and firm crumb mixture)

- Heat the oil to 350 degrees. Cook chicken strips in batches about 4 minutes until deep golden brown and cooked inside.
- Serve chicken strips in tortillas, topped with coleslaw. Serve and eat promptly.

---

110. Cuban Adobo Pulled Pork And Slaw Sandwiches

Serving: Serves 8 to 12, depending on portion size (total - about 8 cups / 1700 grams) | Prep: | Cook: |Ready in:

Ingredients

- Braised Pulled Pork Sandwich
- 3 ½ pounds pork butt or shoulder (with bones, if possible; use 3 pounds if boneless)
- 2 large onions
- 1 tablespoon olive oil
- 5 cloves of garlic, minced
- 1 tablespoon brown sugar
- 2 tablespoons brown mustard (I use a coarse mustard with horseradish)
- 1 tablespoon dried oregano, crumbled
- 1/2 teaspoon ground coriander seed (freshly roasted and ground, if you can)
- 1 tablespoon ground cumin
- 1/8 teaspoon ground allspice
- 3 bay leaves
- 1 tablespoon chopped fresh sage, or 1 1/2 teaspoons dried, and crumbled
- 2 cups crushed plum tomatoes
- 1/4 cup cider vinegar
- 1 tablespoon Worcestershire sauce
- 3 tablespoons chopped cilantro leaves (optional)
- Freshly ground pepper and salt to taste
- 1 teaspoon salt

- 2 limes, juiced
- Whole grain buns
- The Slaw
- 1 medium cabbage - about 1 1/2 pounds
- 3 tablespoons apple cider vinegar (preferably unfiltered organic)
- 3 tablespoons organic mayonnaise
- 3 tablespoons crème fraiche or sour cream
- Juice of 1 lime
- 2 tablespoons maple syrup
- 2 teaspoons Dijon mustard (or coarse brown mustard)
- Kosher salt
- 1 cup grated jicama or apple
- 2 tablespoons celery leaves, chopped (measured before chopping)
- 1 carrot, grated, optional
- 1/4 cup roasted chopped pecans or pumpkin seeds

Direction

- Braised Pulled Pork Sandwich
- Heat oven to 300 degrees Fahrenheit.
- Make the sauce: Thinly slice the onions; sweat them for a few minutes in the oil in a Dutch oven. Add the garlic and stir for a minute or two, until it becomes soft but not brown.
- Add the brown sugar, mustard, spices, bay leaves, oregano, tomatoes, Worcestershire sauce, vinegar, and 1/2 cup of water. Stir well. Simmer gently over low heat while you cut the pork.
- Braise the pork: Cut the meat into 2" cubes; put them in the Dutch oven with the sauce (and the bones, if using them).
- Tightly cover and braise for 2 1/2 hours, or longer if necessary, until the meat can easily be pulled apart with a fork. Check after about two hours, as ovens vary quite a bit. (You can also braise in a slow cooker; I'd put it on high and check after 2 hours, or on low and let it go for 4-5. Be sure to check it though, so the meat does not overcook.)
- As soon as you remove it from the oven, push the meat aside in the Dutch oven and stir the sage and cilantro into the sauce. Let sit for a

few minutes, covered. Pull the pork apart, using two forks. Combine well with the sauce.

- Allow this to sit, covered and refrigerated after cooling, for at least eight hours before serving. The next day, or 2 days later, it will taste even better.
- Before serving, heat through over medium heat on the stove or in the microwave. Check for salt and pepper, and correct, if necessary.
- Serve on soft multigrain buns, or corn or flour tortillas, with slaw. See recipe below. Enjoy! ;o)
- The Slaw
- It's best to start this at least 2 hours before serving. Trim, quarter and finely slice the cabbage. Coarsely chop it after slicing, if you like. Put in a large bowl and toss with 1 teaspoon kosher salt. Let it sit for at least one hour.
- In a small non-reactive bowl, whisk the vinegar, mayonnaise, crème fraiche, maple syrup, mustard and lime juice well, until fully blended.
- Add the chopped cabbage, carrot, jicama or apple, celery leaves and carrot. Toss it well and let it sit for at least an hour. Add a good pinch of freshly ground pepper.
- Before serving, toss again and test for salt and pepper, correcting if necessary.
- Immediately before serving, add the chopped pecans or pumpkin seeds, if using.
- Enjoy!!! ;o)

111.   Curried Chicken Salad Tea Sandwiches

Serving: Makes 16 appetizer servings | Prep: | Cook: | Ready in:

Ingredients

- 1 skinless, boneless chicken breast, cooked & chilled
- 1/4 cup mayonnaise
- 2 teaspoons ground curry powder

- 1/2 teaspoon ground coriander
- 1/2 teaspoon kosher salt (or to taste)
- 1/4 teaspoon coarsely ground black pepper
- 4   slices cinnamon-raisin bread
- 4 teaspoons Major Grey's Chutney
- 16   walnut or pecan halves

Direction

- Pulse chicken in a food processor until finely chopped (or finely shred chicken by hand).
- In a small bowl, stir together mayonnaise, curry, coriander, salt and pepper.
- Stir curry mixture into the chicken until completely combined. If too dry, add another teaspoon of mayo. You want the mixture to hold together without excess mayo oozing out. Set aside.
- Using a 1-1/2 inch biscuit cutter (or a small jar), cut out 4 rounds from each bread slice. Arrange on serving platter in a single layer.
- Place a rounded tablespoon of chicken mixture on each slice. Top each with a 1/4 teaspoon of chutney, then gently press a walnut or pecan half on top. If not serving within an hour, cover with plastic wrap and refrigerate. Remove from the refrigerator about a half-hour before serving.

112.   Curried Egg Salad + Pickled Red Onion Smørrebrød

Serving: Serves 4 | Prep: | Cook: | Ready in:

Ingredients

- Curried Egg Salad
- 6 eggs, hard boiled and peeled
- 1 tablespoon red onion, minced
- 2 tablespoons dijon mustard
- 2 teaspoons mayonnaise
- 2 teaspoons curry powder
- 1 teaspoon ground cumin
- 1/4 cup cilantro, chopped
- Pinch salt

- Pinch freshly ground black pepper
- 4 slices gluten-free rye bread
- 2 tablespoons nigella seeds
- 2 tablespoons fresh dill
- 1/2 cup pickled red onion
- Quick Pickled Red Onions
- 2 cups hot water
- 1 teaspoon maple syrup or honey
- 1/2 teaspoon salt
- 3/4 cup white wine vinegar or apple cider vinegar
- 1 medium red onion, halved, sliced into 1/4-inch half moons

Direction

- Curried Egg Salad
- Roughly chop the eggs and add them to a large mixing bowl.
- Add in the red onion, mustard, mayonnaise, curry powder, cumin, chopped cilantro, salt and pepper. Mix well to combine.
- Top toasted gluten-free rye bread with egg salad and garnish with pickled red onion, nigella seeds, and a few sprigs of fresh dill.
- Quick Pickled Red Onions
- Bring water to a boil in a kettle.
- In a large bowl, whisk together the maple syrup or honey, salt, vinegar, and hot water.
- Place the onions into a jar and pour in the vinegar mixture. Let sit at room temperature for an hour. Can be made a week in advance. Cover and refrigerate.

---

113.   Curried Egg Salad, Radish And Fall Pea Shoot Tartine

Serving: Serves 4 | Prep: | Cook: |Ready in:

Ingredients

- 6 eggs, hard boiled and peeled

- 3 tablespoons mayonnaise, one of the tablespoons should be heaping
- 2 tablespoons bread and butter pickles, minced with some of the onion from the jar
- 1 hot red pepper, I used a cayanne
- 1/2 teaspoon Madras curry powder, I would stick with Madras it has a flavor that goes especially well with eggs
- 12 radishes, scrubbed clean and thinly sliced
- 1 small bunch of tender pea shoots, rinsed and dried
- 1 tablespoon cliantro, coarsely chopped, plus a few leaves for garnish
- roasted walnut oil for drizzling
- 4 slices of great bread of your choice but not rye. I used a multigrain.

Direction

- To make the egg salad place the eggs into a bowl and mash them with a potato masher until you have a mealy mash. Then add the mayonnaise, curry powder, bread and butters, 1 tablespoon of the cilantro and the hot pepper. Season with salt and pepper then mix to combine. Taste and adjust the seasoning if necessary.
- Spread the egg salad across one side of each piece of bread. Place the bread on a plate egg side up.
- Using a mandolin or Japanese slice shave three radishes across the top of each tartine or sprinkle them if you sliced them with a knife.
- Garnish each tartine with pea shoots and a couple of cilantro leaves. Drizzle with walnut oil and give each a few grinds of black pepper, then serve.

---

114.   Curried Halibut Cakes With Apricot Ginger Dipping Sauce

Serving: Makes 6-8 dinner size cakes | Prep: 0hours20mins | Cook: 0hours15mins |Ready in:

Ingredients

- Curried Halibut Cakes
- 3/4 pound cooked halibut
- 1 tablespoon curry powder
- 1/2 teaspoon salt
- 1/2 teaspoon black pepper
- 1/4 cup thinly sliced green onions
- 1/2 cup mayonnaise, or more as needed
- 2 cloves garlic, minced
- 2 teaspoons grated fresh ginger
- 1 cup panko breadcrumbs
- zest of one lemon
- oil for pan cooking
- Apricot Ginger Dipping Sauce
- 1/2 cup apricot preserves
- 1 teaspoon grated fresh ginger
- 2 tablespoons Thai sweet chili sauce
- 1/4 cup white wine, sherry or water

Direction

- To prepare the sauce, in a small sauce pan over low heat, whisk together the apricot preserves, ginger, sweet chili sauce and liquid of choice. Heat until slightly warm and runny, only a few minutes. Then take it off the heat to cool.
- To prepare the Curried Halibut Cakes, in a small bowl, mix together the mayonnaise, garlic and ginger. In a large bowl, add the halibut, curry powder, salt and pepper and lightly mix until incorporated into the flaked fish.
- Next stir in the green onions, lemon juice and lemon zest. Then stir in the mayonnaise mixture.
- Fold in the panko breadcrumbs and stir until well blended. The mixture should be moist enough to form small patties and hold together. If needed, add additional mayonnaise.
- Form 6-8 dinner size patties or 12-16 small appetizer size patties. I use a muffin scoop to form the dinner patties and a cookie scoop to form the appetizer size patties. Lay the formed patties on a parchment lined baking sheet.

- Heat a large skillet over medium low heat and add ghee, olive oil or safflower oil. When the oil is hot but not smoking, add enough patties to fill the skillet but not crowd the pan. Brown on either side.
- Transfer to a paper towel lined platter and sprinkle with a pinch of salt.
- Serve the Curried Halibut Cakes with the Apricot Ginger Dipping Sauce. If you'd like to make a meal, serve these with my coconut rice and a tossed green salad.

115.   Curry Battered Barramundi Fillet Sandwiches With Garlic Mayo And Pickled Cucumbers

Serving: Serves 2 | Prep: | Cook: |Ready in:

Ingredients

- Pan-Fried Barramundi Fillet
- 8 ounces Barramundi fillet
- 2 tablespoons neutral tasting oil, such as canola
- 1 egg, beaten
- 1/2 cup all-purpose flour
- 1/2 teaspoon cumin
- 1/2 teaspoon turmeric
- sea salt
- freshly cracked black pepper
- Sandwich Condiments and Preparation
- 1 15" baguette
- 2 tablespoons mayonnaise
- 1 garlic clove, minced
- 1 cucumber, thinly sliced
- 1/4 cup white distilled vinegar
- 1 teaspoon white miso paste
- 1/2 teaspoon sesame oil
- 1/2 teaspoon soy sauce
- fresh cilantro
- lime wedges

Direction

- Pan-Fried Barramundi Fillet
- In a non-stick frying pan or cast iron skillet on medium heat, heat the oil.
- Pat dry the fillet and cut in half length-wise. Season both sides with salt and pepper.
- In a shallow dish for battering, pour the beaten egg. In another shallow dish for battering, mix together the flour, cumin and turmeric.
- Dip the fillets first into the beaten egg and then dredge with the flour mixture.
- Pan-fry the fillets, about 3-4 minutes on each side. Set aside.
- Sandwich Condiments and Preparation
- In a large bowl, stir together the vinegar, miso paste, sesame oil and soy sauce.
- Mix in cucumber slices and refrigerate at least 30 minutes.
- In a small bowl, mix together the minced garlic and mayonnaise.
- Cut the baguette into two and slice open.
- Spread garlic mayo onto the baguettes and add in the pickled cucumbers.
- Add one fillet to each sandwich, along with cilantro and a splash of lime juice.

---

116.   Curry Chicken Salad

Serving: Serves 2 | Prep: | Cook: |Ready in:

Ingredients

- Chicken Salad
- 1 medium apple (your favorite variety for eating out of hand)
- Juice of one small lime
- 1 tablespoon mayonnaise
- 2 tablespoons plain yogurt
- 1 teaspoon fruit-based or stone ground mustard (or Dijon) (See note below.)
- Salt
- ½ teaspoon curry powder (or more to taste)
- 1/4 teaspoon finely grated ginger (optional) (See note below.)
- 1 ½ cup cooked chicken, in bite size pieces

- ¼ cup chopped celery
- 1 tablespoon finely chopped cilantro
- 1 tablespoon finely chopped celery leaves (I use Chinese celery.)
- Freshly ground pepper to taste
- ¼ cup coarsely chopped pecans, walnuts or almonds (preferably toasted)
- Curry Powder
- 2 teaspoons cumin seed
- 2 teaspoons coriander seeds
- ¼ teaspoon cardamom seeds
- 1 small stick of cinnamon
- 1 teaspoon yellow mustard seeds
- 5 whole cloves
- ½ teaspoon turmeric
- Ground cayenne to taste (optional)

Direction

- Chicken Salad
- Quarter, core and coarsely chop the apple. (Don't peel it.) Toss it with the lime juice.
- Add the mayonnaise, yogurt, mustard, salt, curry powder and grated fresh ginger, if using. Stir well to combine.
- Add the chicken, the celery and the chopped herbs. Toss lightly.
- Test for salt and add more, if necessary. Add pepper to taste and toss again.
- Before eating, add the nuts and toss one more time. If taking this for lunch later, put the nuts on top, then mix them in before eating, if you want them to remain as crisp as possible. (They'll get a bit soggy if they sit in the dressing for more than hour or two.)
- Enjoy!! ;o)
- N.B. I've indicated that the fresh ginger is optional because it actually adds a bit of heat, which some people like, but others really don't. Add it or not, to taste.
- About the mustard: I like to use my own Apple Mustard, or pear Mostarda Mantovana (which I make often during pear season!) in this salad.
- Curry Powder
- Toast the cumin, coriander and cardamom lightly in a small skillet just until fragrant,

shaking the pan frequently. The minute they seem to be turning a darker color, remove all of the seeds right away, lest they burn.

- Break the cinnamon stick into about five or six pieces. Very lightly toast it in the skillet, for no more than a minute or so on medium heat.
- Grind the toasted seeds, the cinnamon stick, the mustard seeds and the cloves to a fine powder. (Check the grinder once or twice to dislodge any cinnamon pieces that may have stuck to the blade.)
- Put into a jar and add the turmeric and the cayenne, if using. Put on the lid and shake well to combine. Use within a few weeks.
- Enjoy!! ;o)

---

117. Curry Dip

Serving: Serves 6 | Prep: | Cook: | Ready in:

Ingredients

- 1 cup soft fresh cream chease
- 1 cup mayonnaise
- 3 tablespoons high quality curry powder
- chips, pita triangles, broken up papadums or cut fresh vegetables

Direction

- Whisk the mayonnaise and cream cheese together in a small bowl until completely blended. Add the curry powder, whisking it in slowly until it too is completely blended. (It will appear to be way too much curry powder, but it is fine.) The dip benefits from an hour's refrigerated rest but it is not essential.

---

118. Dad's Favourite Baked Fish

Serving: Serves 4 | Prep: | Cook: | Ready in:

Ingredients

- 1 pound frozen tilapia filets
- 1   lemon
- 1 cup mayonnaise [do NOT use reduced fat or no fat varieties]
- 1 1/2 tablespoons onion powder [NOT salt]
- 1/2 teaspoon garlic powder [NOT salt]
- 1 tablespoon dried dill [may substitute 2 tablespoons fresh dill]
- 1 teaspoon coarse ground salt
- 1 teaspoon fresh ground pepper
- 1/3 cup shredded Parmesan cheese
- 16   multigrain saltine crackers, finely crushed

Direction

- Preheat oven to 375 degrees F. Line a rimmed baking sheet with aluminum foil, parchment paper or a silicone baking mat. If using foil or parchment paper, spray lightly with nonstick cooking spray. Place fish filets on prepared baking sheet.
- In a small bowl, zest the lemon. Then, cut the lemon in half and squeeze the juice into the bowl. Add the mayonnaise, onion powder, garlic powder, dill, salt, pepper, and cheese to bowl and whisk thoroughly together.
- Use a spoon to spread mayonnaise mixture evenly over each of the tilapia filets. Sprinkle evenly with saltine crumbs. Place baking pan in oven and bake fish for 15-20 minutes or just until fish baked through and opaque. Switch oven over the broiler and broil for 1-2 minutes or just until top is bubbly and golden brown. Serve immediately.

---

119. Deluxe Monte Cristo Sandwiches With Mayo Dijon And Cranberry Sauces

Serving: Makes 2 sandwiches | Prep: | Cook: | Ready in:

Ingredients

- For the Mayonnaise- Dijon sauce
- • 2 tablespoons mayonnaise
- • 2 teaspoons Dijon mustard
- • 1 teaspoon honey
- • 1 teaspoon lemon zest + 2 teaspoons lemon juice
- • 2 teaspoons fresh thyme leaves or parsley, finely chopped
- For the sandwiches
- • 4 slices 2 days old white French bread (preferably purchased from a bakery)
- • 4 thin slices homemade or deli style roasted turkey breast (I like Oven Gold brand)
- • 4 thin slices Premium Black Forest ham
- • 4 slices Italian Fontina cheese
- • 4 slices smoked Gouda cheese
- • 4 teaspoons homemade or the best quality store-bought cranberry sauce + more for serving
- For dipping and frying:
- • 2 large eggs + 2 tablespoons whole milk
- • 1/2 teaspoon salt
- • 1/2 teaspoon freshly ground black or white pepper
- • 1/4 teaspoon freshly ground nutmeg
- • 2 tablespoons clarified butter for frying
- • Strawberries, for garnish (optional)
- • Confectioners' sugar (optional)

Direction

- In a small mixing bowl combine all ingredients for the Mayonnaise-Dijon sauce; whisk until well blended; refrigerate until ready to use.
- To assemble: On a work surface, lay out 4 slices of bread and spread with Mayonnaise-Dijon sauce.
- Top each bottom slice with a slice of Fontina and a slice of Gouda. Place a slice of turkey and then a slice of ham. Spread 2 teaspoons cranberry sauce; then place a slice of ham, a slice of turkey, a slice of Gouda and a slice of Fontina. Cover with the top slice of bread. Repeat the same with the second sandwich.
- Using a sharp knife, cut the crusts off the sandwich (this helps to seal the ends). Wrap the sandwich tightly with plastic wrap and refrigerate for at least 30 minutes and up to 2-3 hours. (Wrapping the sandwiches in plastic wrap, compacts them, and prevents the egg batter from seeping in.)
- In a shallow dish, whisk together eggs, milk, salt, pepper, and nutmeg. Dip each sandwich in the egg mixture, turning to coat well.
- In a large skillet, melt butter over medium-low heat. When butter is hot, add the sandwiches, and cook, turning once, until golden brown on both sides, 6 to 8 minutes total. Cut each Monte Cristo in half, transfer to a platter, and garnish with the strawberries.
- Spoon some cranberry sauce over each half. Serve immediately, dusted with confectioners' sugar (if desired).

120.   Deviled Eggs

Serving: Makes 16 halves | Prep: | Cook: | Ready in:

Ingredients

- 8   Hard boiled eggs
- 4   Slices Applewood Smoked Bacon, cooked, drained, crumbled
- 1/4 cup mayonnaise
- 4 teaspoons yellow mustard
- 1/4 teaspoon Paprika
- 1/4 teaspoon ground black pepper
- 1/2 tablespoon diced fresh parsley

Direction

- Remove egg yolks from whites and smash, leaving small chunks.
- Mix with remaining ingredients except the parsley, slowly adding the mayonnaise and mustard until you get a proper consistency. You can always add more if needed (but remember, you can never take it away, so be careful). Mixture should be smooth but not runny!
- Refill egg halves with yolk mixture.
- Garnish with parsley.

- Bacon can be omitted to make them vegetarian. Use Smoked Paprika instead to add a bacon like flavor to the eggs.

121. Don't Tell My Cardiologist Thanksgiving Leftover Sandwich

Serving: Serves 1 | Prep: | Cook: | Ready in:

Ingredients

- 2 slices challah, preferably homemade
- Good Jewish Chopped Chicken Liver
- Cornbread, Bacon, Onion & Apple Dressing (or your favorite stuffing recipe)
- Leftover Roast Turkey
- Cranberry Sauce
- Mayonnaise

Direction

- Spread each slice of bread with mayonnaise.
- Add a nice thick schmear of chopped liver on one of the slices.
- Press some dressing on one side of the sandwich.
- Spoon some cranberries over the dressing, let the juices sink in.
- Layer some turkey over the cranberries.
- Top with the other slice of mayonnaise's bread.
- Press down a little, just so you can fit it in your mouth. Cut it in half to look polite.
- Enjoy. Once a year. Maybe twice.

122. Earl Grey Cured Salmon With Vanilla Mayonnaise

Serving: Serves 8-10 as hors d'oeuvres | Prep: | Cook: | Ready in:

Ingredients

- 1 1/2 pounds salmon filet, with skin on
- 1/2 cup Earl Grey loose leaf tea, crushed into fine powder
- 1/2 cup kosher salt
- 1/4 cup turbinado sugar
- 1 teaspoon coarsely ground pepper
- 1/4 cup mayonnaise
- 1-2 tablespoons creme fraiche
- 1/2 vanilla bean
- A couple of drops of lemon juice (if needed)
- 2-3 tablespoons grapefruit tears/cells

Direction

- Wash the salmon and pat dry.
- In a small bowl, mix the tea, salt, sugar and pepper.
- Line a large, non-reactive dish with plastic wrap. Pour one third of the cure mixture on the bottom of the dish. Lay the salmon skin-side down, and coat evenly with the remaining cure mixture. Fold the edges of the plastic wrap and wrap the salmon tightly. Weight the salmon down with something heavy (I used a cast iron casserole filled with a 5lb flour bag). Cure in the refrigerator for three days.
- Remove the salmon from the refrigerator and carefully rinse off the cure mixture with cold water. (Even after a careful wash the traces of the cure will remain, and that's ok, it will look pretty when you serve. But if you really take an issue with black speckles, use whole tea leaves without crushing them into powder.) Pat the salmon dry.
- Slice the vanilla bean in half lengthwise and scrape the seeds carefully. In a small bowl, mix the mayonnaise, creme fraiche and vanilla seeds. (Use mayonnaise that has a hint of lemon flavor. If not, add 2-3 drops of lemon juice. Make sure you do not overdo it.)
- With a sharp knife, slice the salmon crosswise off the skin. Serve each slice with a tiny drop of mayonnaise and a couple of grapefruit tears.

123. Egg Salad Sandwich

Serving: Serves 4 | Prep: | Cook: |Ready in:

Ingredients

- 6 large eggs
- 1 to 2 tablespoons mayonnaise
- a few drops of lemon juice or white wine vinegar
- 1 stalk clelery, washed and finely chopped
- sweet curry powder, to taste
- 1 to 2 1 to 2 teaspoons dry mustard, or to taste
- a few sprigs of tarragon, to taste, chopped
- 2 slices white bread, toasted and lightly buttered
- handful of lettuce
- salt and pepper, to taste

Direction

- Prepare an ice bath by filling a bowl with ice water and set aside.
- Place the eggs in a pot, fill with water to cover eggs by about 1/2-inch, and bring to a gentle boil. Turn off the heat, cover, and let sit for 7 – 10 minutes, depending on your preference for doneness. (I let mine sit for 7 minutes since I prefer softer-boiled egg yolks.) Remove and transfer to the ice bath for about 5 minutes to stop the cooking.
- Peel eggs and place in a mixing bowl. Add the mayonnaise, lemon juice or white wine vinegar, and season with salt and pepper. Mash with a fork. Add in the celery, curry powder, dry mustard, and tarragon. Taste and adjust the seasoning, if needed.
- To assemble the sandwich, place a handful of lettuce and a scoop of egg salad between two pieces of bread.

124. Egg Salad With Pickled Celery

Serving: Serves 4 | Prep: | Cook: |Ready in:

Ingredients

- Time consumers: the eggs and pickled celery
- 12 eggs
- 4 celery stalks, diced very small
- 1 cup white vinegar
- 1 cup water
- 2 tablespoons sea salt
- 1 tablespoon granulated sugar
- The add in's
- 1/2 cup mayonnaise
- 1/2 cup Dijon mustard
- 1 tablespoon chopped capers
- 1/4 cup chopped green onion or leeks
- 1 tablespoon chopped fresh chives
- 1 tablespoon chopped fresh tarragon
- a pinches Allepo peppers

Direction

- Place the eggs in a heavy pot, cover by an inch with lukewarm water, and heat on medium high.
- Bring to a boil and then add ¼ teaspoon of kosher salt and a teaspoon of white vinegar.
- Cover the pot and turn off the heat.
- Set a timer for 10 minutes if you like a harder yolk. Set a time for 8 minutes if you like the yolk a bit softer.
- Meanwhile, prepare an ice bath by filling a medium bowl half with water and half with ice to cool the eggs once the timer goes off.
- At that point, transfer the eggs to the ice bath and let them cool completely.
- Gently crack the eggs by rolling them against a counter, using just enough pressure to crack the shells. Do this to all of the eggs and then place them back into the water for at least 15 minutes. This is one of my favorite steps in the recipe because it allows the shells to be more easily removed. Thank you Hugh! I am going

to leave the eggs in the water while I go through the next step, pickling the celery.

- Leave the eggs in the water while going through the next step, pickling the celery.
- Pickle your celery: Combine vinegar, water, kosher salt and sugar in a jar and shake it until the salt and sugar dissolve.
- Add diced celery to jar, cover it and place in the fridge for at least 30 minutes, ideally one hour and up to one week. My pickled celery was bright, crisp, and had a lovely acidity from pickling for only an hour.
- My personal creation: After peeling the eggs, I cut them in half and separate the yolks from the whites with my hands. I use two bowls to separate them.
- I take a potato masher to the egg whites until they are all coarsely "mashed."
- Add the remainder of the ingredients to the yolks. I like to base my assessment of the taste here. I also prefer the yolky part to be creamy.
- Once I add the remainder of the ingredient to the yolks and get them to taste to my liking, I fold the yolks into the whites.
- As for adding my own element into the recipe, I usually add a combo of what is available in the fridge. Occasionally I like to make my egg salad with full fat Greek yogurt. Most of the time, I like mayonnaise. You pick!
- I add Dijon mustard, capers, and one of the members of the allium family, depending on what I have on hand - green onion, red onion, shallot, or sweet onion.
- For spice I keep it simple. I like Celtic sea salt. Sometimes I will use white pepper, too.
- I usually use some French inspired flavored fresh herb like chives or tarragon or both.
- I do all of these ingredients by taste; though to start I will give you some measurements. Then, you can adjust them to match how you like the texture and flavor of your egg salad to be.
- In this recipe I suggest salting to your personal taste. Taste the egg salad before you add any salt. The capers and the pickled celery are bringing brininess to the recipe already. After you have tasted the egg salad, begin adding

salt in ¼ tsp increments. I do the same with pepper. You can always add more salt and pepper. You can never take away what you have already added!!

- Get creative! Other additions could include, but are not limited to: paprika, parsley, garlic chives, cayenne, pickle relish, dill pickles, bread and butter pickles, cornichons, Castelvetrano olives, pickled jalapeños, and the list goes on!!!
- To enjoy on a sandwich, spread on fresh baked rye or sourdough bread with a piece of fresh lettuce, sprouts, or pea shoots. You can make fancy little finger sandwiches to serve as Hors d'oeuvres. Egg salad is also wonderful on cracker or on top of your favorite salad greens. The possibilities for this recipe are endless!

---

125.   Egg And Cheese Salad With Spicy Cilantro Pepitas Aioli

Serving: Makes makes 1 3/4 cups of the salad + enough aioli for one more portion | Prep: | Cook: |Ready in:

Ingredients

- • 3 extra-large eggs, hard boiled, (but the yolk should be still pretty soft), shredded on the large holes side of a box grater
- • 1 cup Aged Sharp White Cheddar or Parmesan cheese, shredded
- • 2 celery ribs with leaves, peeled and thinly sliced
- • Freshly ground black pepper to taste
- • 1/2 cup pepitas (raw pumpkin seeds), lightly toasted
- • 1 cup fresh cilantro leaves
- • 1 large garlic clove, peeled and chopped
- • 1/2 jalapeno chile, seeded and chopped
- • 1/4 teaspoon ground cumin
- • 1/2 teaspoon kosher salt
- • 2 tablespoons olive oil
- • 2 teaspoons each lime zest and juice

- • 1/4 cup Best Foods or Hellman's mayonnaise

Direction

- In a small skillet over medium heat, toast pepitas, shaking pan often, until they begin to pop and are fragrant, but not browned, 3-5 minutes.
- Transfer to food processor or blender. Add cilantro, garlic, jalapeno, salt and cumin. Process, scraping sides frequently, until well-minced. With machine running, gradually add oil, then lime juice, processing until as smooth as possible, and scraping down sides as needed. Transfer to a mixing bowl; whisk in mayonnaise and lime zest. Chill until ready to use.
- In another bowl toss to combine the eggs, cheese, celery and black pepper; gradually add spoonfuls of the aioli until desired consistency; I added about 3 and 1/2 or 4 tablespoons. Can be made ahead and kept refrigerated up to 3 days.

126.   Eggs Benedict Strata

Serving: Makes one 9 x 13 casserole | Prep: | Cook: | Ready in:

Ingredients

- FILLING
- Hard boil 12 eggs; cool and chop them
- Dice 2 cups black forest ham
- 2-1/2 cups coarsely torn day old bread (I have used day old croissants, too)
- 1 cup shredded Gruyere cheese
- 6 tablespoons unsalted butter
- 1/3 cup flour
- 2 cups milk
- 1 tablespoon fresh lemon juice
- 1/2 cup mayonnaise – the good stuff
- 2 teaspoons Dijon mustard
- 1/2 teaspoon garlic powder

- 1 teaspoon dried tarragon
- Cayenne pepper

Direction

- Butter a 9 x 13-inch baking dish. Add the eggs, bread and ham to the baking dish. Set aside.
- Melt the butter in a saucepan over medium-high heat. Stir in the flour and cook until mixture foams.
- Whisk in milk and cook until sauce thickens; remove from the heat.
- Stir in lemon juice, mayonnaise, mustard, garlic powder, and tarragon.
- Season with cayenne – to your taste. If needed, salt, however, the ham and cheese is usually salty enough.
- Pour the sauce over the top of the casserole. Top with the cheese. Cool, cover and refrigerate overnight.
- The next morning: take out the dish to sit at room temperature for a little bit; then bake at 350 degrees for about 35 minutes or until bubbly.
- Note: My technique written above has been changed slightly since it was originally posted.

127.   El Eme's Mythical "Triángulo" Sandwich With Secret Sauce

Serving: Makes 1 sandwich | Prep: 0hours10mins | Cook: 0hours0mins | Ready in:

Ingredients

- For the sandwich
- 1   schmear secret sauce, recipe follows
- 2   slices white sandwich bread
- 1 piece thin-sliced ham
- 1 piece lettuce
- 1   schmear mayonnaise
- For the secret sauce
- 1   alegria riojana or other spicy roasted red pepper

- 1 (non-spicy) roasted red pepper
- 1/2 Italian green pepper, seeds removed
- 1 large tomato, chopped
- 2 oil-packed anchovies
- 1/2 cup extra-virgin olive oil
- 1/2 teaspoon flaky sea salt

Direction

- For the sandwich
- Spread spicy sauce on the bottom piece of sandwich bread. Layer ham and lettuce on top. Spread a healthy coat of mayonnaise on top piece of sandwich bread. Close sandwich, cut diagonally and enjoy.
- For the secret sauce
- Add everything but the last two ingredients to a food processor or blender. Blend on high until smooth.
- Stream in olive oil and blend on medium-low until sauce is completely mixed.
- Add about half of the salt, blend and taste. The anchovies add a good hit of saltiness already, so taste and adjust salt to your liking.

---

128. Endive With Bacon And Buttermilk Ranch Dressing

Serving: Serves 4 | Prep: | Cook: | Ready in:

Ingredients

- For the buttermilk ranch dressing:
- 1/4 cup mayonnaise
- 2 tablespoons sour cream
- 1 teaspoon minced shallot
- 1 clove garlic, crushed and minced
- 1 teaspoon lemon zest
- 1/4 teaspoon mustard powder
- 1/2 cup buttermilk, shaken vigorously
- 1 to 2 tablespoons lemon juice
- 1 splash sherry vinegar
- 2 tablespoons minced parsley, plus more for garnish

- 2 teaspoons minced chives, plus more for garnish
- 1 teaspoon thyme leaves, plus more for garnish
- ground black pepper to taste
- For the salad:
- 1/4 pound thick-cut bacon
- 6 Belgian endives
- sea salt, to taste
- ground black pepper, to taste
- 1 teaspoon minced fresh herbs

Direction

- In a medium bowl, combine mayonnaise and sour cream. Stir in shallot, garlic, lemon zest, and mustard powder. Slowly whisk in buttermilk. Next, whisk in 1 to 2 tablespoons lemon juice (until dressing reaches desired thickness) and the sherry vinegar. Finally, fold in herbs and black pepper. Cover bowl and set dressing in the fridge to chill for at least 20 minutes, but preferably overnight. Recipe makes approximately 1 cup.
- To prepare the salad, cook bacon over medium heat until edges have crisped. Briefly cool on a plate lined with paper towels, and then chop.
- Core endives, remove leaves, and cut into diagonal 1/2-inch strips.
- Set chopped endive in a serving bowl, drizzle with ranch dressing, and toss gently. Scatter bacon and spoon on a bit more dressing. Finish with a pinch each of sea salt and black pepper and a sprinkle of minced herbs. Serve immediately.

---

129. Esquites

Serving: Serves 2 | Prep: 0hours5mins | Cook: 0hours7mins | Ready in:

Ingredients

- 2 cups fresh corn kernels, just cut from cob
- 2 tablespoons unsalted butter

- 1 serrano pepper, diced (about 2 tablespoons)
- 1/2 teaspoon salt
- 2 tablespoons mayonnaise (low fat is fine) or Mexican crema
- 1/8 teaspoon cayenne pepper
- 1/4 teaspoon chili powder
- 2 tablespoons queso fresco or cotija cheese, crumbled
- 1 lime cut into wedges (optional)

Direction

- Heat the butter in a medium pan. Add the serrano pepper and sauté for 2 minutes.
- Add the corn kernels and salt. Sauté for another 4 minutes and remove from heat. Let the mixture cool slightly and stir the mayonnaise in. Move to a serving bowl.
- In a separate small bowl mix the cayenne pepper and chili powder. Sprinkle as much of the powder mixture on top of the corn as you want. Top with queso fresco and lime juice (optional). Serve immediately.

130.　　　Fennel And Asian Pear Salad

Serving: Serves 2 | Prep: | Cook: | Ready in:

Ingredients

- 2 teaspoons sherry vinegar
- 2 tablespoons mayonnaise
- 1/2 teaspoon sugar
- 1 small head fennel
- 1 Asian pear
- 1/4 pecans, toasted and chopped
- 1/4 cup dried cherries
- salt and pepper to taste

Direction

- In a bowl whisk together the vinegar, mayonnaise, sugar and a bit of salt and pepper. Set aside.

- Slice the fennel and Asian pear very thin (a mandolin works very well for this)
- Add the sliced fennel, Asian pear, pecans and cherries to the bowl with the dressing. Stir to combine.

131.　　　Fennel And Scallop Salad With Garlic Creme

Serving: Serves 4 (as a starter) | Prep: | Cook: | Ready in:

Ingredients

- Salad Ingredients
- 8 raw scallops
- 1 tablespoon olive oil
- 1 tablespoon butter
- 2 fennel bulbs (around 1lb together)
- 3 tablespoons freshly squeezed lemon juice
- 1 tablespoon extra virgin olive oil
- 4 tablespoons fresh parsley leaves, finely chopped
- 1/2 teaspoon sea salt
- Garlic Creme
- 3/4 cup creme fraiche or sour cream
- 1/4 cup mayonnaise
- 2 garlic cloves, peeled and finely grated
- 1/8 teaspoon red chilli powder
- 1/2 teaspoon sea salt

Direction

- Prepare the Garlic Creme by mixing all the ingredients in a jar or small bowl. I use 2 garlic cloves to get a pronounced garlic flavor which can kick through the creme fraiche and mayonnaise, but you can use 1 garlic clove if you want to keep it more subtle. Cover and refrigerate until ready to serve. This can be made a day in advance.
- To prepare the fennel, first cut off the fennel stalks at the top (you can save them to flavor stocks or soups). Trim the base slightly (but not so much that the fennel separates). Cut the fennel in half lengthwise and then put the cut

side of each half on the chopping board and cut it in half lengthwise again. Each fennel bulb should now be in quarters. Take a quarter and slice it across as thinly as you can. Do the same with all the other quarters of fennel.

- Place the finely sliced fennel into a bowl and add 3 Tbsps. fresh lemon juice, 1 Tbsp. extra virgin olive oil, 4 Tbsps. finely chopped parsley leaves, and 1/2 tsp sea salt. Mix well and refrigerate until ready to serve. This can be made a day in advance.
- Pan-sear the scallops just prior to serving. Put a large frying pan on high heat with 1 Tbsp. olive oil and 1 Tbsp. butter. While the pan is heating, season your scallops with some sea salt. When the oil and butter is very hot, add the scallops to the frying pan (make sure not to crowd them), and allow them to cook on one side for 2-3 minutes. Do not turn them over too early otherwise they will not be nicely caramelized. When you can see that the golden caramelized color is starting to climb up the sides of the scallop, turn it over and caramelize it on the other side for a another 2-3 minutes (you may need to reduce the heat slightly). Remove the scallops from the pan when they are getting firm and almost cooked through as they will continue to cook off the heat.
- In four individual plates, place some fennel salad, two scallops and a dollop of Garlic Creme. Serve immediately.

| 132. | Filet Mignon Sliders |

Serving: Serves 4-6 people | Prep: | Cook: | Ready in:

Ingredients

- 3 medium yellow onions
- 3 tablespoons olive oil
- 1/2 tablespoon McCormick Barbecue Seasoning
- 1 1/2 tablespoons low sodium soy sauce
- 1 1/2 tablespoons Worcestershire sauce

- 2 tablespoons Dijon mustard
- 2 tablespoons horseradish
- 6 tablespoons mayonnaise
- 2.5 pounds ground filet mignon
- Salt and pepper
- 12 slices cheddar cheese
- 12 mini pretzel buns

Direction

- Barbecue onions: Cut the onions in half vertically. Cut off both ends and peel away the skin. With the middle of the onion face down, cut the onion into ¾ inch wedges. Heat 1½ tablespoons of the olive oil in a pan over high heat. Add the onions (you should hear them sizzle). After a minute or two, lower the heat to medium-low and cook the onions until brown and caramelized, about 10-12 minutes. Stir in the barbecue seasoning, soy sauce, and Worcestershire sauce. Let the flavors blend over low heat for about 10 more minutes. (At this point, the onions are ready to serve. However, you can let them sit longer if necessary. If they start to lose their shape, turn off the heat. You can reheat them over medium heat when everything else is ready.)
- Filet patties: Preheat the oven to 375°F. Form the ground filet mignon into patties, 3½ inches in diameter and ¾ inches thick (about 3.3 ounce portions). Season the patties with salt and pepper. Heat the rest of the olive oil on a flat top grill over high heat. Sear the patties until brown and slightly crisp, about 2 minutes per side. Transfer them to the oven and cook for 6-8 minutes, or until desired doneness is reached.
- Horseradish mayo: Meanwhile, whisk together the mustard, horseradish, and mayonnaise. Reserve in the fridge until ready to serve.
- To serve: When the patties have cooked, place a piece of cheddar on each patty and broil for 30 seconds to melt the cheese. Transfer the patties to the pretzel buns, pile high with barbecue onions, and slather on the horseradish mayo.

133. Fingerling Potato Salad

Serving: Serves 8-10 | Prep: | Cook: |Ready in:

Ingredients

- 1 1/2 pounds fingerling potatoes
- 1 tablespoon cider vinegar
- 1 teaspoon kosher salt
- 1 cup fresh basil leaves
- 1 tablespoon lime juice
- 1/2 cup olive oil
- 2 tablespoons grated Parmesan cheese
- 2 tablespoons honey mustard
- 2 tablespoons 2% Greek yogurt or mayonnaise

Direction

- *Place potatoes in a large pot with enough salted water to fully cover the potatoes. Bring water to boiling and continue to cook potatoes for 10 to 15 minutes, until fork tender. Transfer potatoes to a strainer and rinse with cold water to stop the cooking process.
- *Transfer strained potatoes to a large zip top bag with the cider vinegar and kosher salt. Shake to evenly coat and refrigerate for at least 1 hour, up to one day.
- *Meanwhile, prepare the dressing. In a food processor or blender, combine the basil leaves, lime juice, olive oil, Parmesan cheese, honey mustard, and Greek yogurt or mayonnaise. Process or blend until creamy.
- *Place the refrigerated potatoes in the food processor, with the dressing, and pulse until potatoes are coarsely chopped but not blended. Transfer to serving bowl and sprinkle with salt and black pepper.

134. Fish Tacos With Chili Mango Salsa And Smoked Paprika Mayo

Serving: Makes 8 tacos | Prep: | Cook: |Ready in:

Ingredients

- For the tacos:
- 4 Tilapia fillets (or other white fish)
- 1 tablespoon Extra-virgin olive oil
- 1 tablespoon All-purpose seasoning (Zatarain's, Jamaican Jerk, your choice)
- Salt and pepper to taste
- 1 Recipe Smoked Paprika Mayo
- 1 Recipe Chili Mango Salsa
- 8 Corn tortillas
- 1 bunch Cilantro, chopped
- Fresh limes, sliced
- Smoked Paprika Mayo & Chili Mango Salsa
- 1/4 cup Mayonnaise
- 1/4 cup Mexican Crema
- 1 teaspoon Smoked paprika
- 1 teaspoon Lime juice
- 2 teaspoons Granulated sugar
- 1 Fresh mango, cubed
- 1/4 cup Purple onion, diced
- 1/4 cup Red bell pepper, diced
- 1 tablespoon Cilantro, finely chopped
- 1 Lime, juice and zest
- 1 dash Cayenne pepper
- 1/2 teaspoon Chili powder
- Salt to taste

Direction

- For the tacos:
- Heat a comal or large skillet over medium-high heat. Warm tortillas on each side and keep warm.
- Heat the oil over medium-high heat in a non-stick skillet. Season fish with all-purpose seasoning mix, salt and pepper. Lay fish carefully in the heated pan, seasoning side down. Cook for about 2 minutes. Carefully flip the fish and cook until fish flakes easily. Place all the cooked fish fillets in a bowl and chop

up. Serve 1/2 of each fillet in a corn tortilla, top with smoked paprika mayo and chili mango salsa. Garnish with chopped cilantro and a fresh lime slice.

- Smoked Paprika Mayo & Chili Mango Salsa
- For the smoked paprika mayo: Mix mayonnaise and next 4 ingredients. Refrigerate until ready to use.
- For the chili mango salsa: Combine the mango with the next 7 ingredients. Refrigerate until ready to use.

---

135.   Fish Tacos With Mango Guacamole

Serving: Serves 8-10 | Prep: | Cook: | Ready in:

Ingredients

- For The Spicy Creamy Chipotle Sauce
- 1 cup fat free Greek yogurt
- 2 tablespoons chipotle peppers in adobo sauce
- 3 tablespoons mayonnaise
- 2 cloves garlic, minced
- For The Cabbage & The Fish:
- 1/4 head of fresh purple cabbage
- 2 tablespoons lime juice
- 1 teaspoon cumin
- 1/2 teaspoon cayenne
- 1/2 teaspoon salt & pepper
- 1 tablespoon olive oil
- 12 small corn tortillas
- 3 ears fresh corn, boiled 5 minutes & cut from the cobb
- 1 1/2 pounds halibut filet
- 1 tablespoon cumin
- Salt & pepper
- lime wedges for garnish
- mango guacamole (see our related recipe for this)

Direction

- For The Spicy Creamy Chipotle Sauce

- Using a food processor combine yogurt, Chipotle peppers in adobo sauce, mayonnaise and minced garlic.
- Pulse gently until texture is smooth and creamy.
- For The Cabbage & The Fish:
- Finely shred cabbage, cutting in very thin strips.
- In a small bowl combine cabbage with lime, cumin, cayenne, olive oil, 1/2 teaspoon of salt & pepper.
- Spray each corn tortilla with cooking spray and cook in a hot preheated sauté pan for 30 seconds on each side. Monitor them closely and do not allow them to burn. Set aside.
- Season the halibut with salt, pepper, and cumin.
- Sauté in olive oil over medium-high heat for 3-4 minutes per side.
- Remove from heat and gently cut or break the fish into taco-sized pieces.
- Assemble the tacos, starting with the fish, then adding Mango Guacamole, cabbage mixture, cooked corn, and finish with creamy chipotle sauce. Garnish with fresh cilantro and lime wedges for a hit of citrus.

---

136.   Flank Steak On Texas Toast With Chimichurri

Serving: Serves 4 | Prep: 0hours0mins | Cook: 0hours0mins | Ready in:

Ingredients

- The chimichurri and flank steak
- 1 1 1/2 to 2-pound flank steak
- 1 cup flat leaf parsley cleaned and large stems removed, finely chopped (by hand or use food processor)
- 1/2 cup baby arugula, finely chopped (by hand or use food processor)
- 2 cloves garlic, minced (you can add to parsley and arugula in food processor)

- 1/4 teaspoon dried oregano
- 1/4 teaspoon crushed red pepper flakes
- 1/2 cup 2 tablespoons olive oil
- 2 tablespoons red wine vinegar
- salt and pepper to taste
- Searing the steak and making the sandwich
- 1   brioche pullman loaf or if you prefer a white pullman loaf
- 1/4 cup mayonnaise
- 1   beefsteak or heirloom tomato, sliced
- Soft butter for bread
- salt before you sear and pepper after
- 2 tablespoons Chimichurri to mix with mayonnaise

Direction

- The chimichurri and flank steak
- For chimichurri, place all ingredients except flank steak into a bowl, stir to combine. For the steak, cover both sides of the steak with some of the chimichurri, put in ziplock bag and refrigerate for one or two hours. Cover and refrigerate the rest of the chimichurri.
- Searing the steak and making the sandwich
- Remove steak from refrigerator approximately 45 minutes before you are going to cook it. Scrape off some of the chimichurri, salt the steak and let rest. While steak is resting prepare the other ingredients: slice tomato, slice bread in 1-inch thick slices, mix the mayonnaise and chimichurri.
- To sear the steak: First with a paper towel pat the steak to remove any excess moisture. In a very hot fry pan lay steak, let it sear without disturbing it. Cook approximately 3-4 minutes on each side for a medium rare steak. (You will have to judge exactly how long to sear based on the thickness of the steak.) Remove from pan, lay on cutting board, pepper the steak now, and let rest 5-10 minutes.
- While steak is resting, heat a fry pan (if you have one with ridges it will make nice grill marks on the bread). Spread butter on each side of bread, place in hot pan and grill, about a minute per side.
- When steak has rested, slice thinly, cutting across the grain. To put your sandwich together, spread the chimichurri mayonnaise on each side of bread, lay meat on bread, then add the tomato, put the other slice of bread on top and enjoy.

137.   Free Form Kimbap/onigiri

Serving: Serves 1 | Prep: | Cook: |Ready in:

Ingredients

- 1 cup cooked rice (I like white short grain mixed w/barley, and brown rice is good too)
- 1   small can of tuna packed in olive oil
- 3/4 tablespoon mayonnaise
- sriracha to taste
- salt and pepper to taste
- 1-2   Korean perilla leaves (sometimes labeled as "wild sesame leaves")
- pickled daikon
- 1   single-serving package of toasted seaweed

Direction

- Drain tuna from oil, mix with mayonnaise and sriracha, season with salt and pepper.
- Cut pickled daikon into slices less than 1/4 inch thick. Chiffonade or tear strips of perilla.
- When ready to eat, put some rice on one square of toasted seaweed, top with a portion of the spicy tuna, daikon, and perilla. Fold like a taco and eat!

138.   French Bean Salad With Tarragon And Green Peppercorn

Serving: Serves 4 | Prep: 0hours0mins | Cook: 0hours0mins |Ready in:

Ingredients

- 1/2 pound French green beans, stems removed
- 1   small green zucchini (about 6-8 oz.), julienned lengthwise then cut in half
- 2 teaspoons white wine vinegar
- 4 teaspoons olive oil
- 1 tablespoon mayonnaise
- 1 pinch flaky sea salt, more to taste
- 1 tablespoon chopped fresh tarragon
- 1/2 teaspoon green peppercorns, finely crushed (more to taste)
- 1 teaspoon capers, rinsed and chopped, more to taste

Direction

- Bring a big pot of salted water to a boil on the stove, drop in beans for 1-2 minutes until bright green but still very crisp; drain and soak in an ice water bath to stop them from cooking further; when cool enough to handle, cut in half and add to bowl with the zucchini.
- For the dressing, whisk together vinegar, olive oil, mayonnaise, and a couple pinches of salt; stir in tarragon and peppercorns, reserving a small bit of each for garnish.
- Add enough dressing to the beans and zucchini to lightly coat; stir in capers; transfer to serving bowl and top with a few sprigs of tarragon and a light dusting of pepper.

---

139.   Fried Green Tomato Sandwiches With A Shrimp Spread Filling

Serving: Makes 4 sandwiches, or 8 open faced sandwiches | Prep: | Cook: |Ready in:

Ingredients

- For the Shrimp Spread
- 1/2 pound medium uncooked shrimp
- 1 cup white wine

- juice of 1/2 medium lemon
- Sprig lemon verbena or other herb - thyme is also nice
- 1 tablespoon mayonnaise
- 1 teaspoon ketchup
- 1/2 teaspoon Worcestershire sauce
- 1/4 teaspoon anchovy paste
- 1 tablespoon lemon juice
- Dash Tabasco sauce
- Dash Old Bay seasoning or paprika
- Dash black pepper
- 1 to 2 tablespoons coarsely chopped sour pickles
- For the Avocado Topping and the Fried Green Tomatoes
- 1   ripe yet firm avocado
- juice of 1/2 medium lemon
- olive oil - twice the amount of lemon juice
- 1/4 teaspoon sugar
- salt and pepper to taste
- enough olive oil to pour in a large saute pan to 1/4 inch depth
- 3   green tomatoes, sliced 1/2 inch thick
- 1/2 cup fine corn meal
- Salt and pepper to season the tomato slices

Direction

- For the Shrimp Spread
- Bring the wine, lemon juice, and herb sprig to a boil in a medium sauce pan. Add the shrimp and cook for 1 minute. Immediately take off the heat and plunge the shrimp in an ice water bath.
- Shell and coarsely chop the shrimp.
- Whisk together all the ingredients listed from the mayonnaise on down the list. Taste and adjust the remoulade as you like. Add the sauce and shrimp to the bowl of a food processor, and pulse gently until the shrimp had the consistency of a spread. Taste for seasoning - add extra ingredients to suit yourself. Place in a bowl and refrigerate until ready to use.
- For the Avocado Topping and the Fried Green Tomatoes

- For the Avocado Topping: Chop the avocado coarsely. Place in a plastic container with a sealable top. Mix together the lemon juice, olive oil, sugar, and salt and pepper. Add to the avocado and seal the container top. Shake well and set aside while you fry the green tomatoes.
- For the Fried Green Tomatoes: Heat the olive oil in the sauté pan. While the olive oil is heating, dredge the green tomato slices in the corn meal. Place in the hot oil and salt and pepper the slices. Fry for about 3 to 4 minutes, or until the coating is golden brown. Flip the slices, salt and pepper, and fry until the second side is golden brown. Place on paper towels to drain, and blot.
- Assemble by creating a sandwich with the shrimp spread as the filling. Top with the avocado. You can also create an open faced sandwich by serving the avocado directly upon the shrimp spread.

---

140. Fried Mushrooms With Smoked Paprika Remoulade

Serving: Serves 4 | Prep: 0hours30mins | Cook: 0hours20mins |Ready in:

Ingredients

- For the fried mushrooms
- 2 cups panko
- 6 tablespoons flat-leaf parsley leaves
- 1/2 cup all-purpose flour
- 2/3 cup buttermilk
- Zest of 1 lemon
- 10 button mushrooms, stems removed and sliced 1/4-inch thick
- 1 pinch salt and freshly ground black pepper, to taste
- 1/3 cup olive or canola oil for frying
- For the smoked paprika remoulade
- 1/2 cup mayonnaise
- 2 tablespoons cornichons, capers, or pickles, finely diced
- 1 teaspoon whole-grain mustard
- 1 teaspoon Dijon mustard
- 1 teaspoon smoked paprika
- 1 tablespoon lemon juice
- 1 pinch salt and freshly ground black pepper, to taste

Direction

- To prepare the fried mushrooms, combine the panko and parsley in the bowl of a food processor, then pulse until finely ground. If you've just washed your parsley, dry it before adding it to the food processor.
- Set up a "breading" station with three low bowls. In the first bowl, add flour. In the second, add buttermilk. In the third, add the panko/parsley mixture, then stir in lemon zest and season with salt and pepper. (Set the lemon aside to use later -- see "Optional" note below.) Dunk the mushrooms into each bowl, covering them with flour, then buttermilk, then the panko/parsley mixture. Place the breaded mushrooms aside until ready to be fried.
- In a skillet, heat the oil until simmering. Fry the mushrooms in batches over medium to high heat, turning them, until golden and crispy, about 3 minutes total -- a fish spatula works well to flip the mushrooms without tearing the breading. Drain the mushrooms on a paper towel-lined plate, and sprinkle with salt. To keep the mushrooms warm, transfer them to a baking sheet -- fried mushrooms can be held in an oven at 225º F for 20 to 30 minutes.
- Optional: Instead of throwing away the lemon, add it to the fry. Slice the lemon as paper-thin as possible with a sharp knife or mandolin, then follow the same process as with the mushrooms to bread and fry the lemons.
- To prepare the smoked paprika remoulade, combine the mayonnaise, cornichons, mustards, smoked paprika, lemon juice, salt,

and pepper in a small bowl and mix until combined.

141. Gabrielle Hamilton's Grilled Cheese Sandwiches

Serving: Serves 10 | Prep: | Cook: |Ready in:

Ingredients

- 20 (1/2-inch-thick) slices rustic bread (from about 1 1/2 loaves)
- 1 cup mayonnaise (Hamilton likes Hellmann's)
- 1 pound shredded extra-sharp cheddar cheese

Direction

- Heat the oven to 300°F and arrange a rack in the middle.
- Place half of the bread slices on a work surface and spread with half of the mayonnaise. Flip the bread slices over and evenly divide the cheese among the slices.
- Spread the remaining bread slices with the remaining mayonnaise and place them mayonnaise-side up over the cheese to form 10 sandwiches.
- Heat a large nonstick frying pan or griddle over medium-low heat until hot, about 4 to 5 minutes. Place 2 to 3 of the sandwiches in the pan and cook until the bottoms are golden brown and the cheese is starting to melt, about 5 minutes. Flip the sandwiches and cook until the second sides are golden brown and the cheese is completely melted, about 5 minutes more. Transfer to a baking sheet and place in the oven to keep warm. Repeat with the remaining sandwiches.
- When all the sandwiches are cooked, remove the baking sheet from the oven and place on a wire rack. Let cool 1 to 2 minutes before cutting each sandwich in half.

142. Gallo Salami Rolette With Watercress And Smoked Tomato Aioli

Serving: Serves 3 | Prep: | Cook: | Ready in:

Ingredients

- 12 pieces Thin Slice Gallo Salami
- 2 ounces Watercress leaves
- 1/4 cup Watermelon, Cut into Julienne Matchsticks
- 1 cup Cherry Wood Chips
- 1 cup Roma Tomatoes
- 1 cup Mayonnaise
- 1 tablespoon Garlic, Minced
- 1 teaspoon Kosher Salt
- 1 teaspoon Black Pepper

Direction

- Start by soaking the chips in water for 2hrs next remove and drain water and place onto a hotel pan lined with foil. Set over burners on high heat; next place the tomatoes in a perforated hotel pan and insert it into the first one, cover and allow to smoke for 20 min. next remove tomatoes from smoker and puree. Now whisk in the smoked tomato puree into the mayonnaise add the garlic and season to taste. Now layout the salami and place an equal amount of watercress into each piece and repeat process with watermelon. Now roll the salami making sure to have a tight seal but not overly that the product comes out, secure with a toothpick if necessary. Now arrange the rollete's onto a square plate and serve with a side of the smoked tomato Aioli.

143. Garlicky Roasted Potato Salad

Serving: Serves 3-4 | Prep: 0hours20mins | Cook: 0hours40mins |Ready in:

Ingredients

- 1 pound pound small Potatoes (white or red)
- 3 tablespoons Olive Oil
- 1 1/4 teaspoons Salt
- 1/2 teaspoon Ground Black Pepper
- 4 Cloves of Garlic finely chopped
- 4 tablespoons Mayonnaise
- 1 tablespoon Lemon Juice
- 1 teaspoon Dijon Mustard

Direction

- Preheat the oven to 400 degrees. Cut the potatoes in half or quarters into a bowl. Add 2 tablespoons of the olive oil, 3/4 teaspoon of salt and the pepper. Mix and put on a baking sheet in a single layer. Bake the potatoes for 40 minutes flipping twice during baking. Make sure they turn a nice golden brown. Take out of the oven and allow to cool.
- In a bowl combine 1/2 teaspoon of salt, 1 tablespoon of olive oil, the chopped garlic, mayonnaise, lemon juice and Dijon mustard. Mix and pour over the cooled potatoes.

144. General Tso's Chicken Sliders

Serving: Makes 8 | Prep: 0hours15mins | Cook: 0hours15mins |Ready in:

Ingredients

- 1 box Crazy Cuizine General Tso's Chicken
- 1/4 cup mayonnaise
- 1 1/2 teaspoons sriracha
- 1 1/2 teaspoons General Tso's Chicken sauce (included in Crazy Cuizine box)
- 8 small hamburger buns
- 8 small green lettuce leaves
- 4 scallions, thinly sliced

Direction

- Prepare chicken according to the Crazy Cuisine box instructions, but reserve about 2 tsp of the sauce for the spicy mayonnaise.
- In a small bowl, combine mayo, sriracha and General Tso's sauce. Whisk until smooth. Taste and adjust as needed.
- To assemble your sliders, place a lettuce leaf on each of the bottom buns. Add about 3 pieces of chicken on top of each lettuce leaf. Spoon about 1 tbsp of spicy mayo over the chicken. Garnish each slider with a small amount of scallions. Place top half of buns on sliders.

145. Gibson Gobbler

Serving: Serves 4 | Prep: | Cook: |Ready in:

Ingredients

- Tea-Smoked Turkey
- Leftover turkey, large pieces like legs, thighs, breasts
- 1/2 cup sugar
- 1/2 cup tea leaves (I prefer lapsang souchong, but any tea will do)
- 4 tablespoons salt
- White Bar-B-Q Sauce
- 1 cup good-quality mayonnaise
- 1/2 cup apple cider vinegar
- 2 tablespoons sugar
- 1 tablespoon fresh lemon juice
- 1 teaspoon salt
- 1 teaspoon fresh cracked pepper
- 3 or 4 dashes hot sauce, such as crystal or tobasco

Direction

- Tea-Smoked Turkey
- Line your smoking vessel (a wok or pot) with tin foil so that this process doesn't ruin your pan. You should also line the inside of the lid with foil. Spread sugar evenly over the smoking vessel and layer the salt and tea over. Set a rack (such as a round cake rack or cooking rack) over the mixture, and position the turkey pieces on the rack.
- Place the smoking vessel over high heat. When the tea begins to smoke, cover with the lid and reduce to a medium-low temperature. Let the turkey smoke for 15 minutes, or until the pieces reach a dark, satisfying color.
- Turn off the heat and let the turkey sit for 5 minutes before removing the lid. I recommend opening the lid outside.
- Once the turkey is cool enough to handle, pull into bite-sized pieces. Rough, rag-like shreds are ideal, since they hold the sauce.
- White Bar-B-Q Sauce
- Add mayonnaise to a bowl with the dry ingredients (sugar, salt, and pepper). Mix to combine. Slowly add the wet ingredients (vinegar, lemon juice, and hot sauce), whisking until smooth.
- Pour half of the sauce over the turkey (add more if it looks dry). Pile the saucy turkey onto toasted bread and serve with pickles.

---

146.   Gilding The Lily Heirloom Tomato Tart

Serving: Serves 2 tarts | Prep: | Cook: |Ready in:

Ingredients

- 1   your favorite recipe double pie crust
- 2   large or 6-8 small assorted heirloom tomatoes, peeled
- 1 pound good quality crabmeat, picked over, rinsed, drained and blotted
- 3 cups grated extra sharp cheddar, room temperature

- 1 cup plus 2-3 tablespoons mayonnaise
- 1   scant cup well-chopped onion
- 5 tablespoons chopped fresh basil
- 1/2 teaspoon salt
- 3/4 teaspoon freshly ground black pepper

Direction

- Slice tomatoes 1/2-3/4" thick and place on paper towels to drain well.
- Divide the pie crust dough between two tart pans and bake per your recipe instructions until set, about 15-20 minutes.
- Mix cheddar, 1 cp. mayonnaise, onion, basil, salt and pepper and set aside.
- When the shells come out of the oven, set them aside to cool for about 10 minutes, then cover the bottoms with a thin coating of mayonnaise.
- Spread the crabmeat evenly between the two shells.
- Arrange the tomato slices over the crabmeat, covering as completely as possible.
- Spread the cheddar mixture over the tomatoes.
- Bake at 350 degrees 25-30 minutes. Cool at least 20 minutes before serving.

---

147.   Glazed Five Spice Burger With Gingery Mangos

Serving: Serves 6 | Prep: | Cook: |Ready in:

Ingredients

- Gingery Mangos
- 2 ripe mangos, peeled, seeded, and diced
- 2 finely chopped scallions, white and light green parts only
- 2 teaspoons grated fresh ginger
- 2 tablespoon chopped fresh cilantro leaves
- Juice of 1 lime
- sea salt and freshly ground black pepper
- Glazed Five Spice Burger
- 1/3 cup canola mayonnaise
- 2 tablespoons Dijon mustard

- 1 1/2 pound ground beef
- 1/4 cup red onion, finely chopped
- 2 teaspoons Chinese five spice powder
- sea salt and freshly ground black pepper to taste
- 1/3 cup hoisin sauce
- 6 hamburger buns or Kaiser rolls, split

Direction

- In a medium bowl, toss together mangos, scallions, ginger, cilantro, lime juice, salt and pepper. Let marinate.
- In a small bowl, stir together mayonnaise and Dijon mustard. Keep cold.
- Prepare grill to medium-hot heat. In a medium bowl, combine ground beef, red onion, five spice powder, salt and pepper. Form the meat into 6 patties of even thickness. Thoroughly coat patties with glaze after flipping. Cook until desired doneness. Toast buns lightly, while patties are cooking on the outer edges of the grill.
- To serve: slathering cut side of buns with Dijon mayonnaise. Place patties on bottom half of buns, drizzle with a little more hoisin sauce, top with gingery mangos and top half of buns.

148.   Green Eggs And Ham

Serving: Makes 1 quiche | Prep: | Cook: | Ready in:

Ingredients

- 2 bunches green onions
- 1 cup diced, cooked ham
- 1 tablespoon unsalted butter
- 1/2 cup mayonnaise
- 1/4 teaspoon celery salt
- 1/4 teaspoon lemon pepper
- 3/4 teaspoon cornstarch
- 1/2 cup milk
- 1 egg
- 1 1/2 cups shredded white cheddar cheese
- 2 tablespoons diced green chiles (optional)

- 1 9 inch pie shell

Direction

- Preheat oven to 350.
- Slice only the whites of both bunches of onions.
- Melt 1 tbsp butter in sauté pan. Sauté onions on low until they begin to brown. Add ham and increase heat to medium. Sauté 5 minutes. Remove from heat and set aside to cool.
- Chop the greens from one bunch of onions.
- Place the greens from the second bunch of onions into a food processor. Pulse until finely chopped. Add mayo, spices, and cornstarch. Blend until fully combined.
- Using a fork, whisk milk and egg into mayonnaise mixture. Once fully incorporated, add cooled ham, chopped onion greens, cheese, and green chiles (if using).
- Pour mixture into pie shell.
- Bake at 350 for 45-55 minutes. You'll be able to tell that it's done when the filling is set and the top is slightly browned.
- Remove from oven and let cool for at least 10 minutes before serving.

149.   Green Pea Salad

Serving: Makes 6 cups | Prep: | Cook: | Ready in:

Ingredients

- 4 cups Frozen peas
- 1/2 cup Diced Celery
- 1/2 cup Diced Onion
- 1/2 cup cubed cheddar or jack cheese
- 1/2 cup cubed Velvetta cheese
- 2 Hardboiled eggs, diced
- Lawrys salt to taste
- 1/2 cup Mayonnaise

Direction

- In a large colander, run your frozen peas under water to thaw. Keep them firm but not frozen. Drain well.
- In a large bowl, combine all of your ingredients and gently mix. Add more mayonnaise if you like your salad creamier.

---

150. Grilled (or Baked) Bluefish

Serving: Serves 2 | Prep: | Cook: |Ready in:

Ingredients

- bluefish or rockfish
- mayonnaise
- Dijon mustard
- sea salt and freshly ground black pepper

Direction

- A little mayonnaise coats the fish to keep it marvelously moist. Use this recipe with any fresh local fish such as bluefish or rockfish.
- Lightly season the fish with salt and pepper, then brush 1 part Dijon mustard and 2 parts good mayo all across the fish's flesh to coat. Add chopped dill, if desired and broil it in the oven for about 6-8 minutes. Or, lay it on some heavy-duty aluminum foil and slip it onto a hot grill, close the cover, and cook until opaque and moist on the inside (again about 6-8 minutes for fish less than 1-inch).
- Shopping Tip: Keep bluefish cool on the trip home from market and keep it refrigerated in the coldest part of the fridge until you're ready to use.
- Note: As migratory marine fish, blues are voracious predators that sport fishermen prize for their fighting ability. In the US, they can be found off the coast of Florida and in the Gulf of Mexico in the winter months and in New England waters from June through October, when they then head south again.

---

151. Grilled Asparagus And Prosciutto Panini

Serving: Serves 4 | Prep: | Cook: |Ready in:

Ingredients

- 2 pieces garlic
- 1/2 cup mayonnaise
- 6 pieces asparagus
- 1/2 cup arugula
- 4 pieces prosciutto
- 4 pieces swiss cheese
- 4 (3oz) pieces ciabatta bread

Direction

- Mince garlic
- Mix into mayonnaise
- Brush ciabatta with mayonnaise.
- Layer sandwich with cheese, meat, arugula, and asparagus.
- Grill in a Panini press.
- Enjoy with something filling and light like chilled strawberry soup!

---

152. Grilled Beef Tenderloin Sandwich With Spicy Steakhouse Aioli

Serving: Serves 4 | Prep: | Cook: |Ready in:

Ingredients

- Spicy Steakhouse Aioli
- 3 tablespoons Spicy Mustard
- 1/4 cup honey
- 1 garlic clove
- 1/2 cup mayonnaise
- kosher salt and fresh ground pepper
- Beef Tenderloin Sandwich
- 1 pound beef tenderloin, trimmed of fat
- 5 large mushrooms, cleaned

- 1 large vidalia onion, cut into 1/2 inch slices
- 1 cup baby spinach
- 1/4 cup blue cheese
- 1 ciabatta loaf, split lengthwise
- 3 tablespoons extra virgin olive oil

Direction

- In a mini food processor, add the mustard, honey, garlic and mayonnaise processing until smooth. Season with salt and pepper to taste. Let sit for 30 minutes.
- Coat the tenderloin in 1 tablespoon olive oil and cover liberally with salt and pepper. On a prepared grill, cook the beef over med-high heat, turning occasionally to create a crust. Continue to grill until medium rare, approximately 20 minutes. (Use a grill thermometer to determine temperature, I remove around 125 degrees.) Transfer to a plate and allow to rest for 10 minutes covered with foil.
- Drizzle the onions and mushrooms with olive oil and season with salt and pepper. Grill the onions and mushrooms until soft, approximately 5-7 minutes. Transfer to a plate.
- Brush both cut sides of the ciabatta with olive oil and grill, cut side down, until lightly charred, approximately 5 minutes.
- To assemble: Slice the beef into 1/2 inch slices, set aside. Brush both cut sides of the bread with aioli, top the bottom half with grilled onions and then layer the beef on the onions. Top the beef with the mushrooms, blue cheese, spinach and then the top of the ciabatta. Cut into four sandwiches, serve immediately.

153. Grilled Bread Salad With Broccoli Rabe & Summer Squash

Serving: Serves 4 | Prep: 0hours45mins | Cook: 0hours10mins | Ready in:

Ingredients

- For the mayonnaise marinade
- 1 cup full-fat mayonnaise
- 1/2 cup olive oil
- 2 lemons, juiced and zested (about 1/4 cup lemon juice)
- 2 garlic cloves, mashed into a paste
- 1 tablespoon kosher salt
- 1 teaspoon Aleppo pepper (or 1/2 teaspoon red pepper flakes)
- 1 teaspoon Spanish smoked paprika
- 1 tablespoon cumin seed
- For the grilled vegetables and bread salad
- 2 or 3 mixed summer squash (about 1 1/2 pounds), cut into 1/2 inch-thick rounds
- 1 large bunch broccoli rabe (or young, tender broccoli)
- 4 1/2-inch slices from the center of a loaf of crusty bread (ciabatta or sourdough works well)
- 1/4 cup extra-virgin olive oil for brushing bread
- 1 splash Olive oil for brushing grill grate
- 1 handful torn basil and mint for garnish
- 1/4 cup toasted pine nuts or toasted, chopped almonds
- 1 splash extra virgin olive oil and fresh lemon juice, to taste

Direction

- To prepare the broccoli rabe, remove thick, tough lower ends of stalks. Split lengthwise any stalks that are more than 1/2-inch thick. If you are using young, tender broccoli, prepare it in the same way.
- To prepare the mayonnaise marinade: In a large bowl, whisk the mayonnaise with the olive oil, lemon juice, lemon zest, garlic, salt, smoked Spanish paprika, Aleppo pepper, and cumin seed until smooth and emulsified.
- To prepare the vegetables: To the bowl of marinade, add the summer squash. Rinse the broccoli rabe thoroughly to remove any grit hiding among the leaves. Add it to the bowl with the summer squash, then toss with the

marinade to coat the vegetables evenly. (Don't dry the broccoli rabe after rinsing -- the bit of water clinging to the leaves will thin the marinade and gently steam the stalks as they're grilling, allowing any tough stalks to get tender.) Allow the vegetables to marinate at room temperature for about 30 minutes, tossing once or twice to make sure they're evenly coated.

- To prepare grill: Meanwhile, prepare a gas grill with all burners on medium, or a prepare a charcoal grill with hot coals. Brush the grilling rack with olive oil.

- To grill the vegetables: When the grill is ready, arrange the summer squash rounds evenly across the grill grate. Grill for a few minutes on each side, or until tender and nicely blistered in spots. Remove the squash from grill. Next, arrange the broccoli rabe in a single layer on the grill. Grill for 2 to 3 minutes per side, or until tender and blistered in spots. (Taste if you're unsure if the stalks are tender.) If the stalks are charring quickly but aren't tender, spray or drizzle a few drops of water on them. Remove from the grill and place on a large platter or sheet pan to cool. (You don't want to stack the broccoli rabe while it's still hot because it'll lose its crisp, papery texture.)

- To grill the bread: Brush each slice of bread (top and bottom) with about 1 tablespoon of oil, or enough to evenly and thoroughly coat each side. Season with a pinch of kosher salt and a few grinds of pepper. Grill the bread on both sides, checking frequently, until charred in spots, a few minutes per side. Turn down the heat if needed. You want the bread to be crusty but soft in the middle. When the bread is cool enough to handle, cut it into 1/2-inch cubes.

- To assemble salad: On a large serving platter, place the bread cubes, grilled broccoli rabe, and summer squash. Garnish with toasted nuts, basil, and mint. Season with kosher salt and pepper to taste, then drizzle with extra-virgin olive oil and lemon juice to taste. Serve warm or at room temperature.

<table>
<tr><td>154.</td><td>Grilled Cheese Egg In A Hole</td></tr>
</table>

Serving: Serves 1 | Prep: | Cook: |Ready in:

Ingredients

- 2 slices soft bread, like white or potato
- 1 to 2 teaspoons mayonnaise
- 1 to 2 slices sharp white cheddar cheese or your favorite melty cheese
- 1 large egg
- Freshly ground pepper
- Sea Salt

Direction

- Start heating a non-stick pan on medium-low. Spread a thin layer of mayonnaise on one slice of bread and place the bread mayonnaise-side down in the pan.
- Cut the cheese into thirds. Place one-third on each side of the bread in the pan. Cut the remaining third in half and fill in the top and bottom of the gap between the other slices of cheese, leaving a cheese-less square in the middle. [Editors' note: You want to cover the entire slice of bread except for the square in the center where you'll be cutting a hole through the sandwich.]
- Spread a thin layer of mayonnaise on the other slice of bread and place it on top of the cheese, mayonnaise-side up. Cook the sandwich for a few minutes until the bottom is golden brown.
- Flip the sandwich over. Using a cookie cutter or a drinking glass, cut out a hole in the middle of the sandwich about 2 1/2- to 2 3/4-inches wide. Remove the circle of bread (you can continue grilling this on the side of the pan) and crack the egg into the hole. Cover and cook until the egg is set to your liking.
- Slide the sandwich onto a plate. Season the egg with freshly ground pepper and sea salt (I used a red Alaea salt, which is why the egg looks like it has measles). Serve with tomato soup, if you like.

155. Grilled Mexican Corn

Serving: Serves 6 | Prep: | Cook: |Ready in:

Ingredients

- 6 fresh corn cobs with husk in tact
- 1 lime
- 1/3 cup Kewpie Japanese mayonnaise
- 1 teaspoon Spanish smoked paprika
- 1 teaspoon chili powder
- 4 ounces grated Cotija cheese
- 1/3 cup chopped cilantro

Direction

- Pull the corn husks back from each cob and remove silk, leaving the corn husks attached to the corn. Pull off a small ribbon of the husk and tie the husks back to form a handle.
- Fill a sink full of water and soak the tied corn for at least half an hour. This helps prevent the husks from burning when they are on the grill.
- While the corn is soaking, grate and juice the lime and mix it with mayonnaise, smoked paprika and chili powder. Cover and refrigerate until ready to serve.
- Clean and lightly oil your grill grates and heat to medium-high. Dry the corn and grill until charred on all sides, taking care to keep the husks away from the hottest part of the grill, about 10 minutes.
- When the corn is cooked, remove any lingering silk and generously rub each cob down with the lime-mayo-spice mixture. Sprinkle each cob with the grated Cotija cheese, chopped cilantro, salt, and if you prefer, a little extra chili powder. Serve hot with plenty of napkins.

156. Grilled Pepper Cheese Sandwiches

Serving: Serves 1 (plus extra cheese) | Prep: | Cook: |Ready in:

Ingredients

- For Pepper Cheese Spread
- 12 ounces extra sharp cheddar cheese
- 6 ounces roasted piquillo peppers
- 4 cloves garlic
- 1/2 cup good prepared mayonnaise (Hellman's or homemade)
- For the sandwich
- 2 slices good sandwich bread (my favorite is variations on French country bread like Pain Poilane)
- 1 tablespoon butter (give or take)

Direction

- Break the cheese into large chunks and put it in the bowl of your food processor. Pulse until mixture resembles coarse gravel.
- Add peppers and garlic to food processor. Process until mixture is finely chopped.
- Add mayonnaise, and process until the mixture is smooth. Put into a container for refrigerator storage.
- Lightly butter both sides of the bread and preheat a cast iron skillet.
- Place two slices of bread in the skillet and heat until lightly toasted. Turn over bread.
- Spread about 1/3 c. cheese mixture onto one of the toasted bread surfaces. Place other slice of bread onto the cheese, toasted side facing cheese.
- Cook sandwich, turning, until exterior is toasted and cheese is melt.

157. Grilled Prosciutto And Parmesan Garlic Burger With Marinated Tomatoes

Serving: Serves 6 | Prep: | Cook: | Ready in:

Ingredients

- Marinated Tomatoes
- 3 vine-ripened tomatoes (about 2 cups), seeded and chopped
- 2 tablespoons red wine vinegar
- 1 tablespoon honey
- 1 1/2 teaspoons Dijon mustard
- 1 teaspoon extra-virgin olive oil
- 2 tablespoons fresh basil, chopped
- Grilled Prosciutto and Parmesan Garlic Burger
- 1 1/2 pounds ground beef
- 4 tablespoons finely shredded, not grated, parmesan cheese
- 1 tablespoon Worcestershire sauce
- 2 cloves garlic, minced
- sea salt and freshly ground black pepper to tasted
- 6 slices proscuitto
- 4 ounces fresh mozzarella, shredded
- 6 whole-grain hamburger buns, toasted
- canola mayonnaise

Direction

- In a large bowl, combine the ground beef, parmesan cheese, Worcestershire sauce, garlic, salt and pepper. Use your hands to mix the ingredients until just combined and shape into 6 patties. Place on a lined baking sheet, cover loosely with plastic wrap and refrigerate for 30 minutes.
- To make Marinated Tomatoes: In a small fire-proof skillet, combine olive oil, vinegar, honey, mustard, salt and freshly ground black pepper. Add tomatoes and coat with marinade. When patties are ready to be cooked, preheat your grill on medium-high heat and place the skillet with the marinated tomatoes in it directly on the grill. Sauté 2 to 3 minutes or until thoroughly heated. Remove from heat, and stir in basil. Set aside.
- Grill the burgers, flipping once until desired doneness. Meanwhile, grill the prosciutto slices until slightly crisp, about 1 minute, then flip and grill for another 30 seconds. Set aside.
- To assemble the burger, spread mayonnaise on toasted bun and place a meat patty on top. Layer with a slice of grilled prosciutto, shredded mozzarella, and a heaping tablespoon of marinated tomatoes. Top with toasted bun.

158. Grilled Tuna Nicoise Sandwich

Serving: Serves 2 | Prep: | Cook: | Ready in:

Ingredients

- 1.5 ounces green beans
- 1 tablespoon minced shallot, divided
- 300 grams piece of fresh tuna
- 1 small potato scrubbed well
- 2 teaspoons dry white wine
- boston lettuce leaves
- sliced tomato
- 1 boiled egg
- 1 teaspoon olive oil, plus more for grilling
- 0.75 teaspoons lemon juice, divided
- 0.5 teaspoons dijon
- 2.5 tablespoons mayonnaise
- 1 tablespoon pitted, chopped nicoise olives
- 1 anchovy fillet, chopped finely
- 0.5 tablespoons chopped capers
- sea salt and freshly ground pepper
- thick slices of a crusty, dense bread of choice

Direction

- -Bring salted water to boil in saucepan, then adding green beans, boil for 2-3 minutes. Remove green beans and immediately plunge into iced water. When cool, slice lengthwise and toss with 1/2 tbsp minced shallot. Set aside.

- -Steam or bake potato, then allow to partially cool. While still a little warm, slice and drizzle with 2 tsp white wine and other 1/2 tbsp minced shallots. Allow to cool, then drain excess liquid if needed. Set aside.
- -Mix together 2.5 tbsp mayonnaise, nicoise olives, capers, anchovy fillet, and 0.25 tsp lemon juice. Set aside.
- -Mix together 1 tsp olive oil, 0.5 tsp lemon juice, 0.5 tsp Dijon and salt and pepper. Set aside.
- -Heat a grill pan at medium. Brush sliced bread with olive oil, then grill until toasted.
- -Wipe grill pan and increase heat to medium-high.
- -Season tuna stack with sea salt, pepper and some olive oil. Place in grill pan and cook for 1.5-2 minutes each side. Remove tuna from heat and allow to rest for several minutes, then slice. Set aside.
- -To assemble sandwich: spread mayonnaise mixture on one slice of bread. Top with slices of potato, then sliced grilled tuna. To other slice of bread, add boston lettuce leaves, then green beans, sliced tomato and slices of boiled egg. Drizzle with olive oil/Dijon mixture. Press both sides together, cut and serve. Makes enough for one large sandwich. Ingredients may be made the day prior and kept covered in refrigerator until ready to use.

159. Grilled Mini Swordfish Rolls With Lemon Caper Mayonnaise

Serving: Serves 4 | Prep: | Cook: |Ready in:

Ingredients

- 2 Swordfish Steaks
- 2 tablespoons Olive Oil
- 3/4 cup Mayonnaise
- 2 tablespoons Capers
- 2 tablespoons chopped parsley
- 1 1/2 tablespoons fresh lemon juice
- 1/2 teaspoon lemon zest
- 2 tablespoons salted butter
- 1 lemon for wedges
- 2 New England style hot dog rolls cut in half (split top) or 2 6 inch french rolls cut in half
- 1/2 teaspoon salt
- 1/2 teaspoon pepper

Direction

- In mini food processor combine capers, lemon juice, zest, parsley and mayo till well blended. Season with salt and pepper. Set aside.
- Lightly brush swordfish with oil, salt and pepper. Grill on high for 3-4 minutes per side for medium-well. Cut up swordfish in small chunks.
- Toast buttered buns and brush inside with mayo. Fill buns with swordfish. Garnish with lemon wedges on side. Serve extra mayonnaise in side dish for dipping.

160. HAWAIIAN POTATO SALAD

Serving: Makes a nice big bowl | Prep: | Cook: |Ready in:

Ingredients

- 1/2 cup red wine vinegar
- 1 tablespoon sugar
- 1 teaspoon salt
- 1/2 Maui, Vidalia or red onion, thinly sliced into 1/2 circles
- 2 fresh jalapenos, 1 sliced thin into rings, 1 finely chopped (seeds included)
- 2 pounds new red, or golden fleshed potatoes, halved
- 3/4 cup dry (uncooked) ditali pasta (or other smallish pasta)
- 2 eggs, hard boiled, peeled, smooshed finely with a fork

- 1 cup (scant) crispy celery, thinly sliced
- 1 cup mini cucumbers, quartered lengthwise, chopped into small chunks
- 1 - 1 1/2 cups mayonnaise
- 2 tablespoons whole grain mustard
- Sea salt and freshly ground black pepper

Direction

- In a medium bowl mix together red wine vinegar, sugar and 1 teaspoon salt. Add onions and jalapenos. Marinate at least 30 minutes and up to 2 hours, stirring occasionally. Drain, reserving pickling juice.
- Put potatoes in a large pot, cover with cold water, and add 2 tablespoons salt. Bring to a boil over high heat. Turn down heat to maintain an easy boil and cook until just tender. Drain potatoes and rinse well with cold water to stop cooking and to cool those spuds down. Chop into about 1 inch cubes, and set aside.
- Cook ditali in boiling salted water until just al dente. Drain, rinse thoroughly with cold water.
- Add diced potatoes and cooked ditali to large bowl. Add the eggs, celery, cucumber chunks and drained onion and jalapenos. Add one cup mayonnaise, mustard, 1/2 of the pickling juice and salt and pepper, to taste, to the bowl. Mix gently to combine and evenly distribute dressing. Add more mayo, if mixture is not well covered with dressing. Taste, adjust seasonings, and add more pickling juice, if desired. Refrigerate for at least 2 hours so flavors meet one another and get all friendly. Serve chilled.

---

161.   Halibut Rolls

Serving: Serves 4 | Prep: | Cook: | Ready in:

Ingredients

- Halibut Mixture

- 3/4 pound Halibut, baked
- 2 Celery Ribs, sliced thin
- 1 piece Roasted Red Pepper, diced small
- 8 Black Olives, Large, Sliced
- 2 tablespoons Flat-leaf Parsley, chopped
- 2 tablespoons Herb Mayonnaise (see below)
- 2 Green Onions, sliced
- 1 teaspoon Fresh Ground Pepper
- 4 Croissants
- 4 Lettuce Leaves
- 2 Roma Tomatoes, sliced
- Herb Mayonnaise
- 1 1/2 cups Mayonnaise
- 2 tablespoons Fresh Dill, finely chopped
- 1 tablespoon Thyme, finely chopped
- 1 tablespoon Fresh Oregano, finely chopped
- 1 tablespoon Fresh Basil, finely chopped
- 1 Shallot, finely chopped
- 1 Garlic Clove, finely chopped
- 2 tablespoons Fresh Lemon Juice
- 1 teaspoon Whole Grain Mustard
- couple dashes Tabasco
- Salt and Pepper to taste

Direction

- Flake fish into small pieces in large bowl.
- Add celery, red pepper, olives, parsley, green onions and pepper to fish.
- In a separate bowl, mix all ingredients for the mayonnaise until smooth.
- Add mayonnaise to fish mixture and mix throughly.
- Cut croissants in half and remove some of the interior bread, making room for the fish mixture. Spoon into croissants and top with lettuce and tomatoes.
- Serve with a side of fresh fruit for a great summertime treat!

---

162.   Hawaiian Salmon Cakes With Pineapple Salsa

Serving: Makes 8 salmon cakes | Prep: | Cook: | Ready in:

Ingredients

- For the salmon cakes
- 12 ounces fresh boneless, skinless salmon, cut into 1/2-inch pieces
- 4 - 6 tablespoons mayonnaise
- 2 tablespoons soy sauce
- 1/2 teaspoon toasted sesame seed oil
- 1/2 teaspoon sambal oelek, plus more to taste (if you like it spicy)
- zest of one lime
- 1 medium clove garlic, minced
- 1/2 teaspoon fresh ginger, peeled and minced
- 1/2 cup scallions, finely chopped
- 1 cup panko breadcrumbs
- 1/2 teaspoon sea salt
- 1 tablespoon black sesame seeds
- 3 tablespoons coconut oil, or canola oil
- For the pineapple salsa
- 1 1/2 cups fresh pineapple, diced
- 1/2 small red onion, finely diced
- 1 small jalapeno, seeded and finely chopped
- 1/4 cup cilantro, roughly chopped
- 2 - 3 tablespoons fresh lime juice
- 1 tablespoon fruity extra virgin olive oil

Direction

- For the salmon cakes, freeze the salmon pieces for about 10 minutes. Add half of the chilled salmon to the bowl of a food processor and pulse until roughly chopped, about 8 - 10 pulses. Transfer the chopped salmon to a large bowl and repeat with the remaining half of the salmon (I like my salmon cakes to be a little chunky, so sometimes I only pulse the second half for 5 or 6 pulses). Transfer the remaining half of the chopped salmon to bowl.
- In a small bowl, whisk together 4 tablespoons of the mayonnaise, soy sauce, sesame oil, sambal oelek, lime zest, garlic and ginger. Add the mayonnaise mixture, green onions and ½ cup of panko breadcrumbs to the chopped salmon and gently mix to combine. If the mixture is too dry, add the remaining mayonnaise one tablespoon at a time. Set aside.

- In a shallow bowl or plate, stir together the remaining ½ cup of panko breadcrumbs, salt and black sesame seeds.
- Divide the reserved salmon mixture in 8 balls and form into individual cakes, about 3 inches wide. Gently press each cake into the panko-sesame seed mixture, lightly coating all sides. Place the breaded salmon cakes on a clean plate.
- In a large skillet, heat the coconut or canola oil over medium heat. Add the breaded salmon cakes and cook until the salmon is cooked through and the outside is golden brown and crispy, about 3 - 4 minutes per side. Transfer cooked salmon cakes to a paper towel-lined plate.
- For the salsa, mix all the ingredients together in a medium bowl. Season with salt to taste.
- To serve, arrange the salmon cakes on a platter, or individual plates, and serve alongside the pineapple salsa. Enjoy!

---

163. Hazelnut Crunch Salmon

Serving: Serves 4 | Prep: | Cook: | Ready in:

Ingredients

- 6 tablespoons mayonnaise
- 1.5 tablespoons rosemary, chopped
- 3 tablespoons Dijon mustard
- 4 salmon fillets, center cut, 6 - 8 oz each
- 1 teaspoon garlic, crushed
- 2 tablespoons olive oil
- 1 cup hazelnuts, chopped
- kosher salt and freshly cracked black pepper

Direction

- Preheat the oven to 450*F. Mix the mayonnaise, rosemary, garlic and mustard together in a small bowl with a pinch of salt and pepper. Set aside.
- Heat a large, oven-proof skillet over medium-high. Rub the flesh of the salmon with the

olive oil and season generously with salt and pepper. Place the salmon, flesh side down into the hot skillet. Season the skin side. Let the flesh get a deep sear, about 3 minutes.

- Carefully flip the salmon over. Turn off the flame. Spread the mayo mix over the tops of the salmon fillets, and into the sides. Sprinkle on the hazelnuts and pat into place. Put the skillet into the oven and roast until cooked thru, about 10 minutes for thick fillets.

---

164.   Healthy Teriyaki Burger

Serving: Serves 2 | Prep: | Cook: |Ready in:

Ingredients

- 2 buns
- 6 ounces firm tofu
- 6 ounces chicken breast meat
- 1 teaspoon ginger powder
- 2 tablespoons soy sauce
- 2 tablespoons sweet sake (mirin)
- 2 tablespoons sugar
- 1 teaspoon potato starch
- 30 milliliters water
- 2 tablespoons ketchup
- 2 tablespoons mayonnaise
- 2 pieces red onion
- 2 pieces tomato
- 2 pieces lettace
- 1 egg
- 2 tablespoons sesami oil

Direction

- Heat tofu in a microwave oven for one minute, and squeeze tofu (drain liquid)
- Mix meat, tofu, egg and ginger well
- Make two thick patties and pat it
- Put oil in a frying pan
- Cook until both sides are golden brown, and steam it for five minutes
- Remove patties from frying pan temporarily

- Put soy sauce, sweet sake, potato starch and water in a frying pan, and boil down
- Dress patties with Teriyaki sauce
- Toast buns
- Mix ketchup and mayonnaise, and spread on the buns
- Place vegetables on patties

---

165.   Heirloom Tomato Galette With Burrata

Serving: Serves 6 | Prep: | Cook: |Ready in:

Ingredients

- Galette
- 1 pie crust
- 1/4 cup mayonnaise
- salt and pepper
- 4 cloves garlic, minced
- 1/4 cup grated parmesan cheese
- 2 balls burrata
- Pie Crust
- 2 1/2 cups all-purpose flour
- 1 tablespoon sugar
- 1/4 teaspoon salt
- 2 sticks salted butter
- 8 tablespoons ice water (give or take)

Direction

- Galette: Preheat the oven to 425F and prepare a baking sheet with parchment paper or cooking spray. Sprinkle the tomatoes evenly with salt and pepper and let sit for 15-30 minutes to remove as much liquid as you can. Blot the tomatoes dry and drain the burrata balls on paper towels.
- Roll the pie crust thinly into the shape of a large rough circle about 14 inches in diameter. Transfer the pie crust to the baking sheet.
- Spread the mayonnaise evenly on the pie crust. Layer half of the tomatoes in a large circle on the pie crust, leaving about 3 inches of crust at the edges. Sprinkle with half of the

garlic. Repeat with the remaining tomatoes, heaping them into the center of the dough. Top with the remaining garlic, the parmesan cheese, and the burrata balls, breaking them up lightly in the center of the tomatoes.

- Form the galette by pulling the edges of the pie crust up and a round the tomatoes to form a crust, pinching the dough together as you go. Spray the crust with cooking spray to help it brown in the oven.
- Bake the galette for 45-55 minutes until the crust is browned and crispy and the cheese is bubbly. Let rest for 15 minutes before slicing and serving. Enjoy!
- Pie Crust: Cut the butter into cubes and place in the freezer for 5-10 minutes. While the butter is chilling, pulse the flour, sugar, and salt in the food processor to combine.
- Add the cold butter cubes and pulse about 10 times to break up the butter just a bit. Stream in the water and blend into the flour mixture until a dough just barely starts to come together - it will still be crumbly.
- Dump the dough onto a cutting board sprinkled with a bit of flour. Split the dough into 2 mounds and form each into a flat disk about 1-inch thick. Wrap the disks in plastic wrap or a plastic bag. Refrigerate for 1 hour or until ready to use. Make any pie you like! Enjoy.

---

166.   Heirloom Tomato Pie

Serving: Serves 6 | Prep: | Cook: |Ready in:

Ingredients

- 1 Prebaked deep dish pie shell, or homemade if you have time
- 4 Large Heirloom Tomatoes
- 10 Fresh Basil Leaves, Finely Chopped
- 1/2 cup Green Onion, Chopped
- 1 cup Grated Fresh Mozzarella
- 1 cup Grated Gruyere
- 1 tablespoon Sour Cream

- 1 cup Mayonnaise
- Sea Salt and Cracked Black Pepper for taste
- 1 tablespoon Fresh Grated Parmigiano

Direction

- Preheat oven to 350 degrees.
- Blanch the tomatoes and slice. Place the tomatoes in the strainer to drain.
- In a medium bowl, mix mayonnaise, sour cream, gruyere, mozzarella, salt and pepper.
- Layer the tomato slices, basil and green onion in pie shell. Season with salt and pepper. Spread the mayonnaise and cheese mixture on top of the tomatoes and bake for 30 minutes or until golden brown.
- Sprinkle top with grated Parmigiano and serve.

---

167.   Herbed Soft Scramble

Serving: Serves 2 | Prep: | Cook: |Ready in:

Ingredients

- 4 happy, farm fresh eggs, at room temperature
- 1 tablespoon real mayonnaise, best quality
- 1 tablespoon whole milk, (goat or cow)
- 1/2 tablespoon unsalted butter
- dash of Maldon salt flakes or sea salt
- two turns of fresh milled mixed peppercorns
- 1 teaspoon snipped fresh chives
- small handful of torn cilantro leaves (or Italian parsley if you prefer)
- finishing dash of sweet paprika or Aleppo pepper

Direction

- Gently whisk eggs with mayonnaise and milk until smoothly blended. Add the salt and ground peppercorns.

- Heat butter in the frying pan. Then slowly pour in the egg mixture. Using a fork, gently fluff the eggs.
- As soon as they are scrambled, transfer to warmed plates. Season with a little more salt and pepper if needed. Garnish with the fresh chives and cilantro leaves. Finish with a sprinkle of either sweet paprika or Aleppo pepper. Serve while still warm so you can savor each bite. And don't be one bit afraid of the mayo-you will not taste it.

168. Hoisin Glazed Meatballs With Spicy Coleslaw

Serving: Serves 4 | Prep: | Cook: | Ready in:

Ingredients

- 450 grams / 1 lb minced lamb
- 1 small carrot, grated (about ¼ cup)
- 1 tablespoon fresh ginger, grated
- 2 cloves garlic, minced
- 2 teaspoons sesame oil
- Salt & pepper
- 1 tablespoon vegetable oil
- 2 tablespoons hoisin sauce
- 100 grams / 3.5 oz glass noodles
- 8 baby gem, or other small lettuce leaves
- 250 grams / 2 cups coleslaw mix
- 2 tablespoons mayonnaise
- 1 tablespoon lime pickle (or 2 tsp lime juice + 1 tsp Asian hot sauce, such as sriracha)

Direction

- In a bowl, combine the mayonnaise and lime pickle. Toss in the coleslaw mix until coated and set aside.
- In a large bowl, mix together the lamb, carrot, ginger, garlic, sesame oil, salt and pepper.
- Taking approximately 1 tbsp. at a time, shape into about 24 balls.
- Heat the oil in a large non-stick pan over medium heat and cook meatballs, stirring

occasionally, until browned and no longer pink inside.
- While the meatballs are cooking, cook the glass noodles according to the package directions, then set aside.
- In large bowl, whisk the hoisin sauce with 2 tbsp. water. Add the meatballs and toss to coat.
- Place 2 baby gem lettuce leaves on each plate. Top with noodles, coleslaw and meatballs.

169. Homemade Potato Chips With French Garlic DIp

Serving: Serves 2-3 | Prep: | Cook: | Ready in:

Ingredients

- 6 Potatoes
- 2 tablespoons Mayonnaise
- 1 teaspoon Mustard
- 1/2 teaspoon Thyme
- 1/2 teaspoon Oregano
- 1 piece Garlic

Direction

- First, I recommend peeling the potatoes, but you could also just wash them thoroughly.
- Next, chop the potatoes on thin rings (or chips). Fry a batch of chips in a deep fryer until they get a golden brown color. If you don't have a deep fryer, pour a lot of oil (500 ml – 1000 ml) in a pot and fry them in a pot on high heat.
- Put a napkin on a plate and take out the first batch of chips and put them over the napkin. Then, put a napkin over the first batch of chips and fry the rest of the potatoes. Take out the second batch, and you're done (If you have a larger deep fryer you can make them in one batch).
- The dip is really easy to make. Just chop the clove of garlic as finely as you can and put it in a bowl with the mayonnaise, the mustard and

the rest of the spices. Mix it up a bit with a spoon and there you go.

---

170. Horseradish Caraway Mayonnaise

Serving: Makes 1 cup | Prep: | Cook: | Ready in:

Ingredients

- 3/4 cup good quality mayonnaise
- 3 tablespoons prepared horseradish
- 1/4 teaspoon whole caraway seeds

Direction

- Place the ingredients into a small bowl and mix well. Adjust the amount of horseradish, depending on the strength.
- This mayonnaise can be made and held in the refrigerator for a week.
- Spread it generously on corned beef, roast beef, turkey or lamb sandwiches to add a spicy boost. It can even be used as a dip for vegetables.

---

171. Horseradish Crusted Salmon

Serving: Serves 8 | Prep: | Cook: | Ready in:

Ingredients

- One whole salmon filet
- Skin removed, approximately 3 lbs
- Topping
- 5 ounces prepared horseradish
- 2 cups plus 1/2 cup best-quality mayonnaise
- 1 tablespoon lemon juice
- 1.5 teaspoons worcestershire sauce
- 1 tablespoon dried minced onion

- Not essential, but very helpful: non-stick aluminum foil (Reynolds) or a Silpat mat

Direction

- Place horseradish in a clean dish towel and wring it until liquid no longer comes out. When unwrapped, the horseradish should hold together in a dry, almost solid ball.
- Reconstitute the horseradish by mixing it with 1/2 cup mayonnaise, forming a smooth paste. Combine with remaining topping ingredients.
- Place salmon, flat side down, on a Silpat or non-stick foil-lined baking sheet.
- Cover the entire surface of the fish with the topping, making the topping layer thickest over the thickest part of the fish.
- The surface of the topping may be decorated, the back of a teaspoon was used to make rows of small indentations resembling (?) fish scales.
- Bake at 425 degrees for 30 minutes, or until the topping has been partially absorbed into the fish and turned deep, golden brown. With all of the mayo in the topping, the fish really doesn't dry out.
- When done, carefully remove the layer of oil that has collected on the baking sheet by blotting it with paper towels. Pouring the oil off is pretty risky if the fish is on Silpat or non-stick foil! When the baking sheet is clean, slide the fish onto the serving platter by tilting the baking sheet. Or, leave the oil alone and move the fish using two large spatulas.

---

172. Hot Ham And Cheese With A Secret

Serving: Serves 1 | Prep: | Cook: | Ready in:

Ingredients

- For the Horseradish Sauce
- 3/4 cup mayonnaise
- 1 tablespoon(s) prepared or fresh-grated horseradish

- 1/4 cup sour cream
- Kosher salt
- For the Sandwich
- 1 tablespoon cream, milk or club soda
- 2 tablespoon(s) Horseradish Cream Sauce
- 1 fluffy hamburger bun, split
- 2 ounce(s) thick-sliced ham
- 1 thick (1/4") slice Swiss cheese

Direction

- For the Horseradish Sauce: In a medium bowl, stir together mayonnaise, horseradish and sour cream. Add a pinch of salt and taste, adding additional salt if desired. Makes 1 cup. Set aside at room temperature during use, then store leftovers covered in the refrigerator for up to two weeks. The sauce goes well with beef, too.
- For the Sandwich: Mix one tablespoon of horseradish sauce with one tablespoon of cream, milk or club soda. Stir until smooth. Spread onto the cut sides of the bun.
- Heat a small skillet over medium-high heat. Place bun halves, cut-side down, in skillet and cook until deep golden brown, rotating bun frequently to insure even browning. Remove bun from pan and place, cut-side up, on a serving plate. Place cheese on the bottom of the bun.
- Add ham to skillet and heat it through. When hot, place it on top of the cheese. Dollop with the remaining tablespoon of horseradish sauce and the top of the bun; serve immediately.

173.   Incredible Curry Shrimp Salad

Serving: Serves 5 | Prep: | Cook: | Ready in:

Ingredients

- 1 pound shrimp
- 1/2 cucumber, peeled, cut into slices, quartered

- 2/3 cup salad style green olives
- 3/4 cup corn kernels
- 12 cherry tomatoes, cut in half
- 3 tablespoons mayonnaise
- 1 tablespoon dijon mustard
- 1 tablespoon lemon juice
- 3/4 teaspoon curry powder
- 1 teaspoon dry dill weed
- salt and pepper to taste

Direction

- Put the shrimp, cucumber, olives, corn and tomatoes in a large bowl. Toss gently to combine. Mix together well in a separate bowl the mayonnaise, mustard, lemon juice, curry powder, dill and pepper. Salt and pepper to taste, taste sauce and adjust seasonings if necessary. Add this to the shrimp mixture. Toss again gently to combine. Chill for about 1-2 hours. Serves about 5.

174.   Irish Lady Potato Salad

Serving: Serves 6-8 | Prep: | Cook: | Ready in:

Ingredients

- 2 pounds great potatoes (see headnote)
- 1 cup best mayonnaise, Hellmans or home made
- 8 scallions, chopped on diagonal, green & white
- 1 cup slivered radishes- any kind I love the Easter egg & French Breakfast
- flaked Salt & fresh ground black pepper
- 1/2 cup minced chives + chive blossoms when you can get them

Direction

- Boil potatoes in salted water until very tender, they should mash easily with a fork- same level of done-ness for a mashed potato

- Drain and let cool, but only slightly they should be very warm but not HOT HOT
- Add mayonnaise, I know it may seem wrong, but what happens is the hot potatoes absorb the mayonnaise, and become crazy delicious.
- Mash mayo into potatoes with a fork, you are going for lumpy mashed potato texture
- Mix in scallions and season to taste
- You can serve at this temp or room temp or let cool in the fridge, right before served flutter the radishes and chives on top and an extra bit of crunchy sea salt flakes & black pepper
- This is insanely good with Beer Can Chicken.

---

175. Jamaican Jerk Burger With Chipotle Orange Mayonnaise

Serving: Serves 6 | Prep: | Cook: | Ready in:

Ingredients

- For the Chipotle-Orange Mayonnaise
- 1 cup Mayonnaise
- 3 tablespoons fresh Orange Juice
- 1 tablespoon minced Chipotle Chile in Adobo Sauce
- 1 tablespoon Adobo Sauce
- For the Jamaican Jerk Burger
- 1-1/2 cups coarsely chopped Green Onions
- 1 teaspoon dried Thyme
- 2 Jalapenos, seeded and chopped
- 3 cloves of Garlic
- 1/2 cup Brown Sugar
- 1/2 cup Canola Oil
- 1/2 cup Low-Sodium Soy Sauce
- 1 teaspoon Ground Allspice
- 1-1/2 pounds Ground Beef
- 6 Hamburger Buns
- Condiments: Lettuce, Tomato and Grilled Yellow Onions

Direction

- For the Chipotle-Orange Mayonnaise
- Mix all the ingredients into a small bowl and stir to combine. Cover with plastic wrap and place in the fridge until ready to spread on the burger buns before serving.
- For the Jamaican Jerk Burger
- In a food processor, finely chop the first 4 ingredients. Add the next 4 ingredients and puree until almost smooth.
- Form the burgers into patties and place into a baking dish. Pour 1/2 cup of sauce over all the burgers, toss to coat and let them marinate for 20 minutes. The rest of the sauce will be used for basting the burgers while they cook.
- Grill the onions, slice the tomatoes and tear up the lettuce while the beef marinates. Also, if you choose to make them, start cooking up some fries or potato wedges.
- After 20 minutes, now it is time to grill the burgers! Grill the burgers until desired doneness (about 4 minutes per side), brushing occasionally with the remaining jerk sauce.
- Spread the Chipotle Mayonnaise on both inner sides of the bun. Place the lettuce on the bottom half of the bun with the tomato, burger, onion and then the top half of the bun.

---

176. Japanese Kamaboko (Fishcake) Inspired Gefilte Fish For Passover

Serving: Makes 12 patties | Prep: 0hours45mins | Cook: 0hours0mins | Ready in:

Ingredients

- Fish Cakes
- 1 pound white fish (rockfish, cod, sole, other or a combination) deboned, skinned and finely ground (This will be about 1 1/4 lb pre-ground. See note below)
- 2 egg whites
- 1/4 bunch of chives, finely chopped

- 1/2 of a small carrot, peeled and grated (on the smallest side of a cheese grater)
- 1/2 inch piece of peeled and grated ginger
- 2-1/2 teaspoons kosher salt
- 5 tablespoons potato starch
- 3 tablespoons white wine (or mirin if not kosher for Passover)
- 3 tablespoons sugar
- 6 leaves of finely shredded romaine lettuce
- Olive oil or vegetable oil for shaping, resting and pan-frying
- Sauce
- 1/4 cup Japanese kewpie mayonnaise (Vegenaise or crème fraiche would also work)
- 1 teaspoon apple cider vinegar
- 1 teaspoon wasabi powder
- 1 handful finely chopped dill and chives for garnish

Direction

- Shaping kamaboko gefilte fish. A note about the fish: I used rock cod, but most white fish work well–I especially like the texture and flavor of wild caught. Most kamaboko and gefilte fish are made with a blend of fish–you could even throw in salmon. I highly recommend asking the fishmonger (it will save you loads of time) at the counter to debone, skin and put it through the grinder. You lose about a 1/4 pound to the grinder, so you'll need to purchase a little over a pound to start. If the fishmonger at your local market is not able to do this, carefully debone and skin the fish yourself. Using a food processor, blend until smooth. The other reason I prefer to have the fishmonger do this step for me is that it can be tough on your food processor if you don't have a heavy-duty one.
- Place the ground fish in a large mixing bowl. Add a little bit of salt at a time and mix until well-incorporated. Add the rest of the ingredients and mix well. Let the mixture sit at room temperature for 30 minutes.
- Pour a bit of olive oil into a small bowl. Pour a bit more onto a lined baking sheet and spread it evenly.

- Coat your hands with a bit of oil from the bowl and place about 2 teaspoons of the mixture in your hands. Press lightly and shape them into flat little footballs. You'll need to coat your hands with oil every 2-3 patties. Once you've used up all of the mixture, let them sit on the baking sheet for 30 minutes.
- Heat a large non-stick pan over medium-low heat and melt a bit of oil in the pan. (You can use a regular stainless pan, but make sure the bottom is well coated with a high-heat oil such as ghee, vegetable oil or coconut oil. You may need to clean or wipe down the pan between batches so the bottom doesn't burn.) Once the pan is hot, carefully place fishcakes one by one onto the sizzling pan. Cook for about 3-4 minutes on each side, uncovered, until browned and the center is firm. You can also check for doneness with a toothpick–if it comes out clean, it's cooked.
- Let the fish cakes cool slightly on a paper towel (about 10 minutes). Place them on a bed of shredded romaine lettuce, drizzle with wasabi mayonnaise and garnish with chives and dill. Enjoy!

177. Japanese Potato Salad

Serving: Serves 4 to 6 | Prep: 0hours10mins | Cook: 0hours15mins |Ready in:

Ingredients

- 5 potatoes, Yukon Gold or russet work best
- 1/2 cup mayonnaise, preferably Japanese Kewpie
- 1/2 teaspoon Dijon mustard
- 1 1/2 tablespoons rice vinegar
- 1/2 teaspoon ground black pepper
- 1 tablespoon salt, for seasoning the water, plus 1 teaspoon for the actual mash

Direction

- Peel and quarter the potatoes, and rinse them under cold water to rid them of excess starch. Place the potatoes in a deep pot or saucepan, cover with water, add in 1 tablespoon of salt (or until it's as salty as the sea), and bring it to a boil. Turn it down to a simmer, and let the potatoes cook for 10-15 minutes. The potatoes are done when they can be easily pierced by a knife or a fork.
- Drain the potatoes and leave them for a minute or two to let the excess steam evaporate. Then, mash the potatoes using a ricer, potato masher, or just a fork. Add in the mayonnaise, mustard, vinegar, black pepper, and the teaspoon of salt, and mix it all until the ingredients are well combined. Taste a little, and adjust the seasoning with more vinegar and/or salt as you see fit!
- I like my mash plain, but if you have any leftovers or potato-salad-y ingredients, add them in at this point! Whether it's peas and onions, a bit of ham or chorizo, or that half stick of carrot you had from last weekend's roast, just make sure they're cut into small pieces (and suitably defrosted if they were frozen) before adding them in. This mash will take just about anything you throw into it and end up tasting great!

178.   Japanese Tuna Grilled Rice Balls ("ツナ"焼きおにぎり Tuna Yaki Onigiri)

Serving: Makes 6-8 | Prep: | Cook: |Ready in:

Ingredients

- 1 can tuna
- 2 tablespoons mayonnaise
- 1 1/2 cups cooked Japanese rice
- 4 tablespoons soy sauce
- 1/2 teaspoon butter

Direction

- Filling: Mix tuna and mayonnaise.
- Scoop 1/4 cup of rice onto plastic wrap and flatten rice. In the middle, place filling on top of the rice. Pull plastic wrap together to shape into a ball.
- Under lower to medium low heat, grill each onigiri in a pan with butter until all sides form a crispy crust.
- Brush all sides with soy sauce and re-fry all sides (30 secs per side) until crispy. Be careful as it burns quickly!

179.   Japanese Potato Salad

Serving: Serves 2 | Prep: | Cook: |Ready in:

Ingredients

- 1 potato(8oz.)
- 1 1/2 TBSP. rice vinegar*
- 1/2 TBSP. brown sugar
- 3 TBSP. Kewpie Mayonnaise**
- 1 stalk celery
- 2 slices of your favorite ham
- 2 TBSP. carrot,finely chopped
- 1 TBSP. Parsley, finely chopped
- White pepper to taste

Direction

- Rinse potato in running water. Put into microwave safe glass container, keeping wet. Cover with lid or plastic wrap (microwave safe), and heat in microwave for 7-8 min. Peel the skin using paper towels while the potato is still warm.
- In a medium bowl add potato, and gently smash with masher or fork making sure you leave some chunks. Add sugar, salt, and vinegar, stirring. Last, add and stir kewpie Mayonnaise, and let it cool to room temperature.
- {Meanwhile cut veggies}Peel and thinly slice celery. Salt the celery to dehydrate. Set aside for 5min. Dice ham into 1/2 inch slices.

- Squeeze the water out of celery, and add to the potato bowl. Add the rest of veggies and ham, stirring. Season with pepper.

180. Japanese Inspired Salmon Cakes With Wasabi Yogurt Sauce

Serving: Serves 12-14 cakes | Prep: | Cook: |Ready in:

Ingredients

- Wasabi Yogurt Sauce
- 1 tablespoon wasabi powder
- 1 tablespoon water, room temperature
- 1/2 cup lowfat plain yogurt
- juice of one whole lemon
- black bamboo salt (available at Asian markets, or sea salt)
- Salmon Cakes
- 28 ounces pink or red salmon, well drained (2 cans)
- 1/2 cup daikon, shredded
- 1/2 cup carrot, shredded
- 1/2 cup bell pepper, thinly sliced
- 1/4 cup shoyu (Japanese soy sauce, sweeter and less salty than Chinese soy sauce)
- 1 teaspoon crushed red pepper
- 1 tablespoon fresh ginger, finely shredded
- 6 tablespoons mayonnaise
- juice of half a lemon
- 2 eggs
- 6 slices bread, crust removed, crumbled fine (pref. whole grain)
- 1/2 cup pancake mix or Korean Buchim vegetable pancake mix (has spices)
- oil (I like using unconventional oils, like coconut and avocado)

Direction

- Wasabi Yogurt Sauce
- Mix wasabi powder and water to a paste. Set aside for 15 minutes.
- Mix wasabi paste with yogurt. Squeeze lemon juice and add black salt to taste. Consistency should be in between thick and thin.
- Let sit at room temperature for flavor to develop while preparing the salmon cakes.
- Salmon Cakes
- Mix salmon, vegetables, soy sauce, red pepper, ginger, mayonnaise, lemon juice, eggs and bread in a large bowl.
- Spread pancake mix in a shallow bowl or plate.
- Heat frying pan on high. Lower heat to medium and add about 2 tablespoons of oil.
- Using an ice cream scoop, scoop out salmon mixture. Form the mixture into a patty in your hand, then dredge it lightly through pancake mix.
- Fry the patty for 5 minutes a side or until golden brown. Do not flip over too much or it may crumble. Add more oil as needed.
- Serve hot, drizzled with wasabi yogurt sauce. Good with a side salad.

181. Juicy Bacon Cheese Burgers With Special Sauce

Serving: Serves 4 | Prep: | Cook: |Ready in:

Ingredients

- Burger:
- 1 small Onion, quartered
- 1/8 pound Mushrooms, halved
- 1 1/2 pounds ground beef chuck
- 1/2 cup crushed saltines crackers
- 2 tablespoons Heavy Cream
- 3/4 tablespoon Worcestershire Sauce
- 1 teaspoon kosher salt
- 1 teaspoon ground black pepper
- Special Sauce:
- 1/2 cup Mayonnaise
- 2 tablespoons Heinz Chili Sauce
- 2 tablespoons Asian Sweet Chile Sauce
- 1 1/2 tablespoons Dijon Mustard

- 1/2 tablespoon minced garlic
- 4 slices Sharp Cheddar Cheese
- 4 thick-cut bacon slices, cooked crisp
- Lettuce and Tomato, as desired
- 4 Potato Rolls, split

Direction

- In food processor; process onion until finely chopped. Remove. Process mushrooms until finely chopped.
- Combine beef with onion, mushroom, crackers, heavy cream, Worcestershire sauce, salt and pepper; mix well. Shape into 4 patties.
- Combine mayonnaise, Heinz and Asian Chile Sauces, mustard and garlic; mix well.
- Grill patties until cooked as you like, adding cheese and then bacon on top of burgers; cook to melt cheese. Spread special sauce on both sides of rolls; top with lettuce and tomato. Place burgers inside buns.

182. Kale Slaw

Serving: Serves 6 | Prep: | Cook: | Ready in:

Ingredients

- 1/2 cup good quality mayonnaise or veganaise
- 2 tablespoons red wine vinegar
- 1 tablespoon honey or agave nectar
- 1/8 teaspoon fine sea salt
- 1/4 teaspoon freshly ground black pepper
- 3 green onions, sliced very thin
- 1 bunch green curly kale (6-8 stalks)
- 1 cup Thompson raisins
- 1 cup raw sunflower seeds

Direction

- In a large bowl, add the mayonnaise (or vegenaise), vinegar, honey (or agave), salt and pepper. Whisk until smooth.

- Wash the kale and remove the center ribs and stems from each stalk. Dry the leafy part between kitchen towels or in a salad spinner and then cut into bite-sized pieces.
- Add the kale, green onions, raisins and sunflower seeds to the bowl with the dressing. Toss to combine and refrigerate for at least one hour and up to overnight to let the flavors come together and allow the kale to soften.

183. Kale Slaw For All

Serving: Serves 4-6 as a side | Prep: | Cook: | Ready in:

Ingredients

- 10 cups thinly sliced ribbons lacinato kale (washed and thoroughly dried, thick ribs removed)
- 1/4 cup smoked whole almonds
- 1/4 cup water
- 1/3 cup mayonnaise
- 2 tablespoons freshly squeezed lime juice
- 1 tablespoon white wine vinegar
- 1 teaspoon Aleppo pepper
- salt to taste, if desired
- 1/4 cup whole natural almonds (for serving)

Direction

- Place thinly sliced kale ribbons in a large bowl.
- In a blender, combine smoked almonds and water. Puree until almonds are pulverized and you have a thin paste, stopping to scrape down sides with a spatula as needed.
- Add mayonnaise and puree until combined. Scrape down sides of blender and add lime juice and then vinegar in two additions, pureeing and scraping between each. Add Aleppo pepper and puree one last time. Taste for salt (since the smoked almonds add a good amount of salt, I've never had to add additional salt) and add if desired.
- Pour dressing over mixture, scraping out the blender to get every drop. Using your spatula,

carefully fold the dressing into the kale. Stir slaw a few times, cloaking the greens in dressing. Cover bowl with plastic wrap and refrigerate, at least four hours and up to overnight. Be sure to take the chill off slaw before serving. When ready to serve, toast almonds until fragrant in a dry pan over medium heat. Make sure to stir mixture continuously to prevent burning. Transfer to a plate and let almonds cool. Rough slice almonds and scatter over salad. Serve and enjoy.

184.   Katsu Sando Sandwich

Serving: Serves 2 people | Prep: | Cook: |Ready in:

Ingredients

- Salt and pepper
- 2 boneless pork chops, on the thin side
- 2 tablespoons flour
- 1 large egg, lightly beaten, in a shallow bowl
- 1 cup breadcrumbs
- Oil, for frying
- 4 slices bread
- Mayonnaise, to taste. If you can get a hold of Japanese Kewpie mayo, even better
- Mustard, to taste
- Tonkatsu sauce, to taste

Direction

- Wash the pork chops first and let them rest while you prep everything you need. When you are ready, season both sides of the chops with a little salt and pepper before sprinkling flour gently over them. Then, proceed to dip the chops into the beaten eggs and then to the breadcrumbs. Make sure all sides are coated.
- Heat up about 1.25 cm / half an inch of oil into a large frying pan over medium high heat, and fry the chops until they are golden brown and cooked through. Leave the temperature as is

and flip them once, about a minute on each side.
- Leave the chops to drain on a paper towel while you start to toast the bread. Put one spread of mayonnaise of one slice and the mustard on the other. Then put the Tonkatsu sauce on the chops before putting it all together.
- Slice of the crusts, and enjoy!

185.   Kick In Scallion Sauce Burger

Serving: Serves 4 | Prep: | Cook: |Ready in:

Ingredients

- 1/2 pound Ground Turkey
- 1 tablespoon Sesame Oil
- 4 Burger buns, split
- 4 Slices Tomato
- 8 Torn Green Lettuce Leaves
- 4 tablespoons Chopped Scallions
- 2 tablespoons Mayonnaise
- 2 ounces Cream Cheese, softened
- 1 tablespoon and 1 teaspoons Horseradish Wasabi Sauce
- 1/2 teaspoon Soy Sauce

Direction

- In a bowl, mix together ground turkey, salt and black pepper to taste. Divide into four and shape into a patty.
- In a skillet, heat sesame oil and cook patties until brown. Flip and cook the other side until brown.
- In a small bowl, mix together mayonnaise, wasabi, soy sauce, scallions and cream cheese. Add salt and black pepper to taste.
- On the bottom of each bun, butter lightly, put lettuce, tomato, patty and spread 1/4 of the sauce on the patty. Put the top of bun to cover. Press the top hard and place on a serving plate.

186. Kitchen Sink Chicken Salad

Serving: Makes 5-4 cups | Prep: | Cook: |Ready in:

Ingredients

- 2 cups cooked chicken or turkey, shredded or cut into 1/2" dice
- 1/2 yellow onion or one whole shallot, diced
- about 1 cups chopped celery (I like it fairly fine, so I cut each rib in half lengthwise before dicing)
- 3/4 cup dried cranberries
- 3/4 cup slivered almonds
- 3 tablespoons Dijon mustard
- 1/2 to 1 cups Mayonnaise (to taste, but enough to bind)
- salt and pepper
- 1 apple, cut into about 1/4" cubes

Direction

- Combine all ingredients together and mix to bind. Add salt and pepper, and more mayonnaise or mustard, to taste.

187. Kitchen Sink Pasta With Tuna Sauce

Serving: Serves 4-6 | Prep: | Cook: |Ready in:

Ingredients

- 1/4 cup olive oil
- 2 tablespoons unsalted butter, divided
- 1 small yellow onion, finely chopped
- small handful (4 or 5) spring radishes, trimmed and diced (optional)
- 1 small fennel bulb, finely chopped, or an equivalent amount of chopped celery
- 1/2 teaspoon hot pepper flakes (or to taste)
- 4 garlic cloves, minced
- 6 anchovy fillets
- 1 teaspoon grated lemon zest
- 6-8 ounces can (or jar) high-quality tuna in olive oil, drained and chopped, oil reserved
- 1/2 cup dry white wine
- 1/4 cup capers, drained and rinsed
- 1/4 cup Italin parsley leaves, finely chopped, plus extra for garnish
- 1/2 cup mayonnaise or aioli
- 2 tablespoons wine vinegar or lemon juice, or more to taste
- 2 tablespoons water
- salt and freshly ground pepper to taste
- 1 pound spaghetti or whichever pasta you prefer
- 1 pound quarted artichoke hearts (frozen or jarred if not preparing fresh; optional)
- a few handfuls cooked green or wax beans (optional)
- a few handfuls baby arugula or watercress leaves (optional)

Direction

- Heat the olive oil and 1 tbsp. of the butter in a skillet. Add onions, radishes (if using), and fennel, and sauté on medium-low heat until tender and translucent. Mash garlic cloves, anchovies, and a pinch of salt to a paste in a mortar or on a cutting board using the flat side of your knife. Add to the onion-radish-fennel mixture along with the hot pepper flakes and lemon zest and continue sautéing over medium-low, until the anchovies have dissolved, then stir in the tuna, mashing with the back of a wooden spoon to break up large chunks. Raise the heat to high and add the wine. Cook until almost all evaporated, then lower the heat and stir in the capers and the parsley. Season to taste with salt and pepper. Stir in the remaining tbsp. of butter and remove from heat.
- Bring a large pot of generously-salted water to a rolling boil. (It should be salty enough to taste like sea water.) Cook pasta according to

package directions. Drain, reserving a cup of the pasta water. (You won't need all of it, but just in case.) Return tuna sauce to medium-low heat and toss with pasta, artichokes and/or beans (if using), and some of the pasta water. Remove from heat. Toss with arugula or watercress until just wilted. Garnish with parsley and serve. OR:

- Turn your cooked tuna sauce into tonnato: Prepare the sauce as instructed in Step 1. After removing the pan from heat, allow it to cool to room temperature. Get your pasta water going in the meantime. When sauce has cooled, put it in a food processor or blender along with the mayonnaise/aioli, the vinegar or lemon juice, the water, and the reserved tuna oil, and puree until smooth. You may need to adjust the amounts of acid and/or water depending on taste and desired texture. Toss with cooked pasta, pasta water, and artichokes, beans, and greens (if using). Garnish with parsley and serve.

---

188.   **Korean Fried Chicken Tacos**

Serving: Makes 4 | Prep: | Cook: | Ready in:

Ingredients

- 1 pound chicken, cut into chunks. skin-on has more flavor.
- 4 corn tortillas
- 1/2 cup cornstarch
- gochujang Korean fermented hot pepper paste
- fry oil, such as peanut or vegetable
- apple cider vinegar
- carrots, shredded
- cilantro, chopped
- hot peppers, sliced very thin
- mayonnaise
- sesame seeds, toasted

Direction

- Bring chicken to room temperature (so as not to cool the oil when you put it in the pan). Cut the chicken into chunks if needed, rinse well and pat thoroughly dry. It is very important because the drier the chicken, the better it will fry and the safer you will be from oil splash.
- Season the chicken with salt and pepper and then coat thoroughly in cornstarch.
- Heat the oil in a fry pan until very hot. Once almost smoking, carefully lower the chicken into the oil, and allow to cook for several minutes. Once cooked, take out of the pan and place in a strainer for a minute or two. Then place back into the oil and fry a second time, it makes it crunchier.
- Once finished, allow to dry in the strainer once more. Then take the gochujang sauce and mix with a splash of apple cider vinegar. Microwave for a bit until warm. Warm the tortillas as well.
- Toss the chicken in the sauce until well coated. Place chicken, cilantro, hot pepper, sesame seeds and carrots in the tortillas.
- Use the leftover sauce, combine with a bit of mayonnaise to make a spicy and creamy sauce to top the tacos with. Enjoy and try not to fight over the last one!
- Notes: If you want, you can add or subtract any toppings for the tacos, add corn or mango or coleslaw or kimchi instead it you want. Gochujang is available at Asian markets, or online.

---

189.   **Korean Potato Salad**

Serving: Serves 6 | Prep: | Cook: | Ready in:

Ingredients

- Salad Ingredients
- 5 Russet potatoes
- 1 Gala Apple (finely diced)
- 1 Korean Pear (finely diced)
- 1 stalk celery (finely diced)
- 1.5 teaspoons salt

- 1.5 tablespoons toasted sesame seeds, optional garnish
- Dressing
- 2 cups Kewpie mayonnaise
- 2 tablespoons sugar
- 1 teaspoon white pepper

Direction

- Wash the potatoes then peel and rinse in cold water.
- Cut into about 1 inch by 1 inch cubes (2.5 cm squared) and rinse again.
- Bring a large pot of water to a full boil, add 1/2 teaspoon salt and the cubed potatoes
- Boil until semi tender (Korean chop stick or fork passes through with slight resistance). This will take 8-15 minutes.
- Drain and let cool.
- While the potatoes are cooking, clean the apples and Korean pear, then cut into about 1/2 inch by 1/2 inch pieces (1.25 cm squared) and add to bowl. Toss until well mixed.
- In a medium mixing bowl combine the mayonnaise, pepper and sugar (optional) then mix well.
- Add dressing to potato mix and stir until well mixed. If desired garnish with toasted sesame seed.
- Chill and serve cold or at room temperature.

---

190. Kushiage (Japanese Style Oil Fondue)

Serving: Serves 4 | Prep: | Cook: |Ready in:

Ingredients

- 32 ounces canola oil
- 7 ounces round of beef
- 4 asparagus
- 8 quail eggs
- 4 pearl onions
- 4 shiitake mushrooms
- 1 piece salmon

- 1 piece cod
- 3 ounces minced chicken breast
- 8 pieces perilla leaves
- 1 chicken breast fillet
- 3 eggs
- 1/2 cup all-purpose flour
- 1 cup bread crumbs
- Pinch salt and pepper
- 1/2 zucchini
- 4 scallops
- Pinch ginger powder
- 1 boiled egg
- 3 pickles
- 6 tablespoons mayonnaise
- 4 tablespoons worcester sauce

Direction

- 1 Grind bread crumbs 2 Cut meat and fish 3 Boil quail eggs 4 Mix minced chicken breast with ginger powder 5 Cut half Shiitake mushroom, onion and fill the minced chicken breast 6 Put minced chicken, asparagus on the piece of perilla leave, and roll it 7 Spit everything by bamboo skewer 8 dip everything in the flour, egg and bread crumbs 9 deep-fry everything one by one 10 Mix boiled egg, and add vinegar, pickles and mayonnaise 11 serve Kushiage with Worcester sauce and tartar sauce

---

191. LA VICTORIA® LAYERED DIP

Serving: Serves 4 | Prep: | Cook: |Ready in:

Ingredients

- 2 medium avocados
- 2 tablespoons lemon juice, freshly squeezed
- 1 cup sour cream
- 1/2 cup mayonnaise
- 2 tablespoons taco seasoning
- 16 ounces bean dip (store bought or homemade)

- 6 ounces sliced black olives
- 16 ounces jar of LA VICTORIA Thick'N Chunky Salsa
- LA VICTORIA Nacho Sliced Jalapeños, optional

Direction

- In a small mixing bowl, mash the avocados and mix with lemon juice and salt and pepper. In another bowl, mix together the sour cream, mayonnaise and taco seasoning.
- Assemble the dip by layering the ingredients in a 2-quart casserole dish. Spread the bean dip on the bottom of the dish.
- Top with the olives, cheese, onions, sour cream/mayonnaise mixture, LA VICTORIA® salsa and avocado mixture.
- To make the spider web design, place sour cream in a piping bag or squeeze bottle and draw 4 circles inside each other. Gently drag a bamboo skewer or toothpick outward from the center to create the webbed effect (be sure to clean the skewer/toothpick between lines.)
- Serve with tortilla chips and LA VICTORIA® Nacho Sliced Jalapeños, if desired.
- For a fun twist, make "Scary Chips" by using Halloween cookie cutters to cut bat and ghost shapes out of fresh tortillas.
- Fry chips in 400°F oil for 3 minutes or bake in a 350°F oven until crisp.

---

192.   LEFTOVER TURKEY BÁNH MÌ

Serving: Serves 1 | Prep: | Cook: | Ready in:

Ingredients

- Bánh Mì
- 1 sandwich-sized baguette (light, crisp & airy, if you can find one)
- 1 handful leftover Thanksgiving turkey
- 2 heaping spoonfuls leftover Turkey Liver Pâté (recipe below)

- 1 handful Pickled Carrot and Daikon Radish (recipe below)
- 1 small handful fresh cilantro
- 3-5 slices fresh jalapeño
- 2 spoonfuls mayonnaise (Kewpie, if you can find it)
- Maggi seasoning, to taste
- chili sauce, to taste (optional)
- Turkey Liver Pâté & Pickled Carrot and Daikon (adapted only slightly from J. Kenji López-Alt's Vietnamese Pickled Daikon and Carrots for Banh Mì (Do Chua) Recipe on seriouseats.com)
- FOR THE PÂTÉ
- 1 6-oz turkey liver
- 2 tablespoons cold, unsalted butter
- 1/2 small shallot, finely chopped
- 2 tablespoons Cognac (you can also substitute scotch or brandy)
- 2 teaspoons fish sauce
- 1/4 cup whole milk
- salt and pepper, to taste
- FOR THE PICKLED CARROT AND DAIKON
- 1 large carrot, peeled and julienned
- 1/4 cup granulated sugar
- 1 tablespoon Kosher salt
- 1/2 cup rice wine vinegar
- 1 cup water

Direction

- Bánh Mì
- Preheat oven to 350°. Halve the baguette lengthwise and warm it in the oven for a minute or two.
- Smear the baguette with mayonnaise and optional chili sauce. Add a couple of dashes of Maggi to each side. Spread the pâté over the bread and top with a small heap of turkey. Pile on the cilantro, jalapeños and pickles. Close the sandwich, take a huge bite, and adjust the proportions to your liking.
- Turkey Liver Pâté & Pickled Carrot and Daikon
- FOR THE PÂTÉ

- Cut the turkey liver into 1/2-inch pieces, trimming away any visible membrane or blemishes.
- In a medium skillet, melt 1 tablespoon of the butter over medium heat. Toss in the shallots and sauté for 3 minutes, or until translucent.
- Add the liver pieces to the pan and allow them to sizzle undisturbed for the first 30-60 seconds. Sauté the liver for 4-5 minutes, turning occasionally. You want the pieces to be brown and caramelized on the outside with a rosy (not bloody) center.
- Pour the Cognac into the pan and continue to sauté the shallots and liver for another minute or two. Most of the Cognac will have evaporated.
- Remove the pan from the heat and allow the liver to cool for 5 minutes.
- Scrape the liver, shallots and Cognac into a small blender, and blend them together with the milk and fish sauce. Add the remaining tablespoon of butter and blend one more time. Season with salt and pepper, to taste.
- Transfer the pâté to a small ramekin or serving bowl. Bang the ramekin on the counter to help the pâté settle. Cover and chill for at least 3 hours before serving.
- FOR THE PICKLED CARROT AND DAIKON
- Place the julienned carrot and radish in a medium bowl along with the salt and sugar. Massage the vegetables until the salt and sugar have dissolved. The carrot and radish will have wilted slightly.
- Pack the vegetables and their rendered liquid into a jar and pour in the vinegar and water. Store the jar in the refrigerator until ready to use (30 minutes is my sweet spot).

---

193.   Lambs Liver With Pickled Spring Onions, Speck With Peas & Carrots

Serving: Serves 4 | Prep: | Cook: |Ready in:

Ingredients

- For the pickled onions
- 1 bunch scallions, roots trimmed and whites cut into 2 1/2 inch lengths. You want twelve pieces.
- 1/2 cup water
- 1/4 cup rice vinegar, do not use the seasoned kind
- 3 tablespoons sugar
- 1 teaspoon salt
- For the lamb
- 4 pieces lambs liver, cut 1/2 inch thick, the are small but very rich, you can up the amount if needed
- 4 pieces speck or good smoked bacon
- Kosher salt and fresh ground pepper
- 1/2 cup flour, for dredging
- safflower oil
- 1/4 cup mayonnaise
- 1/2 cup heavy cream
- 1 teaspoon Dijon mustard
- 2 teaspoons pickled onion liquid
- 1/4 cup unsalted butter
- 1/2 cup carrot, small dice
- 1/2 cup onion, small dice
- 1 1/2 cups fresh peas

Direction

- Place the scallions, in a single layer, in a small heat proof container. In a saucepan bring the water, vinegar, sugar and salt to a boil. Pour over the scallions and set aside to cool. This can be done up to a day in advance.
- Season the lamb with salt and set on a rack over a sheet tray with sides. This will catch the juices.
- Combine the mayonnaise, cream, mustard and pickling juice in a mixing bowl and whisk to combine. Season with salt and pepper.
- Reserve 8 of the pickled scallion batons and chop, should have 4, the rest and combine with the dressing.
- Preheat the oven to 250 degrees. Place a heavy bottomed skillet over medium heat and add the bacon. As the fat starts to render turn up

the heat. Cook until nicely crisp. Remove the bacon and the pan from the heat. Place the bacon on a paper towel lined oven proof plate or tray.

- In another pot add the butter, onion and carrots. When the onions start to wilt add kosher salt and pepper. Then add 2 cups of water. Let the carrots cook until tender.
- Place the plate with the bacon into the oven. Season the liver with pepper, remember you already salted them. Dredge the liver pieces through the flour and shake off any excess. Place the bacon pan back on the stove over medium high heat. Add 2 tablespoons of safflower oil.
- When the oil is hot, gently place the liver into the pan.
- Place the peas into the carrot and onion pot and turn the heat to medium high.
- Once the lamb pieces are nicely browned turn them. Be careful not to overcook the lamb. Cook medium rare to medium at most.
- To plate. Place a smear of the sauce onto a plate. Using a slotted spoon place a nice helping of peas next to it. Place a piece of lamb liver onto the sauce. Top with bacon and garnish with pickled spring onions.

194. Leftover Roast Pork

Serving: Serves 2 | Prep: | Cook: | Ready in:

Ingredients

- 2 slices pork loin roast (about 5-6 ounces)
- 2 hard boil eggs
- 2 tablespoons mayonnaise
- 2 scallions
- black pepper
- 1 teaspoon dijon mustard

Direction

- Break pork, cut eggs and put everything in food processor.

- Add mayonnaise, scallion, Dijon mustard and freshly ground black pepper. Pulls till is the way you like.
- Serve with crackers and pickles.

195. Lila's Tomato Pie

Serving: Serves 6 | Prep: | Cook: | Ready in:

Ingredients

- For the filling:
- 1   Single pie crust recipe
- 5-6 Large, ripe but still firm tomatoes
- 1 handful Fresh basil
- Salt and pepper
- The topping
- 3/4 cup Mayonnaise
- 1 1/2 cups Shredded extra sharp cheddar

Direction

- An hour or so before you want the pie to go into the oven, core and slice the tomatoes fairly thickly, close to an inch wide. Either blot thoroughly, without crushing the flesh, with tea towels or paper towels until the flesh has a dry, matte look to it, or lie on racks with towels under them to drain thoroughly. Allow to drain this way for as long as you can, up to an hour.
- Preheat oven to 375. Roll out pie crust and shape into a 9-inch pie plate. If you use a deep dish, increase the tomatoes by two or three and give it a few extra minutes in the oven.
- Line pie crust with parchment or foil, weight, and bake for 10 minutes. The crust will begin to dry and faintly tan at the edges. Remove weights and parchment and set aside. You may fill the crust when it's still warm; no harm will be done.
- Make a single layer of tomatoes in the crust; they should fit snugly. Sprinkle with a pinch of the garlic, and then a pinch of salt and the pepper. Tear up a few leaves of basil and

scatter over. Add another layer of tomatoes and repeat with garlic, s & p and basil. Continue until the shell is full and you've used all the tomatoes.

- Gently but thoroughly mix the cheese and mayonnaise. Drop small spoonfuls of topping over tomatoes and gently press to cover the filling.
- Bake 40-50 minutes until the top is browning and the filling is bubbling, adding time as needed. Begin checking at 30 minutes just in case!
- Allow to rest at least 10 minutes before serving, longer if you can.

---

196. Loaded Potato Salad

Serving: Serves 6-8 | Prep: | Cook: |Ready in:

Ingredients

- 2.5 pounds Yukon Gold potatoes, peeled and cubed
- 8 ounces apple wood smoked bacon ends and pieces
- 1/2 cup sour cream
- 1/2 cup mayonnaise
- 3 fresh chives, thinly sliced
- 1/2 teaspoon ground black pepper
- 1/4 teaspoon kosher salt, or more to taste
- 1/2 cup sharp cheddar cheese, shredded

Direction

- Place potatoes in a stockpot, cover with warm water, and boil for 25 minutes or until potatoes are fork tender. Keep in mind that larger potatoes can take as long as 40 minutes to cook. Transfer cooked potatoes to a bowl of ice water and once cool enough to handle remove the skins. Dice potatoes and set aside.
- Add bacon to a cold skillet, then set heat on medium. Allow to cook until crispy, periodically flipping so it browns evenly. When cooked to desired level remove and set

on a paper towel lined plate to drain. Once cool cut or crumble the bacon and add to diced potatoes.

- In a mixing bowl combine mayonnaise, sour cream, chives, kosher salt, and black pepper. Mix well, then add to diced potatoes.
- Refrigerate at least 6 hours or preferably overnight. Before serving add shredded cheese and stir to combine. Top with additional shredded cheese, bacon, and chives if desired.
- Notes: I like to use bacon ends and pieces because they contain more salt than standard bacon. If you can't find them use an equal amount of sliced bacon and add more kosher salt if you feel it is necessary.

---

197. Lobster Salad

Serving: Serves 4 | Prep: | Cook: |Ready in:

Ingredients

- Garlic Mayonnaise
- 1 garlic clove, minced
- 1 egg yolk, fresh as possible
- 1 heaping tablespoon Dijon mustard
- freshly ground black pepper
- about 1 cup canola oil, or other neutral oil
- a pinch of salt, to taste
- Lobster Salad
- 5 scallions
- 1 pound fresh lobster meat (tail and claw)
- 1 tablespoon fresh lemon juice
- a pinch of cayenne pepper
- 1/3 cup garlic mayonnaise

Direction

- Garlic Mayonnaise
- Add the minced garlic, the egg yolk, the mustard, and the black pepper to a small bowl. Give everything a little stir, to incorporate.
- Slowly incorporate the oil in a very thin stream, while constantly beating with a fork or

mini whisk. (Add a little oil at a time, waiting until the oil has 'disappeared', before adding more.) The whole process should take about 5 minutes--the mayonnaise will have risen in the bowl and turned a paler yellow. You should also be able to tip the bowl over without the mayonnaise falling out.

- Let the mayonnaise rest in the fridge, covered, for at least one hour before use. (This can also be made a night ahead.)
- Lobster Salad
- Wash and thinly slice the scallions. Add them to a medium-sized bowl.
- About the lobster: my fishmonger happens to sell freshly-cooked, whole lobsters. You can also buy live lobsters, and cook them yourself.
- Chop your lobster into bite-sized pieces, and then add them to the medium bowl. Also add: the lemon juice, the cayenne, and the mayonnaise. Gently toss all ingredients together, to incorporate. Serve the salad slightly chilled.

198.   Loup De Mer (Mediterranean Seabass)

Serving: Serves 4 to 6 | Prep: | Cook: | Ready in:

Ingredients

- 2 Mediterranean Seabass, about 1 to 1 1/2 pounds each
- 1 pound shell-on raw shrimp
- 1 onion
- 2 carrots, peeled
- 2 stalks of celery
- 1 leek
- 3 galric cloves, peeled and thinly sliced
- 2 bay leaves
- 2 cups vegetable stock
- a handful of tarragon sprigs
- a quarter sized bundle of chive shoots
- a small handful of parsley
- mayonnaise

Direction

- Before you buy the fish ask the fishmonger if you can smell it, open up the belly flaps and smell and make sure it smells like fresh ocean. Lift the gills and look inside to see they are bright red not gooey or brown or worse removed. Look into the eyes and make sure they aren't sunken and cloudy. If these are all a go buy the fish.
- About an hour before you want to cook the fish salt it making sure to season the stomach cavity.
- Heat the oven to 425 F degrees.
- Using a mandolin or a chef's knife (a mandolin makes really short work of this dish) thinly slice the vegetables. Spread them evenly across the bottom of a 9 x 13 casserole. Add the bay leaves, enough stock to just cover the vegetables, and season with salt and pepper. Slide the casserole into the oven. Set a timer for 10 minutes.
- Meanwhile make two small herb bouquets using tarragon, chive and parsley sprigs. Tuck the bouquets along with a slice of lemon into the stomach cavities of the fish.
- When the timer goes off remove the vegetables from the oven. Place the fish on top of the vegetables. Place a couple of lemon slices on top of each fish. Return the dish to the oven and set the timer for another 15 minutes.
- Again when the timer goes off remove the casserole from the oven. Baste it with the broth from the bottom of the pan then scatter the shrimp around the fish trying to keep them in a single layer. Dab, because dotting isn't enough, the fish with butter. One last time, slide the fish back into the oven for the final 10 minute bake.
- Remove the fish from the oven. Top with tarragon and chives, serve with mayonnaise.

199. Luscious Potluck Cornbread Salad Medley

Serving: Serves 12-15 | Prep: | Cook: |Ready in:

Ingredients

- 1 Package (8-1/2 ounces) corn bread/muffin mix (I use the Jiffy brand Corn Muffin Mix); or any cornbread that you have made for an 8 inch square baking pan.
- 1 cup Mayonnaise
- 1 cup Sour cream (8 oz)
- 1 Envelope (net weight 1.0 oz or 28 grams) ranch salad dressing& seasoning mix (I use Hidden Valley brand, "The Original Ranch" but there are other selections like "Spicy Ranch", "Buttermilk" that you can select)
- 1 Large (or 2 small) garlic cloves, mashed
- 1 tablespoon Juice of a lemon and zest of about half of the lemon
- 1 Can (around 15 oz) black beans, drained and rinsed
- 1 Can (around 15 oz) chickpeas, drained and rinsed
- 2 Cans (around 15 oz each) whole kernel corn, drained (or maybe about 4 cups fresh or frozen/defrosted corn)
- 3 medium tomatoes, chopped
- 1 cup Chopped Green Peppers
- 1/2 cup Cup chopped green onions (scallions) or chives
- 1/2 cup Cup chopped red onions
- 10 bacon strips, cooked until crispy and crumbled
- 1 cup Queso Fresco (or Feta Cheese)*
- 1 cup shredded cheddar cheese (4 oz)*
- * But you can use 2 cups cheddar altogether or your own combination of cheeses instead of the 1 cup queso fresco and 1 cup cheddar cheese.
- 1/4 cup chopped cilantro (my favorite) or parsley

Direction

- Prepare corn bread batter according to package instructions. Place in a greased 8-in. square baking pan. Bake at 400° for 20-25 minutes or until a toothpick inserted near the center comes out clean. Cool.
- In a small bowl, combine mayonnaise, sour cream, garlic, lemon juice and zest, and dressing mix; set aside. Crumble half of the corn bread into a 13-in. x 9-in. dish, followed by half each of the beans, chickpeas, mayonnaise mixture (you may want to use a spatula to spread this as much as possible over entire surface), corn, tomatoes, green peppers, onions, bacon, and cheese. Repeat the layers one more time. Dish will be full. Cover and refrigerate preferably for at least 1 to 2 hours before serving. Sprinkle with chopped cilantro or parsley.

200. Magical Three Ingredient Dressing

Serving: Makes about 1/3 cup dressing | Prep: 0hours1mins | Cook: 0hours0mins |Ready in:

Ingredients

- 2 tablespoons Huy Fong Chili Garlic sauce (or similar)
- 1/4 cup mayonnaise (I use Sir Kensington's or Duke's or Hellman's)
- 2 teaspoons apple cider vinegar
- 1 large pinch salt, plus more to taste

Direction

- Whisk together all ingredients. Taste, and add more salt as needed. Thin with water if desired, or leave as is for a creamier dressing.

201.   Manchego, Grilled Red Pepper + Potato Sandwich With Paprika Mayo

Serving: Serves 4 | Prep: | Cook: |Ready in:

Ingredients

- 2 medium Yukon Gold potatoes (1 pound), sliced 1/4-inch thick
- 4 red bell peppers, cut into planks
- 1 tablespoon olive oil
- Kosher salt and freshly ground black pepper
- 1/2 cup mayonnaise
- 1 garlic clove, finely grated
- 1/2 teaspoon white-wine vinegar
- 1 teaspoon smoked paprika
- 4 tablespoons butter, room temperature
- 4 sandwich buns, split
- 1 plum tomato, halved
- 4 ounces Manchego, sliced

Direction

- Preheat grill or grill pan to medium-high. Fill a medium saucepan to a depth of 2 inches to a boil over high heat. Arrange potatoes in a steamer basket and set the basket in the saucepan. Cover and steam the potatoes until crisp-tender, about 5 minutes.
- Meanwhile, stir together mayonnaise, garlic, vinegar and paprika in a large bowl; season with salt and pepper. Butter the cut sides of sandwich buns. Toss bell pepper with oil and season with salt and pepper.
- Toss cooked potatoes with paprika mayonnaise until coated. Lightly oil grill grates; add potatoes and bell pepper to the grill. Cook potatoes and bell pepper until tender and charred, turning once, about 8 minutes. Add sandwich buns, buttered-side down, to grill to char, 2 minutes.
- Rub cut side of bottom bun with cut tomato. Make sandwiches out of peppers, grilled potatoes and sliced Manchego.

202.   Mango Avocado Shrimp "Ceviche" + Crunchy Tostadas

Serving: Makes 1 quart | Prep: | Cook: |Ready in:

Ingredients

- The "Ceviche"
- 1 pound raw wild-caught shrimp, practically any size will do
- 1 mango
- 1 jalapeno
- 4 limes, juiced
- 1/2 white onion
- 1 avocado
- 1 clove garlic
- 1/2 cup cilantro
- salt & pepper
- 1 teaspoon honey
- To serve
- 6 corn tortillas
- 3 tablespoons sour cream or mayonnaise
- Vegetable or canola oil for frying

Direction

- The "Ceviche"
- Dice up the mango, jalapeno, avocado and onion. Mince the garlic, chop the cilantro and mix all together with the lime juice, honey and salt and pepper.
- Peel and devein the shrimp while bringing a salted pot of water to boil.
- Once water is boiling, add shrimp and cook until pink, approximately 3 minutes.
- Remove shrimp from boiling water and immediately shock in bowl of ice water to stop cooking.
- Roughly chop shrimp and mix in with all other ingredients.
- Place ceviche in covered container into the fridge for at least 2 hours.
- To serve
- Heat a half inch or so of cooking oil over medium high heat.

- Once oil is hot, add one tortilla at a time and fry until crispy, about 1 minute per side.
- To serve, spread each cooled crispy tortilla with a 1/2 tbs or so of sour cream or mayonnaise and top with desired amount of ceviche and share with friends or family. I'd recommend one for a snack and two for a meal!

203. Maple Bacon BLT With Pickled Shallots

Serving: Serves 4 | Prep: | Cook: |Ready in:

Ingredients

- 2   shallots, thinly sliced
- 2 tablespoons red wine vinegar
- 12   slices thick-cut bacon
- 2 tablespoons pure maple syrup
- 8   (1/2-inch thick) slices white bread, toasted
- 2 tablespoons mayonnaise
- 1 cup baby arugula leaves
- 1   plum tomato, cut into 4 slices

Direction

- Toss the shallots with the vinegar in a small bowl. Let marinate at room temperature for 30 minutes.
- Preheat the oven to 400°F. Place a wire rack over a large rimmed baking sheet and arrange the bacon slices on the rack. Bake for 15 to 18 minutes, until the bacon begins to brown. Remove from the oven and brush the maple syrup over the bacon. Bake for 3 to 5 minutes, until the bacon is golden brown and crispy. Transfer to paper towels to drain.
- Place half of the bread slices on a work surface. Spread ½ tablespoon of mayonnaise over each slice. Top each with ¼ cup of arugula, 1 slice of tomato, and 3 slices of bacon. Lift the shallots from the vinegar and distribute among the sandwiches. Place the

remaining bread slices on top. Cut each sandwich in half and serve.

204. Maple Pork Schnitzel With Maple Aoili

Serving: Serves 6 | Prep: | Cook: |Ready in:

Ingredients

- For the Schnitzel:
- 6   boneless pork loin chops pounded to 1/4" thick
- 1 tablespoon dijon mustard
- 2   large eggs
- 1 tablespoon pure maple syrup
- 1 cup homemade whole wheat bread crumbs
- 2 cups panko breadcrumbs
- 1 tablespoon light brown sugar
- 1 teaspoon dried parsley
- 1/2 teaspoon ground allspice
- 1 teaspoon each salt and pepper
- 1/2 cup canola oil, or more if needed
- 2 tablespoons fresh Italian parsley, finely minced
- Maple Aoili:
- 1 cup mayonnaise, regular or lowfat
- 2 teaspoons dijon mustard
- 2 tablespoons pure maple syrup

Direction

- In a shallow bowl, whisk the Dijon mustard, maple syrup and eggs. In another shallow bowl, combine the wheat and panko crumbs, brown sugar, dried parsley, allspice and salt and pepper. Dredge the pork chops first in the egg mixture and then the crumb mixture. Press the crumbs into the meat to adhere.
- In a 12" fry pan, heat the canola oil until shimmering. Add the cutlets, 2 at a time and cook over high heat until golden; about 2 minutes on each side. Add more oil as needed. Place on a serving platter and sprinkle with fresh parsley.

- MAKE THE AOILI: In a medium mixing bowl, whisk the mayonnaise, mustard and maple syrup until smooth. Serve with the pork schnitzel on the side.

205.   Marc Forgione's Salt Cod "Tonnato" With Crudité

Serving: Makes about 1 cup dip | Prep: | Cook: | Ready in:

Ingredients

- For the salt cod:
- 2 pounds salt cod
- 1   bay leaf
- 2   sprigs tarragon
- 2   sprigs thyme
- Peel from 1 lemon
- Olive oil
- 1   onion, cut in half
- 1   rib celery, cut into 3 pieces
- For the tonnato sauce:
- 1/2 cup prepared salt cod
- 1 teaspoon garlic
- 1 tablespoon capers
- 1/2 cup mayonnaise
- 1 teaspoon lemon juice
- 1/4 teaspoon sherry vinegar
- 1/4 teaspoon Tabasco
- Black pepper

Direction

- For the salt cod:
- Place the cod in a large container and completely cover with cold water. Soak for 3 days, changing the water three times a day.
- Preheat oven to 250°F.
- Make a sachet with the bay leaf, thyme, tarragon, and lemon peel.
- Remove skin and bones from the fish. Place the cleaned rehydrated cod in a non-reactive pot with the sachet, the onion, and the celery. Pour in olive oil until it covers the cod. Bring

oil up to 120°F and then place in the oven for 45 minutes. Strain, discard everything except the fish.
- For the tonnato sauce:
- Prepare an ice bath in a large bowl.
- Place cod, garlic, capers, mayonnaise, and lemon juice in a blender. Puree everything until smooth, then pour into a bowl over the ice bath to cool it down. Whisk until cold, then whisk in the sherry vinegar and the Tabasco.
- Transfer to a small chilled bowl. Drizzle with some extra virgin olive oil and a fresh crack of black pepper.

206.   Matcha Potato Salad Tree

Serving: Serves 4 | Prep: | Cook: | Ready in:

Ingredients

- 400 grams Potato
- 2 teaspoons Matcha Powder
- 2 tablespoons Mayonnaise
- 2 tablespoons Milk
- 2 tablespoons Butter
- 2 tablespoons Parmesan Cheese
- 1/2 tablespoon Salt
- Pepper to taste
- Carrot
- Cucumber
- Paprika
- Cream Cheese
- Cheddar Cheese

Direction

- Cook the potatoes in a microwave and mash with mayonnaise.
- Add the matcha powder and other ingredients with the mashed potato and mix well until you get a smooth cream-like texture.
- Heap the potato cream on a plate to make a potato tree. Reserve some for decoration.
- Put the reserved potato cream in a decorating tube and decorate the potato tree.

- Cut out the vegetables and cheese into a small round shape using a straw.
- Decorate the potato tree with the vegetables and cheese as you like!

207. Mediterranean Tuna Salad

Serving: Serves 2 | Prep: | Cook: |Ready in:

Ingredients

- 8 ounces Canned tuna in olive oil, drained
- 1/3 cup cherry tomatoes, halved
- 1/4 cup nicoise olives, halved
- 2 tablespoons diced red onion
- 1 Celery stick, chopped
- 2 tablespoons chopped fresh cilantro
- 1 lime, juiced
- fresh ground black pepper
- fresh ground sea salt
- 1 teaspoon mayonnaise

Direction

- Place the tuna in a bowl and break apart the chunks. Mix in the other ingredients, dress with mayonnaise, lime juice and salt and pepper to taste.
- Serve inside pita bread, on top of your favorite cracker or just by itself, and enjoy in the sun!

208. Melty Mushroom And Robiola Crostini

Serving: Serves 6-8 | Prep: | Cook: |Ready in:

Ingredients

- For the mushroom mixture
- 8 tablespoons unsalted butter,
- 2 teaspoons minced garlic

- 2 tablespoons chopped shallots or green onions
- 1 pound assorted mushrooms, cleaned up and sliced. shiitake work well.
- 2-3 tablespoons cognac
- 1/2 cup heavy cream
- 1/4 cup ricotta cheese
- 1/4 cup mascarpone cheese
- 1 teaspoon each kosher salt and black pepper, plus more to taste
- 1 tablespoon all purpose flour
- Assembly
- 6 tablespoons butter
- 6-8 slices baguette or other chewy bread
- 1 robiola cheese, cut into square inch pieces
- 6-8 teaspoons good quality mayonnaise, preferably homemade
- 6 pieces basil leaves, chopped
- optional truffle oil

Direction

- For the mushroom mixture
- Melt 8 tablespoons of butter in a sauté pan over medium heat. Add garlic and shallots and cook for a few minutes until garlic is soft. Add the mushrooms and all-purpose flour and cook for about 10 minutes.
- Add cognac to pan and let it evaporate. Add cream, mascarpone, and ricotta and let simmer and thicken for a few minutes. Add salt and pepper. Set aside.
- Assembly
- Melt the butter in a skillet and wait until it starts to foam. But the sliced bread into the pan, and cook on low heat. Check it, and flip it over when it's browned. Brown the alternate side. Remove to serving plate.
- To assemble: Spread a teaspoon of mayonnaise on each slice of bread. Layer with robiola cheese, spreading it to the edges, and then top with the mushroom mixture. Top with a sprinkling of basil and a drizzle of truffle oil if desired. Serve warm.
- NB: If you cannot find Robiola cheese, this would work with another soft brie-like cheese. Taleggio, Pierre Robert would be great.

209. Memorial Day Street Corn

Serving: Serves 12 | Prep: | Cook: |Ready in:

Ingredients

- 12 Ears fresh corn, shucked
- 1/4 cup Kosher salt
- 2 cloves garlic, peeled
- 3/4 cup Mayonnaise
- 1/2 cup Fresh lime juice
- 1 Canned chipotle with 2 tablespoons adobo sauce (or more to taste)
- 3/4 cup Creme freche
- 1/4 cup molasses
- 1 cup Cotija cheese, grated
- 1/2 cup Cilantro, minced

Direction

- Add salt to 8 quarts of water in a large pot and bring to a boil. Add garlic and boil 1 minute. Remove garlic and reserve. Add corn to water. Allow to return to a rolling boil, then turn off heat. After 10 minutes, remove corn from water, place on a platter and cover.
- While corn is cooking, add mayonnaise, lime juice, chipotle with adobo, crème fraiche, molasses, and garlic to a blender, and puree until smooth. Pour into a bowl and mix in 3/4 cup Cotija cheese and 1/4 cup cilantro. Cover and refrigerate until ready to use.
- Mix together remaining cheese and cilantro. Cover and refrigerate.
- To serve, place corn on a hot grill, occasionally rotating ears until corn is slightly charred all around. Remove from grill. Brush all around with mayonnaise mixture, sprinkle with reserved cheese mixture and serve

210. Mexican Street Corn Salad

Serving: Serves 4 | Prep: | Cook: |Ready in:

Ingredients

- 6 ears of corn, husks and silks removed
- Olive oil cooking spray
- Salt and pepper
- 1/4 cup mayonnaise
- 1/4 cup sour cream
- Zest and juice of a lime
- 1 teaspoon ancho chili powder
- 1/4 teaspoon onion powder
- 1/4 cup cilantro leaves, plus more for garnish
- 6 ounces cotija cheese, crumbled

Direction

- Preheat oven to broil or prepare grill at high heat. Spray each corn cob with cooking spray and season with salt and pepper. Broil or grill the corn, turning every few minutes to char the kernels. Remove and cool. Cut the corn from the cob into a large mixing bowl.
- In a small bowl, whisk together mayonnaise, sour cream, 1/2 teaspoon salt, lime juice and zest, ancho and onion powders. Pour the dressing over the corn and toss to coat. Stir in the chopped cilantro and place the corn salad onto a large serving platter.
- Top the corn salad with the cheese and serve with some sprigs of cilantro and lime wedges alongside.

211. Mid Century Avocado Toast

Serving: Serves 6 | Prep: | Cook: |Ready in:

Ingredients

- 1 tablespoon Dijon mustard
- 1/2 tablespoon mayonnaise

- 1 tablespoon softened butter
- 1 tablespoon finely grated parmesan
- 12 slices of tiny bread. Use party rye, or your preferred bread (I like sourdough) cut to small size (thinness not required)
- 2 avocados
- 1/3 lemon
- salt and pepper to taste

Direction

- Mix softened butter, mayonnaise, mustard and finely grated parmesan
- Spread mixture in a thin layer on bread slices
- Toast--takes about 6 minutes in a toaster oven
- Cube avocado and mix with a lemon juice. For perfectly ripe avocados I like just a bit of lemon juice with salt and pepper. Younger or older avocados can be improved with more lemon or lime juice and/or some pressed garlic.
- Let toast cool slightly, flip so that parmesan side is on the bottom, and top with avocado mixture.
- Serve--feel free to add other toppings: some of my more common choices include sprouts, sour cream, tomatoes, salsa, pesto, feta, olive oil, or pomegranate seeds.

212.   Mini Crab Cake Appetizers

Serving: Serves 16 | Prep: | Cook: | Ready in:

Ingredients

- 1/2 cup reduced-fat mayonnaise
- 1 tablespoon pickle relish
- 1 teaspoon prepared horseradish
- 1 teaspoon whole-grain mustard
- 1/2 teaspoon hot pepper sauce
- 1/2 teaspoon Worcestershire sauce
- 1/4 cup egg substitute
- 1/4 cup seasoned bread crumbs
- 1/4 cup reduced-fat mayonnaise

- 1 green onion, chopped
- 1 tablespoon whole-grain mustard
- 1/2 teaspoon Old Bay seasoning
- 1/4 teaspoon hot pepper sauce
- minced chives

Direction

- Combine first six ingredients; cover and chill until ready to serve.
- In a large bowl, stir together egg, bread crumbs, mayonnaise, onion, parsley, mustard, Old Bay seasoning and pepper sauce. Fold in crab. Refrigerate for at least 30 minutes. With wet hands, shape mixture by 2 tablespoonfuls into 1/2-in.-thick patties. Cook crab cakes in oil in a large skillet over medium heat, in batches 3-4 minutes on each side or until golden brown. Serve with sauce and garnish with chives.

213.   Mini Crab, Avocado, And Mango Stacks

Serving: Makes 30 servings | Prep: | Cook: | Ready in:

Ingredients

- Crab dressed in Remoulade Sauce
- 1 pound Jumbo lump crab meat, shredded
- 1 1/4 cups mayonnaise (hellman's or kraft)
- 1/3 cup Creole or whole grain mustard
- 1 tablespoon chopped garlic
- 1/2 teaspoon Worcestershire sauce
- 1/4 teaspoon Tabasco sauce
- 1 splash fresh lemon juice
- Assembling the crab stacks
- 2 cups ripe mango, peeled and diced 1/2 inch
- 1 cup yellow or red pepper, diced 1/2 inch
- 1/2 cup red onion, peeled and diced 1/2 inch
- 1 cup ripe avocado, peeled, pitted and diced 1/2 inch
- 2 English (seedless) cucumbers, peeled and sliced into 1/4 inch thick pieces

- optional: you can use a toasted baguette instead of cucumbers

Direction

- Crab dressed in Remoulade Sauce
- Mix the mayonnaise, mustard, garlic, Worcestershire and Tabasco and splash of lemon juice together. Season with black pepper and salt to taste.
- Add 3/4 cup of the remoulade mixture to the shredded crab meat. Refrigerate.
- Assembling the crab stacks
- Mix the mango, onion and red pepper together, set to the side
- Place cucumber slices on serving tray, add a tablespoon of the crab remoulade mixture to each cucumber slice.
- Then layer a few pieces of avocado on top of the crab mixture, lastly sprinkle the mango, onion and red mix on top of the avocado. You are ready to serve.
- Optional- you can drizzle the stacks with Chive Oil. Chive Oil: 1 bunch of chives1/2 cup extra virgin olive oil salt to taste. In a saucepan of boiling water blanch chives 10 seconds and drain in a sieve. Immediately place chives into an ice bath to stop cooking. Remove chives from ice water, squeezing out excess water, and drain on paper towels. Chop chives and purée in blender with oil until smooth. Transfer chive oil to bowl. Chill overnight. Pour oil through a fine sieve into a small bowl, pressing hard on solids. Store in plastic squirt bottle for easy use on stacks.

---

214. Mini Tempeh "Crab" Cakes

Serving: Makes 22 | Prep: | Cook: |Ready in:

Ingredients

- 12 ounces plain tempeh
- 1 tablespoon canola oil
- 1/2 cup finely chopped green bell pepper
- 3/4 cup finely chopped red onion
- 1 tablespoon soy sauce
- 2 teaspoons garlic powder
- 1-1/2 teaspoons Old Bay Seasoning
- 1 teaspoon ground mustard
- 1/2 teaspoon cayenne pepper
- 1 teaspoon kosher salt
- 1/2 cup mayonnaise
- 2 large eggs
- 1-1/2 teaspoons baking powder
- 1-1/3 cups dry bread crumbs or wheat germ or a combination
- Canola oil (if frying)

Direction

- 1. Pulse the tempeh in a food processor until finely minced.
- 2. Heat the oil in a medium skillet. Add the bell pepper and onion and sauté until soft and lightly browned. Add the tempeh and sauté 1 minute. Add the soy sauce, garlic powder, Old Bay Seasoning, mustard, cayenne, and salt and continue cooking for 1 more minute, stirring occasionally.
- 3. Transfer the mixture to a medium bowl and let it cool a few minutes. Add the mayonnaise, eggs, and baking powder and mix well. Add the bread crumbs and blend well. (The mixture should be moist but firm enough to form patties. If necessary, add a little more bread crumbs.) Make patties by taking about 2 tbsp of the mixture, rolling it into a ball, and gently flattening it in the palm of your hands.
- To Bake: Spray a baking sheet with nonstick spray. Preheat oven to 400 degrees. Place the patties on the baking sheet. Bake about 10 minutes; flip them over and cook another 5 minutes. Both sides should be golden brown. To Broil: Spray a baking sheet with nonstick spray. Place the patties on the baking sheet and broil, turning over once, until they are golden brown on both sides, about 3 or 4 minutes per side. To Fry: Heat 1 tbsp oil in a wide pan. Place a few patties in the oil and fry, turning over once, until both sides are brown,

about 2 or 3 minutes per side. Transfer them to paper towels to drain. Repeat with the remaining patties.

- Transfer the patties to a platter with a bowl of dipping sauce of your choice in the center. Serve with tartar sauce, aïoli, or other sauce of your choice.

215.   Mission Kale Salad With Aji Dressing

Serving: Serves 6 | Prep: | Cook: |Ready in:

Ingredients

- 1 large head Dinosaur, Lacinto, orTuscan kale
- 1/2 cup toaste Marcona almonds
- 1/4 cup crisp fried capers
- 1/2 cup gloden raisins
- 1/2 cup crumbled goat cheese
- 1/2 cup baby heirloom tomatoes, halved
- 1/2 cup standard vinagrette
- 2 tablespoons mayonnaise
- 3 tablespoons jarred, sliced banana peppers
- 2 teaspoons honey

Direction

- Cut ribs from the kale and cut into wide chiffonade.
- To make the dressing, prepare a 1/2 cup of classic vinaigrette in a blender. Add the mayonnaise, peppers and honey and blender until smooth.
- Rub the kale manually with 1/4 cup of the dressing. Mound the kale and compose an arrangement of the remaining ingredients on each plate, drizzle decoratively with remaining aji dressing.

216.   Moist Banana Bread

Serving: Serves 8-10 | Prep: 0hours15mins | Cook: 0hours45mins |Ready in:

Ingredients

- 1 cup unsifted, all purpose flour
- 1 cup sugar
- 1 teaspoon baking soda
- 1/2 teaspoon table salt
- 1 cup mashed, ripe banana (about 2 bananas)
- 2/3 cup mayonnaise
- 1/4 cup water
- 1 1/2 teaspoons vanilla extract

Direction

- Preheat oven to 350° F and spray baking pan with non-stick spray
- Stir together the flour, sugar, baking soda, and salt in a large bowl
- Add in the mashed banana, mayonnaise, water, and vanilla. Beat ingredients together with an electric mixer on medium speed for 2 minutes.
- Bake at 350° for 45 minutes- 1 hour until golden brown. A toothpick should come out clean. Eat right away or freeze up to 3 months

217.   Mom's Best Tuna Macaroni Salad

Serving: Serves 10-12 | Prep: | Cook: |Ready in:

Ingredients

- 16 ounces Cavatappi (corkscrew) pasta. You can also use any other large shaped pasta that will hold a chunky salad.
- 2 stalks of celery diced small
- 1 small sweet onion chopped
- 5 hard boiled eggs chopped
- 1 5 oz. can of tuna fish in water - drained
- 1 1/2 cups mayonnaise - I prefer Hellman's

- 1/2 cup Miracle Whip
- 1 squirt of mustard
- 2 tablespoons season salt - I prefer McCormick Season All

Direction

- Cook pasta according to directions and then rinse with cold water.
- In a bowl mix together cooled pasta, tuna fish, celery, onion and egg.
- Mix in mayonnaise, Miracle Whip, mustard and seasoned salt. Stir well. If you taste it and it seems salty, don't worry the flavors will meld in the next step. (I'll be honest that I don't actually measure out these ingredients, but rather eyeball them. So, if it seems a little dry add a bit more mayonnaise/Miracle Whip by the tablespoon)
- Cover and let sit in fridge for at least 4 hours to let flavors absorb and blend. Periodically take it out and stir, if the pasta looks dry add a little more mayonnaise/Miracle Whip. Also if needs more season salt you can add a few shakes to taste.
- Serve cold!

218.   Momma's Potato Salad

Serving: Serves a crowd | Prep: | Cook: |Ready in:

Ingredients

- 2 pounds red potatoes, skins on, cut into halves for boiling in large pot of salted water
- 1/2 Vidalia onion or more to taste, chopped
- 2-3 2 or 3 Kosher dill pickles, chopped
- 1/2 - 3/4 cups Duke's mayonnaise
- 1 - 2 hard-boiled eggs, sliced
- 1/2 tomato, sliced in quarters for garnish
- Salt and pepper, to taste

Direction

- Boil the potatoes until tender (test with a fork). Then drain the potatoes and place them in a large mixing bowl. Set aside to cool.
- When the potatoes are cooled, add in the chopped onions and pickles, as well as the mayonnaise, salt, and pepper.
- Mix all of the ingredients together until well combined and add a little more mayo if you want it creamier (better!).
- Finally, transfer the potato salad to a serving bowl and garnish with the hard-boiled egg and tomato slices.

219.   Mustard Thyme Steak On Tomato Salsa And Rye

Serving: Serves 2 | Prep: | Cook: |Ready in:

Ingredients

- 1 rib eye steak
- Salt
- Pepper
- 1 tablespoon dijon mustard
- Finishing salt, I used Maldon
- 5 stems thyme
- 5 tablespoons olive oil
- 1 handful arugula
- 1 plum tomato, finely chopped
- 1 scallion, finely chopped
- Small bunch chives, finely chopped
- Small bunch parsley, roughly chopped
- 2 tablespoons lemon juice
- Salt
- Pepper
- 2 tablespoons mayonnaise
- 1 tablespoon mustard with seeds
- 2 big slices rye bread

Direction

- When I prepare the meat for grilling I marinate it overnight. Salt, pepper and a tablespoon of good mustard. Rub everything thoroughly in the meat, add enough olive oil to cover the meat, put a lid on and leave it in fridge overnight. Don't forget to bring the meat to the room temperature before grilling! Grilling time depends on how you like your steak to be cooked. After grilling let it rest for 5 minutes, covered with tin foil. Please, don't forget the rest, there is nothing worse than blood on your plate!

- Prepare to cut your steak. On your cutting board, toss some finishing salt, thyme leaves and 2 tbsp. olive oil. Put the steak on that, cut it in slices, mix a little, make sure all the slices are covered with salt, thyme and olive oil.
- Prepare the Tomato salsa. Toss tomato, scallion, chives and parsley together. Add salt, pepper, one tablespoon lemon juice and one tablespoon olive oil. Mix to combine.
- Mix arugula with one tablespoon of olive oil. Set aside.
- Prepare the mustard aioli. Combine mayonnaise, mustard, one tablespoon lemon juice and one remaining tablespoon olive oil, salt and pepper.
- Toast the bread and cut the slices in half. You need one halved slice of bread for one sandwich.
- Now assemble your sandwich.
- First you can dip inner side of the bread in that wonderful juice left from meat, thyme and olive oil on your cutting board. Now put some mustard aioli on the bread.
- Toss the arugula, put some tomato salsa on it, top with steak slices. Cover with other slice of bread.

<hr>

220. My Favorite Fried Egg On Toast

Serving: Serves 1 | Prep: 0hours5mins | Cook: 0hours10mins | Ready in:

Ingredients

- 1 thick piece of a good rustic country-style bread

- 1 tablespoon good-quality mayonnaise, adjusted to taste
- 2 pinches smoked paprika
- 1 generous pat of butter
- 1 large egg (or 2 if you're hungry)

Direction

- Toast your bread until it is nicely golden brown and crisped around the edges. Smear on a thin, but still decidedly noticeable, layer of mayonnaise. Sprinkle a couple of pinches of smoked paprika over the toast.
- Place a small pan — I much prefer to use a pan that is not non-stick, like cast iron — over medium high heat. Add the butter and wait until the butter has melted, foamed up, settled back down and has started to brown. You want the pan to be hot enough that the egg really sizzles when it hits.
- When the pan is hot, crack the egg in. Sprinkle the egg with a good bit of salt. Now, turn the heat down to medium-low, cover the pan and let the egg fry. This will help the white to cook through while the yolk stays runny. When it has reach this stage (cooked white, runny yolk) transfer the egg onto your toast. If there is any remaining browned butter in the pan, scrape that on top too. Sprinkle with some freshly ground pepper and eat.

<hr>

221. My German Mom's Non German Potato Salad

Serving: Serves 8 | Prep: | Cook: | Ready in:

Ingredients

- 4 Large potatoes, diced
- 1 cup chopped celery
- 1/2 cup sliced scallions
- 1/2 cup Minced fresh parsley
- 1/4 cup French salad dressing
- 3/4 teaspoon Salt
- Pepper to taste

- 3 hard boiled eggs, diced
- 3/4 cup Mayonnaise
- 2 1/4 mustard. Mom used ordinary Gulden's. I prefer dijon
- 4 1/2 teaspoons fresh lemon juice

Direction

- Boil the eggs and set aside to cool. Peel and dice the potatoes and boil until barely fork tender, taking care not to overcook. Drain and allow to cool.
- Combine potatoes, celery, scallions, eggs and parsley
- In a separate bowl, mix the French dressing, salt and pepper. Add to the potato mix, stir gently so as not to mash the potatoes and set aside.
- In a separate bowl, combine the mayonnaise, mustard and lemon juice. Add to the potato mix, stirring gently once again. Allow flavors to marry for 30 minutes and serve at room temperature.

222.   My Husband's Broccoli Nut Salad

Serving: Makes about 6 cups | Prep: | Cook: | Ready in:

Ingredients

- 4 cups broccoli florets, chopped into bite-sized pieces
- 2 carrots, peeled then grated
- 1/3 cup finely diced red onion
- 3/4 cup chopped candied walnuts
- 1 cup mayonnaise
- 2 tablespoons wildflower honey
- 1 tablespoon cider vinegar, plus more as desired
- 1/4 teaspoon sea salt

Direction

- In a mixing bowl, toss together the broccoli, carrot, onion, and walnuts. Set aside while you prepare the dressing.
- In a small mixing bowl, whisk together the mayonnaise, honey, and vinegar. Taste the dressing. If it is a little too sweet for you, add another tablespoon of vinegar. Add the salt, combine, and pour over the vegetables and walnuts.
- Toss the salad until the vegetables are well coated. Cover the bowl and refrigerate for several hours or overnight. Before serving, toss the salad once again and serve it chilled.

223.   My Mother's Potato Salad

Serving: Serves 4 to 6 | Prep: 0hours30mins | Cook: 0hours15mins | Ready in:

Ingredients

- 2 pounds baby potatoes, scrubbed and the larger ones halved
- 2 tablespoons apple cider vinegar
- 1/4 cup olive oil
- 1/4 cup best-quality mayonnaise (homemade or store-bought)
- 1 tablespoon whole-grain mustard
- 3 tablespoons finely chopped red onion
- 1/3 cup chopped cornichons
- 2 hard boiled eggs, peeled and chopped
- 1/4 cup chopped fresh herbs (I use tarragon and parsley)
- Salt to taste
- 1/4 cup thinly sliced radishes
- Chives and chive blossoms, for finishing, optional

Direction

- Boil the potatoes in a big pot of salted water until they're fork-tender. Drain, and shock in an ice bath if you want a potato salad that will maintain its shape. (If a few squished potatoes are okay with you, this step is not necessary.)

While the potatoes cook, soak the red onion in a bit of water to soften its bite.

- Place drained potatoes in a large bowl, and sprinkle vinegar on them.
- Mix olive oil, mayonnaise, and mustard together to make your dressing, and set aside.
- To the large bowl, add the drained red onion, cornichon, hard-boiled egg, and herbs. Add the dressing -- starting with half, as you may not use it all -- and toss to coat. (You'll want enough dressing to slickly coat each potato, but you don't want a pool at the bottom of the bowl. If for some reason you find you need more dressing, add an extra splash of olive oil and a dollop of mayo to taste.) Add salt, and/or more vinegar to taste.
- When it's where you want it seasoning-wise, fold in the sliced radishes. Garnish with chives and/or chive blossoms if you like, and serve. It's even better after it's been in the fridge for a day.

---

224. My Ex Mother In Law's Delicious Cole Slaw

Serving: Serves alot | Prep: | Cook: | Ready in:

Ingredients

- 1 bag Cabbage shredded
- 1-2 cups Helman's Mayonnaise
- 1-2 tablespoons Vinegar (your choice)
- 1-2 tablespoons Sugar (white)
- s&p pinches as much salt and pepper as you need.

Direction

- Rinse the Cabbage in cold water and drain. After the cabbage is drained well, add the mayonnaise, and mix well.
- This is the secret to this delicious Cole Slaw, 1-2 Tsp. Vinegar, 1-2 Tsp. Sugar, t is important that you use the exact same amount of sugar and vinegar that is the secret.

- S & p to taste (salt and pepper) to your taste.

---

225. New Age Macaroni Salad

Serving: Serves several | Prep: | Cook: | Ready in:

Ingredients

- FOR THE DRESSING
- 1 cup mayonnaise
- Juice of 1 lemon
- 2 tablespoons Worstershire Sauce
- 1 generous tablespoon whole-grain Dijon mustard
- FOR THE SALAD
- 1 yellow onion, halved, peeled, 1/2? slices
- 4 chicken thighs or 2 chicken breasts, bone-in or boneless
- Olive oil
- Sea or kosher salt and grinds of pepper
- 1 pound ditalini or elbow macaroni, cooked, drained, cooled in cold water
- 4 ribs celery, 1/4? dice
- 1 orange or red bell pepper, 1/4? dice
- 15 ounce can pineapple tidbits, drained
- 2 tablespoons fresh tarragon, minced
- 2 teaspoons sea or kosher salt
- 12 grinds of pepper
- 2 pinches red pepper flakes

Direction

- This is one of those dishes that improves after the ingredients are fully chilled and the flavors have had a chance to meld. You can easily make it 12 hours in advance.
- Light a charcoal fire (my preference), or start a propane grill. While the fire either burns down or heats up, film the bottom of a baking dish with olive oil. Set the onion slices in it and turn them over, seasoning both sides with salt and pepper. Remove them to a baking sheet. Do the same with the chicken pieces. Also remove them to the baking sheet.

- When the fire is ready, arrange the onion slices and the chicken pieces on the grate. The onions will clearly be done sooner than the chicken. Grill the onion slices for about 4 minutes per side, turning them carefully, though honestly, if a few pieces slip into the fire, the flavor of everything being grilled will only be that much better. When done, remove them to a clean platter.
- Continue grilling the chicken pieces until done. Poke them with a fork or knife; when the juices run clear, the meat is done. Remove them to the platter. Allow the chicken and onions to cool while you cook and cool the pasta and prepare the rest of the ingredients.
- Cook the pasta according to the directions on the package, about 10 minutes. When done, strain through a colander then return it to the pot in which you cooked it. Run cold water into the pot, tossing the macaroni with your hands until no residual heat remains, then drain it again. Transfer it to a large salad or mixing bowl.
- Add the celery, bell pepper, pineapple, and tarragon to the bowl. Strip the chicken from the bones, and dice it up. Chop the onions. Add both to the bowl. Toss all the ingredients together with a large spoon.
- Whisk the dressing ingredients together. Don't even bother tasting it; it won't taste like anything by itself. It needs the combination with the salad to bring all the flavors together. Pour the dressing over the salad and toss to distribute it throughout. Stir in the salt, pepper, and red pepper flakes, then taste, and adjust seasonings if necessary.
- When serving outside in hot weather, it's best to serve mayonnaise-based salads in small quantities, with the larger amount refrigerated or kept in a cooler set out of the sun. To serve this salad, spoon some into a bowl that you can set inside a larger bowl filled with ice and a small amount of water. Refill the salad bowl with cold salad as often as you need to, and also keep an eye on the ice.

> ## 226.   New England Lobster Rolls With Lemon Chive Mayonnaise

Serving: Serves 4 | Prep: | Cook: | Ready in:

Ingredients

- Lobster Rolls
- 2 cups cooked, diced lobster meat
- 1/4 cup homemade lemon chive mayonnaise (or other good quality mayonnaise)
- 3 tablespoons finely chopped celery
- Kosher salt and black pepper
- 4   top split hot dog buns
- 3 tablespoons unsalted butter, melted
- 3   leaves Boston lettuce, sliced
- Lemon Chive Mayonnaise (makes 1 cup)
- 1   room temperature egg yolk
- 1 teaspoon dijon mustard
- 1 1/2 teaspoons fresh lemon juice
- 1/8 teaspoon kosher salt
- 6 ounces canola or other neutral-flavored oil
- 2 ounces extra virgin olive oil
- 1 tablespoon water (optional)
- 2 teaspoons chopped chives

Direction

- Lobster Rolls
- To steam your lobster: bring 2 inches of salted water to a rolling boil. Put live lobsters in water, cover the pot, and steam for 8-10 minutes per 1 1/4 pound lobster. They're done when the antennae pull out fairly easily, or the internal temperature of the lobster meat reaches 135 ° F.
- Mix the lobster, mayonnaise, and celery together in a bowl. Season the mixture with salt and pepper to taste.
- Heat a large skillet over medium heat. Brush the inner and outer surfaces of the buns with butter. Open the buns up and toast them in the skillet until golden brown on both sides.

- Arrange some lettuce on each bun and top with equal portions of the lobster mixture. Serve immediately, preferably with a cold beer on the side!
- Lemon Chive Mayonnaise (makes 1 cup)
- Place the egg yolk, mustard, lemon juice and salt in a large bowl and whisk together. Mix the canola and olive oils together in a measuring cup. While constantly whisking the egg mixture in the bowl, slowly pour the oil into the mixture, drop by drop, until an emulsion forms. Continue to whisk as you very slowly pour the oil into the bowl in a thin stream. If the mixture gets too thick, add the water to thin it out. Once about half of the oil is mixed in, you can pour the rest of the oil in a little faster. When all of the oil is in, you should have a smooth mixture with a consistency slightly looser than store bought mayonnaise. At this point, taste the mayonnaise and season it to taste with salt and more lemon juice if desired. Stir in the chives. Store any extra mayonnaise in an airtight container in the refrigerator for no more than a few days.

---

227. New Englandish Chicken Apple Bacon Salad

Serving: Serves 2 as a meal 4 as a starter | Prep: | Cook: | Ready in:

Ingredients

- 2 large size tart apples. I like to use Fuji when available.
- 1 pinch ground black pepper
- 1 tablespoon fresh thyme finely chopped
- 2 teaspoons chopped fresh dill
- 1/2 pound good quality bacon
- 4 tablespoons good quality maple syrup
- 8 ounces good quality apple cider
- 2 bonless skinless chicken breasts
- 1 pound bag of baby spinach leaves drained and rinsed
- 1 head of romaine lettuce drained, risned, and ripped by hand into bite size pieces
- 1/4 cup dried cranberries
- 1/4 cup dried blueberries
- 1 cup roughly chopped previously roasted pecan pieces
- 1 tablespoon Dijon mustard
- 1/4 cup good quality mayonnaise
- 1 teaspoon reserved bacon fat
- 2 tablespoons apple cider vinegar

Direction

- Line the bottom of a baking sheet with aluminum foil.
- Chop apples roughly into 1/2 inch pieces and combine them in a bowl with black pepper, 1 teaspoon dill, and thyme.
- Place the apple pieces on the lined baking sheet.
- Place uncooked bacon pieces on top of apple slices and set aside.
- In a small square baking dish combine 2 tablespoons of the maple syrup with 4 ounces of the apple cider with a fork just until blended.
- Lightly salt and pepper chicken breasts and place in the baking dish and flip to cover breasts on both sides with the apple cider/maple syrup mixture.
- Place both the baking dish and the baking sheet in oven and put the temperature at 400%.
- Cook both items in oven turning both over once halfway through until done. The whole process takes about 20 minutes, with the bacon usually finishing before the chicken.
- Remove both items from the oven and remove the bacon from the apple pieces, crumble it, and set aside.
- At this point, the apples should be soft and a light golden color. Place the apple pieces back in the oven and cook until darker brown, about another 10 minutes, stirring them occasionally.

- While the apples cook, shred chicken breasts with fork in the baking dish and let sit in any remaining liquid in the baking dish.
- Remove apple pieces from oven and set aside to cool.
- In large bowl combine both lettuces, cranberries, blueberries and pecan pieces.
- In another bowl, combine remaining maple syrup, remaining apple cider, mustard, remaining dill, mayonnaise, bacon fat, and cider vinegar. Whisk until just combined. It will be a little runny but that's ok.
- Toss cooled apple pieces in the bowl with lettuce mixture.
- In separate individual bowls place salad/apple mixture and top with the shredded chicken and bacon crumbles. Finish the dish with as much dressing as you would like.

---

228. New Potato And Green Bean Salad With Fresh Fennel And Maybe Some Bacon

Serving: Serves 4 | Prep: | Cook: | Ready in:

Ingredients

- 8 new potatoes (use more like a dozen if using tiny fingerlings)
- 1 tablespoon sea or kosher salt
- 8 ounces green beans, sliced in half, blanched, chilled in ice water
- 1 fennel bulb, thinly sliced
- 1/2 red onion, fine diced
- 4 slices very good bacon baked to very crisp, crumbled (optional)
- 1/2 cup mayonnaise
- 3 tablespoons whole-grain Dijon mustard
- 2 tablespoons finely chopped fennel fronds, plus whole for garnish
- Sea or kosher salt and pepper to taste

Direction

- Wash, cut into 1/2" dice the potatoes and cook them in the salted water until easily pierced with a sharp knife. When done, chill completely in icy water, then drain. This step can be done a day in advance.
- In a large mixing bowl, toss together the potatoes, green beans, sliced fennel, red onion and bacon if using.
- Make the dressing. Whisk together the mayonnaise, mustard, and chopped fennel fronds. Season to taste with sea or kosher salt and pepper. Add to vegetables and toss to blend with a large rubber spatula. Transfer to a serving bowl that will best show off its loveliness. Garnish around the edges with some bunches of fennel fronds.

---

229. No Cook Salad, A Perfect Summertime Meal

Serving: Serves a crowd | Prep: | Cook: | Ready in:

Ingredients

- For the salad
- • 1 (15 oz) can pinto beans, well rinsed and drained
- • 1 cup marinated small white button mushrooms, drained
- • 1/2 to 3/4 cup Korean Carrot Salad
- • 1 (8 oz) can sliced water chestnuts, drained
- • 1/2 pound Canadian bacon, sliced and then chopped in 1-inch lengthwise, 1/4-inch thick pieces
- • 3 whole scallions, thinly sliced on a bias
- • Freshly ground black pepper to taste
- • Half bunch cilantro or parsley, leaves and stems, finely chopped
- • 1/3 cup Best Food or Hellman's mayonnaise + 2 teaspoons of each, lemon zest, juice, finely grated ginger, honey and crushed coriander seeds, whisked together
- For the marinated Mushrooms and Korean Carrot salad

- • 12 ounces small white button mushrooms
- • 3 tablespoons freshly squeezed lemon juice, (1 large lemon)
- • 3 tablespoons fresh thyme leaves
- • 2 tablespoons white wine vinegar
- • 3 tablespoons extra-virgin olive oil
- • 3/4 teaspoon kosher salt
- • 1/2 teaspoon freshly ground black pepper
- For the Korean Carrot salad:
- • 1 pound of fresh (preferably long) carrots, shredded on a mandolin into thin strands
- • 2 garlic cloves, minced
- • 1 large shallot diced
- • 1/4 cup sunflower or canola oil
- • 1 tablespoon whole coriander seeds, crushed
- • 1/2 teaspoon or more to your taste cayenne pepper
- • 3 tablespoons white wine vinegar
- • 1 tablespoon honey
- • 1 teaspoon kosher salt
- • 2-3 teaspoons fresh ginger, finely grated

Direction

- To marinate mushrooms: Using a damp towel, gently wipe dirt from mushrooms. Place mushrooms in a medium bowl, and add the remaining ingredients. Toss to combine. Set mushrooms aside at room temperature, stirring occasionally, to marinate, at least 20 minutes or up to 4 hours. Serve at room temperature.
- To make Korean Carrot Salad: Place the shredded carrots into a mixing bowl. Sauté the shallot in oil until the soft and translucent. Add coriander seeds and cayenne pepper toward the end of the cooking time. When the shallot is done, immediately add it and any leftover oil to the carrots; toss. In a small bowl, mix vinegar, ginger, garlic, honey, and salt. Add dressing to the salad, and mix well. Refrigerate overnight.
- To assemble the salad: Toss to combine all salad ingredients, (except the mayonnaise sauce), in a large mixing bowl; then mix-in the sauce, taste and add whatever is needed. Your salad is ready to eat and enjoy!

230.   Nori, Sesame Seed, And Togarashi Cheese Ball

Serving: Makes 1 cheese ball | Prep: | Cook: |Ready in:

Ingredients

- 8 ounces cream cheese, softened
- 3 tablespoons butter, softened
- 1 tablespoon soy sauce
- 1 tablespoon mayonnaise
- 1/2 sheet nori (dried seaweed)
- 1 teaspoon togarashi, plus more for garnish
- Sea salt and freshly-ground pepper, to taste
- Black and white sesame seeds, for garnish

Direction

- In a stand mixer or in a large bowl with a spatula, whip the cream cheese and butter together until fully incorporated.
- Add the soy sauce, mayonnaise, nori, togarashi, and salt and pepper. Mix thoroughly, and turn onto a sheet of plastic wrap.
- Refrigerate for 2 to 3 hours, or at least until the cream cheese mixture is firm to the touch.
- Remove the cheese ball from the refrigerator, and shape into a ball.
- On a baking sheet, spread out the sesame seeds and additional togarashi and roll the cheese ball in them so that it is fully covered. Serve with crisp cucumbers and crackers.

231.   OYSTERS TOMALES

Serving: Serves about 2 dozen oysters | Prep: | Cook: |Ready in:

Ingredients

- 2 dozen medium or large oysters (at least 6 for each person)
- 1 lb baby spinach, washed and dried
- 1 tbs butter (for sauteeing spinach)
- 3/4 cup mayonnaise
- 1 tbs garlic (minced)
- 1/2 cup grated gruyere (loose)
- 2 tbs fresh lemon juice
- 1/4 cup brandy
- 2 tbs green onions (fine chop) with a little of the green part
- pepper to taste

Direction

- Put the butter in a suitable sized pan and sauté the spinach until wilted. Drain and dry as much as you can. Then chop it up.
- In a bowl, mix the mayonnaise, cheese, lemon juice, cognac, onions, and garlic.
- Using a half oyster shell as a base, put a tbsp. of spinach in the bottom of the shell.
- Add a freshly shucked oyster on top of the spinach.
- Put about 1 tbsp. of the cheese sauce on top of each oyster.
- Heat a broiler.
- Make a bed of rock salt on a baking pan to put the oysters on and to keep them from tipping over.
- Put the baking pan under the broiler about 4-5 inches from the broiler element so that the oysters cook and the topping sauce melts. When the cheese sauce is bubbling they are ready.

232.   Oh Yeah Beef Burger

Serving: Serves 4 burgers | Prep: | Cook: |Ready in:

Ingredients

- 1.5 pounds Ground beef
- .5 pounds Chorizo sausage, removed from casing
- 1 tablespoon pepper
- 1.5 teaspoons salt, reserving .5 for tomatillos
- 1 teaspoon Pilsen seasoning (Found at Spice House, Evanston or Geneva, IL)
- 4 slices pepper jack cheese
- 4 tomatillos, depending on size
- 1 tablespoon canola oil
- 3 jalapenos, rib and seeds removed, sliced
- 1/4 cup mayonnaise
- 1 teaspoon adobo sauce (from can of chipotle)
- 4 Onion brioche rolls, split
- 1 Avocado, mashed

Direction

- Make mayonnaise by combining adobo sauce and mayo. Set aside in fridge.
- To make burgers, bring ground beef (80/20 is best for this application) and chorizo to room temperature or just above. Place both meats in large bowl, adding spices. Mix by hand until combined, but not mushy. Make into patties, creating a small well/dip in the middle to keep the burger's shape. Keep in fridge for 30 mins.
- While beef is resting, slice tomatillos and sprinkle w/ salt and gently toss with canola oil. Place in grill pan or on hot grill to char and tenderize. When tomatillos are fork-tender, remove and place on plate to keep shape. In remaining oil/juices, toss sliced jalapenos until tender and wilted. Keep aside.
- Remove beef/chorizo mixture from fridge 15 mins prior to grilling. During that time, prepare grill for burgers or griddle for flat-top cooking. Place burgers on grill and cook to desired doneness, adding cheese and melting. Butter and grill brioche buns in the last few minutes and spread prepared mayonnaise on buns. Mash avocados when near ready. Place bun on mayo and top with jalapenos, then tomatillos. Spread avocado on top bun. Enjoy!

233.   Okonomiyaki

Serving: Serves 4 | Prep: | Cook: |Ready in:

Ingredients

- Pancake
- 1 cup water
- 2 teaspoons dashi powder
- 1 cup all purpose flour
- 1 teaspoon sugar
- 1 teaspoon baking powder
- pinch   salt
- 1/2 cup onion, thinly sliced
- 1 tablespoon canola oil
- 2 cups cole slaw mix
- 1 1/2 cups cooked chopped seafood, pork, or bacon, or a combination
- 3   large eggs
- 3   green onions, chopped
- Kewpie mayonnaise
- Katsuobushi (bonito flakes - optional)
- pickled ginger (optional)
- Okonomiyaki Sauce
- 3 tablespoons ketchup
- 3 tablespoons horseradish dijon mustard
- 3   Worcestershire sauce

Direction

- Bring the water to a simmer and add the dashi. Stir to dissolve and allow to cool to room temperature.
- In a large bowl, combine the flour, sugar, baking powder, and salt. Slowly add the cooled dashi to the flour mixture, stirring to make a batter. Cover and refrigerate batter for at least an hour and up to three hours.
- While the batter is resting, saute the sliced onion in a bit of canola oil with a pinch of salt until the onion has softened. Stir in shredded cabbage and stir fry for a few minutes until the cabbage gets limp. Remove from heat and set aside.
- After the batter has rested for an appropriate length of time, beat the three eggs and add them to the batter. Drain and discard any liquid that has accumulated from the cabbage and onion mixture; add vegetables to the batter along with any seafood or pork you wish to use. The batter will be very thick.
- Add a tablespoon of canola oil to an 8" nonstick frying pan and heat until it shimmers. Add okonomiyaki batter to a depth of about 3/4" inch. Cover pan and cook over medium-low heat, for about 5-7 minutes. Remove lid. Place a large plate over the pancake and flip out onto the plate. Cover the pancake with another plate and invert, so the pancake is uncooked-side down on the second plate. Carefully slide pancake into the pan. Cook the second side for another 10 minutes or so, turning heat down to medium-low.
- When the pancake is done, transfer to a serving plate. Drizzle with mayonnaise, sprinkle with bonito flakes and scallions, and serve pickled ginger on the side.
- Cut into wedges and serve with Okonomiyaki sauce.
- Okonomiyaki sauce: combine all ingredients in a bowl.

234.   Olivier Potato Salad

Serving: Serves 10+ picnic people | Prep: | Cook: |Ready in:

Ingredients

- 3.5 pounds yellow potatoes, cut into large chunks
- 3   very large carrots, peeled
- 3   hard boiled eggs, chopped (1 of the yolks reserved)
- 4   small kosher dill pickles*
- 8 ounces naturally smoked ham (ideally without nitrates), cubed**
- 1   small red onion, diced
- 3/4 cup Hellman's lowfat mayonnaise
- 2 tablespoons white wine vinegar
- 1   (15~ oz.) can sweet peas, drained (2 tbsp reserved)***

- 2 teaspoons kosher salt, add more to taste

Direction

- In large pot of salted cold water, boil all the potatoes, carrots, and eggs. Take the carrots and eggs out as they become ready. The eggs should approximately 12 minutes and the carrots and potatoes will be ready when a fork pierces through them easily.
- Shell the eggs and peel off the skin off of the potatoes, if you haven't done so already, and let them cool slightly.
- Into a very large bowl, cut your potatoes into irregular shape, but uniform sized small pieces (about 1/2"). Cut your carrots and pickles into 1/4" pieces. Add in your pickles, cubed ham, diced red onions, and add in the chopped eggs and 2 of the yolks. Mix the salad gently. While you may want to cheat and make larger pieces of everything, the reason for making the pieces all small is so that in every bite you will have a little bit of all the flavors.
- Add in the mayonnaise, vinegar, and salt and mix gently. At the very end, add in the drained sweet peas, stirring carefully as to not mush them up. Taste the level of salt and adjust if necessary. (The salt will help bring the flavors out, so don't worry if you think you're adding more than you normally might.)
- Decorate the top of the salad with the reserved chopped egg yolk and the rest of the peas. This salad is best served between the temperature of "tooth cold" and warm. You don't want this sitting out in hot weather for too long. If it does, pop it in the fridge for 5 minutes and serve it again.
- Notes: *I've also made substitutions with canned black olives or capers instead of pickles, but do not include all three in one salad as to keep the level of salt in check. **If you don't have smoked ham on hand, I've used smoked turkey, bologna, or even cut up pieces of hot dog. If you happen to live in the NYC area or have an inclination to come into Astoria, go to Muncan, where they smoke their own meats and sausages without any

fake preservatives. They're the closest thing you can come to your own personal smokehouse without storing sausages in your friend's garage. ***Don't be tempted to use frozen peas, as the texture of frozen, while fresher and notably better in most other things, would lend a completely different tone to this salad where most of the rest of the ingredients might be considered "marinated." It would be like adding a jewel tone color to a salad of earthy hippie colors; it's just wrong. You don't want a fresh crisp pea in here, it wouldn't meld with the other ingredients. The crisp elements are onions and pickles alone and steamed or boiled peas would bring a waxy and watery texture.

---

235.   Open Faced Ham Salad And Cheese Melts

Serving: Serves 2-3 | Prep: 0hours0mins | Cook: 0hours0mins |Ready in:

Ingredients

- 1 cup diced cooked ham
- 1 carrot
- 1/2 small zucchini
- 1-2 cups fresh baby spinach
- mayonnaise
- 1 loaf crusty bread
- old cheddar cheese, sliced
- pepper, to taste

Direction

- Preheat the oven to 400 F.
- Put the diced ham in a medium-sized mixing bowl. Grate the carrot, dice the zucchini, slice the spinach, and add them to the ham. Spoon in a dollop of mayonnaise, and mix it all together. If it needs more mayonnaise, add it now. The vegetables and meat should not be covered in mayonnaise, but it should be just enough to give the salad a little moisture. Give

it a few good grates of pepper, but do not add salt.

- Slice up the bread and pile some salad onto each slice. Arrange the cheese on top. Place the sandwiches on a baking sheet (I cover mine with parchment paper to catch all the drips), and slide into the oven. Bake until the cheese is melted and the bread is toasted, 15-20 mins.

236. Oven Roasted Elote

Serving: Serves 4 | Prep: 0hours10mins | Cook: 0hours35mins | Ready in:

Ingredients

- 4 ears corn on the cob (silks removed, husks pulled back over clean corn)
- 1/2 cup mayonnaise
- 1 teaspoon lime juice
- 1 cup freshly grated parmesan
- 1 dash salt to taste for each cob
- 1 handful chopped cilantro
- 4 lime wedges
- 1 dash Cayenne to taste

Direction

- Preheat the oven to 350°F
- Place each cob directly on the rack of your oven for roughly 30-35 minutes.
- While the corn is roasting, combine the mayonnaise, lime juice, chopped cilantro, and cayenne pepper in a small bowl.
- When the corn is ready, let it cool for a few minutes.
- Then, peel back the husks leaving the core so that the cob is easy to hold on to.
- Lather up each cob with the mayonnaise mixture and a generous sprinkle of Parmesan.
- Finally, add a dash of salt to each cob and additional cayenne as necessary.
- Serve with a lime wedge.

237. Oyster Mushroom Po'Boy

Serving: Makes 2 large or 4 small | Prep: | Cook: | Ready in:

Ingredients

- 1 pound oyster mushrooms
- 1 cup cornmeal
- 3 tablespoons chile powder (without salt)
- 1 teaspoon salt
- 1/4 cup mayonnaise or aioli
- 1/2 teaspoon prepared horseradish with or without beets
- 1/3 cup celery, finely chopped
- 1 scallion, chopped
- 1/2 teaspoon cayenne pepper
- juice of 1/4 lemon
- 1/2 teaspoon mustard
- 2 eggs
- 2 french rolls
- bread and butter pickles
- sliced tomatoes
- 1 cup shredded iceberg lettuce

Direction

- Break eggs into a bowl and beat them well.
- Mix together cornmeal, chile powder and salt and pour onto a plate.
- Preheat oven to 450 degrees, Cover a cookie sheet well with oil.
- Mix together mayonnaise or aioli, horseradish, mustard, cayenne pepper, lemon juice, celery and scallions in a separate bowl.
- Remove stems from mushrooms. Dip each mushroom in egg, then press into cornmeal on each side and place on baking sheet.
- Spray the tops of each mushroom with oil -- if you don't have a spray bottle, just dab a little bit of oil on the top of each mushroom.
- Bake mushrooms until they are browned and crisped on the top.
- Split open rolls and toast them in the oven. Remove and slather with sauce, fill with

mushrooms, and add sliced tomatoes, pickles, and shredded lettuce as desired.

---

238.   PLT Crostini

Serving: Makes 40 pieces | Prep: | Cook: | Ready in:

Ingredients

- 20 Plum tomatoes
- 3 tablespoons Extra virgin olive oil
- 1/2 teaspoon Granulated sugar
- Kosher salt
- Freshly ground black pepper
- 1/2 pound Pancetta (sliced thin)
- 1 bunch Frisee lettuce
- 1 tablespoon Dijon mustard
- 2 Garlic cloves
- Juice of half a lemon
- 1 cup Mayonnaise
- 1-2 Baguettes (depending on size)

Direction

- Center a rack in the oven and preheat the oven to 250 degrees. Line a baking sheet with foil and pour 2 tablespoons olive oil evenly over the pan. Sprinkle the oil with salt and pepper. Cut each tomato in half, lengthwise, and remove the seeds. Lay the tomato halves cut side down in the pan. Using a pastry brush, give the tops of the tomatoes a light coat of olive oil. Season the tops of the tomatoes with salt and pepper and a little sugar. Slide the pan into the oven and bake the tomatoes for 2 ½ hours - they should be tender but still able to hold their shape. About half way through the cooking process, carefully turn the tomatoes over. Once the tomatoes are done, pull them out of the oven and allow them to cool to room temperature in the pan. (If you are doing this ahead of time, stack the cooled tomatoes in a jar or other resealable container. Pour whatever oil remains in the pan over the tomatoes and refrigerate until ready.

- While the tomatoes are in the oven, prepare the garlic mayonnaise. Combine the mayonnaise, lemon juice, and Dijon mustard in a small bowl. Using a micro plane, grate the garlic cloves in the bowl and mix everything together. Transfer the mixture to a plastic squeeze bottle and refrigerate until ready for use. (Note: This makes more than enough for 40 pieces, but I like to use the extra for sandwiches.)

- For the crostini you can either use store-bought or make your own. If you're making your own, slice the baguette at a 45-degree angle into roughly 1/2 inch slices and arrange them on a sheet pan. Brush them lightly with olive oil and bake at 375 degrees for 12-15 minutes.

- Bake the pancetta on a cookie sheet in an oven preheated to 450 degrees for about 10-15 minutes. Once the pancetta is crisp, place them on a paper towel or wire rack to cool and drain any excess fat.

- To assemble, place a confit tomato on each crostini (cutting them to fit, if necessary). Place a dot of the garlic mayonnaise on each tomato to allow the pancetta to stick. Break off a piece of pancetta and place on each crostini atop the tomato. Squeeze the garlic mayonnaise over the tomato and pancetta and then place a bit of frisee lettuce on top.

---

239.   PLT Sandwich (Provolone Lettuce Tomato)

Serving: Serves 1 | Prep: | Cook: | Ready in:

Ingredients

- 3 Slices of Smoked Provolone cheese
- 2 Slices of your favorite bread
- Mayonnaise to taste
- Lettuce
- 2 slices of Tomato

Direction

- Heat a nonstick skillet on medium heat until warm but not too hot. Sprinkle the blackening season in the skillet. Place the cheese on the seasoning. Sprinkle more seasoning on the top of the cheese so it is there when you flip it. Fry until it bubbles and the bottom is starting to brown. The longer you fry it the crispier it gets and the fat renders out like bacon.
- Spread the bread with mayonnaise put the tomato slices on. Put the lettuce on. When the cheese is browned on both sides, put it on and enjoy. My Non-vegetarian friends love this as much as I do.

---

240. Parmesan Dijon Crusted Cod On Burst Tomatoes

Serving: Serves 4 | Prep: | Cook: | Ready in:

Ingredients

- 2/3 cup mayonnaise
- 2 teaspoons Dijon mustard
- 1/2 cup grated Parmesan cheese
- 1/2 teaspoon lemon zest
- 1/2 teaspoon garlic salt
- 1 tablespoon olive oil
- 1 garlic clove, peeled, but left whole
- 2 cups cherry tomatoes
- 1/4 cup thinly sliced onion
- 1 cup corn kernels, thawed if frozen
- 1 cup shelled edamame, thawed if frozen
- salt and pepper to taste
- 4 cod fillets
- salt and pepper again, to taste

Direction

- Preheat the oven to 375 degrees F.
- Mix the mayonnaise, Dijon, parmesan, zest and garlic salt together in a small bowl. Set aside.
- Heat the oil in a large skillet on medium high heat. Toss in the tomatoes, garlic clove, onions, corn and edamame. Season with salt and

pepper and add the water. Cook, stirring often, until the tomatoes burst, about 8-10 minutes. Remove and discard the garlic clove. Remove the skillet from heat and keep warm.
- Season the cod fillets with salt and pepper on both sides and place on a parchment lined baking sheet that has been sprayed with cooking spray. Place ¼ of the Parmesan-Dijon topping on each filet and bake for 8 minutes if they are thin, 10 if they are thick. Turn the oven heat up to broil and broil for 2 minutes or until the topping becomes lightly golden.
- Serve each fillet on a bed of the burst tomato mixture.

---

241. Patatas Bravas

Serving: Serves 3 | Prep: | Cook: | Ready in:

Ingredients

- 1 pound baby yukon gold potatos, cleaned
- 1 tablespoon salt
- 8 cups water
- 1 cup canola oil
- 2 tablespoons olive oil
- 2 cloves of garlic, minced
- 1 shallot, minced
- 1/2 cup tomato sauce
- 1 tablespoon Sriracha, or your favorite hot sauce
- 1 teaspoon Spanish paprika
- 1/2 cup mayonnaise
- 1/4 teaspoon salt, to taste
- 1 pinch cracked black pepper, to taste

Direction

- Start by adding water to a medium-sized pot. Add about a tablespoon of salt, then add in the whole potatoes. Bring this to a medium-high heat, and cook for about 25 minutes, or just until the potatoes begin to soften. Drain the potatoes and set aside to let them cool. Once the potatoes have cooled, cut them in half, then cut the halves in half. Basically you are shooting for one-inch cubes. During this time, make the sauce.

- To another pot, add the olive oil, and bring up to medium-high. Add in the garlic and shallot and let those begin to sweat for a few minutes, stirring along the way. Toss in the paprika, hot sauce, and tomato sauce. Give a good stir and let the sauce simmer for a few more minutes, then set aside to cool. Once the sauce has cooled a bit, add in the mayonnaise. Stir, then season with salt and pepper to taste. Cover and place in the refrigerator until you are ready to use on the potatoes. Let's just say the sauce is awesome, and you will want to start putting this on everything!
- Heat a cup of canola oil on medium-high heat in a pot, or large skillet. After a few minutes, add in the chopped potatoes, and cook them, stirring along the way, until they are golden brown and crisp. Remove them from the oil with a slotted spoon and let them drain on a plate lined with paper towel. Season the potatoes with salt and pepper. Place the potatoes onto your serving dish, then drizzle the sauce all over the potatoes. Now, dig in!

242. Patty Melt

Serving: Serves two burgers | Prep: | Cook: | Ready in:

Ingredients

- 1 lb 85/15 ground beef (yes, I use grass fed, which I don't believe Friendly's does)
- 2 teaspoons Worcestershire sauce
- 1 teaspoon Dijon mustard
- ½ teaspoon kosher salt
- ¼ teaspoon ground pepper
- 3-4 Tablespoons butter, softened and divided
- 6 button mushrooms, sliced
- ½ sweet onion, sliced thin, half-moon slices
- 4 slices of oval-shaped, light rye bread
- 4 ounces, thinly sliced Gruyere cheese
- Mayonnaise (optional)

- Pickles (absolutely crucial garnish)

Direction

- Mix ground beef, Worcestershire sauce, Dijon mustard, salt and pepper thoroughly. Divide mixture and form into two, oval patties. I like to make thinner patties, but shape them so that when they are fully cooked, they cover almost the whole bottom piece of rye bread as this is a sandwich in which each bite should have all the elements. Refrigerate the patties for about an hour or so.
- In a large frying pan, melt one tablespoon of butter over medium high heat and add the mushrooms. Make sure all the of the mushrooms get coated with butter, but then leave them untouched for 3-4 minutes so that one side gets some nice color before you stir them around so the other side can get some color.
- Remove the mushrooms from the pan. Add 2 tablespoons butter and the onion to the pan and cook slowly over medium to low heat for 10-15 minutes until the onions are soft and somewhat caramelized. Remove the onions from the pan and keep them warm with the mushrooms.
- Increase the heat to medium high and fry the burgers to desired doneness. I like mine medium rare, which typically takes 3-4 minutes per side to achieve.
- While the burgers are cooking, put a second skillet over medium heat and butter one side of each piece of rye bread. Put the bread buttered side down on the hot skillet until you see some nice color. On two of the slices of bread, place two ounces of Gruyere cheese.
- When the burgers are done and the bread nicely browned, assemble your burgers: Bottom piece of bread with cheese, beef patty, onions, mushrooms, optional mayonnaise and top piece of bread. I like to give them a firm press and then slice each in half before serving with a pickle.

243. Pearl's Lobster Rolls

Serving: Serves 4 | Prep: 0hours0mins | Cook: 0hours0mins | Ready in:

Ingredients

- 4 1 lb Lobster (or 1 lb. lobster meat)
- 1/4 cup Mayonnaise
- 1/4 cup chopped celery
- 1 tablespoon lemon juice
- 1/4 teaspoon sea salt
- 1/8 teaspoon ground pepper
- 1 tablespoon unsalted butter
- 4 Hotdog buns
- 2 tablespoons chopped chives (optional as garnish)

Direction

- Throw your lobsters into a big pot rapidly boiling water. Cook for 8-10 minutes, or until done. Plunge lobsters into ice cold water bath for 10 minutes to stop cooking, and cool thoroughly. Drain and separate tail and claws. Bash the shells and remove all meat, and chop meat into 1/2 inch pieces.
- Combine lobster meat, mayonnaise, and next four ingredients. Cover and chill until ready to serve.
- Melt butter in large nonstick skillet over medium high heat. Press open buns, and place in skillet, turning to coat both sides. Cook buns until golden brown on both sides.
- Fill buns lobster filling, and sprinkle with chopped chives, as an option.

244. Pecan Chicken Pasta Salad

Serving: Serves 6 | Prep: | Cook: | Ready in:

Ingredients

- 2 cups protein-enriched rigatoni pasta
- 1 cup light mayonnaise
- 1 tablespoon white vinegar
- 2 teaspoons fresh lemon juice
- 1/4 teaspoon salt
- 3 cups smoked chicken, shredded or chopped
- 1 cup celery, chopped
- 1 yellow onion, chopped
- 1/2 cup pecans, toasted and chopped

Direction

- Cook pasta according to package directions. Drain and rinse with cold water.
- In large bowl, combine mayonnaise, vinegar, lemon juice, and salt. Add chicken, celery, bell pepper, and onion. Tossing to combine. Refrigerate until ready to serve.
- Sprinkle salad with pecans before serving. Note: For testing purposes only, we used Barilla Plus Rotini.

245. Peekytoe Crab Dip

Serving: Serves 6-8 as a hors d'oeuvre | Prep: | Cook: | Ready in:

Ingredients

- 1 pound Peekytoe crab meat (or substitute another kind of crab)
- 1 tablespoon mayonnaise
- 3 ounces cream cheese, softened
- 1 teaspoon Dijon mustard
- 3 tablespoons creme fraiche
- 1/4 cup freshly grated parmesan cheese, plus additional
- pinch of cayenne
- salt and pepper
- 2 scallions, finely chopped
- sweet paprika
- crackers or toast points for serving

Direction

- Heat the oven to 350 degrees. Check the crab meat for shells, being careful not break it up too much. Squeeze handfuls of the crab meat gently to get rid of any excess moisture and set aside in a medium bowl.
- In another bowl, combine the mayonnaise, cream cheese, mustard, crème fraiche, 1/4 cup parmesan, cayenne and salt and pepper to taste. Stir until smooth. Stir in the scallions and gently fold in the crabmeat until just combined. Taste and add more salt if necessary.
- Spoon the crab mixture into a shallow oven-proof serving dish. Sprinkle more parmesan over the top to cover, followed by a dusting of paprika. Cover with foil and bake for 15 minutes, until warmed through. Uncover the dip, turn on the broiler and broil until the top is golden brown, watching carefully. Let sit for a few minutes to cool slightly before serving with water crackers, Triscuits or toast points.

246. Pepper Crusted Salmon Cakes With Horseradish Sauce

Serving: Makes 6 fish cakes | Prep: | Cook: | Ready in:

Ingredients

- 1 pound salmon (wild caught)
- 1/2 cup creme fraiche
- 1 tablespoon prepared horseradish
- 1 teaspoon lemon juice
- sea salt and fresh ground pepper
- 2 tablespoons finely chopped red bell pepper (use a food processor)
- 2 tablespoons finely chopped flat leaf parsley (you can food process this too)
- 1/2 teaspoon salt
- 1 teaspoon prepared horseradish
- 1 tablespoon (generous) coarsely ground/cracked black pepper
- 1 teaspoon Dijon mustard
- 1/4 cup mayonnaise

- 1 cup Panko bread crumbs, divided
- olive oil for frying

Direction

- Preheat your oven to 350F. Place the salmon in a baking pan with a half-inch of water. Bake/poach until just cooked through, 20-25 minutes. Remove from the pan and allow to cool slightly. Blot dry with a paper towel and remove the skin.
- In the meantime, in a small bowl combine the crème fraiche, 1 Tbs. horseradish and lemon juice with a pinch of salt and pepper. If you'd like a slightly garlicky sauce, you can add a smashed piece of garlic and let it sit with the garlic in it while you prepare everything else. Then, fish the garlic out before serving. (I tried it both ways and decided I liked it better without garlic, but that's just a personal preference.) Set sauce aside.
- Put the salmon in a bowl, add the minced bell pepper, parsley, salt, mustard, mayonnaise, and a half cup of breadcrumbs. Stir with a fork to combine well and fluff. If it seems too wet or too dry to be able to form cakes, add mayo or bread crumbs as needed. This is something I do totally by feel, so I can't say for sure exactly the quantities I wind up using.
- Form the salmon mixture into 6 patties, place them on a wax paper lined baking sheet and refrigerate for 30 minutes. (During this time you can prep any vegetable you are going to have on the side.)
- Mix together the remaining half cup of Panko and the cracked pepper on a plate or in a shallow bowl. Heat a large splash of olive oil in a large frying pan over medium high heat. Gently dip the salmon cakes in the pepper mixture, lightly coating both sides (be careful when you handle them, as they are a bit fragile at this point). You may need to add a touch more breadcrumbs and pepper depending on how thickly you coat your cakes. Fry the salmon cakes until golden brown on both sides, about 3-4 minutes per side.

- Serve with the horseradish sauce for spooning all over them. We had ours with some roasted asparagus (totally jumping the gun on the seasons, but we're kind of aching for spring around here), and I wound up drizzling the horseradish sauce all over those too!

247. Perfect Pub Fries With Smokey Spicy Aioli

Serving: Serves 4 | Prep: | Cook: | Ready in:

Ingredients

- 2 pounds russet potatoes, peeled
- 2 tablespoons white household vinegar
- 2 quarts water
- 2 tablespoons kosher salt
- 2 quarts oil
- 1 cup mayonnaise
- 2 teaspoons minced fresh garlic
- 1 teaspoon ground cumin
- 1 teaspoon smoked paprika
- 1/2 teaspoon salt
- 1/4 teaspoon fresh ground black pepper
- Dash ground red pepper

Direction

- Cut potatoes into 1/3 inch thick pieces. Place potatoes, vinegar, water and salt in saucepan. Bring to a boil over high heat. Boil for 7 minutes until tender, but not falling apart. Drain potatoes in colander and spread on paper towel-lined rimmed baking sheet. Allow to dry thoroughly, about 5 minutes.
- Meanwhile, heat oil in Dutch oven or deep fryer to 400°F. Add fries to hot oil; cook 10 minutes until crisp and browned. Drain on paper towel-lined trays. Serve with Aioli
- To Make Aioli: Combine mayonnaise and remaining ingredients in small bowl. Serve with Pub Fries.

248. Perfect Roast Salmon

Serving: Serves 2 | Prep: 0hours5mins | Cook: 0hours0mins | Ready in:

Ingredients

- For the salmon
- 2 5 to 8-ounce filets of salmon, preferably wild-caught, skin-on, pin bones removed
- 2 teaspoons mayonnaise
- Salt & freshly ground black pepper
- 1/4 teaspoon dill pollen (or dillweed)
- Sauce
- 1 small garlic clove, peeled
- 1/4 teaspoon salt
- 4 to 5 basil leaves
- 1/2 cup Greek yogurt
- Salt to taste
- Lemon juice to taste

Direction

- Preheat oven to 475° F. Line a sheet pan with foil. DO NOT oil or grease. Place fish skin-side down on the pan. Skim coat with mayonnaise (you may need more or less depending on size of filets—you're looking for a thin coating). Sprinkle with salt and freshly ground pepper and top with dill pollen.
- Roast for 10 to 12 minutes depending on thickness of filets, until rare.
- Meanwhile make sauce (can be done in advance and refrigerated): Smash the garlic and salt and basil in a mortar and pestle until you have a rough paste. Add yogurt and season with salt and lemon juice to taste.
- When fish is done, slip a spatula under the fish to remove from foil, leaving skin behind. Serve with sauce and/or lemon.

249. Pimento Cheese Hominy

Serving: Serves 8-10 people | Prep: | Cook: |Ready in:

Ingredients

- 16 ounces Cheddar, coarsely shredded
- 1/2 cup Mayonnaise
- 8 ounces Pimentos, small dice
- Salt, to flavor
- 80 ounces Hominy, cooked

Direction

- Preheat the oven to 350 degrees Fahrenheit. Lightly oil or butter a 7 x 11 inch casserole dish. Grab a mixing bowl and wooden spoon.
- To make the pimento cheese, combine the shredded cheddar, mayonnaise, and pimentos in the mixing bowl with wooden spoon. Add salt to taste, then gently mix in the hominy.
- Scoop into prepared casserole dish. Bake for 30 minutes or until cheese is bubbly and the top is browned.

250. Pimento Cheese Sandwich With Fried Pickles & Ranch Dressing

Serving: Serves 6 | Prep: | Cook: |Ready in:

Ingredients

- For the pimento cheese and buttermilk ranch dressing:
- 2 cups sharp yellow cheddar cheese, coarsely grated (about 8 ounces)
- 2 cups extra-sharp white cheddar cheese, coarsely grated (about 8 ounces)
- 1 cup drained pimentos or roasted red peppers, finely chopped
- 3/4 cup mayonnaise, divided
- 1/2 teaspoon celery salt
- Salt and freshly ground black pepper
- 2 tablespoons sour cream
- 1 teaspoon minced shallot
- 1 clove garlic, crushed and minced
- 1 teaspoon lemon zest
- 1/4 teaspoon mustard powder
- 1/2 cup buttermilk, shaken vigorously
- 1 to 2 tablespoons lemon juice
- 1 splash sherry vinegar
- 2 tablespoons minced parsley
- 2 teaspoons minced chives
- 1 teaspoon minced thyme leaves
- For the fried pickles and the assembly:
- 1 cup all-purpose flour
- 1 cup milk
- 1 egg, beaten
- 1 pinch cayenne
- 1 cup cornmeal
- 1/2 teaspoon smoked paprika
- 1 teaspoon salt, plus more for seasoning
- 1/2 teaspoon freshly ground black pepper
- 1 jar whole dill pickled, slice 1/2-inch thick on the bias
- Peanut oil, for frying
- Rolls or subs, for making sandwiches

Direction

- For the pimento cheese and buttermilk ranch dressing:
- To make the pimento cheese, mix ingredients through celery salt in a large bowl, using only 1/2 cup of the mayonnaise. Season with salt and pepper to taste. Can be made 3 days ahead.
- To make the dressing, combine remaining 1/4 cup mayonnaise and sour cream. Stir in shallot, garlic, lemon zest, and mustard powder. Slowly whisk in buttermilk. Next, whisk in 1 to 2 tablespoons lemon juice (until dressing reaches desired thickness) and the sherry vinegar. Finally, fold in herbs and season with black pepper. Cover bowl and set dressing in the fridge to chill for at least 20 minutes, but preferably overnight.
- For the fried pickles and the assembly:
- Set up three shallow bowls or baking dishes: In one, pour the flour. In the second, beat together milk, egg, cayenne, and a splash of

pickle juice. In the third, mix together the cornmeal, paprika, salt, and pepper.

- Thoroughly dry pickle slices with paper towels, then dredge the slices by transferring them through the shallow dishes: flour, egg mixture, cornmeal mixture.
- Heat an inch of peanut oil in a Dutch oven over medium-high heat until it reaches 375° F. Working in batches to avoid crowding the pot, fry the pickle slices until golden brown, about 1 1/2 to 2 minutes. Transfer to a sheet tray lined with paper towels and immediately season with salt.
- To assemble the sandwiches, spread pimento cheese on the buns or rolls. Top with fried pickles, then drizzle with the buttermilk ranch.

251. Pimento Cheese Stuffed Pretzel Bites

Serving: Serves 50 bites | Prep: | Cook: | Ready in:

Ingredients

- Classic Pimento Cheese
- 1/2 pound Extra-sharp white cheddar
- 1/2 pound Extra-sharp (yellow) cheddar
- 1 (7) ounces Jar pimentos, drained and finely chopped
- 1/2 teaspoon Salt
- 1/2 teaspoon Pepper
- Cayenne to taste
- 2/3 cup Mayonnaise
- Pimento Cheese Stuffed Pretzel Bites
- 1   Package active dry yeast
- 1 1/2 cups Warm water
- 1 tablespoon Sugar
- 2 teaspoons Kosher salt
- 4 1/2 cups All-purpose flour
- 4 tablespoons Unsalted butter
- 12 cups Water
- 2/3 cup Baking soda
- 1   Egg
- 1 tablespoon Water

- Frozen pimento cheese balls

Direction

- Classic Pimento Cheese
- Finely grate cheeses into a large bowl. Stir in pimentos, black pepper, cayenne, and salt with a fork. Stir in mayonnaise, mashing mixture with fork until relatively smooth.
- Scoop rounded teaspoons onto a baking sheet lined with parchment. Freeze for at least two hours, or overnight.
- Pimento Cheese Stuffed Pretzel Bites
- In the bottom of a stand mixer, combine water, sugar and salt. Sprinkle yeast over. Let set for 5 minutes until foamy. Add in flour, salt, and melted butter. Using the dough hook, mix the dough until combined on a low speed, Increase the speed to medium and mix for 5-7 minutes until dough becomes smooth and pulls away from the sides of the bowl.
- Rinse bowl off and then grease with canola oil. Place dough back in the greased bowl and cover with a clean kitchen towel on your counter, in a warm spot for 1 hour.
- Once the dough has risen, cut dough into 8 equal pieces. Roll dough into a rope 1-inch thick. With a sharp knife, cut into 1-inch bites. Using your palm, flatten the bite and fill with one heaping teaspoon of the chili. Close dough around a frozen cheese ball and re-form into the pretzel bite shape, if needed, roll to smooth edges. Repeat with remaining dough.
- Preheat oven to 450 degrees. Bring a large stock pot to a rolling boil. Add baking soda. Working in batches as necessary, add bites to the boiling water. Cook for 1 minute, flipping halfway through.
- Transfer pretzels to a greased baking sheet. Whisk egg and water together in a small bowl. Brush pretzels with egg wash and then sprinkle with kosher salt.
- Bake until golden brown, about 12-15 minutes.

252. Pizza Appetizers

Serving: Serves 12 | Prep: | Cook: | Ready in:

Ingredients

- 2 cups shredded sharp cheddar cheese
- 1 cup chopped black olives
- 1 cup Hellmann's mayonnaise
- 2 tablespoons finely chopped onion
- 1 packet cocktail party rye bread
- bacon pieces (I use bottled Hormel, but you could crisply cook and crumble your own bacon)

Direction

- Preheat oven to 350 degrees F. In a large bowl, mix together the cheese, olives, mayonnaise, and onion.
- Spread about a tablespoon of the mixture on each piece of cocktail rye bread. Place the pieces on a baking sheet lined with parchment paper, making sure to not crowd them too close together. Sprinkle the bacon pieces on top of the pieces.
- Bake in the preheated oven for 10 minutes. Allow to cool a minute before transferring to a plate with a spatula. Enjoy!

253. Poached Salmon In Light Basil Sauce Over Butternut Squash Latkes

Serving: Serves 12-15 | Prep: | Cook: | Ready in:

Ingredients

- Salmon
- 1 large salmon
- 1 cup German Riesling, or some other white wine
- 1/2 cup cider vinegar
- 4 spring onions, chopped
- 3 cloves garlic
- 2 carrots, chopped
- 2 tablespoons coriander seeds
- 1 handful fresh basil stems
- 1/2 cup light cream
- 1/3 cup mayonnaise
- 1/4 teaspoon ground ginger
- 1/2 teaspoon salt
- 1 tablespoon black pepper
- 1/2 cup fresh basil leaves, finely chopped
- Butternut Squash Latkes
- 2 large butternut squash
- 2 onions
- 2 eggs
- 1 teaspoon lemon juice
- 2 1/4 cups flour
- 2 tablespoons cornstarch
- 1/4 teaspoon garlic powder
- 1 teaspoon salt
- 1/2 teaspoon Cayenne pepper
- 1/2 cup grapeseed oil

Direction

- Salmon
- Remove the inner grill from a fish poacher, and pour the white wine and vinegar into the pan. Add the onions, garlic, carrots, coriander seeds, and basil stems; grease the grill, and replace it in the pan. Place the salmon on the grill.
- Poach over a medium-high heat for 8-12 minutes until the salmon turns a light- to gray-pink color.
- Mix the cream, mayonnaise, ginger, salt, pepper, and basil leaves in a small food processor until spreadable.
- Place a piece of salmon on a Butternut Squash Latke (see below)
- Slather spoonsful of the basil sauce over the salmon when serving.
- Butternut Squash Latkes
- Peel and grate the squash; strip the onions and grate them also. Transfer the squash and onions to a colander and press out any excess moisture. In a separate bowl, combine eggs, lemon juice, flour, cornstarch, garlic powder, salt, and Cayenne; add the squash and onions,

and mix well. (If the mixture is too wet, add a bit more flour.)

- Heat the grapeseed oil in a large frying pan. Drop a heaping spoonful of the mixture into the oil and press down with a spatula to flatten. Fry until brown and crispy on the edges, cooking each side for about 3-5 minutes. Drain on paper towels placed on a large platter and keep warm until serving.

254. Pomodorini Ripieni

Serving: Serves as many as you wish | Prep: | Cook: | Ready in:

Ingredients

- cherry tomatoes
- tuna in olive oil
- mayonnaise
- capers
- flat leaf Italian parsley
- salt and pepper

Direction

- Wash cherry tomatoes and slice the tops off of them.
- Carefully core the cherry tomatoes with a paring knife and scoop out the seeds and pulp with a small spoon.
- Set the hollowed tomatoes upside down unto a baking tray and allow the juices to drain.
- Dice the tomato pulp, and add it along with the juices and seeds into a bowl.
- Drain the tuna and stir into the tomato mixture. We used between 1 and 2 cans of tuna for each pint of cherry tomatoes.
- Add a few spoonfuls of mayonnaise to the creaminess level of your preference.
- Rinse a handful of capers quickly under water, dice them add them to the mixture. You can use more or fewer capers according to preference.

- Chop a bunch of flat leaf parsley finely, and stir it into the mixture.
- Salt and pepper to taste.
- Carefully stuff the tuna mixture into the cherry tomatoes, taking care not to tear the tomato walls.
- If you wish, garnish with a small dollop of mayonnaise.

255. Pork Bacon Burger With Bourbon Onion Mayonnaise

Serving: Makes 4 burgers | Prep: | Cook: | Ready in:

Ingredients

- 4 Omaha Steaks Pork & Bacon Burgers
- 4 Onion Buns
- 2 teaspoons Omaha Steaks All Natural Seasoning
- 1/2 cup Bourbon Onion Mayonnaise
- 4 Green Leaves
- 4 Beefsteak Tomato Slices

Direction

- Clean and preheat grill to high (600°F). Season burgers as desired with Omaha Steaks All Natural Seasoning. Grill for 5-6 minutes per side until internal temperature reads 160°F.
- Lightly toast the Kaiser Rolls and spread 1 Tbsp. of Bourbon Onion Mayonnaise on each half of buns.
- Place burgers on buns and top with green leaf and tomato slice.

256. Portobello Burgers With Arugula, Peppers And Garlic Mayonnaise

Serving: Serves 4 | Prep: | Cook: | Ready in:

Ingredients

- 2 large portobello mushrroms
- 2 teaspoons balsamic vinegar
- 2 cloves garlic, chopped
- 4 tablespoons olive oil
- 2 teaspoons fresh thyme leaves, chopped
- 1 red bell pepper
- 1/4 cup mayonnaise
- 4 bread rolls, halved lengthwise
- 2 teaspoons sherry vinegar
- 1 cup baby arugula
- Kosher salt and freshly ground pepper

Direction

- Wash and dry the portobellos. Cut into 1/2-inch-thick slices. Set aside.
- Combine the balsamic vinegar and half of the garlic in a large bowl. Let sit 5 minutes. Stir in 2 tablespoons of the olive oil and the thyme. Add the portobello slices and carefully mix with the garlic mixture. Let sit.
- Preheat a grill to medium-high heat.
- Place the bell pepper directly on the grill and cook until blackened on all sides, about 12 minutes, turning as needed. Put in a bowl and cover with plastic wrap. Let sit for 10 minutes.
- Mix the mayonnaise and the remaining garlic together in a small bowl. Set aside.
- Put the rolls on the grill, crust-side up and cook until lightly toasted, 1 to 2 minutes. Transfer to a platter and spread equal amounts of the garlic-mayonnaise over the bottoms.
- Whisk together the sherry vinegar and the remaining 2 tablespoons of olive oil in a large bowl. Peel and cut the peppers into 1/4-inch strips. Add the peppers and arugula to the bowl and toss to coat evenly. Season to taste with the salt and pepper. Arrange even amounts over the top of each roll bottom.
- Season the mushrooms with salt and pepper and place on the grill and cook, covered, until browned, about 3 minutes. Turn and cook the other side until browned, about 3 minutes. Put one on top of each bread roll. Put the top on and serve with lots of napkins.

Serving: Serves 6 to 8 people | Prep: 0hours15mins | Cook: 0hours40mins |Ready in:

Ingredients

- 4 large eggs
- 2 pounds red potatoes
- 3 tablespoons freshly squeezed lemon juice
- 1 1/2 teaspoons kosher salt, divided
- 1/2 cup mayonnaise
- 2 tablespoons whole-grain mustard
- 1/3 cup finely diced kosher dill pickles
- 1/2 cup finely diced celery
- 1/4 cup finely sliced chives, plus an extra handful to garnish
- 1/4 teaspoon freshly ground black pepper
- 3/4 teaspoon onion powder

Direction

- Fill a medium pot with water and bring to a boil. Use a mesh strainer to gently add the eggs to the boiling water. Boil the eggs for exactly 10 minutes, then drain and immediately cool in an ice bath or under cold running water. Peel the eggs under water and store in the refrigerator if you aren't using right away.
- Cut the potatoes into bite-size pieces (about 1-inch cubes). Add the potatoes to a large pot, and add cold water to cover the potatoes by about 1 inch. Bring the potatoes to a boil, then reduce the heat and gently simmer for 6 to 10 minutes, until they are just tender—they're done when a paring knife easily pierces the center, but the potato doesn't fall apart. Strain the potatoes and add them to a large mixing bowl. Add the lemon juice and salt while the potatoes are warm, then transfer them to the refrigerator for about 20 minutes, until they are cool.

- Add the remaining ingredients into a large mixing bowl and stir to combine. Chop the hard-boiled eggs into bite-size pieces. Gently fold the potatoes and the eggs into the mayonnaise dressing. Taste and adjust with more salt and/or lemon juice as necessary. You can store this potato salad in the refrigerator for up to a few days, or eat it immediately.

258. Potato Salad Á La Cornwall

Serving: Serves many, many servings | Prep: | Cook: | Ready in:

Ingredients

- 2 pounds little new, red potatoes
- 1 cup Hellmann's mayonnaise thinned with milk
- 1 bunch green onions, chopped
- Sea salt and pepper to taste

Direction

- Boil the potatoes until tender. While warm (but not still steaming hot - I have melted my fingerprints slicing too early and my life of crime may start any minute now) slice potatoes and begin to layer them in a large bowl - one layer potatoes then a handful of green onions and salt and pepper. Pour on some of the mayonnaise mixture. Repeat. Gently stir until all the potatoes are coated. You may need to add more mayonnaise mixture when you are ready to serve, as the potatoes absorb the liquid. Put on the table and stand back - the stampede might knock you down!

259. Pseudo Psaesar Salad With Avocado And Herbs

Serving: Serves 8 | Prep: | Cook: | Ready in:

Ingredients

- 2 heads of romaine lettuce, washed, chilled and crisp
- 2 ripe avocados, divided, peeled and chunked
- 2 tablespoons white wine vinegar
- 2 teaspoons lemon and/or lime juice
- 1/2 cup mayonnaise
- 1 teaspoon anchovy paste or 1 chopped oil-packed anchovy
- 2 tablespoons parsley leaves
- 2 tablespoons tarragon, coarsely chopped
- 2 tablespoons other herbs of choice (basil, thyme, oregano, cilantro?)
- 1 small shallot, chopped
- 1 clove garlic, crushed and chopped
- 1/2 cup good-quality olive oil
- 1 tablespoon chives, coarsely chopped
- 1 cucumber, peel and seeds removed, thinly sliced
- 4 ounces smoked whitefish, trout or salmon, cut into bite-size pieces
- Coarsely ground black pepper

Direction

- Tear the romaine into manageable pieces and divide among eight salad plates. Set aside
- In a processor, blend ONE avocado with vinegar, citrus juices, mayonnaise, anchovy, parsley, tarragon, the selected other herbs, and the garlic until smooth. Then add the garlic and blend again.
- Slowly add the olive oil while processing. As soon as it is blended in, stop.
- Add the SECOND avocado and the chives and barely process to make a chunky dressing.
- Divide the dressing among the salad, spooning it over the romaine. Garnish each sled with cucumber slices and smoked fish. Sprinkle with coarsely ground black pepper.

260.   Ramp Rice Cakes

Serving: Serves 7 | Prep: | Cook: |Ready in:

Ingredients

- 2 cups sticky rice (sushi rice), cooked
- 1   egg, beaten
- 1/2 cup matzo meal
- 1/2 cup jack cheese, grated
- 1 1/2 cups ramps, chopped
- 1   heaping tbsp chopped garlic
- 1   heaping tbsp chopped ginger
- 1 tablespoon sriracha or other chili sauce
- 2 1/2 tablespoons garlic mayonnaise or aioli
- 1 tablespoon soy sauce
- 2   vegetarian or meat bacon strips, fried crisp and crumbled
- 1/2 inch   olive or other oil

Direction

- Sauté ramps, garlic, and ginger for 2-3 minutes.
- Combine ramps, garlic, ginger, rice, matzo meal, egg, jack cheese, and bacon in a mixing bowl.
- Mix well, then form into seven patties by hand. Season well.
- Heat 1/2 inch olive or other oil in a skillet. Pan-fry ramp rice cakes till golden on both sides. Drain on a paper towel.
- In a small bowl, mix garlic mayonnaise, sriracha, and soy sauce thoroughly. Season with a little black pepper.
- Serve ramp rice cakes with dipping sauce while still hot from frying.

261.   Ranch Tzatziki Sauce Or Dressing

Serving: Makes 4 cups | Prep: | Cook: |Ready in:

Ingredients

- 3 cups greek yogurt
- 1   english cucumber, chopped and drained
- 1/2 teaspoon salt
- 1   lemon, juiced (app. 2-3 TB)
- 2 teaspoons crushed garlic
- 2 tablespoons fresh dill or mint
- salt and pepper to taste
- 1/2 cup mayonnaise
- 1/4 cup milk
- 1/2 packet ranch dressing mix

Direction

- Chop the cucumber and place in a paper towel lined strainer over the sink. Sprinkle with salt and let drain for 1/2 hour. Draining the cucumbers will keep the tzatziki sauce from becoming watery.
- In a large bowl, combine yogurt, cucumbers, lemon juice, garlic, dill or mint, and salt and pepper to taste. This is the completed tzatziki sauce.
- To make ranch tzatziki sauce, put sauce in the food processor and process until smooth. Add mayonnaise, milk and ranch dressing packet and pulse until combined. Refrigerate until thickened.

262.   Red Curry Chicken Burgers With Grilled Pineapple

Serving: Serves 4 | Prep: | Cook: |Ready in:

Ingredients

- Juice and zest of 1/2 lime
- 1/4 cup mayonnaise
- 1 pound ground chicken

- 2 tablespoons red curry paste
- 1 medium red onion, peeled and sliced into 4 thick slices
- 1/2 fresh pineapple, cored and sliced into 1-inch thick slices
- Nonstick cooking spray
- 4 hamburger buns

Direction

- Preheat grill for direct grilling over medium-high heat. In small bowl, stir together lime juice and zest, and mayonnaise. In medium bowl, combine chicken and curry paste. Form into 4 patties, making sure not to over-work the meat mixture.
- Spray both sides of chicken patties, onion and pineapple with nonstick cooking spray. Transfer patties, onion and pineapple to hot grill rack. Cook onion and pineapple for 4 to 6 minutes or until dark grill marks appear, turning once; transfer onion and pineapple to plate as they finish cooking. Cook burgers for 6 to 8 minutes, or until internal temperature of 165 degrees F is reached, turning once.
- Assemble burgers using hamburger buns, chicken patties, grilled onion and pineapple, and lime mayonnaise.

263.   Reuben Cheese (and A Beet Reuben)

Serving: Makes 1½ cups spread; 1 sandwich | Prep: | Cook: | Ready in:

Ingredients

- 3 cups Swiss cheese, grated (12 ounces)
- 2 tablespoons sweet onion, finely grated
- 2 tablespoons ketchup
- 1/4 cup mayonnaise
- 2 tablespoons sweet pickle relish
- 1 teaspoon Sriracha (optional)
- 1/4 teaspoon sweet paprika

- 1 large beet, sliced (canned; or boiled or roasted if using fresh beets)
- 1 tablespoon butter, softened
- 2 slices bread (such as rye or pumpernickel bread)

Direction

- Combine the grated cheese, grated onion, mayonnaise, relish, paprika, and Sriracha (if using) in a mixing bowl with a spatula until smooth and spreadable. Cover and refrigerate until ready to use. It will last for about 1 week.
- To make a Reuben sandwich, spread both sides of the bread thickly with the cheese spread (about 2-3 tablespoons, or to taste — there will be leftover spread for more sandwiches). Top with sliced beets (or other protein) and sauerkraut, as desired.
- Preheat a cast-iron griddle or skillet over medium-low heat. Spread each side of the bread with softened butter. Griddle on each side until deeply golden brown and the cheese is fully melted, about 5 minutes per side.

264.   Rhonda's Tomato, Corn And Cheese Tart

Serving: Serves 8 to 10 people | Prep: | Cook: | Ready in:

Ingredients

- pie dough for a single crust pie, rolled thin, fitted into a 12-inch tart pan and chilled for 30 minutes
- 1 1/2 pounds ripe tomatoes - halved grape/cherry tomatoes or cored and sliced larger tomatoes
- 1 ear's-worth fresh corn kernels, raw or cooked
- 1/3 cup plus 3 T fresh basil leaves, divided
- 1/3 cup scallions, chopped fine
- 5 cups grated cheese (sharp Cheddar, aged Provolone, Fontina, Monterey Jack, etc. - I tend to use a mix of whatever is in the fridge)

- 1/4 cup mayonnaise
- 1 large egg, beaten
- 2 tablespoons heavy cream
- 1 teaspoon kosher salt
- 1/2 teaspoon freshly ground black pepper
- 1/2 cup grated Parmesan or Romano cheese
- 4 ounces fresh mozzarella, torn into 3/4-inch chunks or 4 oz fresh goat's milk cheese, roughly crumbled

Direction

- Preheat your oven to 375 degrees.
- Use a fork to pierce the pie crust all over, then line the crust with foil and fill the pan with dried beans or pie weights. Blind-bake the pie shell for 8 minutes, till slightly firmed up. Place on a rack to cool and remove the foil and weights. Keep the oven set to 375 degrees.
- Roughly chop 1/3 c basil leaves and place in a large bowl. Stack the other 3 T basil leaves, roll into a cigar shape and slice thinly into chiffonade. Set aside.
- To the large bowl with the chopped basil, add the corn, scallions, grated cheese, mayonnaise, egg, cream, salt and pepper. Mix well and spread into the tart shell.
- Top cheese mixture with tomatoes, pressing them gently into the cheese mixture. If using small, halved tomatoes, place tomatoes cut-side down.
- Sprinkle the grated Parmesan over the tart and dot with the chunks of mozzarella or goat's milk cheese.
- Bake 25-30 minutes until crust is golden brown and the cheese is bubbly.
- Remove to a rack to cool for at least 10 minutes before serving. Serve warm or room temperature, sprinkling with the basil chiffonade before serving.

265. Roasted Achiote Chicken With Potatoes, Broccoli, And Tangerine Aioli

Serving: Serves 8 | Prep: | Cook: |Ready in:

Ingredients

- 2 tablespoons achiote paste
- 3 tangerines, zested and juiced
- 8 garlic cloves, minced
- 1 teaspoon cumin
- 2 teaspoons chili powder
- 8 whole chicken legs (thigh and leg)
- 2 pounds fingerling potatoes
- 1 pound broccoli
- 1/2 red onion, sliced
- 1/2 cup mayonnaise
- 1 teaspoon chili garlic sauce
- Parsley, for garnish

Direction

- Mix achiote paste, garlic, cumin, chili powder, 1/3 cup tangerine juice, and 1 tablespoon zest in a blender. Rub all over chicken (you might want to wear gloves or plastic bags -- otherwise your hands will be yellow) and refrigerate overnight.
- Heat oven to 450° F. Wash potatoes well and cut into similar sizes, about 2 inches each. Cut broccoli into large florets. Toss broccoli, potatoes, and onion with a drizzle of olive oil and season well with salt and pepper. Place on the bottom of a 9x13 baking dish or casserole. Season chicken with salt and pepper and arrange on top of vegetables. Cover tightly with foil and bake for about 30 minutes. Remove foil and bake another 30 to 40 minutes until skin is brown and crisp. Take a look after a while to make sure the vegetables are not burning on the bottom.
- Mix 1 tablespoon tangerine juice and 1 teaspoon zest with mayonnaise and chili garlic sauce. Salt if needed and serve on the side.

266. Roasted Eggplant Rounds Topped With Olive Tapenade And Artichoke Roasted Red Pepper Spread

Serving: Serves 6-8 | Prep: | Cook: |Ready in:

Ingredients

- For the eggplant rounds and olive tapenade
- • 3 medium uniform eggplants cut into 1/2-inch rounds, unpeeled
- • 1/2 cup pure olive oil
- • 5 garlic cloves, peeled and slightly smashed
- • 3 anchovy fillets, rinsed, patted dry and chopped
- • 1 cup pitted Kalamata or green olives, drained, patted dry
- • 2 teaspoons lemon juice
- • 2 teaspoons prepared mayonnaise
- For the Artichoke-Roasted Red Pepper spread
- • 1 package (12 oz) frozen artichoke hearts, thawed
- • 2 roasted red peppers, homemade or prepared, chopped
- • 1 medium onion, finely chopped
- • 4 garlic cloves, diced
- • 3 tablespoons extra virgin olive oil
- • 2 tablespoons balsamic or red wine vinegar
- • 1 teaspoon dried Italian seasoning mix
- • 1/4 teaspoon red pepper flakes
- • Coarse salt and freshly ground black pepper, to taste
- • Fresh flat- leave parsley, to finish the spread and for plating
- • Capers, drained, rinsed, pat dry (optional)

Direction

- Place a large, preferably flat colander over a bowl; lay out the eggplant rounds and sprinkle liberally with salt each row. Cover with a slightly smaller plate and place something heavy on top. Set aside for about 1 hour.
- To make the spread: In a large skillet heat the extra virgin oil on medium heat. Add onion, salt, red pepper flakes and the Italian seasoning and cook stirring occasionally until softened; add garlic, cook for 2 minutes; then add artichokes, mix well and cook until the artichokes are very tender, about 15-20 minutes.
- Add roasted red pepper and vinegar; cook, stirring occasionally, until all liquid is evaporated, taste and if needed, add some salt. Turn of the heat; mix in black pepper and about a tablespoon of chopped parsley.
- Using a food processor for a smooth consistency or a potato masher for a coarser, whirl or mash until the spread is homogeneous. Set aside.
- To roast the eggplants and make the olive tapenade: Rinse a few times eggplants rounds and pat them dry. Preheat the oven to 400 degrees F.
- In small sauce pan heat the 1/2 cup of the pure olive oil; add the anchovy and cook on medium heat until completely dissolved. Turn down the heat, add garlic and continue cooking until garlic is soft and just starts to brown. Remove from stove and strain thru a fine strainer to a small bowl. Reserve garlic.
- Using a pastry brash generously spread the anchovy and garlic infused oil on both sides of eggplants rounds, place them on a cookie sheet (you may need two cookie sheets), lined with parchment paper, transfer to the oven and roast until softened and golden brown, about 25 minutes. Cool to room temperature.
- To make the olive tapenade: Place olives in the bowl of a small food processor; pulse until finely chopped. Add the reserved garlic and pulse to combine. Scrape down sides of processor and add the remaining infused olive oil, lemon juice and mayonnaise; pulse to combine.
- To assemble the appetizer: Divide olive mixture evenly between eggplant rounds, spreading to cover; then put a heaping teaspoon of artichoke-red pepper spread.

- If using Capers, sauté them for a few minutes until they warmed throw; then sprinkle on top of the spread.
- The olive tapenade and artichoke-red pepper spread can be made 1 day ahead, kept refrigerated and brought to room temperature before serving.

267.   Roasted Mexican Street Corn Salad

Serving: Serves 6 as a side dish | Prep: | Cook: | Ready in:

Ingredients

- 6 ears of sweet corn, silks and husks removed
- Nonstick cooking spray
- 4 ounces diced green chiles
- 2 small garlic cloves, minced
- 1/2 small red onion, finely chopped (about 1/2 cup)
- 3/4 cup crumbled cotija or feta cheese, divided
- 1/4 cup coarsely chopped fresh cilantro
- 3 tablespoons fresh lime juice
- 2 tablespoons mayonnaise
- 2 tablespoons sour cream
- 1/2 teaspoon chili powder
- 1/8 teaspoon cayenne pepper (or 1/4 teaspoon if you'd like it more spicy)
- 1/4 teaspoon kosher salt

Direction

- Preheat oven to 375°. Cut corn kernels from cobs. Spray rimmed baking pan with nonstick spray. Spread corn in single layer on prepared pan. Roast 30 to 40 minutes or until golden brown, stirring twice.
- Meanwhile, in large bowl, stir together chiles, garlic, onion, 1/2 cup cheese, cilantro, lime juice, mayonnaise, sour cream, chili powder, cayenne and salt.
- Let corn cool slightly, then toss with mayonnaise mixture until well combined.

Serve sprinkled with remaining 1/4 cup cheese.

268.   Roasted Red Pepper & Garlic Panini

Serving: Serves 2 | Prep: | Cook: | Ready in:

Ingredients

- Roasted Red Peppers and Roasted Garlic
- 1 large organic red pepper
- 1 whole garlic
- 2 tablespoons Olive Oil
- For the Rest of the Sandwich
- 2 tablespoons organic mayonnaise
- 1/2 tablespoon honey
- 1 sprinkle mustard powder
- 1/4 teaspoon freshly ground black pepper
- 1/4 teaspoon sea salt
- 1 loaf ciabatta
- 6 thin slices mozzarella
- 4 leaves fresh basil, cut in chiffonade
- 1 1/2 tablespoons red onions, finely chopped

Direction

- Preheat oven to 450 degrees
- Thoroughly wash peppers
- Cut out the stem and seeds
- Grease a roasting pan (or a sturdy baking sheet) with 1 tablespoon of olive oil
- Thoroughly dry pepper halves, and place into pan, cut side down
- Remove a few of the dry layers of skin around the garlic, leaving the closest layers intact
- Cut the top of the garlic off, ensuring that each peg has been "opened"
- Place garlic onto a piece of foil, large enough to fully envelop it, and pour the remaining tablespoon of olive oil over the garlic
- Fold the foil up around the garlic and place into the roasting pan, away from the peppers

- Place pan into the oven, and allow to roast for 15 minutes
- After 15 minutes, check on peppers to see if they have begun to brown. If so, allow to roast for another 10 minutes, or until there are more patches of dark brown/ black across the surface of the peppers, at which point, remove from oven and set aside to cool, allowing garlic to remain
- 10 minutes later, remove the garlic
- When cool, remove the skins of the pepper. In some areas you can use a teaspoon to coax the skin off. Fingers also work well. Once the skin is off, set aside.
- Place the mayo into a small mixing bowl.
- Add the honey, mustard powder, salt and pepper and mix
- Holding the garlic at the base (ensure that it is cool) squeeze the soft roasted pegs into the mayonnaise mixture.
- Using a fork, crush the garlic as much as possible
- Add the basil and stir
- If you have a Panini maker or grill pan, begin heating it up
- Cut two sandwich-sized pieces of the ciabatta, keeping in mind the size of each slice of pepper
- Cut each piece in half to create a sandwich
- Spread the mayo mixture generously onto each slice, a little heavier on each bottom slice.
- Place 2 slices of mozzarella onto each bottom slice.
- Add the pepper over the cheese
- Top with onions and remaining cheese
- Complete sandwiches by placing the top slice of bread
- Place sandwiches into Panini maker of grill pan one at a time
- When the bread appears perfectly crisp and the inside of the sandwich has melted, you are ready to go!

---

269. Roasted Red Pepper Sandwiches With Spicy Chipotle Lime Carrot Slaw

Serving: Serves 2 | Prep: | Cook: | Ready in:

Ingredients

- 4 slices sourdough (or similar) bread
- 8 ounces roasted red peppers, drained and patted dry
- 4 slices white cheddar cheese
- 1 avocado, sliced
- 4 large leaves of romaine lettuce
- 1 cup grated carrot (about 2 carrots)
- 3 tablespoons light mayonnaise
- 1 tablespoon adobo sauce
- 1 teaspoon lime juice

Direction

- In a small bowl, mix together grated carrot, mayonnaise, adobo sauce, and lime juice.
- Place lettuce, sliced avocado, red peppers (patted dry with a paper towel), one layer of sliced cheese, and carrot slaw on bottom slices of bread, in that order. Top with remaining slices of bread and cut with a serrated knife.

---

270. Roasted Red Pepper And Pomegranate Patatas Bravas

Serving: Serves 4 | Prep: 0hours30mins | Cook: 0hours30mins | Ready in:

Ingredients

- 1.5 pounds potatoes
- 5 tablespoons olive oil, divided
- 1 onion, diced
- 1 teaspoon ground coriander
- 1 teaspoon smoked paprika
- 1/4 cup blanched almonds
- 1/4 cup white wine
- 2 red peppers, well roasted

- kosher salt to taste
- pomegranate molasses, mayonnaise, and chopped parsley for garnish

Direction

- Heat oven to 400°. Toss potatoes with about 2 tablespoons of olive oil, sprinkled with sea salt and lay in a single layer on a baking sheet.
- Roast potatoes for 25-30 minutes, turning every 10, until potatoes are golden and easily pierced with a fork. You can turn off the oven and leave them inside to warm while you finish the sauce. When ready, move to a dish.
- Meanwhile, prepare the spicy red pepper sauce. Heat 3 tablespoons olive oil on medium high and sauté onion until golden.
- Add chopped garlic and sauté for a minute or so, then add salt, paprika, ground coriander, cayenne, and almonds, and cook, stirring, until spices are fragrant and almonds are slightly toasted. Add white wine and cook until liquid evaporates.
- Remove the mixture from heat and puree in a blender with the red peppers and enough water to thin it to a thick sauce, about 1/4 cup. Return to heat and gently heat through.
- Pour the sauce over warm potatoes. Garnish with a drizzle of pomegranate molasses and a drizzle of mayonnaise, and generous sprinkled of parsley. Serve hot.

271. Roasted Root Vegetable And Chicken Tacos With Chili Mayo

Serving: Serves 4 | Prep: | Cook: | Ready in:

Ingredients

- For the tacos:
- 2 large beets, peeled and chopped into 1 inch pieces
- 3-4 large carrots, peeled and chopped into 1 inch pieces

- 2 pounds chicken thighs
- olive oil
- Kosher salt
- freshly ground black pepper
- 6-8 flour tortillas, warmed up
- 1 avocado, sliced thin
- 4 ounces feta
- cilantro for garnish
- For the sauce:
- 1/2 cup mayonnaise
- 2 teaspoons chili powder
- 1/2 teaspoon paprika
- juice from 1/2 a lemon

Direction

- Preheat oven to 425.
- Place vegetables on a baking dish in a single layer, drizzle with olive oil and then sprinkle with salt and pepper. Toss to coat, then bake for 20-25 minutes, until vegetables are tender.
- Meanwhile, heat 2 tablespoons olive oil in a large skillet over medium high heat. Sprinkle chicken thighs with salt and pepper, then transfer to skillet. Cook on each side until nicely browned. Transfer to a cutting board and allow to cool slightly, then shred using two forks.
- While chicken and vegetables are cooking, make the sauce. Combine mayonnaise, chili powder, paprika, and lemon juice in a small bowl and whisk together. Taste and adjust seasoning.
- Assemble tortillas with a little bit of the vegetables, chicken, avocado, and feta. Top with chili mayo and cilantro.

272. Roasted Squash & Cauliflower Salad With Tahini Dressing

Serving: Serves 5 | Prep: | Cook: | Ready in:

Ingredients

- Salad
- 1/2 medium butternut squash, cut into 1/2" dice (about 6 cups)
- 1 small cauliflower, cut into small florets (about 6 cups)
- 2 teaspoons olive oil
- 1 teaspoon each cumin, coriander
- 1/2 teaspoon smoked paprika
- 1 cup chickpeas, drained and rinsed
- 1/2 cup each fresh mint & cilantro, lightly packed
- 1 cup pomegranate seeds
- Tahini Dressing
- 1/4 cup tahini
- 1/4 cup Hellmann's Organic Mayonnaise
- 1/4-1/3 cups water
- 2 tablespoons fresh lemon juice
- 1 garlic clove, minced
- 1/2 teaspoon salt

Direction

- Preheat oven to 400°F.
- Divide squash and cauliflower pieces between two baking trays. Drizzle with olive oil and toss with spices and seasoning. Place in the oven until golden brown and tender, 20 to 25 minutes.
- While vegetables are roasting, make the dressing. Blend together tahini, mayonnaise, 1/4 cup water, lemon juice, garlic and salt until smooth. If dressing seems a bit thick, add a bit more water.
- Put roasted vegetables on a large serving platter. Toss with chickpeas, mint, cilantro and pomegranate seeds. Drizzle with dressing and toss to combine.

273.   Rosemary Cornmeal Crusted Zucchini With Grapefruit Aioli

Serving: Serves 6 | Prep: | Cook: | Ready in:

Ingredients

- Rosemary Cornmeal Crusted Zucchini
- 4 medium zucchini, slice in 1/4 to 1/3-inch rounds
- 1 cup cornmeal
- 1/2 cup whole wheat flour
- sea salt and freshly ground black pepper to taste
- 2 eggs
- extra-virgin olive oil
- 1 tablespoon chopped fresh rosemary leaves
- Grapefruit Aioli
- 1 grapefruit, juice and 1 teaspoon zest
- 1/2 cup canola mayonnaise
- 1/2 cup sour cream

Direction

- Preheat the oven to 425 degrees.
- Mix cornmeal, whole wheat flour, rosemary, sea salt and black pepper. Beat eggs in a small bowl. Dip zucchini into egg and then into rosemary cornmeal.
- Oil a parchment-lined baking sheet with extra-virgin olive oil. Place zucchini on the baking sheet. Bake for about 10 minutes per side, until golden brown.
- Meanwhile, make the grapefruit aioli. In a small bowl, stir together grapefruit juice and zest, mayonnaise, and sour cream.
- Keep grapefruit aioli refrigerated until serving time. Rosemary cornmeal crusted zucchini rounds can be served hot or at room temperature with grapefruit aioli drizzled on top or separate as a dipping sauce.

274.   Ruth Reichl's Diva Of A Grilled Cheese

Serving: Makes 1 sandwich | Prep: | Cook: | Ready in:

Ingredients

- Any combination of shallot, leek, scallions, onion (any color)
- 1 clove garlic
- 1/4 pound cheddar cheese, divided
- Butter
- 2 slices thickly sliced, sturdy sourdough bread
- Mayonnaise

Direction

- Gather a group of shallot, leek, scallions, and onion—as many members of the allium family as you have on hand—and chop them finely into a small heap. Add a minced clove of garlic. Grate a few generous handfuls of the best cheddar you can afford. (Montgomery is particularly appealing), set a little aside, and gently combine the rest with the onion mixture.
- Butter one side of thickly sliced bread and heap as much of the mixture as possible between the slices (butter facing in). Spread a thin layer of mayonnaise on the outside of the bread (this will keep it from scorching on the griddle). Press the reserved grated cheese to the outside of the bread, where it will create a wonderfully crisp and shaggy crust, giving your sandwich an entirely new dimension. (For less mess, it helps to apply the mayonnaise and cheese first on one side only, lay that side on the griddle, and then quickly do the remaining top side while the bottom is sizzling.)
- Fry on a heated nonstick griddle or in a nonstick skillet about 4 minutes a side, until the cheese is softly melted.

275. SPINACH STUFFED CHICKEN BREAST RECIPE: THE ULTIMATE

Serving: Serves 4 | Prep: 0hours10mins | Cook: 0hours20mins | Ready in:

Ingredients

- 4 chicken breasts
- 1,5 cups fresh spinach, chopped
- 1/2 cup cream cheese, softened
- 1/4 cup grated Parmesan
- 2 tablespoons mayonnaise
- 1 teaspoon olive oil
- 1 teaspoon paprika
- salt teaspoons salt
- 1/4 teaspoon garlic powder
- 1/4 teaspoon onion powder
- 1 teaspoon garlic, minced
- 1/2 teaspoon red pepper flakes

Direction

- Preheat oven to 375 °F.
- Spread the chicken breasts onto a cutting board. Use a sharp knife and slice halfway into the side of each breast to create a pocket. That's where the stuffing will go.
- Spread olive oil onto the breasts with your fingers or a brush.
- Mix paprika, garlic powder, onion powder and half a teaspoon of salt in a small bowl. Sprinkle the mixture on both sides of the breasts.
- Mix cream cheese, Parmesan, mayonnaise, chopped spinach, garlic, pepper flakes and the remaining salt in a bow. Stir well.
- Fill the pockets on the chicken breasts with the mixture created in step 5.
- Place the breasts onto a baking dish and bake for 20 minutes, or until you see the breasts turn slightly brown.

276. Salad Nachos

Serving: Serves 6 to 8 | Prep: | Cook: | Ready in:

Ingredients

- Salad Nachos
- 1 bag (13 ounce) tortilla chips

- 1 cup black beans
- 1 cup refried beans (vegetarian if serving this to vegetarians)
- 16 ounces cheese, shredded (I used half pepper jack and half cheddar)
- 1/2 cup white onion, diced
- 4 to 5 cups finely shredded romaine lettuce
- 3/4 cup thinly sliced grape tomatoes (or halved cherry tomatoes)
- 1/4 cup sliced or chopped green olives
- 1 to 2 avocados, diced
- Hot sauce (optional)
- Cllantro-Sour Cream Dressing
- 1   small garlic clove, minced
- 1/3 cup chopped cilantro (small stems are okay)
- 2 tablespoons mayonnaise
- 1/3 cup buttermilk
- 1/3 cup sour cream
- 1 teaspoon fresh lemon juice
- Fine-grain sea salt

Direction

- Combine garlic, cilantro, mayonnaise, buttermilk, sour cream, and lemon juice in a mini processor. Add a pinch of salt and process until smooth. Taste and add more salt if necessary. (An immersion blender would work for this, too!)
- Line a half sheet tray (18 x 13 inches) with aluminum foil and turn on your broiler (or heat oven to 500°F).
- Follow thirschfeld's advice and open your chips over the lined tray from the bottom of the bag rather than the top. This keeps the small broken bits hidden on the bottom. Spread out the chips.
- Sprinkle about half of the cheese over the chips, then sprinkle with black beans, little blobs of refried beans, and the onions. Cover with the rest of the cheese.
- Broil the chips until all of the cheese has melted, 4 to 5 minutes. (This step might take a few more minutes if you're baking them.)
- While you're broiling the chips, add the lettuce, tomatoes, olives, and avocado to a

medium bowl. Toss with about 2/3 of the dressing, then add more dressing if desired and toss again.

- Once the chips are done, remove from the oven and scatter the dressed salad over the top of them. Serve with hot sauce. And plenty of napkins.

277.   Salad Olivier

Serving: Serves 8 to 10 | Prep: | Cook: | Ready in:

Ingredients

- • 1lb of roasted chicken breast (on the bone and with the skin on)
- • 1cup fresh sweet peas, blanched
- • 3 medium potatoes, baked or boiled
- • 3 medium carrots diced into small cubes and blanched in lightly salted water
- • 5 large hard boiled eggs
- • 5-6 medium pickles (kosher dill pickles in brine without vinegar, that is important)
- • Salt & freshly ground black pepper to taste
- • 1 cup of the best quality or homemade Mayonnaise
- • 1 full teaspoon spicy brown mustard
- • About 1 tablespoon of lemon juice or to taste

Direction

- All the vegetables, eggs, pickles, and chicken breast should be diced into the same size small cubes about ¼-inch. Potatoes and chicken should be still worm; they will better absorb the Mayonnaise sauce.
- Salt and pepper the chicken breast, put on a baking sheet; pour a little olive oil over the skin, and rub it in. Roast in a preheated 350 degrees oven for about 40 minutes. Remove from the oven and let it rest and cool for 15 minutes, then remove skin and bones. Boil potatoes unpeeled until fork tender.

- Blanch the peas for 2 minutes; then diced carrots for about 8-10 minutes until al dente. Cook and peel the eggs, peel potatoes and I also always peel the pickles and squeeze-out gently the excess brine.
- When all the vegetables and chicken breast are ready and diced, transfer them to a large bowl, season with salt and pepper. Pour 1 tablespoon olive oil to moisten the ingredients, and separate them. Gently mix to combine.
- In a small bowl whisk together Mayonnaise, mustard, lemon juice into a smooth sauce. Pour ¾ of the sauce over the salad, carefully mix-in, smooth out the top and spread the rest of the sauce. Garnish with chopped chives, fresh peas, and nicely cutout carrots. Now your Russian Salad Olivier is ready to be served!

278. Salami And Blue Cheese Sandwich

Serving: Serves 4 | Prep: | Cook: |Ready in:

Ingredients

- Vinaigrette
- 1 tablespoon french dijon mustard
- 1 clove garlic, minced
- ½ lemon, juice only
- ¼ teaspoons salt
- ? cups extra virgin olive ol
- freshly ground black pepper
- The Sandwich
- 1 loaf crusty chewy bread
- ¼ cups good quality brand mayonnaise
- 2 tablespoons vinaigrette
- 16 slices italian salami
- 4 ounces creamy blue cheese, sliced or crumbled
- 1 large handful arugula mesclun mix
- fresh black pepper and extra virgin olive oil

Direction

- Vinaigrette: Mix the mustard, garlic, lemon juice, salt and pepper in a bowl. Slowly whisk in the olive oil. You want it to be the consistency of thick cream so if it's too thick, add a few drops of water to thin it down.
- The Sandwich
- 1. Slice the bread into ¼' thickness. Lay them on your counter top or chopping board. Spread the mayonnaise on each slice of bread.
- 2. Scatter the arugula mesclun salad over the bread and lightly drizzle the vinaigrette over it. Try to avoid getting the bread wet. The idea is to keep the moist ingredients away from the bread.
- 3. Layer the salami, 4 per sandwich, and the blue cheese onto half of the bread slices. Grind some fresh black pepper and a light drizzle of good quality extra virgin olive oil over the filling.
- 4. Put the sandwiches together without squashing them. They can be assembled a couple of hours ahead of eating which makes them great for a picnic.

279. Salmon BLT's

Serving: Serves 2 | Prep: | Cook: |Ready in:

Ingredients

- 4 slices whole wheat bread, toasted
- 2 6 oz salmon fillets, skin on
- 3 scallions, roughly chopped
- 1/2 tablespoon capers
- small handful italian parsley, chopped
- juice from 1 lemon
- zest from 1 lemon
- 3/4 cup mayonnaise
- salt and pepper to taste
- olive oil
- 6 slices habanero bacon
- 2 thick slices of tomato
- 2 large lettuce leaves

Direction

- Start by making your lemon-caper mayo. In a bowl of a food processor, combine scallions, capers, parsley, lemon juice, lemon zest, and mayonnaise. Pulse a few times until everything is combined well. Season with salt and pepper to taste and transfer to small bowl.
- Light a charcoal grill under medium high heat. Rub small amount of olive oil onto salmon fillets. Season with salt and pepper. Spread desired amount of lemon mayo on salmon fillets. Grill salmon fillets, skin side down first, on direct heat for about 3-4 minutes per side.
- To assemble sandwiches, place a good amount of leftover lemon mayo onto bottom slice of toast. Place lettuce leaf atop mayo and add salmon fillet. Top with tomato and 3 sliced of bacon. Close sandwich with remaining piece of toast and enjoy!

---

280.   Salmon Burger Avocado Tartar Sauce

Serving: Makes 4 | Prep: | Cook: | Ready in:

Ingredients

- 1   canned Pink Salmon, in water, chunk style, skinless boneless (5oz) drained
- 1   Egg
- 1/2 cup Panko
- 2 tablespoons All Purpose Flour
- 1/2 cup Minced Onion
- 1   Garlic clove, grated
- 1 tablespoon Parmesan Cheese
- 1 tablespoon Mayonnaise
- 1 teaspoon Oregano Leaves
- 1 tablespoon Minced Parley
- 2 tablespoons Olive Oil
- 1/2 Avocado
- 1   Boiled Egg, chopped
- 5 tablespoons Mayonnaise
- 2 tablespoons Milk

- 1 teaspoon Lemon Juice
- 1 tablespoon Dijon Mustard
- 4 pieces American Cheese
- 4   Plain Bagels

Direction

- In a bowl, beat egg and add canned salmon, panko, flour, minced onion, grated garlic, parmesan cheese, mayonnaise, oregano and minced parsley. Mix all together until well blended. Form into patties
- In a skillet, heat olive oil and cook patties until browns. Let cool
- Make avocado tartar sauce. Scoop avocado pulp and mash in a bowl. Add mayonnaise, boiled eggs, milk, lemon juice and Dijon mustard. Mix well
- Put American cheese onto the cut sides of the bagel spread mayonnaise lightly, salmon patties and spread avocado tartar sauce. Cover with the other half of the bagel.

---

281.   Salmon Tacos With Miso Broccoli Slaw And Apricot Salsa

Serving: Serves 4 | Prep: | Cook: | Ready in:

Ingredients

- 1 pound boneless salmon fillets, cut into 1 inch strips, sprinkled with salt and pepper
- 1 tablespoon olive oil
- 8-12   corn tortillas
- 2 cups broccoli slaw (about 1/2 of a 12 oz package)
- 1/2 cup red onion, thinly sliced
- 10   radishes, sliced
- 1 tablespoon miso
- 2 tablespoons mayonnaise
- 1 tablespoon rice vinegar
- 1 teaspoon sugar
- 1 tsp   freshly grated ginger
- 2 tablespoons sesame seeds
- 1 cup fresh apricots (about 8), halved & pitted

- 2 jalepenos, seeds removed
- 1/4 red onion
- 1/4 cup cilantro
- juice of 1/2 lime
- 1/2 teaspoon salt

Direction

- To heat the tortillas, pour 1/2-inch water into the bottom of the steamer that is lined with a clean, heavy kitchen towel. Lay the tortillas on the towel and fold the edges of the towel over the tortillas to cover them. Cover the steamer with the lid and bring the water to a boil. Let the water boil for only 1 minute, then turn off the heat and let the tortillas stand in the steamer covered.
- Combined the miso, mayonnaise, rice vinegar, sugar and ginger together in a bowl to make the dressing for the broccoli slaw and set aside.
- Put broccoli slaw, sliced onions, radishes and sesame seeds into a bowl. Toss to combine and set aside.
- Put apricots, jalapenos, onion, cilantro, lime juice and salt into the bowl of a food processor and pulse until the ingredients are chopped to a desired consistency, about 20-30 pulses.
- Heat the olive oil in a pan on high until it is almost smoking. Carefully place salmon pieces into the pan, skin side down. Cook for about 2-3 minutes and then shake gently to loosen the salmon from the pan. Flip the salmon pieces and cook the other side for 2-3 minutes. Remove from pan and set aside on a plate.
- Add the dressing to the slaw mixture and set aside.
- To assemble the tacos, put a piece of salmon on each tortilla and top with the slaw and salsa.

282. Savory Sausage Breakfast Cake

Serving: Serves 8 - 9 | Prep: | Cook: | Ready in:

Ingredients

- 1 pound ground pork sausage
- 1/2 cup chopped onion
- 1 cup finely grated cheddar cheese
- 1 teaspoon chopped fresh sage leaves
- 1 egg, lightly beaten
- 1 cup all-purpose flour
- 1 teaspoon baking powder
- 1/2 teaspoon baking soda
- 3/4 cup milk
- 1/4 cup mayonnaise

Direction

- Preheat the oven to 400 degrees. Grease an 8 by 8 inch baking dish.
- Break the sausage into pieces and place in a skillet. Cook the sausage until it is beginning to brown and has rendered some of its fat, breaking it into small pieces as you cook. Add the onion and continue to cook until the sausage is browned and no longer pink in the middle and the onions are soft. Drain well and leave to cool slightly.
- Place the cooled sausage and onion into a bowl and add the cheddar cheese and sage. Toss to combine. Add the lightly beaten egg and stir to mix everything together well.
- In another bowl, stir the flour, baking powder and baking soda together with a fork. Add the milk and mayonnaise and stir with the fork to combine. Pour 1/2 of the batter into the prepared pan and spread to cover the bottom. Spread the sausage and cheese mixture evenly over the batter in the pan, then spread the remaining batter over the top. Do the best you can, but it will not cover the top of the sausage mixture and that's fine.
- Bake the cake for 20 – 25 minutes until firm and golden. Serve warm.

283. Savory Southern Deviled Ham

Serving: Makes 3 cups | Prep: | Cook: | Ready in:

Ingredients

- 1/2 pound diced cooked ham, about 2 cups (not from the deli)
- 1/3 cup diced white onion
- 1 stalk celery, diced
- 1/3 cup mayonnaise, or more as needed
- 2 tablespoons dijon mustard
- 1 tablespoon worcestershire sauce
- 1 tablespoon brown sugar
- 2 tablespoons hot sauce or more to your taste, such as tabasco or your favorite
- 1 tablespoon whole grain mustard
- zest of one lemon + 1 tablespoon juice

Direction

- Add the ham, onion, celery, Dijon mustard and 1/3 cup mayonnaise to the bowl of a food processor, pulse several times until ham is a spreadable consistency. If the mixture is too dry add 2-3 more tablespoons of mayonnaise and blend again. Add the lemon zest, brown sugar and hot sauce and blend again until well combined.
- Transfer to a bowl and stir in the whole grain mustard and 1 tablespoon lemon juice. Serve as a sandwich spread or on crackers.

284. Scallop Mousse With Fresh Basil

Serving: Makes 4 to 6 plated first course servings -- (or about 20 "baby" scallops [in madeleine pans]for passed hors d'oeuvre, or fills one copper scallop shell for a stationary selection on a cocktail buffet) | Prep: 0hours45mins | Cook: 1hours30mins |Ready in:

Ingredients

- 1 1/4 pounds dry pack scallops (may be sea, bay or cape scallops), poached and cooled
- 1 tablespoon chopped fresh chives
- 1 large shallot, chopped
- 3 tablespoons chopped fresh basil
- 1 packet unflavored gelatin, dissolved in 1/4 cup dry French Vermouth
- 3/4 cup homemade mayonnaise made with fresh lime juice
- 2/3 cup crème fraîche (can sub sour cream)
- 1/4 teaspoon fine sea salf
- a few grinds of fresh white pepper
- 6 drops hot pepper sauce (I use Louisiana Hot Sauce)

Direction

- In the food processor fitted with the metal blade, chop the basil fine. Remove and set aside.
- With the motor running, drop the chives and shallot through the feed tube, and process until very finely chopped. Add mayonnaise and pulse three times to mix. Now add all the ingredients except the basil and the gelatin mixture, and pulse five or six times to incorporate well, then process until smooth.
- Add basil and gelatin mixture, and pulse several times, to blend thoroughly.
- Pour or spoon mixture into the prepared mold(s) you have chosen. [I use standard Madeleine pans for plated first course, miniature Madeleine pans for the really tiny scallops that fit on crackers.]
- Chill until firm, about 1 1/2 hours minimum for the large mold. (The "babies" take almost no time at all!)
- Unmold onto appropriate serving dish, and garnish with fresh basil leaves or sprigs. (I like to serve the "babies" on a Bremner wafer, on top of a small basil leaf.)
- Wine Tip: The wine that consistently compliments this mousse to perfection is Vision Cellars' California White – a juicy blend of Sauvignon Blanc and Pinot Gris. If you'd

like a sparkler, I'd choose Iron Horse Wedding Cuvée, my favorite domestic bubbly.

285.   Scallop Tataki

Serving: Serves 4 | Prep: | Cook: |Ready in:

Ingredients

- 6 very fresh large scallops
- 4 tablespoons sesame seeds, black and/or white
- 2 teaspoons wasabi paste
- 1 tablespoon lime zest
- 1 tablespoon finely chopped chives
- 1 tablespoon lime juice
- 1 teaspoon toasted sesame oil
- 1 tablespoon sugar
- sunflower or vegetable oil
- Sushi ginger
- Good quality mayonnaise

Direction

- Roll each scallop in the sesame seeds until coated.
- Wrap each scallop tightly in cling film and chill in the fridge for 45 minutes.
- Spray a frying pan with a little oil and put it on a high heat.
- Pan fry each whole scallop for exactly 30 seconds, turning constantly with a tongs so it is lightly seared on all sides but still basically raw inside (this is why they need to be very fresh).
- Put the scallops on a plate and put in the freezer for 15 minutes (don't leave them in longer or they will freeze, this is just to stop them cooking further)
- Meanwhile, mix the wasabi and mayonnaise together in a bowl.
- Mix the lime zest and chive together in a bowl.
- Mix the soya sauce, lime juice, sugar and sesame oil together in a saucepan and heat gently on a low heat to combine.

- Remove the scallops from the freezer and slice each scallop so you are left with 4-6 thin circular slices.
- Divide the scallop slices between four plates, fanning them out.
- Sprinkle the scallop slices with the mixed chive and lime zest, and serve with some sushi ginger and a dollop of the wasabi mayonnaise.

286.   Scallop And Apple Tartare

Serving: Serves 2-4 as an appetizer or many more as an hors d'oeuvre | Prep: | Cook: |Ready in:

Ingredients

- 1 tablespoon mayonnaise
- heaping 1/4 teaspoon chili sauce, like sriracha
- 10 drops toasted sesame oil
- 6 dry large sea scallops, foot removed
- 1 scallion, trimmed, white and green parts thinly sliced
- 1/2 firm apple, cored (I used a pink lady)
- 2-3 shakes shichimi togarashi (Asian 7-spice blend), plus more for serving
- 1/2 juicy lime

Direction

- In small bowl, stir together mayonnaise, chili sauce and sesame oil.
- Cut scallops crosswise into three layers; cube into 1/2" pieces. Peel apple; dice into 1/4" pieces. Add scallops, scallion and apple to mayonnaise mixture; stir, using a rubber spatula, to combine.
- Squeeze lime over scallops. Add the shichimi togarashi and a pinch of kosher salt; stir to combine. Adjust all seasonings, if necessary.
- Transfer decoratively to plate and top with an extra sprinkle of the shichimi togarashi. The scallops can also be served in small spoons, on

a very crisp thin cracker or over sliced cucumber. It should be served immediately.

287. Seafood Salad Stuffed Avocado

Serving: Serves 4 | Prep: | Cook: | Ready in:

Ingredients

- 1 pound Crab and Lobster Meat (you can also use one or the other)
- 5 tablespoons Mayonnaise
- 1/2   Medium Onion, diced
- 2   Medium Avocado
- 1 1/2 teaspoons Salt
- 1 1/2 teaspoons Pepper
- 1   Medium Tomato, chopped
- 1   Cucumber, skinned and diced
- 1   Lemon, juiced
- 1 tablespoon Olive Oil
- 1/2 teaspoon Garlic, minced

Direction

- Mix Crab, Lobster, 4 Tablespoons of Mayonnaise and Onion. Cover and Refrigerate
- Lightly Season Avocado, Cucumber and Tomato with 1 teaspoon of Salt and 1 teaspoon of Pepper.
- Grill Avocado (flat side down) until slightly warm with grill marks on the flesh of the avocado.
- Stuff each Avocado Half with 1/4 of the Seafood Salad Mixture and arrange on plates with Diced Cucumber and Tomato.
- Whisk Together Lemon, Olive Oil, Garlic, Remaining Mayonnaise, Remaining Pepper and Remaining Salt. Pour over Stuffed Avocado, Tomato and Cucumber. Serve Chilled.

288. Sergey's Mayonnaise

Serving: Makes 1 jar mayonnaise | Prep: 0hours10mins | Cook: 0hours0mins | Ready in:

Ingredients

- 1 large egg
- 1 tablespoon sugar
- 1 teaspoon salt
- 2 tablespoons white vinegar
- 1 tablespoon Dijon mustard
- 1 cup neutral oil (like vegetable or canola)

Direction

- Place the egg, sugar, salt, vinegar, and mustard in the bowl of a blender or food processor. Pulse the ingredients to combine.
- With the blender or food processor running, slowly drizzle a thin stream of oil into the other ingredients. It may look like a runny, oily mess at first, but don't stop.
- By the time you pour in 3/4 of the oil, you will see it start to thicken. Keep adding the oil in a thin stream until you have added all of the oil.
- You can use the mayonnaise right away or transfer it into a storage container. It can be stored in the refrigerator, covered, for up to a week.

289. Serious Potato Salad

Serving: Serves 16 | Prep: 0hours30mins | Cook: 0hours30mins | Ready in:

Ingredients

- 4 pounds potatoes
- 2 tablespoons sugar
- 2 tablespoons kosher salt
- 7 tablespoons rice wine vinegar, divided
- 1 1/4 cups mayonnaise
- 1 cup diced red onion
- 3/4 cup diced celery

- 6 scallions, sliced thinly
- 3 tablespoons whole grain mustard
- To Taste: salt and pepper

Direction

- Peel and cut potatoes in 3/4 inch cubes.
- Place in large pot with 2 quarts cold water, 2 tbsps. sugar, 2 tbsps. salt and 2 tbsps. rice vinegar. Bring to a boil over high heat, then simmer until just tender, approximately 12 minutes.
- Drain and spread out on rimmed baking sheet in single layer. Sprinkle with 3 tbsps. of rice vinegar. Let cool on counter for 30 minutes.
- In a large bowl place 2 tbsps. rice wine vinegar, mayonnaise, mustard, red onion, celery and scallions. Mix thoroughly.
- Add potatoes. Coat with sauce, season to taste with salt and pepper. Refrigerate for at least 2 hours.

290. Shakshuka Sandwich

Serving: Serves 1 | Prep: | Cook: | Ready in:

Ingredients

- 2 slices olive bread, lightly toasted
- 1 teaspoon olive oil
- 1/4 onion, chopped
- 1/4 green pepper, chopped
- 1 clove garlic, minced
- 1/4 teaspoon ground cumin
- 1/4 teaspoon hot smoked paprika
- 4 ounces chopped tomato (can use canned, drained)
- 1 large egg
- salt and pepper
- 1 ounce crumbled feta cheese
- 1.5 tablespoons harissa sauce
- 1.5 tablespoons good quality mayonnaise
- boston lettuce

Direction

- Add 1 tsp of olive oil to a small non-stick pan, bring to medium heat.
- Add onions and green pepper to oiled pan along with spices. Cook for several minutes until vegetables have softened. Add tomatoes and cook until liquids have reduced somewhat (the time will depend on whether you have used fresh or canned tomatoes)
- When vegetables have cooked down, crack the large egg over top, add a pinch of sea salt and a grind of pepper. Cover and cook for a minute or two.
- Remove cover from pan and sprinkle the feta over the egg. Return cover and cook for an additional 3-4 minutes, until egg yolk is set and feta has melted slightly. Remove from heat.
- Mix harissa sauce and mayonnaise together and spread on both slices of olive bread. Place boston lettuce leaves on one slice of bread.
- Spoon egg and tomato mixture onto the slice of bread without the lettuce. Press remaining slice of bread to make the sandwich. Plate up and enjoy!

291. Sheet Pan Bacon And Egg Breakfast Sandwiches With Overnight Focaccia

Serving: Makes 12 sandwiches | Prep: | Cook: | Ready in:

Ingredients

- Overnight Focaccia
- 4 cups (512 g) all-purpose flour
- 2 teaspoons kosher salt
- 1 teaspoon instant yeast
- 2 cups lukewarm water, made by mixing 1/2 cup boiling water with 1 1/2 cups cold water
- 4 tablespoons olive oil
- sea salt
- Egg Sandwich
- 1 to 1.5 pounds bacon
- 12 eggs

- kosher salt and pepper to taste
- splash cream
- 4 ounces grated Cheddar cheese
- 1/4 to 1/2 cups finely chopped chives
- lettuce
- hot sauce, mayonnaise, and other condiments for serving

Direction

- Overnight Focaccia
- In a large bowl, whisk together the flour, salt, and instant yeast. Add the water. Using a rubber spatula, mix until the water is absorbed and the ingredients form a sticky dough ball. (If you need to use active dry yeast instead, proof it in the lukewarm water with a pinch of sugar first for about 10 minutes, until foamy, before adding to the other ingredients.)
- Cover the bowl with a damp tea towel or plastic wrap and set inside your refrigerator. (See notes for leaving dough on the counter if you don't have space in the refrigerator and for making non-overnight focaccia.)
- The following morning (or 8 to 10 hours later), remove the bowl from the fridge. Line a rimmed sheet pan with parchment paper or coat with nonstick cooking spray. Pour 3 tablespoons oil on the sheet pan. Using two forks, deflate the dough by releasing it from the sides of the bowl and pulling it toward the center. Rotate the bowl in quarter turns as you deflate, turning the mass into a rough ball. Use the forks to lift the dough onto the prepared sheet pan. Roll the dough ball in the oil to coat it all over. Let it rest without touching it for 1 hour.
- Set a rack in the middle of the oven and preheat it to 425°F. With lightly greased hands, press down on the dough, using all 10 fingers to dimple and stretch the dough outward. Pull gently on the ends and stretch them toward the corners of the sheet pan. When the dough begins to resist being stretched, let it rest for 5 minutes, then stretch it again, continuing until it fits most of the sheet pan.
- Drizzle the remaining tablespoon of oil over the surface of the dough. Sprinkle all over with sea salt. Let stand another 20 minutes, then transfer the sheet pan to the oven and bake for 20 to 25 minutes, until the underside is golden and crisp. Remove the pan from the oven, and transfer the focaccia to a cooling rack. Let it cool for at least an hour before cutting.
- To cut the focaccia for the slab sandwich, trim off the very outer edges—this exposes the crumb, which makes it easier to halve. I like to start the halving process by cutting through each corner, then running the serrated knife through the short end until I get to the midway point, then starting from the other short end until I get to the midway point. A sharp, serrated knife is helpful. Try to keep your knife as parallel to the bread as possible, and I find if I hug the top layer as opposed to aiming for the center, I get a more even cut.
- Egg Sandwich
- Preheat the oven to 425°F. Lay the bacon on a sheet pan. If you are using 1.5 pounds bacon, you will have to overlap pieces and lay pieces on top of one another to start, but don't worry, they will shrink. Cook 10 minutes, remove pan from oven, and, using forks, spread out/separate the slices of bacon. (This is unnecessary if you are using 1 pound of bacon only.) Return pan to the oven, cook for 10 more minutes, remove pan from the oven, and separate the slices again if necessary. Return pan to the oven and cook for 5 more minutes or until the slices are looking crispy. Remove pan from the oven and transfer crisp slices to a paper-towel lined plate. If necessary, drain off some of the fat, and return the pan to the oven one last time to crisp up the remaining pieces. Transfer bacon to plate.
- Turn oven off to let it cool down faster. You can leave the door open, too, to expedite the cooling. You need it to be at 300°F. Grease a half sheet pan (I use a cheap, nonstick Baker's Secret sheet pan purchased from a grocery store—it measures 11x16.5 inches) very well with butter. Crack all 12 eggs in a big bowl, add salt and pepper and the splash of cream,

then whisk until well combined. Add the chives, and gently fold until mixed. Pour the mixture into the prepared pan. Sprinkle with cheese evenly. Bake until the eggs are just set, about 15 minutes.

- Transfer the bottom half of the focaccia slab onto a cutting board. When the eggs have cooked, use an offset spatula to loosen them from the pan, then transfer to the bread. Trim off any excess, overhanging eggs (and save! see notes above). Lay the bacon on top. Scatter the lettuce on top. Top with the top half of bread. Cut the sandwich into 12 pieces (2 cuts through the short end; 3 cuts through the long end). Serve with hot sauce, mayonnaise and any other condiments you like.

292. Shiso Slaw

Serving: Serves 4, if you can find it in your heart to share this . . .. | Prep: | Cook: |Ready in:

Ingredients

- ½ of a medium napa cabbage, finely sliced
- Pinch of salt
- ¼ cup finely sliced green shiso leaves
- 1-2 teaspoons chopped Thai basil (optional)
- 1 large tart apple (I used a Granny Smith), cut into medium julienne (without peeling)
- 1/4 cup apple cider vinegar
- 2 tablespoons organic mayonnaise (regular or vegan), or more to taste
- Pinch of sugar
- Salt and pepper to taste

Direction

- In a large bowl, toss the cabbage with a pinch of salt.
- In a small bowl, toss the julienned apple with the vinegar.
- Reserving the vinegar, add the apple pieces to the bowl with the cabbage.

- Add the shiso, and Thai basil, if using, and toss well.
- Stir the sugar into the vinegar. Then, whisk the mayonnaise into the vinegar; pour over the salad. Toss well to combine. When you think you're done, keep going for another 10 or 12 strokes. It may not look like much dressing, but you really don't need a whole lot.
- Let it sit for at least an hour; then, toss the slaw well. Check for salt and pepper and correct, if necessary.
- Toss again before serving.
- I hope you try this, and like it.

293. Shrimp Rice Paper Roll

Serving: Makes 6 rice paper rolls | Prep: | Cook: |Ready in:

Ingredients

- Zesty Shrimp Filling
- 1/4 cup mayonnaise
- 1 tablespoon chopped Italian flat leaf parsley
- 2 teaspoons wasabi paste
- 1 teaspoon soy sauce
- 1 teaspoon fresh lime juice
- 1/2 teaspoon lime zest
- 8oz   cooked shrimp, coarsely chopped
- 6   round rice paper wrappers (8.5-inch diameter)
- 6   romaine lettuce leaves
- 1   large carrot, peeled and julienned
- 1   cucumber, peeled and julienned
- 1   avocado, thinly sliced
- 2 tablespoons chopped fresh basil
- Wasabi Dipping Sauce
- ¼ cups mayonnaise
- 2 teaspoons soy sauce
- 1 teaspoon wasabi paste
- 1 teaspoon fresh lime juice

Direction

- For the shrimp rice paper rolls, in a medium bowl, combine mayonnaise, parsley, wasabi paste, soy sauce, lime juice and lime zest. Stir well to combine. Add shrimp and mix together. Place 1 rice paper sheet in a shallow bowl of hot water just until softened, about 1 minute. Lay rice paper sheet on a damp tea towel. Place lettuce leaf down the center of the rice sheet, leaving a 1-inch border at the top and bottom. Place 2 heaping tablespoons of the shrimp mixture lengthwise on the lettuce leaf, followed by carrots, cucumber, avocado and a sprinkling of basil. Fold up the bottom 1-inch border of rice paper placing it over the filling. Fold in the right side, followed by the left side and then the top, forming a tight cylinder. Repeat with remaining rice paper sheets and filling. Serve with dipping sauce.
- For the dipping sauce, in small bowl, whisk together mayonnaise, soy sauce, wasabi paste and lime juice. Serve with rice paper rolls

- Line a baking sheet with parchment paper.
- Arrange half of the tortillas in a single layer over the parchment paper. Divide shredded cheese evenly among the tortillas and top with a second tortilla. Bake for about 5 minutes, until tortillas are warm and cheese has melted.
- Meanwhile, heat olive oil in a large skillet over medium heat until hot. Add shrimp; cook and stir until shrimp are pink and just cooked through, 2 or 3 minutes. Remove from heat. Squeeze lime half evenly over shrimp and season to taste with salt and freshly ground black pepper.
- To make the spicy slaw, add mayonnaise, sour cream and sriracha to the bottom of a medium bowl and whisk to combine. Add shredded cabbage and toss to coat.
- Top each double tortilla shell with 3 shrimp then divide the slaw evenly among the tacos. Add a sprig of cilantro to each taco if desired. Serve.

294. Shrimp Tacos With Spicy Sriracha Slaw

Serving: Serves 2 | Prep: | Cook: | Ready in:

Ingredients

- For the tacos:
- 8   small flour or corn tortillas
- 2 ounces mozzarella cheese, shredded
- 1 tablespoon olive oil
- 12   medium shrimp, peeled and deveined
- 1/2   lime
- For the spicy slaw:
- 2 tablespoons mayonnaise
- 2 tablespoons sour cream
- 2 teaspoons sriracha sauce (or more)
- 2 cups shredded green cabbage
- several sprigs of cilantro (optional)

Direction

- Preheat oven to 350°F.

295. Shrimp And Crabmeat Bake

Serving: Serves 4-6 | Prep: | Cook: | Ready in:

Ingredients

- 2 pounds raw cleaned shrimp
- 1 pound lump crab meat
- 1   can cream of shrimp or cream of mushroom soup (I use cream of shrimp)
- 1 cup mayonnaise
- 1   small onion chopped or grated (I like to grate mine)
- 1   small green pepper
- 1   stick of butter
- 2   sleeves of Ritz crackers crushed
- salt and pepper to taste
- Old Bay Seasoning to taste

Direction

- Preheat oven to 350 degrees. Spray 9x12 baking dish or casserole dish with nonstick spray.
- In a large bowl mix shrimp, crabmeat, onion, green pepper or you can use red pepper, with soup and 1/2 can water, mayonnaise, salt pepper and Old Bay.
- Put in bottom of baking dish.
- Mix melted butter and crushed Ritz crackers, and sprinkle on top of mixture.
- Bake at 350 degrees for 45 mins or less.
- Serve over hot rice or pasta.

296. Shrimp Smoked Salmon Mousse

Serving: Serves about 3 cups | Prep: | Cook: | Ready in:

Ingredients

- 1 packet unflavored gelatine
- 1 cup plain non-fat yogurt
- 1/2 cup mayonnaise
- 1/4 pound smoked salmon scraps
- 1/4 cup red onion, coursely chopped
- 3/4 cup cooked shrimp, coursely chopped
- 1/2 teaspoon lemon juice
- 1 egg white
- 1 teaspoon dried dill weed

Direction

- Soften gelatin. In a medium size bowl containing 1/4 cup cold water.
- Add 1/2 cup hot water. Stir until gelatin is dissolved. Then stir in the yogurt and mayonnaise.
- Refrigerate until slightly gelled.
- Meanwhile, in food processor, chop onions and smoked salmon until fine. Then add shrimp and chop briefly, but do not puree. (The shrimp should be lumpy) Stir in lemon juice and dill.
- When yogurt mixture is jiggly, remove from fridge and whip it with an electric hand mixer.

- Whip egg white separately until stiff.
- Mix/fold all ingredients and pour into an oiled 3-cup fish-shaped mold, or individual molds.
- Chill until set.
- Unmold onto a serving dish, garnish with fresh dill, and serve with toasted baguette slices or crackers.

297. Simple Grilled Swordfish Steak

Serving: Serves 4-6 | Prep: 0hours5mins | Cook: 0hours15mins | Ready in:

Ingredients

- 2 pounds Swordfish
- 6 teaspoons Mayonnaise
- 2 lemons, halved
- 1 pinch Kosher salt
- 1 pinch Fresh cracked pepper

Direction

- Plan on 6-8oz. of swordfish per person. Heat the grill to medium-high heat.
- Rinse and pat dry the swordfish. On one side of the steak spread 3 teaspoon of the mayonnaise and sprinkle 1-2 pinches of kosher salt and 1-2 pinches of freshly cracked black pepper. Repeat this on the other side.
- Place the swordfish on the grill and grill it for 7 minutes per side. At the very end you can grill it for an additional 30 seconds per side to create a crosshatch pattern if desired. Remove from heat, divide swordfish amongst plates for serving. Give everyone half a lemon to squeeze over their fish. Feast!

298. Simple Lobster Rolls

Serving: Serves 4 | Prep: 0hours0mins | Cook: 0hours0mins | Ready in:

Ingredients

- 1 pound lobster meat (a 1 pound lobster has about 1/4 pound meat)
- 1/2 cup melted butter, divided
- 1/2 cup mayonnaise
- 1 dill pickle, finely chopped
- juice of 1/2 a lemon
- 1/4 red onion, finely chopped
- 1 tablespoon parsley, finely chopped
- 4 split-top frankfurter rolls (see below for substitute)

Direction

- First, you need to cook your lobster. I just used tails and claws for this recipe (I did not have a full, live lobster). Either way, live or not, bring a large pot of water to a boil, then drop in your lobster or lobster pieces. Boil for 10 minutes, until the shells are bright red, then remove from the water. If you have a full lobster, twist off the tails and claws and remove the meat. Discard the intestinal vein that runs along the length of each lobster tail. Discard the body. Chill the meat in a clean bowl, covered, in the refrigerator, for about 30 minutes.
- Combine 1/4 cup of butter, 1/2 cup of mayonnaise, pickles, red onion, lemon juice, parsley and black pepper in a medium sized bowl. Add in the chilled lobster meat and toss lightly to combine. Taste and add any additional salt, if needed.
- Toast your frankfurter rolls*, then spread evenly with the remaining melted butter. Fill each roll with the lobster mixture and serve.
- *If you can't find split-top rolls, you can simply slice off a bit of the side of regular hot dog buns to give them the same look as the split-top rolls.

299. Smoked Salmon With Honey Mustard Sauce Blobs

Serving: Serves 2 | Prep: | Cook: | Ready in:

Ingredients

- 4 slices multi-grain bread
- 4 teaspoons cream cheese
- 4 slices smoked salmon
- 1 tablespoon chopped dill
- freshly grounded black pepper
- freshly squeezed lemon juice
- 2 tablespoons mayonnaise (heaped)
- 1 teaspoon Dijon mustard
- 1 teaspoon fluid honey

Direction

- Spread the cream cheese over the bread slices.
- Lay a slice of smoked salmon on each creamed bread cut.
- Sprinkle with lemon juice, black pepper and dill weeds.
- In a small bowl mix well mayonnaise, mustard and honey.
- Add one blob of honey-mustard-mayo mix on top of each salmon-bread slice.

300. Smoked Whitefish Deviled Eggs (Dibbuk* Eggs)

Serving: Serves 4-6 | Prep: | Cook: | Ready in:

Ingredients

- 4 Hardboiled eggs
- 6 tablespoons Smoked whitefish salad (best quality, or homemade)
- 1 teaspoon Chopped fresh dill
- 1 teaspoon Prepared white horseradish (or to taste)
- 2 teaspoons Mayonnaise (optional)

Direction

- Halve the eggs lengthwise, and scrape the yolks into a bowl. Mash well.
- Stir the whitefish salad into the mashed yolks. If the mixture seems too thick, add mayonnaise to loosen it a bit. Mix in the dill, and horseradish to taste - start with a little bit - and blend well.
- Mound the mixture into the egg white halves. If you're fancy, pipe it in. Sprinkle a little chopped dill, or chives, on top. Refrigerate, covered, until ready to serve.

---

301.   Smoky Sweetcorn Tostadas

Serving: Makes 12 | Prep: | Cook: | Ready in:

Ingredients

- 2 corn on the cob
- 4 wheat tortillas
- sunflower oil
- 2 spring onions
- 80 grams mayonnaise
- 1/2 teaspoon smoky paprika powder
- 2 limes
- 4 teaspoons parmesan, grated
- fresh coriander, chopped
- salt and pepper

Direction

- Put the corn on the cob into a saucepan with boiling, unsalted water. Cover and cook for 8 minutes.
- Meanwhile, cut out small tostada rounds by pushing down an 8cm serving ring or glass onto each tortilla – you should get three tostadas per tortilla.
- Over the base of a frying pan with sunflower oil and heat the oil until a piece of leftover tortilla dropped into it starts sizzling right away. Fry the tostada rounds in batches for approximately 1 minute each, until they're golden. Drain on kitchen paper and set aside.

- After 8 minutes, drain the corn on the cob.
- Drain the sunflower oil from the frying pan, leaving a thin film of oil for frying the cooked corn on the cob. Put back on the heat and fry the corn on the cob on all sides until they have some lightly charred patches and look like they've just come from a barbecue. Leave to cool for 5 minutes.
- Meanwhile, trim the spring onions and cut into thin slices.
- In a small bowl, mix the mayonnaise with the smoky paprika powder and set aside.
- Place a soup bowl upside into a large mixing bowl, so that it sits like a cupola inside the bowl. Place one corn on the cob onto the platform of the soup bowl and cut down alongside the corn on the cob, so that the corn kernels fall down into the bowl. Alternatively, place the corn on the cob on a chopping board and cut the kernels off on there – this might be messier than using the bowl trick.
- Slice one lime in half and squeeze half the juice into the bowl with the sweetcorn. Add the spring onion slices and season with salt and pepper to taste.
- Lay out the crisp tostadas on a serving plate and top each tostada with a portion of sweetcorn. Then, top with a dollop of smoky mayonnaise, and sprinkle with parmesan and coriander
- Cut the remaining lime into wedges and serve with the tostadas.
- TIP: The tostadas taste just as good with cold sweetcorn, so you could prepare everything in advance and assemble the tostadas when your guests arrive.

---

302.   Southern Deviled Egg Salad

Serving: Serves 8 | Prep: 0hours0mins | Cook: 0hours0mins | Ready in:

Ingredients

- 1 dozen eggs, boiled and peeled
- 1/3 cup mayonnaise (preferably Duke's)
- 3 tablespoons heaping, sweet relish (preferably Mount Olive)
- 1 tablespoon prepared yellow mustard
- 1 tablespoon grated onion
- 1 teaspoon white vinegar
- 1/2 cup salted sunflower seeds
- 1 teaspoon paprika

Direction

- Cut peeled boiled eggs in half. Scoop out the yolks and place them in a large bowl. Set egg whites aside.
- Once all the yolks have been scooped out, add mayonnaise, relish, mustard, grated onion, vinegar, and paprika to the bowl. Whisk vigorously until the yolks are broken up and mixture is somewhat creamy, the texture similar to ricotta.
- Roughly chop egg whites. Add to bowl with mayo-mustard mixture. Toss with a wooden spoon until egg whites are coated. Let sit for at least 30 minutes and up to overnight.
- When ready to serve, sprinkle with paprika-covered sunflower seeds. To make, simply combine seeds, paprika, and a drop of oil in a small frying pan or cast iron skillet. Heat over medium-low heat, shaking and tossing constantly until seeds are covered and paprika fragrant. Let cool.
- Serve by itself, on a sandwich, or with toast points or crackers.

303. Speck And Mozzarella Baguette With Homemade Mayonnaise

Serving: Serves 4 | Prep: | Cook: |Ready in:

Ingredients

- Homemade Mayonnaise
- 2 egg yolks, at room temperature
- pinch salt
- 1 cup canola oil
- 2 tablespoons lemon juice
- Sandwich Assembly
- 1/4 pound Speck
- 1 pound fresh mozzarella
- Homemade mayonnaise
- 1 Large Baguette
- Freshly cracked black pepper

Direction

- Homemade Mayonnaise
- Using a hand or stand mixer on medium speed, beat the egg yolks and salt until the yolks turn pale yellow and thick. With the mixer still running, very slowly add the canola oil a little at a time. Wait until the oil that you added in has been incorporated until adding more. Continue adding oil until the mixture becomes very thick. Add 1 teaspoon of lemon juice and continue beating. This will help to thin out the sauce a little. Add more oil, making sure to stop from time to time to make sure the sauce is absorbing the oil. When it becomes very thick again, add more lemon juice to thin out. Continue alternating between oil and lemon juice until all the oil has been incorporated and the mixture is at the desired consistency. Taste for salt...it will most likely need it!
- Sandwich Assembly
- Split baguette down the middle. Spread homemade mayonnaise on each side of the bread. Slice mozzarella into rounds of desired thickness and layer on top of the baguette. Liberally pepper the surface of the mozzarella, then arrange the speck on top of that. Cut into four sandwiches and enjoy!

304. Spicy Deviled Eggs

Serving: Serves 8-10 | Prep: | Cook: |Ready in:

Ingredients

- 10 large eggs
- 1/4 cup mayonnaise
- 1 tablespoon Sriracha Sauce
- 3 cornichons, minced
- 4 ounces goat cheese, at room temperature
- 2 teaspoons Dijon Mustard
- 1 1/2 teaspoons shallot, minced
- 2 teaspoons chives, snipped
- 1 dash kosher salt and pepper to taste
- 1 ounce prosciutto, torn into 20 pieces

Direction

- In a large saucepan, cover the eggs with cold water and bring to a boil over high heat. Remove from the heat and let the eggs stand in the hot water for 12 minutes. Transfer the eggs to an ice water bath until chilled, about 5 minutes.
- In a medium bowl, mix the mayonnaise, Sriracha sauce, cornichons, goat cheese, mustard, shallot and 1 teaspoon of the chives. Peel the eggs and halve them lengthwise. Add the yolks to the bowl, mix until smooth and season with salt and pepper.
- Set the egg whites on a serving platter. Scrape the egg yolk mixture into a pastry bag fitted with a large round tip and pipe the filling into the whites; alternatively, use a plastic ziplock bag with a corner snipped off or spoon in the filling with a teaspoon. Top each egg with a piece of prosciutto, sprinkle with the remaining 1 teaspoon of chives and serve.

305. Spicy Deviled Eggs With Piment D'Espelette

Serving: Makes 24 | Prep: | Cook: | Ready in:

Ingredients

- 12 large eggs
- 1 cup mayonnaise
- 1 tablespoon sriracha sauce (or more)
- salt to taste

- Piment d'Espelette

Direction

- Place eggs in large saucepan and add enough cold water to cover. Bring to a low boil. Remove from heat, cover, and let stand 9 minutes.
- Drain eggs; cover with cold water and add several ice cubes.
- Once eggs are cool enough to handle, peel and cut in half lengthwise. Spoon yolks out into a small bowl and arrange whites on serving platter.
- Grate yolks with a fine grater into a medium bowl. Add mayonnaise and sriracha sauce to yolks and whisk until smooth. Season to taste with salt and more sriracha if you like.
- Spoon or pipe filling into egg white halves. Cover and refrigerate eggs for 2 hours or more (up to 1 day). Once chilled, sprinkle generously with Piment d'Espelette and serve.

306. Spicy Shrimp Sashimi At Home

Serving: Serves 4-6 | Prep: | Cook: | Ready in:

Ingredients

- mayonnaise,chili oil,Sriracha,Wasabi,Cooked Shrimp,Tenkasu
- 1/2 cup mayonnaise
- 1/8-1/4 teaspoons chili oil or to taste
- 1/8-1/4 teaspoons Sriracha,or to taste
- 1/2 teaspoon prepared Wasabi or powdered to taste
- 1 pound cooked Shrimp or a fatty fish like Salmon or Tuna
- 1/2 cup Tenkasu
- Romaine Lettuce Leaves,Avocado slices

Direction

- Combine first 6 ingredients. Add the mayonnaise preparation to the shrimp and gently toss. Leave at room temperature not more than 20 minutes or if desired it can be served cold. Just prior to serving add the 1/2 cup Tenkasu so that the crispiness is there with every chopstick bite. Dip in soy sauce if desired; pickled ginger as well.
- Optional: also plated some of the Sashimi on crisp Romaine Lettuce leaves and topped that with slices of Avocado.
- As well, while shopping at the Japanese Grocery store I saw vacuum packed Tempura which are ready to fry. I bought this on a lark to see the taste and when fried a la minute (to order) it was really tasty. Remember frying oil must be between 300-350 to get the crispiness quickly so that your Tempura does not soak up the oil***I have a fear of tapeworm - an illogical fear. Before I make any uncooked fish at home whether for Sashimi or Sushi I freeze my fish overnight or longer. Then I defrost it and use it raw. The freezing kills the Parasites that cause tapeworm. I don't even trust my fishmonger - as I said it is an illogical fear.

---

307. Spicy Thai Basil Asiago Stuffed Petites Potatoes

Serving: Serves 4 to 5 | Prep: | Cook: | Ready in:

Ingredients

- 16 Small Red Bliss Potatoes
- 1 cup Grated Asiago Cheese (or Parmesan, Pecorino Romano or Dry Jack which can substitute for the Asiago)
- 1/2 cup Mayonnaise (not the light or reduced calorie version)
- 5 tablespoons Chopped Thai Basil Leaves, divided (found in Asian stores, but if you can't find, use 5 tbsp regular basil combined with 1-2 tsp fresh mint leaves)
- 1/4 cup Olive Oil
- 3 Medium Garlic Cloves
- 1 tablespoon Fresh Lime Juice
- 1/4 teaspoon Grated lime Zest
- 2 Thai Red Chili Peppers, minced*
- Salt and Pepper to taste
- *Taste after the first pepper is added and add the 2nd one or even more based on your taste buds; note that I have not asked to remove the seeds. Also if you cannot find Thai red chili pepper, use Asian hot sauce, preferably Sriracha, starting with 1/2 t

Direction

- Preheat oven to 350°F with rack in middle.
- Generously cover potatoes and 1 tablespoon salt with cold water in a medium pot, then simmer until tender, about 12 minutes. Drain potatoes and rinse with cold water. Cool to room temperature in refrigerator, about 40 minutes.
- Meanwhile, cook garlic cloves in oil at a bare simmer in a small heavy saucepan, stirring occasionally, until tender and golden. Drain garlic, reserving oil for another use, then mash to a paste.
- Mix the mayonnaise with the mashed garlic paste, 3 tbsp chopped basil leaves, cheese, lime juice and zest, and salt and pepper to taste. Taste cheese mixture before adding salt since the cheese is already a bit salty. Last, add the first minced Thai red chili pepper (or ½ tsp Sriracha) and taste before adding more based on your spiciness tolerance. Of course, if you are not at all adventurous you can skip these ingredients or start with even less.
- Using a small melon-ball cutter or a teaspoon, scoop out a hole in each cooled potato, but making sure bottom of potato is not pierced. Stuff potatoes with cheese mixture. By the way, I don't think you will have leftover, but just in case you do, save it to eat it with some crackers or bread.
- Bake in a baking sheet until cheese is melted and bubbling, about 20 minutes. Prior to serving, sprinkle the remaining 2 tbsp chopped basil on top of the potatoes.

308.　　Spicy Tuna Burger

Serving: Makes 4 | Prep: | Cook: | Ready in:

Ingredients

- 1 pound fresh, sushi-grade tuna steak
- 1 scallion, finely chopped
- 2 tablespoons cilantro, minced
- 2 teaspoons ginger, minced
- 1 Thai bird chile, minced
- 1/2 avocado, mashed
- 3/4 teaspoon kosher salt
- 1/4 teaspoon freshly ground black pepper
- 2 tablespoons extra-virgin olive oil
- 4 sesame seed buns
- 1 1/2 tablespoons wasabi paste
- 1/2 cup mayonnaise
- 3 limes, juiced (about 6 tablespoons)
- 1 tablespoon fish sauce
- 1 tablespoon orange juice
- 2 teaspoons rice vinegar
- 1 clove garlic, minced
- 1 1/4 cups romaine lettuce, shredded

Direction

- Dice the tuna into 1/4-inch chunks and put in a large bowl. Add the scallion, cilantro, 1 teaspoon ginger, chile, avocado, salt, and pepper. Gently work the mixture with your hands to incorporate all of the ingredients. Divide the contents of the bowl into 4 equal portions and shape them into 1-inch thick patties. Cover and refrigerate for 20 minutes, and up to 2 hours.
- In the meantime, make the wasabi mayonnaise. In a small bowl, add the wasabi paste, mayonnaise, the juice of one lime, and 1 teaspoon of ginger. Stir well to combine. Cover and refrigerate until ready to use.
- Just before you're ready to cook the tuna burgers, make the dressing. In a medium-sized bowl, add the juice of two limes, fish sauce,

orange juice, rice vinegar, and garlic. Stir well, then add in the shredded lettuce and toss to coat. Set aside until ready to use.
- Heat the oil in a large skillet over medium-high heat. Cook the tuna burgers for 2 to 3 minutes per side -- don't overcook or they will be dry. Transfer to a clean plate to rest.
- With the remaining oil in the pan, toast the hamburger buns for 1 minute, adding more oil if needed.
- To assemble, place the burgers on the bun bottoms. Top each with wasabi mayo and dressed lettuce. Cover each burger with the bun tops and serve immediately.

309.　　Spicy And Sweet Chicken Apple Salad With Pomegranates And Pecans

Serving: Serves 8+ | Prep: | Cook: | Ready in:

Ingredients

- 1/4 cup scallion, thinly sliced
- 1 lemon, juice and zest
- 2 teaspoons salt
- 1 cup apple cut into small dice
- 1 cup pear, cut into small dice
- 1 cup celery, thinly sliced
- 1/2 teaspoon turmeric
- 1-1.5 pounds cooked chicken
- 3 tablespoons mayonnaise
- 1/4 teaspoon sriracha or other hot sauce
- pomegranate seeds for garnish
- chopped pecans for garnish
- baby spinach or arugula leaves for garnish

Direction

- In a large mixing bowl, combine the scallions, lemon juice and zest and salt. As you dice the apples the apples and pears add them to the bowl and mix to coat with the lemon juice to prevent browning. Add the celery and turmeric, mix again to combine all ingredients thoroughly.

- Add the chicken, mayonnaise and hot sauce to the bowl and fold together with the other ingredients to mix without breaking the chicken too much. Adjust the seasoning to taste with more salt and hot sauce as needed.
- To serve, make a bed of greens (spinach or arugula) in the center of each plate, greens may be dry or lightly dressed with olive oil and vinegar or lemon juice. Place a large spoonful of the chicken salad on top of the greens. Scatter toasted pecan pieces and pomegranate seeds over each plate.

310. Spicy, Garlicky Broccoli Sandwich

Serving: Serves 2 hungry people | Prep: | Cook: | Ready in:

Ingredients

- 1 head broccoli
- Mayonnaise
- Sriracha
- 1 lime
- Smoked paprika
- Olive oil
- 2 cloves garlic, minced
- 1/2 red onion, thinly sliced into half moons (or sub in an equivalent amount of quick-pickled red onions)
- 1 very fresh baguette that you're excited to eat
- Ricotta salata, grated or crumbled
- Sun-dried tomatoes, chopped
- Cilantro

Direction

- Cut the broccoli into small florets—you want the florets to be small enough to cook quickly on the stovetop and not be cumbersome balanced on a sandwich.

- Make the spicy mayonnaise: Squirt or dollop mayonnaise into a small bowl, squeeze Sriracha over top, then add a squeeze of lime juice to thin plus a sprinkle of smoked paprika. Whisk, taste, and adjust accordingly. You'll need enough to spread over the inside of all pieces of bread.
- Now cook the broccoli: Over medium-high heat, get a cast-iron pan hot and coat the bottom with olive oil. When the oil is hot, add the broccoli florets. When they're sizzling and seared, flip the florets to brown the other side. Stir them around, checking to make sure they've browned, then cover the pan so that you cook the broccoli all the way through,
- If you're using raw red onion instead of pickled (both are good; raw is easier), add the onion slivers and a sprinkle of smoked paprika, then stir and cover for another minute or so, until the onion has softened a bit. Remove the pan from the heat, add the minced garlic, stir so that the garlic cooks in the residual heat of the pan, and squeeze some lime juice over top. Season with salt to taste.
- Cut the baguette into sandwich-sized lengths (whatever that means to you and your hunger!), then cut each length down its belly. To build a sandwich, spread both the top and bottom piece of bread with the spicy mayonnaise. Add the ricotta salata, either grated or crumbled, on the bottom bread, then top with broccoli, sun-dried tomatoes, and pickled red onions, if using. Sprinkle with torn cilantro leaves and close the sandwich with the top piece of bread. Eat!

311. Spinach Artichoke Dip

Serving: Serves 4-6 | Prep: | Cook: | Ready in:

Ingredients

- 1 tablespoon coconut oil
- 1 BOU Vegetable flavored Bouillon cube
- 1.5 cups medium white onion, finely chopped

- 3 cloves garlic
- 9 ounces package artichoke hearts, defrosted, rinsed, dried, finely chopped
- 10 ounces package frozen chopped spinach, defrosted, excess liquid squeezed out
- 1/2 cup fresh part skim ricotta
- 2 tablespoons mayonnaise
- 1/2 cup reduced-fat cream cheese
- 1/2 cup shredded part-skim mozzarella cheese
- 1/2 teaspoon nutmeg
- 1/2 teaspoon salt
- 1/4 teaspoon fresh ground pepper

Direction

- Preheat oven to 375 degrees F
- Heat the oil in a sauté pan over medium heat. Add onions and cook stirring occasionally, 4 to 5 minutes. Add garlic and Bou and cook an additional 3 to 4 minutes, or until onions are light golden. Remove from heat and cool.
- In the bowl of a food processor combine artichoke hearts, spinach, ricotta, mayonnaise, cream cheese, mozzarella, nutmeg, salt and pepper. Process until smooth. Add cooled onion-garlic mixture to the food processor and pulse a few times to combine.
- Transfer mixture into an 8-inch glass square baking dish or 9-inch glass pie plate which has been lightly sprayed with cooking spray. Bake for 15 to 20 minutes or until heated through. Serve with tortilla chips.

---

312. Spiralized Firecracker Hot Dogs

Serving: Makes 6 hot dogs | Prep: 0hours0mins | Cook: 0hours0mins | Ready in:

Ingredients

- 6 hot dogs
- 1/2 cup hot sauce, divided (I prefer Frank's)
- 1/2 cup mayonnaise

- 1/4 cup sour cream
- 1/2 teaspoon celery seed
- 6 hot dog buns
- Crumbled blue cheese, for topping
- Finely chopped celery and celery leaves, for topping
- Finely chopped red onion, for topping
- Finely chopped or shredded carrot, for topping

Direction

- To spiralize the dogs, place the skewer through the center on the dog so it's on a stick, like a corn dog. Place the stick part in your hand and angle the hot dog down so that the tip of the dog is touching the counter top. With your other hand, grab a paring knife and place it at the tip of the dog holding it at a 90 degree angle. While twirling the hot dog with your other hand, cut up the side of the dog to make a spiral cut running up the sides of the dog. Remove the dog from the skewer and repeat with the rest of the dogs.
- To make the firecracker sauce, mix 1/4 cup of the hot sauce with mayonnaise, sour cream and celery seed. Set aside.
- Heat a grill to a high heat. Once the grill is hot, place the dogs on the grill and grill for a couple minutes turning them occasionally until they begin to char. For the last few minutes of grilling baste the hot dogs with the remaining 1/4 cup of the hot sauce. Remove from grill and cover with foil to keep warm.
- To build a firecracker dog, place one hot dog into a bun and top with blue cheese, celery, celery leaves, onion, carrot and slather of the hot dog sauce.

---

313. Spring Fling Potato Salad

Serving: Makes approx. 12 cups | Prep: | Cook: | Ready in:

Ingredients

- For the salad
- 3 pounds red and gold waxy potatoes, cubed
- 1 1/2 cups green peas, frozen or fresh
- 1/3 cup dried cranberries
- 2 small cucumbers, seeded and diced
- 4 scallions, sliced
- 1/4 cup sliced almonds
- For the dressing
- 3 tablespoons white balsamic vinegar
- 2 tablespoons pomegranate molasses
- 2 teaspoons kosher salt
- generous handful fresh basil
- leaves from a few springs of fresh mint
- 3/4 cup buttermilk, plus additional as needed
- 3/4 cup mayonnaise

Direction

- Boil the cubed potatoes until just fork tender, about ten minutes. Drain and reserve.
- While potatoes cook, bring a second pot of water to a boil and blanch peas for one minute, then drain and plunge them into an ice water bath to shock and stop the cooking. Set aside.
- To make the dressing, place vinegar, pomegranate molasses, salt, and herbs in the small bowl of a food processor and pulse until leaves are minced. Combine this mixture with the buttermilk and mayonnaise in a jar with a tight-fitting lid and shake until dressing is well mixed. Thin dressing with additional buttermilk as needed.
- In a large bowl, place potatoes, peas, cranberries, cucumbers, scallions, and sliced almonds. Toss with enough of the dressing to coat. Chill until ready to serve.

314.   Summer Sliders

Serving: Serves 6 | Prep: | Cook: |Ready in:

Ingredients

- 1 pound grass-fed organic ground beef, 92% lean

- 1 tablespoon chipotle in adobo sauce
- 1 medium red onion, sliced, 1/4" rounds
- 1 tablespoon butter
- 1 tablespoon olive oil
- 2 medium peaches, halved and pitted, sliced, 1/4" thick
- 1/2 cup mayonnaise
- 1 teaspoon lime zest
- juice from 1/2 lime
- 6 basil leaves
- salt and pepper
- 6 slider rolls, grilled/toasted

Direction

- Heat outdoor grill or indoor cast-iron griddle to high.
- Meanwhile, melt butter and oil in pan on medium high heat. Add onions and cook until caramelized, approximately 5-6 minutes.
- While onions are caramelizing, fold in chipotle into ground beef. Note: do not over-work/mix the beef.
- Once onions are caramelized, remove from heat. Start to form sliders, approximately 6 sliders per 1 pound of beef. Feel free to make sliders as big or as small as you like.
- Salt and pepper the sliders and place on hot grill. Cook to desired temperature. We like medium-rare which is approximately 3 minutes per side.
- While sliders are grilling, add mayonnaise, lime zest, lime juice and basil to food processor and blend until combined. Season with salt and pepper to taste. Note: the sauce will be a lovely light green color.
- Once you are 1 minute away from sliders being done, place peach slices on grill and cook for 1 minute until grill marks appear but peaches do not soften.
- Remove peaches and sliders from heat. Let sliders rest but remember there will be some carry-over cooking so internal temperature will still rise.
- To assemble: spread sauce on bottom half of slider roll. Next, stack slider, peach, onion (in

that order). Spread more sauce on top half of roll and place on top of slider stack.

315. Summer Squash Chicken Salad

Serving: Serves 2 | Prep: | Cook: |Ready in:

Ingredients

- 2 Small organic zucchini, skin on, grated
- 1 Small organic yellow squash, skin on, grated
- 1 Small organic carrot, grated
- 2 cups Roasted, skinless chicken breast, diced
- 1/2 Small white onion, finely chopped
- 3 tablespoons Mayonnaise
- 1/2 teaspoon Freshly squeezed lemon juice
- 1/2 teaspoon Kosher salt
- 1 tablespoon Rice wine vinegar
- 1/2 teaspoon Sugar
- 1/2 teaspoon Fresh tarragon, finely chopped
- 1/4 teaspoon Fresh lemon thyme, chopped
- 1 teaspoon Fresh chives, finely chopped
- 1/2 teaspoon Garlic, minced
- 1/4 cup Fresh blueberries
- Fresh chives for garnish

Direction

- In a medium-sized bowl, place grated zucchini, yellow squash and carrot, chicken, and onion.
- In a small bowl, whisk mayonnaise, lemon juice, salt, rice wine vinegar, sugar, herbs and garlic until blended.
- Top salad with dressing, and then gently mix. Chill for at least 1 hour before serving. Just before serving, add blueberries and again gently toss. Garnish with chives.

316. Super Easy Coleslaw

Serving: Serves at least 6 as a side | Prep: | Cook: |Ready in:

Ingredients

- 1 cup mayonnaise
- 1 cup greek yogurt (I always go with full fat)
- 2 tablespoons dijon mustard
- 2 tablespoons apple cider vinegar
- 3 teaspoons celery salt
- 1/2 teaspoon salt
- 1/2 teaspoon ground pepper

Direction

- Roughly chop entire cabbage, to about 1/2 inch thick ribbons. Put aside in a large mixing bowl.
- Mix the rest of the ingredients the together and taste (if you like more celery salt/salt/pepper, go for it!)
- Pour mayonnaise/yogurt mixture onto chopped cabbage and mix together until the all of the cabbage is completely coated. You can use tongs (the most useful kitchen appliance) or if you just don't care (like me) feel free to use your hands (actually the most useful kitchen appliance)
- Cover with saran wrap and let sit for at least a half hour in the fridge (more if you can wait!)

317. Surprise Sandwich

Serving: Serves 4 | Prep: | Cook: |Ready in:

Ingredients

- 2 eggs
- 150 grams ricotta
- 2 tablespoons mayonnaise
- 1 teaspoon curry
- 1/2 red apple in a small pieces
- 1 shallot, finely chopped

- 2 tablespoons chopped parsley
- A little drops of vinegar
- Salt and pepper

Direction

- Crush the ricotta with a fork, add the mayonnaise, curry and vinegar, salt and pepper. Chop the eggs, and add them to the folder, as well as the remaining ingredients.
- Serve this folder in your favorite bread in sandwiches, barring bread and putting on top, tomato, lettuce and avocado (optional as it may opt for other ingredients).

---

318.   Takoyaki

Serving: Makes 54 balls | Prep: | Cook: | Ready in:

Ingredients

- 10.5 ounces Cake Flour
- 3 Eggs - beaten
- 4.25 cups Ice Cold Water
- 1/2 teaspoon Salt
- 1 teaspoon Hondashi Granules
- 2 teaspoons Ponzu or Yuzupon Sauce
- 1/2 pound Boiled Octopus Legs (cut into 1/2" pieces)
- 4 Green Onions Minced
- 1 bunch Pickled Ginger Minced
- 1 cup Rice Crispy Cearal
- Oil
- Aonori (Dried Seaweed Powder)
- Takoyaki Sauce
- Mayonnaise
- Bonito Flake

Direction

- Blend the ice water and dashi stock granules until dissolved. Add the sauce and eggs. Add the flour, and mix together gently. Do not over mix, the batter will be slightly lumpy.

- Wad up a paper towel into a fat cigar shape and soak one end with oil. Oil each hole in the pan as well as the surface. Pour batter into each hole 2/3rds full. (Pour in a clockwise direction starting at 12:00 so you remember where you started) Add 1 piece of octopus to each hole and sprinkle in a little bit each of the following: green onion, ginger and cereal. When finished fill each hole to the top with batter.
- Use wooden chopsticks to sweep the edge of the first hole you poured. Once it starts to release (about 3 minutes total) sweep the chopstick under to flip the takoyaki on its side 90 degrees. Let the uncooked batter on top fall into the bottom the flip the takoyaki the whole way. Continue cooking and spinning the balls until they are evenly golden brown on all sides. (An additional 4-5 minutes total from the 90 degree flip)
- Top with takoyaki sauce, mayonnaise, bonito flake and aonori. Enjoy!

---

319.   Tangy Zangy Roasted Potato Salad

Serving: Serves 6 to 8 | Prep: | Cook: | Ready in:

Ingredients

- 16 to 20 new, waxy potatoes
- 2 tablespoons olive oil
- 1/3 cup red onion, thinly sliced
- 1/2 cup diced celery, or cut into thin half-moons
- 1 handful of fresh celery leaves, chopped roughly
- 1/2 cup plain yogurt
- 1/4 cup mayonnaise
- 1/4 cup creole mustard (I like Zatarain's; use grain mustard if you can't find it)
- 1/2 teaspoon paprika
- 2 tablespoons red wine vinegar

- 6 to 8 dashes of tabasco, or your favorite hot sauce
- salt and pepper, to taste

Direction

- Preheat oven to 375 degrees.
- Scrub potatoes, leave skin on. Cut in half and toss with olive oil, light salt and black pepper. Arrange on a baking sheet lined with parchment paper, cut side down. Roast for 15 to 20 minutes. Flip. Roast for another 10 to 15 until tender. Set aside to cool slightly.
- Drain onions and pat dry. Peel strings off celery stalk with a vegetable peeler before chopping. Combine onion and celery with yogurt, mayonnaise, mustard, vinegar, paprika, and hot sauce.
- Taste the dressing with a celery leaf, and adjust for seasoning. The mustard and tabasco can make the sauce a little salty, so try first and adjust to your liking.
- As soon as you can handle the potatoes (but while they are still hot), cut into bite-sized pieces and mix well with dressing. Add celery leaves.
- Eat warm or cold. Enjoy!

---

320.   Tarragon Pecan Chicken Salad

Serving: Makes approximately 2 pounds | Prep: | Cook: | Ready in:

Ingredients

- 24 ounces Boneless Chicken Breast
- 1/4 cup Beau Monde Seasoning
- 1 cup Heavy Cream
- 1/2 cup Celery, diced
- 1/2 cup Roasted Red Peppers, diced
- 2 ounces Dried Tarragon, crushed
- 1 cup Kahlua Roasted Pecans, chopped
- 1 cup Mayonnaise--Duke's or Hellman's
- Salt and Peper to taste

Direction

- Rinse and pat dry chicken breasts. Coat with Beau Monde seasoning (made by Spice Island brand, a must to make this chicken salad sooo delicious) and a touch of salt and pepper. Place on a roasting pan with a lip and pour heavy cream over chicken. Bake at 350 degrees for 12-15 minutes until cooked through. Let sit to cool and then dice.
- To make the Kahlua pecans: roast pecan pieces or halves in an oven for 5 minutes on 350 degrees. Remove from oven and toss with Kahlua (yes the beverage) or any other coffee flavored liquor and a touch of salt. Place back in the oven for another 5 minutes or until the liquid has evaporated.
- In a bowl, toss together the celery, red pepper, chicken, pecans and tarragon. Add mayonnaise slowly, you just want enough mayo to coat the product and hold everything together. Adjust seasoning with salt and pepper.
- To make the yummy grilled chicken salad sandwich you will need the following: some kind of hearty whole grain bread, cheddar cheese and a touch of whole grain mustard. Heat a skillet and add some butter. Put the mustard and cheese on the bread, place open faced in the hot skillet when cheese has melted take out and make sandwich with chicken salad. You can put back in the skillet after you've added salad if you want, but I like the contrast between the cold chicken salad and the warm gooey cheese.

---

321.   Tart & Tangy Broccoli Slaw

Serving: Makes about six heaping cups of slaw | Prep: | Cook: | Ready in:

Ingredients

- For slaw

- 2 heads of broccoli
- 2 carrots, peeled
- 1 apple, cored
- 1/2 cup thinly sliced almonds, toasted
- 3 T fresh mint, thinly sliced
- 3/4 cup pomegranate arils (or substitute dried cherries or cranberries)
- For yogurt dressing
- ¼ cup finely chopped shallot
- 1 T apple cider vinegar
- ¾ cup plain yogurt (regular or Greek); full-fat recommended
- ¼ cup mayonnaise
- 1 T lemon juice
- 2 T pomegranate molasses
- 1/4 tsp Aleppo pepper, or to taste
- kosher salt, to taste

Direction

- Wash and trim broccoli and cut florets away from stems. Either by hand or with your food processor's slicing blade, thinly slice / shave the florets and cut into small bite-size pieces. Peel the stems, and coarsely grate them (either with box grater or food processor's grating blade). Also coarsely grate the carrots and apple. Toss them together in a large bowl, then add the toasted almonds, mint and arils (or dried cranberries) and toss again.
- Combine chopped shallot and apple cider vinegar in a small bowl; let it sit for about 5 minutes so it lightly pickles. Meanwhile, in a small bowl, combine the yogurt, mayonnaise, lemon juice, pomegranate molasses, Aleppo pepper and kosher salt. Whisk together until well incorporated, then add the shallot-apple cider vinegar mixture.
- Pour your dressing over the slaw and toss. Add more salt to taste. Cover and chill at least one hour so all of the flavors meld together. Taste again for seasoning and balance – you may want to add a splash of lemon juice right before serving for brightness. Covered tightly and refrigerated, the slaw keeps well for at least a day.

322.   Tartar Sauce

Serving: Makes about 1/2 cup | Prep: 0hours3mins | Cook: 0hours0mins | Ready in:

Ingredients

- 1/3 cup mayonnaise
- 3 tablespoons roughly chopped cornichon pickles
- 2 tablespoons roughly chopped capers
- 1 tablespoon finely chopped dill
- 2 tablespoons freshly squeezed lemon juice or white wine vinegar

Direction

- Combine all of the ingredients in a small bowl or jar. Store in an airtight container in the fridge for up to 6 months.

323.   Tender Turkey Meatballs And Orzo With Whole Lemon Vinaigrette

Serving: Serves 6-8 people | Prep: | Cook: | Ready in:

Ingredients

- Turkey Meatballs
- 2 pounds ground turkey (dark meat recommended)
- 1/2 cup mayonnaise
- 3 cloves garlic, minced
- Finely grated zest from 1 large lemon (saving juice for the orzo)
- 1/2 cup parsley, finely chopped
- 1/2 cup grated Parmesan cheese
- 2 teaspoons kosher salt
- Freshly ground black pepper
- 2 tablespoons olive oil, plus more for greasing pan
- Orzo with Whole-Lemon Vinaigrette

- 1 pound orzo
- 2 tablespoons mayonnaise
- 2 tablespoons finely chopped shallots (from 1 small shallot)
- 1 cup green olives, such as Castelvetrano, pitted and coarsely chopped or torn
- 1 large lemon, quartered, seeds removed, and finely chopped (peel and flesh)
- Kosher salt
- Freshly ground black pepper
- 1/3 cup olive oil
- 1/2 cup grated Parmesan, plus more for serving
- 4 cups coarsely chopped greens (such as spinach, arugula, kale, or a mix)
- Freshly squeezed lemon juice, to taste (from the lemon you zested for the meatballs)

Direction

- Turkey Meatballs
- Heat broiler and place top oven rack below heat source.
- In a large bowl, combine turkey, mayonnaise, garlic, lemon zest, parsley, Parmesan, salt, and a few grinds of black pepper. Mix together with your hands until well combined.
- Line a large sheet pan with foil and, using your hands, rub olive oil over the entire surface.
- Shape turkey mixture into small meatballs, about 2 tablespoons each or 1 1/2-inches wide, and place them on the foil-lined sheet pan. It's fine if they're close together. Drizzle the meatballs with 2 tablespoons of olive oil. Broil meatballs about 8 to 10 minutes, flipping them once, until they're browned on both sides and cooked through. Remove from oven; cover with foil to keep warm.
- Orzo with Whole-Lemon Vinaigrette
- Bring a large pot of salted water to a boil. Add orzo, and cook according to package directions. Drain (do not rinse) and transfer to a large bowl. Immediately add mayonnaise, and stir until evenly incorporated.
- While orzo is cooking, make the whole-lemon vinaigrette: in a bowl, combine shallots, olives,

and chopped lemon. Season with kosher salt and few grinds of black pepper. In a small skillet or saucepan, heat olive oil over medium-low heat. Add lemon-olive mixture, and cook, stirring frequently, until ingredients are warmed through and the shallots have softened but not browned, about 3 to 5 minutes.

- Pour the whole-lemon vinaigrette over the warm orzo and mayonnaise, and toss to combine. Add Parmesan and chopped greens, and toss again. Taste the orzo, and add salt, pepper, and lemon juice to taste.
- Gently toss in the meatballs, or place them on top of the orzo. Serve warm, with more grated Parmesan if desired.

324.　　　　Teriyaki Salmon Burgers

Serving: Serves 4 people | Prep: | Cook: | Ready in:

Ingredients

- For the patties:
- 1 pound salmon, cooked or raw, minced
- 1 egg
- 1/3 cup panko breadcrumbs
- 1/2 teaspoon toasted sesame oil
- 1 small lemon, juiced
- 1/2 large orange, juiced
- 1 teaspoon soy sauce
- 1 teaspoon garlic powder
- 1 teaspoon ground ginger
- salt and pepper to taste
- 2 tablespoons vegetable oil
- For the sauce and remaining ingredients:
- 1/4 cup soy sauce
- 2 tablespoons orange juice
- 1 tablespoon honey
- 2 teaspoons rice vinegar
- 1/4 teaspoon chili powder
- 2 teaspoons cornstarch
- 1 splash water
- 1 can of pineapple rings

- 4 butter lettuce leaves
- 1 tomato, sliced
- 4 pairs of hamburger buns
- mayonnaise or other plain spread of choice

Direction

- Spread mayonnaise on the hamburger buns and toast in a large pan over medium heat until lightly golden and remove. If desired, drain and dry the pineapple rings and cook in a grill pan until slightly charred. Remove to a plate.
- In a large pan, heat the vegetable oil over medium heat until waves appear.
- Meanwhile, in a food processor or by hand, combine salmon, panko breadcrumbs, egg, sesame oil, lemon juice, orange juice, soy sauce, garlic powder, ginger, and salt and pepper. Mix until everything comes together, but do not over mix. Divide the mixture into four portions and form into patties. Set aside.
- In a small bowl, combine the ¼ cup soy sauce, orange juice, vinegar, chili powder, cornstarch, and water. Whisk until there are no lumps.
- Gently slide the patties into the pan and cook for about 5 minutes until a light golden crust forms. Carefully flip over and cook for another 5 minutes. Add the sauce mixture and cook together, spooning the sauce over the patties. Flip the patties over again to coat in the sauce. Continue cooking until it thickens. Remove from heat.

325.   Thai Shrimp Cakes

Serving: Makes 4 cakes | Prep: | Cook: | Ready in:

Ingredients

- Shrimp Cakes
- 8 ounces Shrimp, peeled, deveined, coarsely chopped
- 1 tablespoon Mayonnaise
- 1/4 teaspoon Salt

- 1/4 t teaspoons Pepper
- 1/2 cup Panko breadcrumbs
- 1/3 cup Unsweetened dried coconut, minced, divided
- 2 tablespoons Scallions, minced
- 2 tablespoons Cilantro, finely chopped
- 2 teaspoons Fish sauce
- 2 teaspoons Siracha
- 1 1/2 teaspoons Fresh ginger, grated
- 1 teaspoon Fresh lime juice
- 1 Large garlic clove, minced
- 1 tablespoon Olive oil
- Sauce
- 1 tablespoon Soy sauce
- 2 tablespoons Fish sauce
- 2 tablespoons Fresh lime juice
- 1 tablespoon Seasoned rice vinegar

Direction

- Place one-third of shrimp (2.5 oz.), mayonnaise, salt and pepper in a food processor and pulse until shrimp are finely chopped and have formed a paste, about 10 pulses.
- Add remaining two-thirds of shrimp (5.5 oz.) to shrimp mixture in processor and pulse until coarsely chopped, about 5 pulses, scraping down sides of bowl. Transfer shrimp mixture to bowl and stir in 1/4 cup panko, 2T coconut, scallions, cilantro, fish sauce, Sriracha, ginger, lime juice and garlic.
- Combine remaining 1/4 cup panko and remaining coconut in a bowl. With wet hands form 4 patties 3/4" thick. Dredge both side of patties in panko mixture pressing to flatten. The patties can each also be pressed into a 3" ring to help form. Chill patties on a sheet pan for at least 30 minutes or for several hours.
- In a large skillet heat oil and sauté patties till golden browned about 3 to 5 minutes per side.
- Meanwhile combine sauce ingredients and serve with patties.

326.   The August Year

Serving: Makes 4 sandwiches | Prep: | Cook: | Ready in:

Ingredients

- 8   slices of Capicola
- 12   Cherry Tomatoes
- 2 tablespoons Ricotta Cheese
- 2 tablespoons Mayonnaise
- 2 tablespoons softened Cream Cheese
- 8   Fresh Basil leaves
- 1   Small sweet onion (A Vidalia works well)
- 8   slices of hearty bread (I used 12 grain)

Direction

- Mix Ricotta, Mayonnaise, and Cream Cheese together
- Slice up the cherry tomatoes. Cut the Basil into thin long strips (Chiffonade) and dice the Onions and Capicola.
- Spread the Ricotta, Mayo, and Cream Cheese mixture on all pieces of bread. Add basil on the top halves, and the onions and tomatoes on the bottom halves. Add the Capicola on either half. Put the two halves together and cut diagonally.
- Eat and make sounds of appreciation.

327.   The Best Broccoli Salad Of My Life

Serving: Makes 4 cups | Prep: | Cook: | Ready in:

Ingredients

- 1/4 cup of buttermilk
- 1/4 cup of good mayonnaise
- 1 tablespoon of red wine vinegar or cider vinegar
- 1/2 teaspoon of sugar
- 1/4 teaspoon of salt
- 1/2   shallot, finely chopped
- 1   head of broccoli

- 1/4 cup of toasted sliced almonds
- 1/8 cup of dried cranberries, coarsely chopped
- Freshly ground black pepper

Direction

- In a small bowl, whisk the buttermilk, mayonnaise, vinegar, sugar and salt until smooth. Stir in the shallot. Allow the shallot to mellow out in the dressing for 10 minutes.
- Meanwhile, trim the broccoli, and chop it into large chunks. Then cut chunks into thin slices (you could do the slicing with a mandolin, just watch your fingers!) Toss the broccoli with almonds and cranberries.
- Pour the dressing over the broccoli mixture, and add a generous amount of freshly cracked black pepper. Stir the salad until all of the components have been evenly coated. This salad can be served immediately or lasts 3 days in the fridge.

328.   The Cuban

Serving: Makes 4 good-sized sandwiches | Prep: | Cook: | Ready in:

Ingredients

- The Cuban
- 4 good Cuban sandwich rolls (I posted a separate recipe for these here on food52.)
- 1 pound roasted and sliced Cuban Adobo Roasted Pork Shoulder (recipe is below)
- 4 - 6 generous slices good Swiss cheese
- 4 - 6 ounces finely sliced Black Forest or similar deli ham
- Mayonnaise to taste
- Four half-sour pickles, thinly sliced
- Hearty brown mustard (I like a coarse mustard with horseradish)
- Cuban Adobo Pork, Braise Roasted
- 1 3-pound pork shoulder
- 5 medium garlic cloves, peeled and mashed

- 2 teaspoons Kosher salt
- 1 ½ - 2 teaspoons freshly ground cumin seeds
- 2 tablespoons finely chopped fresh sage leaves
- 1 tablespoon finely chopped fresh oregano leaves
- ½ teaspoon freshly ground black pepper (I like Malabar) or white pepper
- 2 - 3 tablespoons olive oil
- 2 medium onions, peeled and thickly sliced
- 1 – 2 cups of chicken stock, heated
- 3 or 4 medium carrots, peeled and cut into bite-sized chunks (strictly optional, but nice to serve with the sauce)

Direction

- The Cuban
- Heat Panini press or other top and bottom grilling device for sandwiches.
- Slice the rolls lengthwise and spread one side with mustard and the other side with mayonnaise.
- Layer the ham, cheese, pork and pickles in whatever order you like. Press the two sides together.
- Cook in the Panini press until the grill lines are dark brown and sandwich is nice and warm.
- Enjoy!! ;o)
- Cuban Adobo Pork, Braise Roasted
- Score the pork shoulder a few times about ¼ inch deep on each side.
- Using a mortar and pestle, mash the garlic with the salt to make a paste. Add the cumin and sage leaves and pound a few times to mix it into the garlic and salt. Add the pepper and the olive oil and stir to combine.
- Rub the herb paste all over the pork should and into the crevices. Some people like to tie their pork shoulders up, but I generally don't, as I find you get more crispy bits that way. You certainly may, if you wish.
- Put the roast in a bowl you can cover or a lidded glass storage container and refrigerate for at least six hours or, preferably, overnight. Bring the meat to room temperature for about an hour before roasting.
- Preheat the oven the 375 degrees.

- Put the onion slices in a braising pan or Dutch oven. Put the meat in on top of that. Cook for about 20 minutes, then add the stock. It should come up about ¼ of the way up the meat. If it doesn't, add a bit of water.
- Cook the roast for another hour, then turn the roast over. Add more stock or water if what you put in earlier has evaporated.
- Cook for another half hour, then turn the roast over again and add more liquid if necessary. The onions will have released quite a bit, but depending on how much space there is on the bottom of the pan, it's not uncommon for the pan to dry out. Add the carrots now, if using.
- Return the roast for yet another half hour, then check the meat with a fork. It should be very tender and should pull apart easily. At this point, I usually flip the roast over again and cook it for at least another 15 – 20 minutes. The USDA says the internal temperature should be 160 degrees. Some respected cooks take the roast out at 145. It's up to you.
- Let the roast sit for at least 20 minutes after removing it, before slicing.
- The onions can be pureed with the pan juices, and more stock if you like, using an immersion or other blender, to make a nice sauce for the roast.
- Enjoy!!

---

329. The Cuban Burger

Serving: Serves 1 | Prep: | Cook: | Ready in:

Ingredients

- 1/2 pound ground chuck
- 1 teaspoon salt
- 1/2 cup shaved ham
- 1 tablespoon mayonnaise
- 5 pieces dill pickles, cut in ovals
- 2 slices of Swiss cheese
- 1 sturdy hamburger bun
- 1 tablespoon unsalted butter

Direction

- Begin by shaping your hamburger patty. Lay down a bit of wax paper on a plate, shape the patty, and then lay down another piece of wax paper on top of it. Lay a dinner plate on top of the patty and press down lightly -- that should press it into a uniform shape. Season it liberally with salt.
- Preheat your cast iron skillet over medium-high heat. Once heated, add the patty, salt-side down. Let the burger cook, untouched, for a few minutes. Flip it, then cook to your desired level of doneness.
- Slice your buns, then add a bit of butter to each side. Toast them on a preheated skillet, then set aside.
- Add the mayonnaise to the bottom of one bun. Add the mustard to the other bun. To the bottom bun, add the ham, then one slice of Swiss cheese. Top with the cooked patty. Add the pickles, then top with the remaining Swiss cheese. Add the top bun.
- Wipe the skillet, and return it back to the burner, setting the temperature to low. Put the burger in the skillet and weigh it something down with something heavy. After a minute or so, take a look at the bottom to make sure that you're not burning the bread. Flip the burger again and cook until the buns are crispy and the cheese is gooey. Enjoy!

| 330. | The Fabulous, Legendary Fried Provolone And Tomato Sandwich |

Serving: Makes 2 sandwiches | Prep: 0hours15mins | Cook: 0hours0mins | Ready in:

Ingredients

- 2 to 4 1/4-inch slices provolone cheese
- 1 splash Olive oil for frying (doesn't have to be your best bottle)

- 4 tablespoons your favorite mayonnaise, plus more as needed
- 4 1/2-inch thick slices sturdy, country-style bread
- 1 medium-sized ripe tomato, preferably heirloom
- 1 pinch Flaky salt and freshly cracked black pepper, to taste

Direction

- Add a thin layer of olive oil to the bottom of a heavy-bottomed skillet and heat until shimmering. Carefully add the slices of provolone and let them fry until crusty and golden on the outside but still gooey in the center, about 2 to 3 minutes total, carefully flipping them halfway through. (Flipping them is tricky and messy, and you'll probably curse my name, but it can be done—just be careful not to splatter yourself. Using a nonstick pan is also helpful.) Once it's done, carefully remove it from the pan, allowing any excess oil to drip back into the pan, and blot it gently on a paper towel.
- Spread the mayonnaise evenly across four slices of bread, adding more as desired. Core the tomato and cut it into 4 slices. Place the fried cheese on 2 of the slices of bread, layer 2 tomato slices on each piece of bread, sprinkle with salt and pepper, then top with the 2 remaining slices of bread. Grab lots of napkins and dig in.

| 331. | The Ultimate Tomato Sandwich, With Jammy Eggs & Herby Mayo |

Serving: Serves 1 | Prep: 0hours15mins | Cook: 0hours6mins | Ready in:

Ingredients

- 2 eggs, plus 1 egg yolk
- 1 teaspoon white vinegar

- 1/2 teaspoon lemon juice
- 1 teaspoon Dijon mustard
- 1/2 teaspoon kosher salt
- 1 teaspoon room-temperature water
- 1 cup safflower oil (or another neutral oil)
- 1/2 cup loosely packed basil and chives, very finely chopped (I like to blitz mine in a food processor, for ease); plus more for sprinkling
- 2 slices rustic, crusty bread
- 1 large ripe tomato (I like beefsteak), sliced roughly 1/2-inch thick
- 1 pinch each flaky salt and freshly ground pepper
- 1 tablespoon olive oil for drizzling

Direction

- Set a pot of water over high heat. Once it reaches a rolling boil, gently add two eggs. Let them boil for six minutes exactly. Meanwhile, fill a bowl with ice and a large splash of cold water, and place it nearby. After six minutes, transfer the eggs to this ice bath.
- Make the herb mayonnaise. In a bowl, whisk together the egg yolk, white vinegar, lemon juice, Dijon, kosher salt, and water. While whisking like your life depends on it, begin to dribble in the oil a few drops at a time, checking that it's fully distributed before adding more. Go slowly! Once you've added about a third of the oil this way, you'll have the beginnings of a thick, creamy mayonnaise. Stream in the rest of the oil steadily, continuing to whisk frantically as you go. Once you've added all of the oil, fold in the herbs. Set aside as you prepare the other elements. (Note: Mayonnaise can be made a few days in advance and kept in the refrigerator—wait to chop and add the herbs until you're ready to serve.)
- Toast the bread slices however you like (I prefer to do it in the stove at 450° F for 4 minutes). While the bread is toasting, peel the soft-boiled eggs in the ice bath.
- To compile your sandwich, slather one side of each piece of toast with herb mayo. Layer tomato slices on top, and drizzle with olive oil

and a pinch each of flaky salt and pepper. Slice the soft-boiled eggs lengthwise and immediately layer on top of the tomatoes, so you don't lose any yolky dregs! Garnish with a sprinkling of herbs, serve open-faced, and eat immediately.

332.   Three Cheese Garlic Bread

Serving: Serves 8 | Prep: | Cook: |Ready in:

Ingredients

- 2 tablespoons mayonnaise
- 2 tablespoons butter, unsalted, room temperature
- 4 cloves garlic, minced
- 3/4 cup green onions, thinly sliced
- 3/4 cup feta cheese, crumbled
- 3/4 cup monterey jack cheese, shredded
- 1/2 cup Parmesan, grated, divided
- 1 loaf focaccia bread, 10-12 ounces

Direction

- Preheat oven to 375 and line a baking sheet with aluminum foil. Place rack in the center of the oven.
- Mix together the mayonnaise, softened butter and garlic in a medium sized mixing bowl.
- Blend in the onions, feta, Monterrey Jack and 1/4 cup of Parmesan. Spread mixture onto the bread.
- Top with remaining Parmesan and bake until cheese is golden, about 15 minutes. Let cool slightly before slicing.

333.   Thrice Cooked Potatoes

Serving: Serves 6 | Prep: | Cook: |Ready in:

Ingredients

- 4 large russet or Yukon Gold potatoes, scrubbed and cut into 1/2-inch-thick batons
- Sea salt
- 1 quart peanut oil or fresh lard
- 2 thin slices pancetta or bacon
- Mayonnaise or ketchup, for serving

Direction

- Place the sliced potatoes in a large pan of cold water and soak for half an hour. This removes excess starch, giving the potatoes a lighter texture.
- Rinse and place the potatoes in a pan with cold water seasoned generously with sea salt. Bring to a boil and cook for 8 to 10 minutes, or until you can insert a knife easily through the center of the largest chip. Drain and run the chips under very cold water to prevent further cooking. Place the potatoes back in the pan, cover with a lid and shake the pan vigorously to rough up the edges. Spread the potatoes on a tea towel to dry and arrange on a baking sheet lined with parchment paper. Place the baking sheet in the freezer for 30 minutes. You want the potatoes very cold, if not nearly frozen, before you drop them into the hot oil to fry.
- Fill a medium saucepan a third full of oil or lard (about 1 quart) and heat it to 270 degrees. If using oil, add the pancetta and cook until crisp; use a slotted spoon to remove the pancetta (eat once cool!). Remove the potatoes from the freezer and carefully lower into the hot oil in batches of 8–10, cooking for 4–6 minutes, until they start to color. Drain on paper towel and continue cooking the remaining potatoes before cooling them in the freezer for another 30 minutes. Alternatively, prepare up to this stage a day in advance and leave them in the freezer overnight.
- For the final cooking, heat the same oil to 350 degrees and again, lower small batches of the potatoes into it. Cook for 2–3 minutes or until crisp and golden. As they come out of the oil, drain on paper towel and give each batch of

fries a good sprinkling of sea salt. Serve with mayonnaise or ketchup and eat while hot.

---

334. Tingly Szechuan Tots

Serving: Serves 4-6 | Prep: 0hours5mins | Cook: 0hours20mins | Ready in:

Ingredients

- one 32-ounce package frozen tots
- 1 tablespoon Szechuan peppercorns
- 1 1/2 teaspoons red pepper flakes
- 1 teaspoon dried garlic flakes
- 1 teaspoon salt
- 2/3 cup mayonnaise
- 1 tablespoon sesame oil
- Black sesame seeds, for garnish
- Scallions, chopped, for garnish

Direction

- Preheat oven or tabletop fryer to package directions to cook your tots. While the tots cook, prepare the spice mixture.
- In an electric spice grinder, grind the Szechuan peppercorns, red pepper flakes, fried garlic flakes, and salt to a fine but not quite powdery mixture — something like sand. Set aside.
- To make the dipping sauce, mix together the mayonnaise and sesame oil. Set aside.
- Once the tots are cooked and still hot, place them into a large mixing bowl and sprinkle the spice mixture over the top, tossing well to coat. Place onto a plate and sprinkle black sesame seeds and scallions over top. Serve with dipping sauce on the side.

---

335. Tofu Bacon Avocado Bahn Mi

Serving: Makes 4 | Prep: | Cook: | Ready in:

Ingredients

- 14-16 ounces Firm Tofu
- 2 tablespoons Fresh Ginger
- 2 teaspoons Sugar
- 1 teaspoon Fresh Ground Pepper
- 1/4 cup Soy Sauce
- 3 tablespoons Sesame Oil
- 1 tablespoon Olive Oil
- 4   Bread Rolls, we used Bolillo from our local Mexican grocery
- 2   Zuchini, cut lengthwise into 1/4" slices
- 3 tablespoons Mayonnaise
- 4 teaspoons Srisacha (or more if you like spicey!)
- 1 bunch Cilantro, chopped
- 1/4   Head of Red Cabbage, finely shopped
- 1   Lime, squeezed
- 4 pieces Bacon, cooked until crispy
- 1   Avocado, sliced
- 1   Jalapeno, seeded and chopped

Direction

- Cut tofu into pieces about 1/2 inch thick and put into gallon Ziploc to marinade. Micro plane the ginger and whisk together with the soy sauce, sesame oil, olive oil, sugar, and pepper. Pour into the Ziploc bag and make sure it's covering all tofu. Marinade overnight.
- Heat your grill or cast iron pan on high and seat tofu until grill marks appear and the tofu is heated through, turn once. Reserve the marinade and put your slices of zucchini into the bag that held the tofu and let it sit in the marinade for a few minutes before grilling the zucchini until tender and browned.
- Prep your remaining sandwich ingredients. Slice the avocado into thin slices and cook the bacon until crispy. Combine the mayonnaise and sriracha in a small bowl until blended well for spreading on your sandwich. In another bowl, combine your cilantro, cabbage, and jalapeno with the lime juice.
- Cut the sides of your bread toast to your liking, you could do this in the oven or on the grill, just until it's crisp. Now you're ready to assemble your sandwich! Spread the Sriracha mayo on both sides of the bread and layer your tofu, zucchini, bacon, avocado, and cilantro cabbage slaw. This sandwich is quite the mouthful, so we recommend cutting it in half first! Enjoy!

336.   Tonnato Sliders

Serving: Makes 6-12 patty-cakes | Prep: | Cook: | Ready in:

Ingredients

- 1/4 cup olive oil
- 2 tablespoons unsalted butter, divided
- 1   small yellow onion, chopped
- 1   small fennel bulb, chopped
- handful of spring radishes (5 or so), trimmed and chopped
- 1 teaspoon hot pepper flakes, or to taste
- generous pinch of caraway seeds
- 6   garlic cloves, chopped (remove and discard any green shoots)
- 9   anchovy fillets
- big handful of Italian parsley leaves, chopped (to yield a 1/4 cup or so)
- 3 6-8 oz cans good-quality tuna in olive oil, darined and chopped, oil reserved
- 1/2 cup dry white wine
- 1/4 cup capers, drained and rinsed
- 1/2 cup mayonnaise or aioli
- 2 tablespoons wine vinegar or lemon juice
- 2 tablespoons water
- salt and freshly ground pepper, to taste

Direction

- Heat the olive oil and 1 tbsp of the butter in a large skillet over medium-low heat. Add onions, fennel, and radishes, and sauté until tender and translucent. Add pepper flakes, caraway, garlic, and anchovies, and continue sautéing until anchovies have dissolved, then stir in the tuna, mashing with the back of a wooden spoon to break up any large chunks. Raise the heat to high and add the wine. Cook until almost all evaporated, then lower the heat and stir in the capers and the parsley. Stir in the remaining tbsp of butter and remove the pan from heat. Let the mixture cool completely.

- Transfer half of the skillet mixture to a food processor with the mayonnaise (or aioli), vinegar (or lemon juice), and water. Measure out and add 2 tbsp of the tuna oil, discarding the remainder. Pulse until you achieve a pasty consistency. Transfer to a mixing bowl and lightly mix with the remaining skillet mixture. Refrigerate several hours or overnight.

- When you are ready to cook, form the mixture into patties of roughly equal size and heft. I think slider-size is ideal, but feel free to go big. Heat a large non-stick skillet and slick with a light coat of olive oil. When it shimmers, add the patties in batches, taking care not to overcrowd. Pan-fry until browned, then flip and cook until heated through. Serve on mini-brioche buns, or better yet, mini croissants, perhaps with some arugula or watercress and a little cheddar melted over. (Do this open-faced for tuna melt-style.)

337.	Tortilla With Chive And Garlic Aioli

Serving: Serves 6 as an hors d'oeuvre or 2 for lunch (with salad) | Prep: | Cook: | Ready in:

Ingredients

- 1 3/4 pounds white or baking potatoes
- 6 tablespoons olive oil, plus more for cooking the tortilla
- Salt
- 6 large eggs
- Freshly ground black pepper
- 1/2 bunch chives cut into 1-inch-long slices
- 5 garlic cloves

- 1/2 cup Hellmann's mayonnaise, or homemade

Direction

- Heat the oven to 375 degrees. Peel the potatoes, then rinse them. Slice them as thinly as possible (1/16 inch thick) on a mandoline, and discard the nubby ends. Spread the potato slices on a baking sheet, sprinkle with 2 tablespoons olive oil, season with salt and toss to coat -- do this with your hands, which is the only way to coat them evenly; plus it's good for your skin.

- Roast the potatoes for 15 minutes. Turn the potatoes with a spatula and roast for another 10. The potatoes are done when they're tender and the ones on the perimeter are getting brown and crisp. Remove from the oven and let cool.

- Crack the eggs into a large bowl and whisk until blended and frothy. Add the cooled potatoes and a good bunch of pepper (I like it coarse). Blend with your hands, taking care to separate the potato slices without breaking them.

- Generously coat the base of a well-seasoned 9-inch cast iron (or nonstick) skillet with olive oil and set over medium heat. Crush two of the garlic cloves and add to the pan. When they begin sizzling, slide in the egg and potato mixture. Arrange and press the potatoes so they're mostly lying flat. Reduce the heat to low (or medium-low if you have a meek stove) and let cook for 20 minutes. Check from time to time, slipping a spatula under one edge and lifting, to see if the tortilla is cooking too slowly or too quickly. By the end of 20 minutes, the base should be golden brown.

- Now get ready to turn it -- this is the only tricky part about making tortilla. Get a baking sheet without a raised edge (or thin cutting board) and lay it, inverted, over the skillet. Then using oven mitts on both hands, lift the skillet, holding the pan on top and take it over to your sink, then swiftly invert the two, so the tortilla falls onto the baking sheet. Set down on the counter. Breathe.

- If any pieces stick to the skillet, pry them off and either patch up the tortilla or eat the bits. Add more oil to the skillet if needed, then slide the tortilla back into the skillet (browned side up) and place back on the heat to cook the other side, 15 minutes.
- Now don't hate me, but I'm going to have you flip the tortilla again and cook it for 10 more minutes on the first side. Then you can shut off the heat and call it done. Serve it at room temperature, inverted onto a platter.
- Time to make the aioli: combine the chives and remaining 3 cloves garlic in a food processor or blender. With the machine running, slowly drizzle in the oil through the feed tube and let it purée until the chives are fully pulverized. You may need to scrape down the sides of the bowl once or twice. Season with salt.
- Put the mayonnaise in a bowl. Add the chive-and-garlic oil, 1 tablespoon at a time (to taste), and blend with the mayonnaise. Adjust seasoning as desired. Serve alongside the tortilla, which should be cut into wedges.

338.   Triple Sandwich

Serving: Makes 4 personal triples or 36 mini bites | Prep: | Cook: |Ready in:

Ingredients

- 2 avocados peeled and cut into thin slices
- 1 cup home-made mayonnaise
- juice of 1 lime
- 3 slices of bread for every sandwich
- salt and freshly ground pepper
- 2 tomatoes cut into very thin slices
- 3 boiled eggs cut into thins slices

Direction

- Place on a cutting board the sliced tomato, egg and avocado, peeled and thinly sliced too.

Add salt and pepper and squeeze over the lime juice.

- Take three slices of bread and spread mayonnaise on them.
- Place avocado over a slice first, pressing with a fork to make it compact. Be generous.
- Cap. Put mayonnaise.
- Add egg slices (3) and 4 tomato sliced very thin. Cap.
- Cut into 3 vertical rows and 2 horizontal and you've got many small addictive Triple bites. Cut in diagonally and you've made one just for you!!

339.   Trout Kabayaki With Avocado

Serving: Serves 2 | Prep: | Cook: |Ready in:

Ingredients

- For the trout:
- 1 medium shallot, chopped
- 1 tablespoon ginger, chopped
- 1/4 cup soy sauce
- 1/4 cup mirin
- 2 tablespoons sugar
- 2 trout fillets
- For the accoutrements:
- 1/4 cup rice vinegar
- 1/2 teaspoon sambal (hot chili sauce)
- 2 teaspoons sugar
- 1 teaspoon salt
- Pepper, to taste
- 2 carrots, julienned
- 1 cucumber, julienned
- 1 jalapeño, seeded and julienned
- 1 avocado
- 2 tablespoons mayonnaise
- 1 tablespoon sweet chili garlic sauce
- 1/2 teaspoon soy
- 1/2 lime, juiced
- Sesame seeds, for garnish
- Cooked rice, for serving

- Cilantro, for garnish
- A green side (asparagus, sugarsnap peas, kale, spinach), cooked quickly in oil with garlic

Direction

- Start with the accoutrements: Mix together the vinegar, sambal, sugar, salt, and pepper until dissolved. Add the carrots, cucumber, and jalapeño, then toss and set aside. (This can be done a day or two ahead and stored in the fridge.)
- Preheat broiler. While it heats, cook the shallots over medium-low heat in a pan with a bit of oil until they're medium brown. Add the ginger and cook for few minutes, then add the soy, mirin, and sugar and simmer on low for about 12 minutes, or until the sauce is thick. Be careful not to burn it. Cool the sauce and blend it using an immersion blender (or transfer the sauce to a blender). Set aside.
- Broil trout skin side-up for a couple of minutes, then remove the skin. Slather the sauce on the trout and broil the fish for a couple additional minutes, slathering twice more as it cooks. Gently flip the fillets and cook them for few more minutes, again slathering twice. Set aside.
- Mash avocado and mix with mayonnaise, sweet chili sauce, soy, lime juice, and salt and pepper to taste.
- Mound rice on a plate and top with trout, pickled vegetables, your green vegetable of choice, and mashed avocado. Garnish with sesame seeds and cilantro.

340.   Tsuyu Candied Kabocha With Bonito

Serving: Serves 2-3 | Prep: | Cook: | Ready in:

Ingredients

- 1/2 small kabocha squash, seeded and cut into 1-inch wedges

- 2 tablespoons bottled tsuyu*
- 4 tablespoons sweet mayonnaise (Kewpie, if you have it)
- 1 tablespoon bonito flakes, to serve

Direction

- Preheat the oven to 400 degrees F. Line a large baking sheet with parchment paper.
- Whisk together the tsuyu and mayonnaise until well combined. Dip the kabocha wedges into the tsuyu mixture to coat on both sides, allowing the excess to drip off and reserve the remaining mixture. Place the coated wedges on the lined baking sheet.
- Bake for 20 minutes, brush with some of the remaining tsuyu mixture and continue baking at 375 degrees F for another 10 minutes. Brush again and bake for another 15 minutes, or until bubbly and fully caramelized.
- Top with bonito flakes and serve with steamed rice and sliced avocado to round out the meal.
- * If you're unsure about tsuyu, "[it] is the delicious soup stock used for most Japanese noodle dishes, hotpots and can even be used as a rich dipping sauce for tempura. Tsuyu has become an increasingly popular condiment in Japan and is made from a blend of dashi soup stock and a mixture of soy sauce, mirin and sugar."

341.   Tuna Avocado Okra Cannelloni With Red Shiso Gazpacho

Serving: Serves 4 dinner or 8 first-course servings | Prep: | Cook: | Ready in:

Ingredients

- Tuna Avocado Filling
- 2 Avocados (plus 1/2 for backup plan)
- 1 tablespoon lemon juice (1/4 lemon freshly squeezed)

- 1 cup green or spring onions, thinly sliced, starting at green tops
- 1/4 cup Greek yogurt
- 2 tablespoons Mayonnaise, I prefer Kewpie; if using a thick type add another 1/4 of lemon
- 6   pods okra (optional) microwaved or steamed, sliced
- 1   cucumber, diced in 1/4 in cubes, OPTIONAL
- 1/2 pound fresh Tuna, sushi grade, (250 g)
- salt, to taste
- 16   cannelloni tube pasta (250 g), or 8 lasagna sheets
- Red-Shiso Gazpacho
- 2   Large, very-ripe tomatoes
- 3   medium-size Tuscan purple tomatoes
- 1/4   red bell pepper
- 1   large clove garlic
- 1/2   knob fresh ginger (or 2 myoga ginger flowers) scraped, sliced
- 10-12   red shiso leaves (purple perilla) about 2 inches in size
- 1/2 teaspoon soy sauce, to taste
- 1/2 teaspoon horseradish

Direction

- Put tomatoes, bell pepper, garlic, ginger, and shiso leaves in the blender and give it a whirl. When mixed, add soy sauce and horseradish. Put the whole blender jar in your fridge to chill for about 2-3 hours.
- Cube the softest avocado and mix with the lemon juice.
- Slice onions, and move to the side of cutting board or another bowl.
- Add yogurt, mayonnaise, and pepper to the avocado. Mix until the avocado is slightly smashed and mixture will be greenish. Put the wasabi on the edge of the bowl and mix a little bit into the yogurt/mayo, slowly increasing until all mixed. Taste here and if the wasabi goes "zzznnnttt" up your nose, it is the right strength. If you pass out or gag, it is probably too strong.
- Cube the other avocado.

- Check if you have enough onions, the spring onion pile should be about the same volume as your two cubed avocados. Add onions to the yogurt/ mayo/avocado mixture and mix well.
- Add the optional cucumber now. It does add a pretty green color, but even finely diced it was too crunchy. We liked the smooth velvet-iness of the avocados without it. On the other hand, okra, avocados, and tuna are delicious together. Add okra here if you are using, save some for decorations.
- Then slowly, gently add the second avocado. Chill.
- You can add the tuna now if you want the flavors to meld, but the lemon juice will begin to 'cook' the tuna, turning it a little grayish on each piece. I prefer my cubes to be red, so I add the tuna right before plating.
- About 20 minutes before serving: Boil cannelloni or lasagna noodles. I used Barilla Cannelloni-8 minutes is recommended. We like el dante but these noodles need to be softer to eat, but not so delicate they keep falling apart.
- Add cubed tuna to the avocado mixture. Taste test the filling. Need more wasabi? Salt? If too strong, add another half of an avocado. Spoon or pipe in the filling. Carefully lay on plates with lasagna noodles seam-side down.
- Whirl gazpacho in blender right before serving. Check seasonings. Spoon over filled cannelloni.
- NOTE: Wasabi POWDER needs to be blended with water in a little bowl. Turn the bowl upside down until you use it. Wasabi also comes in tubes already mixed. Both types do not have salt added. If you don't like wasabi, or really love horseradish, you can substitute it but it does have salt. Make either the cannelloni or the gazpacho "HOT" and leave the other half as a cooling effect. In Japanese, horseradish is known as 'Western wasabi'.

342.   Tunisian Sandwich (Bonito, Cured Lemon & Harissa Mayo Sandwich)

Serving: Makes 1 sandwich plus lots of extra harissa |
| Prep: 0hours10mins | Cook: 0hours10mins | Ready in:

Ingredients

- 2 ounces dry-packed sun-dried tomatoes, sliced
- 1 teaspoon each whole coriander and cumin seeds
- 1/2 teaspoon caraway seeds
- 2 long narrow hot red fresh peppers, seeded, trimmed and coarsely chopped
- about 8 Fresno peppers, seeded, trimmed and coarsely chopped
- 3 fat fresh garlic cloves, coarsely chopped plus one garlic clove, unpeeled, cut in half diagonally
- 1/4 cup extra-virgin olive oil
- kosher salt to taste
- 1/2 teaspoon ground Aleppo or other mildly spice ground red pepper
- 2 thick slices of crusty sourdough or country bread, preferably hand-sliced
- 1 tablespoon prepared mayonnaise
- 1 squirt lemon juice
- 1 hard-cooked egg, sliced lengthwise in an egg slicer
- 1/2 can (~2 oz. total) best-quality tuna in olive oil such as Ortiz Bonito del Norte
- 1/4 cured Moroccan-style lemon, rinsed and diced
- 1 handful washed baby arugula as garnish
- sliced very ripe tomato
- 3 thin slices ripe avocado
- 2-3 pitted marinated black or red-black olives (optional) such as kalamata

Direction

- To make the harissa:
- Bring a kettle of water to the boil. Cool slightly. In a heat-proof bowl, pour boiling water over sun-dried tomatoes to reconstitute.

Let sit 10 minutes while you continue with recipe.
- Toast spices lightly in a heavy skillet until fragrant; empty into bowl of mini-processor. Cover, start motor and grind them coarsely.
- Add chopped peppers and garlic to spice grinder. Drain tomatoes, reserving soaking water for another use, and pat dry with paper towels. Add tomatoes to puree; cover and whiz until pureed. Add olive oil, a few tablespoons at a time, whizzing until blended. Add a pinch or two of salt and Aleppo pepper and blend. Scrape into a container. Makes extra harissa.
- To assemble sandwich:
- Toast bread lightly
- Take each half of the cut clove of garlic and rub crusts and inner face of each slice of toasted bread.
- In a small bowl, whisk 1 tablespoon mayonnaise, 1 teaspoon harissa and a squirt of lemon juice.
- Spread harissa mayonnaise generously on each slice. Layer bottom half with tomato, 3-4 slices of egg, a few spoonful of tuna (drained and flaked), finely chopped cured lemon, optional chopped olives, and arugula. Top with remaining slice of bread. Press together slightly, cut in halves on the diagonal, secure each half with a decorative toothpick if desired, and serve.

343.   Turkey Banh Mi Sandwich

Serving: Serves 6 | Prep: | Cook: | Ready in:

Ingredients

- 1 pound leftover turkey
- 6 baguettes
- 1 daikon radish, cut into matchsticks
- 3 carrots, cut into matchsticks
- 1/4 cup white vinegar

- 1/4 cup unseasoned rice vinegar
- 1 cup water
- 1/4 cup sugar
- 1 tablespoon salt
- 1 cup mayonnaise
- 2 tablespoons sriracha, or more for added spice
- 2 teaspoons Maggi seasoning
- 1 english cucumber, chopped
- 1 jalapeno peppers, chopped
- 1 bunch cilantro, chopped

Direction

- Make the pickled vegetables (called do chua): Put the white vinegar, rice vinegar, water, sugar, and salt into a canning jar or container with a lid and stir until the sugar is dissolved. Add the daikon radish and carrot matchsticks. Make sure all the vegetables are covered. Refrigerate up to a month.
- Make the "special" sauce: Mix mayonnaise, sriracha and Maggi seasoning together until combined. Refrigerate. I put the finished sauce in a squirt bottle for convenience. Maggi sauce is available at grocery stores and is widely used in Asian recipes.
- Chop up cucumbers and jalapeno into bite sized pieces. If you like it spicy, leave the seeds in the jalapeno. Set aside.
- Chop up cilantro, including stems, and set aside.
- Slice up the turkey into sandwich slices. Slice open the baguettes and toast under the broiler under browned.
- To assemble the banh mi: Line up the toasted baguettes. Spread on the "special" sauce, then add the sliced turkey. Add the pickled vegetables, and top with a few chopped cucumbers, jalapenos, and chopped cilantro. Squirt or place approximately 1/4 tsp. more "special" sauce on top and serve!

---

344.   Turkey Peanut Dip

Serving: Serves 4-6 | Prep: | Cook: | Ready in:

Ingredients

- 1 pound Ground Turkey
- 2 Garlic Cloves
- 1.2 Small Onion
- 1/4 cup Peanut Butter
- 1 tablespoon Soy Sauce
- 3 tablespoons Mayonnaise
- 3 teaspoons Chili Powder (if you like spicy taste, add more)
- 2/3 cup Crushed Peanuts
- 2 tablespoons Olive Oil

Direction

- Mince onion and garlic cloves.
- Heat olive oil in a skillet and cook onion and garlic until tender. Then add ground turkey and cook until browned.
- Add peanut butter and soy sauce. Stir to coat well. Then turn off the heat and add mayonnaise, chili powder and peanuts. Stir until well blended.

---

345.   Twice Baked Potatoes With Lobster And Shrimp

Serving: Serves 4 | Prep: | Cook: | Ready in:

Ingredients

- 4 large russet baking potatoes
- 125 grams cream cheese, softened to room temperature
- 1/4 cup mayonnaise
- 1/4 cup milk
- 1/2 teaspoon white truffle oil
- 1/4 teaspoon black pepper
- 1 tablespoon chopped fresh chives
- 12 large shrimp, peeled and de-veined
- 2 whole lobster tails

- 1 tablespoon butter
- 1/4 teaspoon sea salt
- 1 cup shredded Gruyere cheese

Direction

- Preheat oven to 425.
- Wash potatoes, prick with a fork, and bake directly on your oven rack for 1 hour until tender
- Trim off potato ends, halve, and let rest until cool enough to handle. Gently remove the baked potato from the skins and mash well. Reserve the potato skin for stuffing later.
- Add the softened cream cheese, and mayonnaise and whip using an electric mixer. Add the milk and continue to whip until potatoes are smooth without lumps. Blend in the white truffle oil.
- Remove shrimp and lobster from shells. Chop meat into bite size pieces and sauté over medium high heat in butter for 1-2 minutes until cooked through. Add the salt. Add the seafood to the potatoes along with a half cup of the cheese and the chives. Stir well.
- Spray a baking sheet with cooking spray. Spoon the potato mixture back into the potato skins and place on the prepared baking sheet. Top the potatoes evenly with the remaining Gruyere cheese and bake in a 350 oven for 30 minutes or until the cheese topping is golden.

346.   Uncluckingbelievable Chicken Salad

Serving: Serves 8 | Prep: | Cook: | Ready in:

Ingredients

- Roasting the chicken
- 2 4 lb. Whole Chickens, preferably kosher
- 6 tablespoons Ground cumin
- 4 tablespoons Black peppercorns, smashed
- 2 tablespoons Kosher salt
- 8 Carrots, peeled, trimmed and cut into 2" pieces
- 2 Heads of fennel, trimmed and sliced
- 1 White onion, peeled and cut into eight pieces
- 1 Butternut squash, peeled, trimmed and cut into 1" cubes
- 4 tablespoons Olive oil
- Making the Chicken Salad
- 2 tablespoons Fig preserves
- 4 tablespoons Mayonnaise

Direction

- Roasting the chicken
- Mix cumin, salt and pepper. Drizzle 2 Tb. of oil over chickens. Rub chickens inside and outside with spice mixture. Reserve around 1/4 of mixture.
- Toss vegetables with remaining olive oil and spices.
- Heat oven to 450 degrees. Place chickens in large roasting pan. Put vegetables around chicken. Roast approximately 1 hour until juices run clear, turning chickens after half an hour. When chicken is done, remove and let cool. If vegetables are not soft and caramelized, continue cooking until they are succulent.
- When cool enough to handle, remove chicken meat from the bones and cut into big chunks (where possible). Coarsely chop vegetables.
- Making the Chicken Salad
- Combine chicken, vegetables, preserves and mayonnaise in bowl. Salt and pepper to taste. Salad is best when flavors can meld for at least an hour.

347.   Vegan Sushi

Serving: Makes 6 rolls (approximately 50 pieces) | Prep: | Cook: | Ready in:

Ingredients

- Sushi rice
- 2 cups sushi or short grain white rice
- 2 1/4 cups cold water
- 5 tablespoons rice vinegar
- 2 tablespoons raw sugar
- 1/2 teaspoon fine sea salt
- Fillings
- 6 sheets nori
- 1/4 cup mayonnaise (vegan if necessary)
- 1 ripe avocado, sliced
- 1 small cucumber, sliced
- 2 tablespoons toasted sesame seeds
- pickled ginger, wasabI, and gluten-free soy sauce, to serve

Direction

- Sushi rice
- Place the rice in a bowl, cover with water, and massage it with your hands. You will see the water turn white as the starch is washed off the grains. Drain the rice, then repeat this 2 to 3 more times until the water is almost clear.
- Transfer rice to a sieve and set it aside to drain for 20 to 30 minutes. Transfer it to a medium saucepan, then cover with the 2 1/4 cups of cold water. If time allows, set the rice aside to soak for 30 to 60 minutes. Otherwise, continue on with the recipe right away.
- Cover the saucepan with a lid and bring to a boil over high heat. As soon as the water boils, turn the temperature down to the lowest setting, making sure the lid is still on, and cook for 12 minutes. Remove the pot from the heat, leaving the lid firmly on; don't be tempted to peek or you'll run the risk of the steam escaping and the rice not cooking completely. Let the rice stand for 15 minutes.
- Combine the rice vinegar, sugar, and salt in a small saucepan. Bring the mixture to a boil over a medium-low heat, stirring to dissolve the sugar. Boil for 1 to 2 minutes until syrupy, then remove from the heat and set aside to cool. Stir the seasoned vinegar through the rice, then turn it out onto a flat tray to cool to room temperature.
- Fillings

- Place a sheet of nori, shiny-side down, on a bamboo sushi mat. Have a small bowl of water nearby and wet your hands to stop the rice from sticking.
- Divide the cooled rice into 6 portions. Using your wet hands, gently spread one portion of rice over the nori, leaving a good amount of space on the top and bottom. Don't press the rice down firmly -- just pat it into place.
- Spread a little mayonnaise down the center of the rice, then sprinkle with sesame seeds. Arrange a few strips of cucumber and avocado on top. Wet your finger and rub it along the edge of nori furthest away from you (this will help seal your sushi roll).
- Using the bamboo mat for assistance, lift the end of the sushi closest to you up and over the filling, gently squeezing the mat as you go. Continue rolling the mat forward to complete the roll.
- Repeat this process with the remaining nori, rice, and filling until you have 6 rolls. To slice, run a sharp knife under cold water and cut each roll into 8 to 10 slices. Serve with pickled ginger, wasabi and soy sauce.

348.   Vegetarian "Reuben"

Serving: Makes 2 sandwiches | Prep: 0hours10mins | Cook: 0hours20mins |Ready in:

Ingredients

- 4 slices rye or pumpernickel bread
- 4 slices Swiss cheese (lacey, baby, or regular)
- 10 to 15 button mushrooms (cleaned and sliced)
- 1/4 head red cabbage (sliced)
- 2 cloves garlic (minced)
- 3 tablespoons mayonnaise
- 2 tablespoons Dijon mustard
- 2 tablespoons dill pickle relish
- 2 tablespoons prepared horseradish
- 1/4 cup apple cider vinegar

- 1 pinch sea salt and freshly ground black pepper
- 1 serving unsalted butter, for spreading
- 1 splash Olive oil

Direction

- The first step in assembling this grilled cheese is to prepare all your ingredients. Heat two sauté pans over medium heat. Add some olive oil to each pan. In one pan, add the mushrooms, garlic, and black pepper. Let cook for 5 minutes.
- In the second pan, add the red cabbage, salt, and pepper and let cook in oil for 2 minutes. Add the vinegar and horseradish and let cook for 5 more minutes.
- While both the mushrooms and cabbage are cooking, mix up the dressing. Combine mayonnaise, Dijon, and relish in a small bowl.
- Butter one side of 2 pieces of bread generously. On the other side of the buttered pieces of bread, spread the dressing. Add mushrooms to each sandwich. Add a slice of cheese on top of the mushrooms. Cover the cheese in cabbage. Add one more slice of cheese on top of the cabbage.
- Heat a skillet over medium heat. Place the slices of bread, buttered side down, on the skillet. Add the second slice of bread to the top of the sandwich and place a couple cubes of butter on top of each slice. Put the pan you used to cook the mushrooms or cabbage on top of the sandwiches (unless you have a foil-covered brick or some other cool device).
- Flip after a few minutes and cook the other side without the pan. The bread should be nice and crusty, and cheese should be melting out the sides.

---

349.   Veggie Masala Burgers With Cilantro Chutney Aioli

Serving: Makes 8 to 10 burgers | Prep: | Cook: | Ready in:

Ingredients

- Masala Burger
- 4 cups shredded cauliflower (yield from one medium size head)
- 2 cups shredded carrot (yield from about 4-5 medium size carrots)
- 1 cup onion, finely diced
- 2 green chilies
- 2 tablespoons ginger-garlic paste
- 2 teaspoons cumin powder
- 2 teaspoons coriander powder
- 1 teaspoon chili powder (additional teaspoon if you like it spicy)
- 1.5 tablespoons Madras curry powder
- 3/4 cup chopped cilantro
- 3/4 cup breadcrumbs (can be replaced with chick pea flour for gluten free version)
- 1 large egg
- 1 cup plus 2 tbsp canola oil
- Salt and Pepper to taste
- 8-10 toasted buns
- Cilantro Chutney Aioli
- 1 bunch fresh cilantro
- 3 small green chilies
- 1-2 cloves of garlic
- 1 inch piece of fresh ginger
- 1 tablespoon cumin seeds
- 1 pinch asafetida
- 1/4 cup canola oil
- 1 lime, zested and juiced
- salt and pepper to taste
- 3 tablespoons mayonnaise

Direction

- Masala Burger
- In a large skillet over medium heat, fry the onions, green chillies, and ginger garlic paste in the 2 tbsps. of oil.
- Add cumin, coriander and chili powders and continue to saute until spices have been absorbed by the oil.
- Mix in the shredded cauliflower and carrots into the mixture and allow to sweat for a few minutes before seasoning well with salt and pepper.

- When cauliflower begins to look slightly transparent add the curry powder and saute until fully incorporated. Cook the mixture until fork tender but not mushy. Place in a large mixing bowl to cool.
- Add the chopped cilantro, breadcrumbs, and egg and mix well. The mixture should not appear too wet, and you should be able to form rough balls.
- Divide mixture into 8 to 10 balls based on the size of the buns you're using and form in patties.
- In a large skillet on medium-high heat pour enough oil to cover the bottom of the pan by 1/4 inch.
- In batches, gently place the patties around the pan giving enough room to flip over. Sear the bottom of each patty until completely brown before flipping over and repeating on the other side. The patties should be crisp, hinging on the side of burnt, on the top and bottom. Sear sides as well for extra texture if desired. Remove from pan and blot off excess oil before placing on toasted buns.
- Cilantro Chutney Aioli
- In a food processor or blender, puree the ginger, garlic, lime juice and zest, cumin seeds, and asafetida.
- Add the cilantro and blend on low while drizzling in the canola oil. Add water if needed to bring it to a consistency of a thin paste.
- Season with salt and pepper. Store in an airtight container in the fridge for future use
- Take 4 tablespoons of the fresh chutney and mix with 3 tablespoons of mayonnaise. Spread over the top of all the toasted buns.

| 350. | Vietnamese Banh Mi Burgers |

Serving: Serves 4 | Prep: | Cook: | Ready in:

Ingredients

- 2 carrots, shredded
- 1/4 cup rice vinegar
- 1 tablespoon sugar
- 1/2 cup mayonnaise
- 2 tablespoons Frank's Red Hot sauce
- 2 teaspoons tomato paste
- 1 garlic clove, minced
- salt and pepper
- 1 & 1/2 pounds ground beef
- 1 & 1/2 teaspoons curry powder
- 2 tablespoons vegetable oil
- 2 tablespoons unsalted butter
- 4 Ciabatta Rolls
- 10   sliced jalapeños

Direction

- Preheat oven to 400 degrees F. In a small bowl, combine the carrots, jalapeños, rice vinegar, and sugar. Toss to combine and let sit for about 10 minutes. Drain, then set aside.
- In another small bowl, mix the mayonnaise, tomato paste, hot sauce, garlic, salt, and pepper. Mix well and set aside.
- Patty up the beef into 4 large burgers. You could go as thick or thin as you want, but I just quartered my ground beef and made a patty out of each one. It made for a decent size patty. Season each patty with curry powder, salt, and pepper. It's pretty simple seasoning here, but I think the curry powder really adds a depth of flavor.
- In a large skillet, heat the oil under medium-high heat. Add the patties and cook until nicely browned on each side. Flip only once, took about 15 minutes or so, depending on how thick your patties are.
- While the patties are cooking, you can start crisping up your ciabatta rolls. Cut each roll in half and spread butter on cut sides of bread. Set bread, cut side up, and bake for about 5 minutes so you get a nice, lightly toasted roll.
- Spread spicy mayo on side of roll, then place patty on roll, and top with pickled carrots and jalapeños.

351.   Vietnamese Flavored Chicken Salad Lettuce Wraps With Spicy Cucumbers

Serving: Serves 6 | Prep: | Cook: |Ready in:

Ingredients

- Vietnamese Flavored Chicken Salad Wraps
- 3 cups Cooked shredded chicken
- 1 cup Shredded carrots
- 1/2 cup Sliced garlic scapes or scallions
- 1/4 cup Chopped cilantro
- 1 cup Mayonnaise
- 2 tablespoons Sriracha
- 1 tablespoon Fish Sauce
- 1 1/2 tablespoons Lime juice
- 6   Bibb Lettuce Leaves
- Spicy cucumbers (recipe follows)
- Spicy Cucumbers
- 1   Cucumber, peeled, split lengthwise and seeded
- 1 teaspoon Salt
- 1 tablespoon Lime juice
- 1 tablespoon Soy sauce
- 1 tablespoon Fish Sauce
- 1 tablespoon Sugar
- 1 1/2 teaspoons Sambal Olek

Direction

- Vietnamese Flavored Chicken Salad Wraps
- Combine the chicken, carrots, garlic scapes or scallions, and cilantro in a bowl.
- Whisk together the mayonnaise, Sriracha, fish sauce and lime juice. Add to chicken and combine well. Serve the chicken salad in the lettuce leaves topped with the cucumbers.
- Spicy Cucumbers
- Cut the cucumber into 1/2-inch thick slices. Toss with the salt and set aside for 1 hour. Drain the cucumbers in a colander, rinse well with cold water, and dry.
- Whisk together the lime juice, soy sauce, fish sauce, sugar, and sambal oelek. Toss the sauce

with the cucumbers and chill for at least 20 minutes.

352.   Warm Steelhead And Roasted Beet Salad With Crispy Potatoes

Serving: Serves 4 | Prep: | Cook: |Ready in:

Ingredients

- 4   small Steelhead trout fillets
- 2   small yukon gold potatoes (or other starchy potatoes, like russets), sliced very thinly
- 3   beets
- 3 - 5   radishes (depending on size), thinly sliced
- 150   grams of guanciale, sliced into small cubes
- 1   clove garlic, minced
- 1   shallot, minced
- 3 cups mixed salad greens
- 0.25 cups fresh dill, chopped
- 2 tablespoons mayonnaise
- 2 tablespoons dijon mustard
- Olive oil
- Salt and freshly cracked pepper

Direction

- Preheat your oven to 350 degrees. Remove the stems and leaves from the beets, wash thoroughly, then roast until softened, about 45 minutes. Let the roasted beets sit for about 10 minutes, then remove the skins (they should easily slide off) and slice into bite-sized wedges.
- Lay the potato slices out on a baking sheet – they should not be overlapping. Brush thoroughly with olive oil, then sprinkle with salt and freshly cracked black pepper. Roast for about 10 minutes, then flip each slice over and roast for another 10 – 15 minutes or until the edges are beginning to turn brown and crispy (this will depend on how thinly you've

sliced the potatoes – you want to aim for slices about 2 millimeters thick).

- Heat a pan over medium heat. Sauté the shallot until translucent, then add the garlic and continue to sauté for another 1 – 2 minutes. Remove from the pan and set aside. Now add the guanciale to the pan and sauté until crispy, then set aside.
- In a small bowl, stir the mayonnaise and the mustard until well mixed.
- Place the steelhead fillets on a baking sheet. Brush lightly with olive oil and sprinkle with salt and pepper, then bake until no longer translucent, about 10 – 12 minutes.
- In a bowl, combine the salad greens, shallot, garlic, guanciale, radishes, beets and dill. Drizzle lightly with olive oil (or, if you're feeling adventurous, a little bit of the fat that's rendered off of the guanciale – it'll add extra depth of flavor to the salad) then toss to combine. Add a handful of the salad to each plate, then add several potato slices and top with a steelhead fillet. Add a spoonful of the Dijon mayonnaise on top, then serve.

---

353.   Warm Summer Shrimp Salad

Serving: Serves 4-6 | Prep: | Cook: | Ready in:

Ingredients

- 2 pounds large shrimp (21/25 count), peeled and deveined, shells reserved
- 2 tablespoons coarse salt
- freshly ground white pepper
- 4 cups water
- 6 ears fresh sweet corn, kernels scraped (about 3 cups)
- 1 tablespoon corn oil, preferably unrefined, or pure olive oil
- 2-3 medium to large tomatoes, preferably heirloom, cored and chopped
- 2 lemons (finely grated zest and juice of 1, and 1 quartered)
- 1/4 cup mayonnaise, or to taste
- 1 small bunch basil leaves, chopped
- 1/2 cup loosely packed microgreens or arugula

Direction

- Place the shrimp in a bowl. Rub and toss with 1 tablespoon of the coarse salt. Wash under cold running water. Rub once again with the remaining 1 tablespoon salt, wash well under cold running water, and then drain in a colander. Pat dry with paper towels. Season the shrimp generously with the white pepper. Set aside. Combine the shrimp shells and water in a saucepan. Bring to a boil over medium-high heat. Decrease the heat to simmer and let cook until the shells are pink and the broth is fragrant, about 3 minutes. Strain, reserving the broth and discarding the shells. Wipe the saucepan clean.
- Return the strained broth to the now-clean saucepan. Add the corn and season with salt and pepper. Bring to a boil over medium-high heat. Decrease the heat to simmer and cook until the corn is tender, about 3 minutes. Drain in a fine-mesh sieve. Place the corn in a medium bowl. Set aside.
- Heat the oil in a large skillet over high heat until shimmering. Add the reserved shrimp and cook until pink and opaque, 3 to 5 minutes. Add the shrimp and chopped tomatoes to the corn. Add the lemon zest, lemon juice, mayonnaise, and basil. Stir to combine. Taste and adjust for seasoning with salt and pepper. Divide among chilled plates. Garnish each with micro greens and a wedge of lemon. Serve immediately.
- Brilliant: Presentation Served with Popcorn. This recipe is already about building layers of flavor -- using shrimp stock to cook the corn, using corn oil to cook the shrimp. To elevate this simple and elegant, yet basic recipe to Brilliant, add popcorn to take it a step further. Prepare the recipe as for Basic and spoon onto

room-temperature serving places. Scatter each plate with 1/4 cup freshly popped, lightly salted popcorn. This popcorn enhances the already present flavor of the corn as well as mixing up the textures and temperatures.

354. Whole Fish Roasted With A Medley Of Vegetables

Serving: Serves 6-8 | Prep: | Cook: | Ready in:

Ingredients

- Ingredients for the fish and vegetables:
- • 2 whole fish about 2 ½ pounds each, such as Red Snapper or Striped Bass or any fish with a white flash, and not a lot of bones (scaled, gutted and gills removed)
- • 1 cup Pure olive oil plus 11/2 tablespoons
- • 1 cup good quality dry white wine (Sauvignon Blank)
- • 1 tablespoon white wine vinegar
- • 2 medium size onions sliced thickly
- • 2 medium eggplants(unpeeled) sliced in half, and then cut in half-moon pieces about 1/3 of an inch
- • 3, 4 large ripe but firm meaty tomatoes cut in ¼ inch rounds
- • 1 red bell pepper sliced in strips
- • 1 yellow or orange bell pepper sliced in strips
- • 3 carrots and 2 parsnips, sliced in strips
- • ½ teaspoon dry pepper flakes
- • 4 cloves of garlic finally grated plus 4 cloves unpeeled and smashed
- • 8 lemon slices
- • 2 bundles fresh herbs, such as thyme, parsley, and dill, plus a lot of extra (chopped)
- • Kosher salt and freshly ground black pepper
- Lemon Sauce:
- • 3 lemons, juiced
- • 1 tablespoon prepared mayonnaise
- • 1 teaspoon Dijon mustard
- • 1 tablespoon honey

- • Salt and freshly ground black pepper
- • 1/2 cup olive oil
- • 1 tablespoon chopped fresh herbs

Direction

- Prepare the fish and marinate over night before roasting. Wash and dry with paper towels the fish inside and the skin. Cut three (3) diagonal slits about 1/3-inch deep on each side of the fish.3. Mix salt, pepper, the grated garlic, and 2 tablespoons of olive oil; smear this mixture all over the fish, and also inside the slits and fish. Cover and transfer to the refrigerator. Marinate over night.
- Preheat the oven to 400 degrees F. Cut the eggplants, sprinkle with salt and let them drain in a colander for about 30 minutes. Meanwhile prepare all the other vegetables, then wash of the salt from the eggplants and dry them of with paper towels. Transfer all vegetables (leave out only the tomatoes), and the unpeeled garlic cloves to a large bowl. Wisk the wine, vinegar, oil, salt, black pepper and dry pepper flakes in a small bowl (taste for seasoning). Mix all the freshly chopped herbs. Pour 2/3 of this vinaigrette over the vegetables and mix well to cover them all, sprinkle with herbs, and spread in one layer in a not to deep roasting pan lined with aluminum foil and parchment paper. Top with a layer of tomatoes, sprinkle with some salt and pepper. Cover with parchment paper. Transfer to the oven for 25 to 30 minutes.
- Get the fish out of the refrigerator to take of the chill. Stuff the insides with herb bundles, 3 slices of tomatoes, and 1 lemon slice cut in half.2. Take out the roasting pan with the partly roasted vegetables; with a large spatula push gently the soften vegetables to the sides of the roasting pan. Orange the fish in the middle; pour the remaining vinaigrette over the fish. Lower the temperature to 375 degrees F., and return the roasting pan to the oven uncovered. Bake for another 30, 40 minutes or until the fish and vegetables are golden brown but not burned. Remove from oven, present

on an oval large platter. Surround the fish with the vegetables (discard the unpeeled garlic cloves). Garnish with freshly chopped parsley, dill, olives and lemon slices, filet and serve.
- Lemon Sauce: Whisk together lemon juice, mayonnaise, mustard, honey, salt and pepper in a medium bowl. Slowly whisk in the oil until emulsified and stir in the herbs.

355.   Wild Garlic New Potato Salad

Serving: Serves 4 | Prep: | Cook: | Ready in:

Ingredients

- 2 teaspoons Dijon Mustard
- 2 teaspoons Honey
- 2 tablespoons White wine vinegar
- 1 cup Mayonnaise
- 1 pinch Sugar
- 12   Wild garlic leaves, finely chopped
- 16   Cooked (cold) New Potatoes, quartered
- a couple   Cherry tomatoes (for optional garnish)

Direction

- In a mixing bowl, whisk together the mustard, honey, vinegar, oil, salt, pepper and pinch of sugar, until it emulsifies (just like how you would normally make vinaigrette).
- Mix the Mayonnaise and wild garlic into the other ingredients until well combined. Mix the potatoes into the finished sauce (not too vigorously! You don't want to mash the potatoes!).
- Season to taste with salt and pepper, and serve, with some quartered cherry tomatoes for presentation if desired!

356.   Wilted Scallions With Lemon Mayonnaise

Serving: Serves 4-6 as a side dish | Prep: | Cook: | Ready in:

Ingredients

- 3 bunches scallions
- 1 tablespoon olive oil
- 2 tablespoons mayonnaise (your favorite brand, or if you feel like making aioli, go for it)
- 1   fresh lemon

Direction

- If using a grill, prepare the grill. If using an oven, heat the oven to 450°F.
- Wash and dry the scallions. Trim off any funky ends or stray layers of onion skin. Leave the root end intact.
- For grilling: Toss the scallions with the olive oil in a large bowls. Place the scallions on a grill (at the risk of being way too obvious, set them perpendicular to the grate) over a medium-hot area. Grill until they are charred and wilted, turning them frequently, about 5-8 minutes.
- If using the oven, toss the scallions with the olive oil on a large, rimmed baking sheet. Roast for 20-25 minutes, turning occasionally until the scallions are wilted and have some browning on them.
- When the onions are ready, place them on platter. Zest a little bit of the lemon directly onto the scallions. In a small bowl, mix the mayonnaise and enough fresh lemon juice to make a thin sauce. Serve the sauce alongside the scallions.

357.   Yum Dogs

Serving: Makes 6 dogs | Prep: | Cook: | Ready in:

Ingredients

- Bean Sprout Slaw
- 1 pound (approximatey 4 big handfuls) bean sprouts
- 2 teaspoons kosher salt
- 1 large carrot, grated on the large holes of a box grater
- 1 small red onion, very thinly sliced
- 1 jalapeño pepper, seeds and ribs removed, very thinly sliced (keep some of the ribs and seeds if you'd like your slaw a little spicier)
- 1/2 cup roughly chopped cilantro
- 1/3 cup rice wine vinegar
- 1 tablespoon sugar
- 1/2 teaspoon freshly ground black pepper
- Yum Dogs
- 1/2 cup mayonnaise or aioli
- 2 tablespoons Sriracha
- 6 good quality hot dogs of choice (I use a very juicy organic chicken dog)
- 6 slices good quality bacon of choice (I have found maple bacon particularly luscious)
- 6 hot dog buns or rolls, preferably ones that are large and sturdy
- 4 scallions, thinly sliced
- 1/2 cup roasted, salted peanuts, roughly chopped

Direction

- Bean Sprout Slaw
- In a large colander, thoroughly wash the bean sprouts, then shake off the excess water. Set the colander over a bowl or in the sink. Toss the salt with the bean sprouts to distribute evenly, then let the liquid drain from the sprouts, turning them periodically. Let the sprouts drain for at least 30 minutes. Their volume should decrease significantly.
- In a large bowl, combine the sprouts and the rest of the ingredients. Adjust seasoning as necessary. Keep refrigerated until ready to use.
- Yum Dogs
- Combine the mayonnaise and Sriracha and keep covered in the refrigerator until ready for use.

- Heat a cast iron skillet over medium heat. Score each hot dog a few times. Wrap each hot dog in a slice of bacon, starting at one end and corkscrewing it around to the other. If you find the bacon isn't adhering, you can use a wooden toothpick to pin it to the ends of hot dog.
- Cook the dogs, rotating to cook the bacon thoroughly on all sides. Depending on the thickness of your meats, this will probably take 2-4 minutes on each side. Transfer the hot dogs to a newspaper- or paper towel-lined platter. If you used toothpicks, remove them.
- Depending on the size or density of your buns (tee hee hee), you might need to hollow them out a little or not. Spread each bun generously with the Sriracha mayonnaise, then fill them with the Bean Sprout Slaw (I use tongs to gently squeeze out excess liquid).
- Place the dogs on the slaw and top with scallions and peanuts. Then open wide! It's a mouthful!

358.   Zeltner's Potato Salad

Serving: Serves 6-8 | Prep: | Cook: |Ready in:

Ingredients

- 3 pounds Waxy Potatoes
- 1-2 Green peppers, diced
- 1 small Red onion, diced
- 1 cup Fresh parsley, minced
- 1 1/2 cups Good quality mayonnaise, like Hellman's
- 5-6 tablespoons Apple cider vinegar
- Salt and pepper, to taste

Direction

- Boil potatoes in generously salted water until tender. (The amount of time will depend on the size of your potatoes.)

- While the potatoes are cooking, whisk apple cider vinegar into the mayonnaise to create a pourable dressing.
- Once the potatoes are tender -- and be careful about checking your potatoes too often because they can become water-logged if you poke too many holes in them -- drain them in a colander.
- As soon as the potatoes are cool enough to handle, chop them into bite-size pieces. (You can peel them or not, as you choose. My grandmother always did, but I sometimes do not.)
- While the potatoes are still warm, toss them with the mayonnaise and vinegar mixture. (Warm potatoes will absorb the mixture better.)
- Add green pepper, red onion, and parsley and combine gently so as not to break up the potatoes. Add salt and pepper to taste.
- Allow to stand for 10 minutes or so, so the potatoes can absorb the dressing. Serve warm (my favorite) or cold.

---

359.   Zippy Salsa Tonnato (Cold Tuna Sauce)

Serving: Serves 4 to 6 | Prep: | Cook: | Ready in:

Ingredients

- 3 tablespoons olive oil
- 3 tablespoons unsalted butter, divided
- 1   small yellow onion, finely chopped
- 1 small   fennel bulb, trimmed, cored, and diced
- 4 or 5   (1 small handful) spring radishes, trimmed and diced
- 1/2 teaspoon hot pepper flakes (or more to taste)
- 4   garlic cloves, minced
- 6   anchovy fillets
- 6- to 8- ounces can (or jar) good-quality tuna in olive oil, drained and chopped, oil reserved
- 1/2 cup dry white wine
- 1/4 cup capers, drained and rinsed
- 1/4 cup Italian parsley leaves, finely chopped, plus extra for garnish
- 1/2 cup mayonnaise or aioli
- 2 to 4 tablespoons red wine vinegar or lemon juice (start with 2 and adjust from there — I prefer more tang)
- 2 to 4 tablespoons water
- Salt and freshly ground pepper, to taste

Direction

- Heat the olive oil and 2 tablespoons of the butter in a skillet or saucier. Add onion, fennel, and radishes, and sauté on medium-low heat until tender and translucent. Add hot pepper flakes, garlic, and anchovies and continue sautéing over medium-low, until the anchovies have dissolved, and then stir in the tuna, mashing with the back of a wooden spoon to break up any large chunks. Raise the heat to high and add the wine. Cook until almost all evaporated, then lower the heat and stir in the capers and parsley. Swirl in the remaining 1 tablespoon of butter and remove from heat.
- Allow to cool slightly, then transfer to a blender or food processor. Add the mayonnaise (or aioli), vinegar (or lemon juice), reserved tuna oil, and water, and process until smooth. Then let it go some more, until it is super light and airy. (You can also do this directly in the pan with an immersion blender.) Adjust for salt, pepper, acid, and — if you prefer a little extra zip — hot pepper. You may need to add a little more olive oil or water if the purée is too thick. Serve as a dip, or tossed with pasta and a little pasta water (and something assertive and green, like arugula), or as a crostini topping, garnished with chopped parsley. [Editors' note: We spread the tomato on a plate, then topped it with boiled potatoes, blanched asparagus and snap peas, and raw radishes and Romanesco.]

360. Zucchini Frites With Lemon Basil Mayonnaise

Serving: Serves 4 | Prep: | Cook: |Ready in:

Ingredients

- 3 cups zucchini batons, approx. 2 1/2 inches long and 1/4 to 3/8 inch square, you want to use firm and relatively seed free zucchini
- 1 cup all purpose flour
- 2 1/2 tablespoons fresh basil, minced
- 1/2 teaspoon garlic powder
- 1/2 teaspoon paprika
- 1/2 teaspoon kosher salt
- 1/4 teaspoon black pepper
- 1 cup milk, maybe more
- 1/2 cup mayonnaise
- 2 teaspoons lemon juice
- 1 teaspoon lemon zest
- peanut oil for frying
- kosher salt and fresh ground pepper

Direction

- Place the zucchini batons into a strainer set over a bowl and toss them lightly with a teaspoon of kosher salt. If you are using table salt use 1/2 teaspoon. Let them sit for at least 30 minutes and up to an hour. This step is important because by getting rid of the moisture in the zucchini it allows for a crispier fry that doesn't go soggy quite as quick.
- Place the flour, 1 1/2 tablespoons of basil, garlic powder, paprika, salt and pepper into a large plastic or paper bag. Pour the milk into a bowl or small casserole.
- Combine the mayonnaise, lemon juice, zest and basil in a bowl and mix. Season with a pinch of salt and pepper. Mix, taste and adjust the seasoning. Set the sauce aside. The sauce can be made in advance and stored in the fridge.

- Place a 4-quart heavy bottomed pot on the stove. Fill it no further than 1/3 full with peanut oil, seriously, you don't want the oil to boil over and catch fire and even if it doesn't catch fire a half cup of oil will clean up like it is a gallon of oil.
- Turn the heat to medium high and insert a fry thermometer into the oil. Bring the oil to 350°F. Adjust the flame as necessary.
- When the oil is at about 300°F take the zucchini and drain them. Then place them on a towel and thoroughly dry them. This will help to keep the grease from splattering.
- Drop the zucchini into the flour and twist the bag. Shake the zucchini around to get them good and coated.
- Remove the zucchini from the flour to the milk and turn them coating them then drain them and put the zucchini back into the flour. Shake gently to coat them again.
- Dry the strainer you used to salt the zucchini. Place it back over the dried-out bowl used for draining and dump the zucchini into the strainer. Gently shake the strainer to remove the excess flour.
- Take the bowl with strainer over to the oil which should be at 350? F now. If you lowered the heat turn it back up to high, the oil temp will drop dramatically and you want it to recover its temp as quickly as possible for non oily fries, so make sure the flame is on high, and add the zucchini. Fry the zucchini until golden brown and delicious. Remove to a rack or a brown paper bag lined sheet tray, season them with salt and serve immediately with the basil mayonnaise.

361. Avocado River Boats

Serving: Makes 24 | Prep: | Cook: |Ready in:

Ingredients

- 12 avocados

- 3 pounds frozen peeled pre-cooked small shrimp
- 5   ripe slicing tomatoes
- 1   fresh jalapeno
- 3 tablespoons mayonnaise
- 2   fresh limes
- 3 dashes fresh ground pepper
- 1 pinch sea salt

Direction

- Thaw frozen shrimp, and rinse. Set aside and keep cool.
- Slice each avocado in half lengthwise. Remove pits, and keep three. Cube avocado and scoop gently into a large bowl; add the three reserved pits (this keeps the avocado from turning brown while you do the rest of the prep or toss a few horseshoes). Reserve intact peels.
- Dice tomatoes and finely dice the jalapeno.
- Squeeze limes and whisk into mayonnaise. Add salt and pepper.
- Remove avocado pits and discard. Stir shrimp, avocado, tomatoes, jalapeno, and mayo together gently. Mound into avocado peel "boats." no fork necessary because the boat acts as a scoop. Beer, however (or a nice swig of tequila) is a must.

362.   Brussel Fennel Apple Slaw

Serving: Serves 6 | Prep: | Cook: | Ready in:

Ingredients

- 3/4 pound brussel sprouts, roots trimmed, shredded
- 1   granny smith apple, (skin on) seeded and cored, shredded
- 1   carrot, peeled and shredded
- 1/2   fennel bulb, cored and shredded
- squeeze of lemon juice
- 1 teaspoon fennel seed

- 4 teaspoons sugar
- 2 tablespoons distilled white vinegar
- 2 tablespoons mayonnaise
- 1/4 cup sliced almonds

Direction

- Preheat oven to 350. Lay almonds in a single layer on a sheet pan. Bake for 6-8 minutes until lightly toasted. Set aside.
- There's a lot of shredding in this slaw -- for the ultimate ease - use the shredder attachment on your food processor. Otherwise, a box grater or mandoline work well.
- Combine the shredded Brussels sprouts, apple, carrot and fennel in a large bowl. Add the lemon juice and toss to combine.
- In a small skillet, toast the fennel seeds until warm, fragrant, and beginning to pop. Remove from heat and use a mortar and pestle, spice grinder or a heavy rolling pin to crush the seeds.
- Add the mayonnaise mixture to the slaw and toss thoroughly to combine.
- Just before serving, sprinkle with the almonds -- if you add them too early, they'll get soft.

363.   Egg N' Cheese Sandwich With Zesty Lime Baked Fries

Serving: Serves 1 | Prep: | Cook: | Ready in:

Ingredients

- egg n' cheese sandwich
- 1   egg
- 2 pieces toast
- 1 piece cheese
- 1/2   onion, thinly sliced
- 1 tablespoon herb butter
- 2 tablespoons extra-virgin olive oil
- zesty fries and lime zest aioli
- 1   large potato, julienne
- 2   lime zest
- 1   lime juice

- 3 tablespoons mayonnaise
- 1/2 garlic clove, finely chopped
- 1/2 teaspoon cayenne pepper powder
- 3 tablespoons extra-virgin olive oil

Direction

- Egg n' cheese sandwich
- Preheat a frying pan with 2 tbsp. of olive oil, add onions and cook until the onions are translucent and caramelized on medium-low heat. This should take about 5-10 minutes. Set aside.
- Using the same frying pan, add a little oil (if needed) under medium-low heat, pour in the whisked egg, season. The scrambled egg should be done in less than 3 minutes.
- Butter the toasts and combine the egg, cheese, and caramelized onion to make a sandwich.
- Zesty fries and lime zest aioli
- Soak the fries in cold water for at least 30 minutes or overnight then rinse with water after.
- Pat dry and mix the fries with 2 tbsp. extra-virgin olive oil, season with salt, pepper, lime zest, and cayenne pepper.
- Transfer the seasoned fries to a baking dish with 2 tbsp. of olive oil on the baking sheet and lay them evenly on the baking dish without overlapping.
- Preheat the oven at 180°C.
- Bake the fries for 30-40 minutes until crispy. Check occasionally to avoid burning by using a spatula to move the fries or flip them to the other sides.
- Add 3 tbsp. of mayonnaise with chopped garlic, lime zest and lime juice. Mix well. Feel free to add a little cayenne pepper powder for a little extra kick.

364. Lemon Herb Buttermilk Dressing

Serving: Makes 1 1/2 cups | Prep: | Cook: | Ready in:

Ingredients

- 1 cup buttermilk
- 2/3 cup mayonnaise
- 1 teaspoon lemon zest
- 2 tablespoons lemon juice
- 1 tablespoon chopped chives
- 1 tablespoon chopped thyme
- 1 tablespoon chopped tarragon
- 1 tablespoon chopped parsley
- 1 1/2 teaspoons kosher salt
- 3/4 teaspoon black pepper

Direction

- Combine buttermilk and mayonnaise in a medium bowl. Whisk to combine.
- Stir in lemon zest and juice. Add herbs and stir to combine. Add salt and pepper.
- Chill one hour to thicken before serving.

365. Loaded Chicken Salad

Serving: Serves 6 | Prep: | Cook: | Ready in:

Ingredients

- 2 stalks celery, diced
- 1/4 cup minced red onion
- 2 1/2 cups diced cooked chicken breast
- 1 cup seedless grapes, halved lengthwise
- 1 small apple, peeled, seeded and diced
- 1/2 cup pecans
- 2 tablespoons lemon juice
- 1/2 cup mayonnaise
- 1 tablespoon whole grain dijon mustard
- 1/4 cup freshly chopped tarragon leaves
- salt and pepper to taste

Direction

- Preheat oven to 300 degrees.
- Lay pecans on a baking sheet and bake for 10-12 minutes until lightly toasted and fragrant. Set aside to cool.

- Add celery, onion, chicken, grapes and apple to a large bowl and toss to combine.
- In a small bowl stir together lemon juice, mayonnaise and whole grain mustard. Stir in chopped tarragon and taste for seasoning -- adding salt and pepper as needed.
- Add mayonnaise mixture to chicken. Using a large spoon or spatula, fold the mayonnaise into the chicken until well coated.
- Roughly chop the pecans, add them to the salad and stir to combine.
- Great served with toasted bread or on a bed of greens.

Index

Conclusion

Thank you again for downloading this book!

I hope you enjoyed reading about my book!

If you enjoyed this book, please take the time to share your thoughts and post a review on Amazon. It'd be greatly appreciated!

Write me an honest review about the book – I truly value your opinion and thoughts and I will incorporate them into my next book, which is already underway.

Thank you!

If you have any questions, **feel free to contact at:** *author@shellfishrecipes.com*

Ebony Garcia

shellfishrecipes.com

Printed in Great Britain
by Amazon

14000921R00127